# New to This Editio

D1305937

This new edition of *The Essential Elements of Public Speaking* is a major revision with several important changes that make this text more user friendly than ever before. Here are some of the key changes.

- A more thoroughly integrated and developed "steps" theme (consisting of an easily managed system of ten steps to public speaking) runs throughout the book. These ten steps are covered in brief in Chapter 3 and then—in coordinated fashion—followed in Chapters 4–9 with detailed coverage of each of the ten steps.

- A variety of types of sample speeches are included in this edition. Model speeches with annotations show how the speaking concepts covered in the text are applied in a real speech. Two poor speeches, both with annotations, address common public speaking problems and offer potential correctives. A variety of new special occasion speeches appear in Chapter 12.

- "A Primer of Small Group Communication," a new section included in Chapter 12, offers succinct, but highly usable coverage of the nature and functions of small groups, membership, and leadership.

- Interior photos now present Public Speaking Choice Points—points in the public speaking process where you have to analyze your options and ultimately say something (or, of course, decide to say nothing—which is still communicating a message).

- Revisions and updates to each chapter, including materials instructors using the text requested, as well as new research, speech excerpts, and examples.

- Major content changes include discussion of scholarly and popular journals (Chapter 4), guidelines for using each of the forms of supporting material (Chapter 6), additions to the benefits of organization (Chapter 7), principles of persuasion and fallacies of reasoning (Chapter 11).

- A more detailed description of the changes in this edition is presented on pages xvi–xviii.

# The Essential Elements of Public Speaking

**Fourth Edition**

**JOSEPH A. DEVITO**

Hunter College of the
City University of New York

**Allyn & Bacon**

Boston  Columbus  Indianapolis  New York
San Francisco  Upper Saddle River
Amsterdam  Cape Town  Dubai  London  Madrid
Milan  Munich  Paris  Montreal  Toronto
Delhi  Mexico City  Sao Paulo  Sydney  Hong Kong
Seoul  Singapore  Taipei  Tokyo

Editor-in-Chief, Communication: Karon Bowers
Editorial Assistant: Megan Sweeney
Director of Development Manager: Meg Botteon
Senior Development Editor: Carol Alper
Marketing Manager: Blair Tuckman
Associate Development Editor: Angela G. Mallows
Media Producer: Megan Higginbotham
Production Manager: Raegan Keida Heerema
Associate Managing Editor: Bayani Mendoza de Leon
Managing Editor: Linda Mihatov Behrens
Project Coordination, Text Design, and Electronic Page Makeup: Nesbitt Graphics, Inc.
Cover Design Manager: Anne Bonnano Nieglos
Cover Designer: Manuel Morales
Cover Illustration: Vance Vasu
Image Permission Coordinator: Lee Scher/Annette Linder
Photo Researcher: Bill Smith Group
Senior Manufacturing Buyer: Mary Ann Gloriande

Printer and Binder: R.R. Donnelley/Willard
Cover Printer: Coral Graphics Services Inc.

For permission to use copyrighted material, grateful acknowledgment is made to the copyright holders on page 308, which is hereby made part of this copyright page.

Printed in the United States of America

10 9 8 7 6 5 4 3 2 1 RDW 14 13 12 11

**Allyn & Bacon**
**is an imprint of**

ISBN-10: 0-205-00594-2
ISBN-13: 978-0-205-00594-9

# Brief Contents

Detailed Contents   vi
Specialized Contents   xiv
Welcome to *The Essential Elements of Public Speaking*   xvi

**PART ONE   Fundamentals of Public Speaking   1**

1   Introducing Public Speaking   1
2   Listening and Criticism   21

**PART TWO   Preparing and Presenting Public Speeches   46**

3   Preparing and Presenting a Public Speech
    (Steps 1–10, in Brief)   46
4   Select Your Topic, Purposes, and Thesis (Step 1)   64
5   Analyze and Adapt to Your Audience (Step 2)   84
    Research Your Speech (Step 3) [Covered in Research Links
    Throughout]
6   Collect Supporting Materials and Presentation Aids
    (Step 4)   105
7   Organize Your Speech (Steps 5, 6, and 7)   129
8   Word Your Speech (Step 8)   167
9   Rehearse and Present Your Speech (Steps 9 and 10)   191

**PART THREE   Types of Speeches   212**

10   Informing Your Audience   212
11   Persuading Your Audience   233
12   Speaking on Special Occasions   269

Glossary   292
References   297
Index   301

# Detailed Contents

*Specialized Contents* xiv

*Welcome to* The Essential Elements of Public Speaking xvi

## PART ONE  Fundamentals of Public Speaking 1

### 1  Introducing Public Speaking 1

**The Benefits of Public Speaking** 2
Improved Public Speaking Abilities 2
Increased Personal and Social Abilities 3
Enhanced Academic and Career Skills 3
**The Essential Elements of Public Speaking** 4
Speaker 5
Audience 5
Message 5
Noise 6
Context 8
Channel 10
Ethics 10
**Plagiarism** 11
What Is Plagiarism? 11
Why Is Plagiarism Unacceptable? 12
How Can You Avoid Plagiarism? 12
**Managing Your Apprehension** 13
The Nature of Communication Apprehension 13
Reverse the Factors That Cause Apprehension 15
Restructure Your Thinking 16
Practice Performance Visualization 17
Desensitize Yourself 17
Essentials of Introducing Public Speaking 18
Essential Terms 19
Public Speaking Exercises 19
LogOn! MySpeechLab 20

## 2 Listening and Criticism 21

**Listening in Public Speaking** 22
Receiving 22
Understanding 23
Remembering 23
Evaluating 24
Responding 24
**Guidelines for Listening** 26
Listen Actively 26
Listen for Total Meaning 27
Listen with Empathy 28
Listen with an Open Mind 29
Listen Ethically 29
**Criticism in Public Speaking** 30
**Guidelines for Criticism** 32
Giving Criticism 33
Responding to Criticism 36
**Listening, Criticism, and Culture** 37
Listening and Culture 37
Criticism and Culture 42
**Essentials of Listening and Criticism** 44
**Essential Terms** 44
**Public Speaking Exercises** 44
**Log*On!* MySpeechLab** 45

## PART TWO Preparing and Presenting Public Speeches 46

## 3 Preparing and Presenting a Public Speech (Steps 1–10, in Brief) 46

**Getting Started with Public Speaking** 47
Popular Beliefs about Public Speaking 47
Starting Early 48
The Public Speaking Class 49
**Step 1: Select Your Topic, Purposes, and Thesis** 50
Your Topic 50
Your General Purpose 51
Your Specific Purpose 51
Your Thesis 52
**Step 2: Analyze Your Audience** 52
**Step 3: Research Your Topic** 53
**Step 4: Collect Supporting Materials** 54
**Step 5: Develop Your Main Points** 55
**Step 6: Organize Your Speech Materials** 56

**Step 7: Construct Your Introduction, Conclusion, and Transitions**  57
  Introduction  57
  Conclusion  58
  Transitions  58
**Step 8: Word Your Speech**  59
**Step 9: Rehearse Your Speech**  59
**Step 10: Present Your Speech**  59
Essentials of Preparing and Presenting a Public Speech  62
Essential Terms  63
Public Speaking Exercises  63
Log*On!* MySpeechLab  63

## 4  Select Your Topic, Purposes, and Thesis (Step 1)    64

**Your Topic**  65
  A Good Public Speaking Topic  65
  Finding Topics  67
  Limiting Topics  69
**Your Purposes**  72
  General Purpose  72
  Specific Purpose  72
**Your Thesis**  74
  What Is a Thesis?  76
  How Do Thesis and Specific Purpose Differ?  76
  Wording and Using Your Thesis  77
Essentials of Selecting Your Topic, Purposes, and Thesis  82
Essential Terms  83
Public Speaking Exercises  83
Log*On!* MySpeechLab  83

## 5  Analyze and Adapt to Your Audience (Step 2)    84

**Audiences and Audience Analysis**  85
  The Audience: Two Basic Characteristics  85
  Learning about Your Audience  86
**Analyze Audience Sociology**  89
  Age  89
  Gender  90
  Affectional Orientation  91
  Educational Levels  91
  Religion and Religiousness  92

Cultural Factors    93
Other Audience Factors    93
Context Characteristics    94

**Analyze Audience Psychology    96**
How Willing Is Your Audience?    96
How Favorable Is Your Audience?    97
How Knowledgeable Is Your Audience?    99

**Analyze and Adapt during the Speech    100**
Focus on Listeners as Message Senders    101
Use Answers to Your "What If" Questions    101
Address Audience Responses Directly    101

**Essentials of Analyzing and Adapting to Your Audience    102**
**Essential Terms    103**
**Public Speaking Exercises    103**
**Log*On!* MySpeechLab    104**

## Research Your Speech (Step 3) [Covered in Research Links Throughout]

## 6  Collect Supporting Materials and Presentation Aids (Step 4)    105

**Supporting Materials    106**
Examples, Illustrations, and Narratives    106
Analogies    108
Definitions    108
Testimony    110
Numerical Data    112

**Presentation Aids    114**
Types of Presentation Aids    115
Using Presentation Aids    117
Computer-Assisted Presentations    119

**Essentials of Collecting Supporting Materials and Presentation Aids    127**
**Essential Terms    127**
**Public Speaking Exercises    128**
**Log*On!* MySpeechLab    128**

## 7  Organize Your Speech (Steps 5, 6, and 7)    129

**The Benefits of Organization    130**
**Develop Your Main Points (Step 5)    131**
Select Your Main Points    131
Limit the Number of Main Points    132

Focus on Your Audience   132
Word Your Main Points   133

**Organize Your Main Points (Step 6)   135**
Topical Pattern   135
Temporal Pattern   135
Spatial Pattern   137
Problem–Solution Pattern   138
Cause–Effect Pattern   139
The Motivated Sequence   139
Cultural Considerations in Organization   144

**Construct Your Introduction, Conclusion, and Transitions (Step 7)   145**
Introductions   145
Conclusions   150
Transitions   153
Common Faults in Introductions, Conclusions, and Transitions   154

**Outlining the Speech   155**
Constructing the Outline   155
Sample Outlines   159
**Essentials of Organizing Your Speech   165**
**Essential Terms   165**
**Public Speaking Exercises   166**
**Log*On!* MySpeechLab   166**

## 8   Word Your Speech (Step 8)   167

**How Language Works   168**
Language Varies in Directness   168
Language Varies in Abstraction   169
Language Varies in Objectivity   169
Language Varies in Orality   171
Language Varies in Accuracy   171

**Choosing Words   175**
Clarity   175
Vividness   178
Appropriateness   180
Personal Style   185

**Phrasing Sentences   186**
Use Powerful Sentences   186
Use Short Sentences   187
Use Direct Sentences   187
Use Active Sentences   188
Use Positive Sentences   188
Vary the Types of Sentences   188
**Essentials of Wording Your Speech   189**
**Essential Terms   190**
**Public Speaking Exercises   190**
**Log*On!* MySpeechLab   190**

## 9  Rehearse and Present Your Speech (Steps 9 and 10)    **191**

**Rehearse Your Speech (Step 9)**    192
Rehearse the Speech as a Whole    192
Time the Speech    192
Approximate the Actual Speech Situation    192
Incorporate Changes and Delivery Notes    193
Rehearse Often    193
Undertake a Long-Term Delivery Improvement Program    193

**Deliver Your Speech (Step 10)**    194
What Is Effective Presentation?    194
Methods of Presentation    195

**Effective Vocal Delivery**    198
Volume    198
Rate    200
Pitch    201
Pauses    202
Articulation    202
Pronunciation    204

**Effective Bodily Action**    204
General Appearance    205
Eye Contact    205
Facial Expression    206
Posture    206
Gestures    206
Movement    207
Proxemics    207
Using Notes    208
Handling Questions    208

**Essentials of Rehearsing and Presenting Your Speech**    210
**Essential Terms**    211
**Public Speaking Exercises**    211
Log*On!* MySpeechLab    211

## PART THREE    Types of Speeches    **212**

## 10  Informing Your Audience    **212**

**Principles of Informative Speaking**    213
Focus on Your Audience    213
Stress Relevance and Usefulness    213
Limit the Amount of Information    215
Adjust the Level of Complexity    215
Relate New Information to Old    216
Vary the Levels of Abstraction    216
Make Your Speech Easy to Remember    217

**Speeches of Description    218**
Thesis    218
Main Points    218
Support    219
Organization    219

**Speeches of Definition    222**
Thesis    222
Main Points    223
Support    223
Organization    223

**Speeches of Demonstration    228**
Thesis    228
Main Points    229
Support    229
Organization    229

**Essentials of Informing Your Audience    231**
**Essential Terms    232**
**Public Speaking Exercises    232**
**Log*On!* MySpeechLab    232**

## 11    Persuading Your Audience                                    233

**Goals of Persuasive Speaking    234**
To Strengthen or Weaken Attitudes, Beliefs, or Values    234
To Change Attitudes, Beliefs, or Values    234
To Motivate to Action    235

**The Three Persuasive Proofs    235**
Logical Proof    235
Emotional Proof    242
Credibility Proof    245

**Principles of Persuasive Speaking    249**
Focus on Your Audience    250
Identify with Your Audience    250
Secure a Yes Response    250
Anticipate Selective Exposure    251
Use Positive Labeling    251
Ask for Reasonable Amounts of Change    251
Provide Social Proof    252
Motivate Your Listeners with Limited Choices    252

**Culture and Persuasion    253**
Individualist and Collectivist Cultures    254
High- and Low-Power-Distance Cultures    254
High- and Low-Uncertainty-Avoidance Cultures    254
Masculine and Feminine Cultures    255
High- and Low-Context Cultures    255
Short- and Long-Term Oriented Cultures    255
Indulgent and Restrained Cultures    255

Persuasive Speeches on Questions of Fact 256
  Thesis 256
  Main Points 257
  Support 257
  Organization 258
Persuasive Speeches on Questions of Value 258
  Thesis 259
  Main Points 259
  Support 259
  Organization 260
Persuasive Speeches on Questions of Policy 260
  Thesis 260
  Main Points 261
  Support 262
  Organization 262
Essentials of Persuading Your Audience 267
Essential Terms 267
Public Speaking Exercises 268
Log*On!* MySpeechLab 268

12  Speaking on Special Occasions                          269

The Speech of Introduction 270
The Speech of Presentation or Acceptance 271
The Speech to Secure Goodwill 273
The Speech of Dedication 274
The Commencement Speech 275
The Speech of Inspiration 277
The Eulogy 278
The Farewell Speech 279
The Toast 281
Presenting the Group's Thinking 282
  General Speaking Guidelines 282
  Speaking in the Panel Group 283
  Speaking in the Symposium and Team Presentations 283
  Oral and Written Reports 284
The Special Occasion Speech in Cultural Perspective 285

A PRIMER ON SMALL GROUP COMMUNICATION 286

Essentials of Speaking on Special Occasions 290
Essential Terms 291
Public Speaking Exercises 291
Log*On!* MySpeechLab 291

*Glossary* 292
*References* 297
*Index* 301

# Specialized Contents

## RESEARCH LINKS

*The Research Links spread throughout the text explain the principles of effective and efficient research and identify lots of resource materials that you'll find useful in researching your speeches as well as throughout your college and professional career. Each of these sections ends with a reference to the next Research Link so you can read them in sequence as you would a chapter.*

Beginning Steps in Public Speaking Research (Chapter 1, p. 7)
Interviewing for Information (Chapter 2, p. 25)
Libraries (Chapter 3, p. 55)

Primary, Secondary, and Tertiary Source Material (Chapter 4, p. 75)
Scholarly and Popular Journals (Chapter 5, p. 94)
General Reference Works (Chapter 6, p. 111)
The Government (Chapter 7, p. 134)
News Sources (Chapter 8, p. 174)
The Web (Chapter 9, p. 199)
Evaluating Internet Resources (Chapter 10, p. 220)
Integrating and Citing Research (Chapter 11, p. 239)
Museum Collections and Exhibits (Chapter 12, p. 289)

## ETHICAL CHOICE POINT

*These ethics boxes explain the principles of ethics and present you with an ethical dilemma that asks what you would do in this situation.*

Plagiarism Detection (Chapter 1, p. 13)
Open Listening (Chapter 2, p. 35)
Using Research (Chapter 3, p. 57)
Thesis Appropriateness (Chapter 4, p. 80)
Audience Interests (Chapter 5, p. 85)

Misleading Your Audience (Chapter 6, p. 107)
Constructing an Outline (Chapter 7, p. 161)
Can You Sidestep Opposing Arguments? (Chapter 8, p. 170)
To Correct an Error, or Not? (Chapter 9, p. 208)
Informing or Persuading? (Chapter 10, p. 217)
Fear as a Persuasive Strategy? (Chapter 11, p. 245)
Telling the Truth (Chapter 12, p. 277)

## PUBLIC SPEAKING EXERCISES

*These exercises, presented at the end of each chapter, are designed to stimulate you to think more actively about the concepts and skills covered in the chapter and to help you practice your developing public speaking skills.*

1.1 A Model of Public Speaking (p. 19)
1.2 Cultural Beliefs and Your Audience (p. 19)
2.1 Do You Really Remember What You Hear? (p. 44)
2.2 Listening to New Ideas (p. 45)
3.1 Theses (p. 63)
3.2 Preparing and Presenting a Speech (p. 83)
4.1 Brainstorming for Topics (p. 83)
4.2 Limiting Topics (p. 83)
5.1 How Well Do You Know Your Audience? 103
5.2 Analyzing an Unknown Audience (p. 104)

6.1 Supporting Materials (p. 128)
6.2 Galileo and the Ghosts (p. 128)
7.1 Generating Main Points (p. 166)
7.2 Constructing Introductions and Conclusions (p. 166)
8.1 Creating Figures of Speech (p. 190)
8.2 Giving Life to Your Sentences (p. 190)
9.1 Communicating Vocally but Nonverbally (p. 211)
9.2 Checking Your Pronunciation (p. 211)
10.1 Defining Terms (p. 232)
10.2 A Two-Minute Informative Speech (p. 232)
11.1 Constructing Motivational Appeals (p. 268)
11.2 Questions of Fact, Value, and Policy (p. 268)
12.1 Developing the Speech of Introduction (p. 291)
12.2 Developing the Special Occasion Speech (p. 291)

## PUBLIC SPEAKING SAMPLE ASSISTANT

*A variety of speeches are presented to help teach you the principles of public speaking. The speeches in Chapters 2 and 4 are purposely poor examples, and are designed to illustrate what not to do. Research finds this is an effective if not obvious instructional method (Hesketh & Neal, 2006; Goldstein, Martin, & Cialdini, 2008). The remaining speeches are excellent and are designed to illustrate effective techniques and strategies.*

A Poorly Constructed Informative Speech (Chapter 2, p. 38)
A Speech of Introduction (Chapter 3, p. 60)
A Poorly Constructed Persuasive Speech (Chapter 4, p. 78)
A Slide-Show Speech (Chapter 6, p. 120)

A Preparation Outline with Annotations (Topical Organization) (Chapter 7, p. 157)
Preparation Outline with Annotations (Motivated Sequence Organization) (Chapter 7, p. 160)
A Template Outline (Topical Organization) (Chapter 7, p. 162)
A Phrase/Key-Word Delivery Outline (Chapter 7, p. 164)
An Informative Speech (Chapter 10, p. 224)
A Persuasive Speech (Chapter 11, p. 263)
Speech to Secure Goodwill (Apology) (Chapter 12, p. 275)
Speech of Dedication (Chapter 12, p. 276)
Speech of Inspiration (Chapter 12, p. 278)
Eulogy (Chapter 12, p. 280)

# Welcome to *The Essential Elements of Public Speaking*

*T*he Essential Elements of Public Speaking will guide you through one of the most important courses you'll take in your entire college career. I know you've heard that before, but this time it's true. Public speaking is a course that will prove exciting, challenging, and immensely practical. It is also a course that is likely to create some anxiety and apprehension; this is normal. Fortunately, the anxiety and apprehension can be managed, and we'll deal with that challenge right at the beginning (in Chapter 1).

This text and this course will help you master the skills you'll need to give effective informative, persuasive, and special occasion speeches. It will also teach you to listen more critically to the speeches of others and to offer constructive criticism. It will help you increase your personal and professional communication abilities and will enhance a wide variety of academic and career skills such as organization, research, and language usage.

This book is purposely short but not simplified or "dumbed down." An "essentials" book is not an elementary book; it's an *efficient* book. And that's what this edition aims to be—an efficient tool that will help you learn the essential elements of public speaking, specifically, the skills to prepare and present effective informative, persuasive, and special occasion speeches to an audience.

## What's New in This Fourth Edition?

This revised edition makes a major effort to focus more clearly than ever on the *essentials* of public speaking. Revisions designed to achieve that end include a variety of both general and chapter-by-chapter specific changes.

### General Changes

The most important change in this edition is the coordination of the steps in public speaking. They are presented in brief in Chapter 3 (Chapter 2 in the previous edition), with Chapters 4–9 presenting the steps in greater detail. The chapter opening photos and quotations encourage the student to reflect on the steps covered in that chapter and on the process of achievement in steps.

The interior photos now present Public Speaking Choice Points. These are points in the public speaking process where you have to analyze your options and ultimately say something (or, of course, decide to say nothing—which is still communicating a message).

New speeches and speech excerpts have been integrated into this edition and are detailed in the chapter-by-chapter changes.

The chapters have been rearranged so that the introduction to public speaking, listening, and criticism are covered in the first two chapters.

## Chapter-by-Chapter Changes

Each chapter has been revised to achieve greater clarity, to include materials instructors using the text requested, and to incorporate new research and updated examples. Here are some of the major changes.

## Part One: Fundamentals of Public Speaking

*Chapter 1* **Introducing Public Speaking** changes include integrating culture and gender into the discussion of context, a revised diagram of the public speaking process (which gives a clearer focus on remote audiences), and an updated discussion of time management. A brief account of fair use is included in the discussion of plagiarism, which is now integrated into the text narrative. *Chapter 2* **Listening and Criticism** changes include a reorganization of listening and criticism and the guidelines for effectiveness. A new "poorly constructed speech" has been added, with annotations covering both problems and correctives.

## Part Two: Preparing and Presenting Public Speeches

*Chapter 3* **Preparing and Presenting a Public Speech (Steps 1–10, in Brief )** changes include newly coordinated steps for public speaking in brief, with the steps in detail covered throughout the remainder of the book. *Chapter 4* **Select Your Topic, Purpose, and Thesis (Step 1)** changes include a new, "poorly constructed persuasive speech" with annotations of problems and correctives. There is also a new Research Link on scholarly and popular Journals. *Chapter 5* **Analyze and Adapt to Your Audience (Step 2)** changes involve a totally updated sociology of the audience section. *Chapter 6* **Collect Supporting Materials and Presentation Aids (Step 4)** changes include a unified discussion of examples, illustrations, and narratives, as well as a new organization in which supporting material is discussed first in terms of type and second in terms of guidance for usage. There is also a broadened discussion of statistics to "numerical data," and a new, easy-to-read table on the media of presentation aids. *Chapter 7* **Organize Your Speech (Steps 5, 6, and 7)** changes include a new section on the benefits of organization and incorporating additional patterns of organization in a table along with their uses and sample outlines. *Chapter 8* **Word Your Speech (Step 8)** changes include a new section on avoiding language that disparages people with disabilities and a new section on powerful sentences.

**1** Select your topic, purposes, and thesis

**2** Analyze your audience

**3** Research your topic

**4** Collect supporting materials

**5** Develop your main points

**6** Organize your speech materials

**7** Construct your introduction, conclusion, and transitions

**8** Word your speech

**9** Rehearse your speech

**10** Present your speech

*Chapter 9* **Rehearse and Present Your Speech (Steps 9 and 10)** changes include new sections on the characteristics of effective presentation, handling questions, and undertaking a long term delivery program.

### Part Three: Types of Speeches

*Chapter 10* **Informing Your Audience** changes include the discussion of a new principle of informative speaking (focus on your audience). *Chapter 11* **Persuading Your Audience** changes include a total reorganization in which the three major proofs are covered as a major unit and each section (logical, emotional, and credibility appeals) now includes a discussion of listening to such appeals with an integration of the fallacies that may accompany each of the uses of proof. Other changes include several new principles of persuasion (for example, securing a *yes* response, social proof, and positive labeling), a new table summarizing and comparing questions of fact, value, and policy, and a streamlined version of the motivated sequence as a persuasive strategy table. *Chapter 12* **Speaking on Special Occasions** changes include the addition of a variety of new speeches. A new section, "A Primer of Small Group Communication," discusses the nature of small groups, membership, and leadership.

## Main Features of *The Essential Elements of Public Speaking*

Among the main features of this text are:

1.  An easy-to-understand and follow ten-step system for preparing and presenting public speeches and an early, brief overview of the steps in public speaking.

2.  Research Links that explain the research process and research strategies.

3.  Extensive coverage of ethics and culture as foundation concepts of public speaking.

4.  Public Speaking Sample Assistant boxes to illustrate the dos and don'ts of public speaking.

5.  Learning aids to make your study of public speaking more efficient and more effective.

In addition, each chapter concludes with a summary, a list of essential terms, two public speaking exercises, and an invitation to visit MySpeechLab (**www.myspeechlab.com**; access code required) for additional materials to help you master the skills of public speaking.

# *Ten Steps to Public Speaking* guide you in the preparation and presentation of a public speech.

The **ten-step system** makes the process more efficient by breaking the process into discrete, manageable steps that are addressed in detail throughout the book.

The third chapter, "Preparing and Presenting a Public Speech (Steps 1–10, in Brief)," presents the **10 steps in brief.** Here you'll learn to accomplish everything from selecting a topic to organizing your materials, rehearsing, and presenting your speech. This chapter is purposely short so that you can read it in one sitting, get a picture of the entire process of public speaking, and start giving speeches almost immediately. The remaining chapters parallel the steps outlined in this chapter and elaborate on each step—helping you to gradually refine and perfect your public speaking skills.

---

Getting Started with Public Speaking    **47**

This chapter answers the FAQs you're likely to be wondering about by providing a brief overview of the public speaking process. By following the 10 steps outlined in this chapter and diagrammed in Figure 3.1, you'll be able to prepare and present an effective first speech almost immediately. The remainder of the text elaborates on these steps and will help you fine-tune your public speaking skills. But first we'll look at some issues to get you started.

## Getting Started with Public Speaking

Before we launch into the step-by-step process of public speaking, consider a few popular beliefs about public speaking and then ponder some helpful advice.

### Popular Beliefs about Public Speaking

Do you think each statement is true or false?

1. Good public speakers are born, not made.
2. The more speeches you give, the better you'll become at it.
3. It's best to memorize your speech, especially if you're fearful or apprehensive about speaking before an audience.
4. If you're a good writer, you'll be a good public speaker; a poor writer, a poor speaker.
5. The First Amendment allows the public speaker total freedom of expression.
6. Like a good novel, play, or essay, a good speech is relevant to all people at all times.

**FIGURE 3.1**
**The Steps in Preparing and Presenting a Public Speech**
This figure presents the 10 steps in a linear fashion. The process of constructing a public speech, however, doesn't always follow such a logical sequence. So you'll probably not progress simply from Step 1, to 2, to 3, through to 10. Instead, after selecting your topic, purpose, and thesis (Step 1) you may progress to Step 2 and analyze your audience. On the basis of this analysis, however, you may wish to go back and modify your purpose or thesis, or both. Similarly, after you research the topic (Step 3), you may want more information about your audience. You may, therefore, return to Step 2.

1. Analyze your
2. Research your topic
3. Collect supporting materials
4. Develop your main points
5. Organize your speech materials
6. Construct your introduction, conclusion, and transitions
7. Word your speech
8. Rehearse your speech
9. Present your speech
10.

---

- **Give your full attention to the speaker.** Avoid playing games on your laptop, texting, or surfing during class and especially during a student's speech. Turn off your cell phone or at least put it on vibrate.
- **Offer constructive criticism.** The norm of most public speaking classrooms is that criticism is expected; it's a useful learning device for the speaker, the critic, and, in fact, for everyone in the course. Keep in mind the suggestions for giving and receiving criticism discussed in the previous chapter.
- **Come to class regularly.** Although class attendance is important in all courses, it's doubly important in the public speaking course. The reason is simply that speakers need audiences, audience feedback and criticism, and the interaction that only an audience can provide. In addition, you'll learn a great deal from observing the efforts of others.

## Step 1: Select Your Topic, Purposes, and Thesis

Your first step is to select your topic, your general and specific purposes, and your thesis (or main idea).

### Your Topic

The first step in preparing a speech is to select the **topic** (or subject) and the overall purpose you hope to achieve. Let's look first at the topic. For your classroom speeches—where the objective is to learn the skills of public speaking—there are thousands of suitable topics. Suggestions [for finding topics] are everywhere. Take a look at the Topic Generator [at AllWords.com]; it will provide you with lots of suggestions [for "interesting topics." Additional suggestions are provided...]

What makes a topic "suitable"? First...

---

## Step 2: Analyze Your Audience

In public speaking your audience is central to your topic and purpose. In most cases, and especially in a public speaking class, you'll be thinking of both your audience and your topic at the same time; in fact, it's difficult to focus on one without also focusing on the other. Your success in informing or persuading an audience rests largely on **audience analysis**—the extent to which you know your listeners and the extent to which you've adapted your speech to them. Ask yourself, Who are they? What do they already know? What would they want to know more about? What special interests do they have? What opinions, attitudes, and beliefs do they have? Where do they stand on the issues you wish to address? What needs do they have?

For example, if you're going to speak on social security and health care for the elderly or on the importance of the job interview, it's obvious that the age of your listeners will influence how you develop your speech. Similarly, men and women often view topics differently. For example, if you plan to speak on caring for a newborn baby, you'd approach an audience of men very differently than an audience of women. With an audience of women, you could probably assume a much greater knowledge of the subject and a greater degree of comfort in dealing with it. With an audience of men, you might have to cover such elementary topics as the type of powder to use, how to test the temperature of a bottle, and the way to

**PUBLIC SPEAKING CHOICE POINT: Audience Analysis**
Stella is planning to give a speech on the need for developing wind energy sources. She has no information about the audience's knowledge of wind energy or their political attitudes. What are some of the things Stella can do

## *Research Links* provide a useful guide to researching your speeches in easy-to-master segments.

Research is essential to an effective public speech—as it is, of course, to your entire college and professional career. Knowing how to conduct research and how to evaluate it are crucial skills that are essential to, but not limited to, public speaking. Rather than appearing in a traditional dense chapter that often gets skipped over or puts you to sleep, discussions of research appear throughout the text in **Research Link** boxes. These Research Links are presented in a progression—from general research principles in early chapters, to more specialized topics in later chapters.

Because public speaking students need to conduct research for speeches throughout the term, we cover a small set of research strategies in each chapter that you can use immediately and thus internalize more effectively. You'll find that in this way, you'll be better able to digest the information and gradually practice the research strategies. By the end of the course, you'll have mastered a detailed arsenal of research techniques that will help you throughout your college courses and into your professional life. Each Research Link ends with a note identifying and locating the next Link so that, if you wish, you can read them as an entire chapter. A complete list of the Research Links is also presented in the Specialized Contents.

# Coverage of ethics and culture broaden your speaking experience.

## Ethical Choice Points

Because public speaking is a powerful medium that can have enormous consequences, it has important ethical or moral implications. In this book, ethics is introduced in Chapter 1 as an essential element of public speaking; in addition, each chapter contains an **Ethical Choice Point** box describing a situation that raises an ethical issue and asking you to identify the choices you have available. One of the major ethical issues, plagiarism, is addressed in Chapter 1. By the end of the text, you should have formulated a clear and defensible ethical standard to govern your own public speaking. A list of these Ethical Choice Point boxes appears in the Specialized Contents, page xiv.

**ETHICAL CHOICE POINT**

### Using Research

You recently read an excellent summary of research on aging and memory in a magazine article. The magazine is a particularly respectable publication, so it's reasonable to assume that this research is reliable. But you feel that citing the original research studies will give your speech greater persuasive appeal and will make you look more thorough in your research. You want to use research honestly but you wonder if this would just be a waste of time. ➤*What are your ethical options in this case?* ➤*What would you do if you were in this situation?*

## Culture

The effectiveness of public speaking principles varies from one culture to another. Depending on cultural factors, different audiences may respond to speakers in different ways. For example, in some cultures an audience will respond positively to a speaker who appears modest and unassuming; in other cultures the audience may see this speaker as weak and lacking in confidence. A direct style will prove clear and persuasive in some cultures, but may appear invasive and inappropriate in others.

As a result of the tremendous cultural variations in the ways in which people respond to public speeches and speakers and the fact that we are all now living in a multicultural world, **cultural insights** are integrated into each of the 12 chapters. Among the issues discussed are how members of different cultures give and respond to public criticism (Chapter 2), the cultural factors a speaker should consider when analyzing different audiences (Chapter 5), and the cultural differences in audience responses to emotional and credibility appeals (Chapter 11).

### Listening, Criticism, and Culture

Culture influences all aspects of public speaking and listening and criticism are no exceptions. Here are some ways in which culture exerts this influence.

#### Listening and Culture

Listening is difficult, partly because of the inevitable differences between the communication systems of speaker and listener. Because each person has had a unique set of experiences, each person's communication and meaning system is going to be different from the next person's system. When speaker and listener come from different cultures the differences and their effects are naturally much greater. Here are just a few areas where misunderstandings can occur.

## *Public Speaking Sample Assistant*—sample speeches and outlines—provide models that show the speaking concepts in action.

Throughout the text, **Public Speaking Sample Assistant** boxes contain speeches and outlines along with annotations. The speeches in Chapters 2 and 4 were purposely written to illustrate what *not* to do. These speeches include dual-annotations that cover both the common problems students may encounter as well as suggested correctives to improve the speeches. All of the other speeches and outlines are models of effectiveness and will show you what good speeches look like. The annotations will help further guide you through the essential elements of public speaking. A complete list of the sample speeches and outlines appears in the Specialized Contents, page xiv.

---

**78**    CHAPTER 4   Select Your Topic, Purposes, and Thesis (Step 1)

### PUBLIC SPEAKING SAMPLE ASSISTANT

#### A Poorly Constructed Persuasive Speech

This speech was written to illustrate both broad errors as well as some subtle errors that a beginning speaker might make in constructing a persuasive speech. First, read the entire speech without reading any of the "Problems/ Correctives." As you read the speech consider what errors are being demonstrated and how you might correct them. Then, after you've read the entire speech, reread each paragraph and combine your own analysis with the "Problems/Correctives" annotations.

| Speech | Problems/Correctives |
|---|---|
| Title:   Prenups | This title sounds like an informative speech title and doesn't give the idea that a position will be argued. In addition, the topic, purpose, and thesis are not clearly focused or appropriately worded. |
| Topic:   Prenuptial agreements | |
| Purpose:   Prenuptials are bad. | A more appropriate title might be something like "Prenups have got to go" or "The dangers of prenups." The topic would need to be narrowed by citing some qualification such as "The negative aspects of prenuptial agreements." The purpose should be stated as an infinitive phrase: to persuade my audience that prenuptial agreements should be declared illegal. The thesis needs to be stated as a declarative sentence: Prenuptial agreements should be declared illegal. |
| Thesis:   Why do we need pre-nuptial agreements? | |

**INTRODUCTION**

You're probably not worried about prenuptial agreements yet. But, maybe you will be. At any rate, that's what my speech is on. I mean that prenuptial agreements should be made illegal.

This opening is weak and can easily turn off the audience. After all, if they're not worried about it now, why listen? The speaker could have made a case for the importance of this topic in the near future, however. It appears as if the speaker knows the topic's not important but will speak on it anyway.

A more effective introduction would have (1) captured the audience's attention—perhaps by citing some widely reported celebrity prenup; (2) provided a connection among the speaker-audience-topic—perhaps by noting the consequences one might suffer with a prenup; and (3) orient the audience as to what is to follow.

**BODY**

Here, a transition would help. In fact, transitions should be inserted between the introduction and the body and between the body and the conclusion. Using transitions between the main points and signposts when introducing each main point would help.

The speaker might have said something like: "There are three main reasons why prenups should be banned."

Prenuptial agreements make marriage a temporary arrangement. If you have a prenuptial agreement, you can get out of a marriage real fast—and we know that's not a good thing. So if we didn't have prenups—that's short for prenuptial agreements—marriages would last longer.

This is the speaker's first argument but it isn't introduced in a way the audience will find easy to understand. Abbreviations should be introduced more smoothly.

A simple signpost like, "My first argument against prenups is . . ." would make the audience see where the speaker is and get a visual image of the outline. To introduce the abbreviation that will be used throughout the speech, the speaker might have incorporated it into the first sentence—"Prenuptial agreements—for short, prenups—make a marriage. . . ."

---

Outlining the Speech   **157**

### PUBLIC SPEAKING SAMPLE ASSISTANT

#### A Preparation Outline with Annotations
(Topical Organization)

**Self-Disclosure**

eneral purpose:   To inform.

ecific purpose:   To inform my audience of the advantages and disadvantages of self-disclosing.

esis:   Self-disclosure has advantages and disadvantages.

**INTRODUCTION**

e all heard them:

m in love with my nephew.

ly husband is not my baby's father.

m really a woman.

e all disclosed.

ometimes it was positive, sometimes negae, but always significant.

nowing the potential consequences will help s make better decisions.

ook at this important form of communication ee parts:

rst, we look at the nature of self-disclosure.

econd, we look at the potential rewards.

hird, we look at the potential risks.

look first at the nature of this type of comunication.]

**BODY**

I. Self-disclosure is a form of communication (Petronio, 2000; Erber & Erber, 2011).

   A. S-D is about the self.

      1. It can be about what you did.

      2. It can be about what you think.

   B. S-D is new information.

   C. S-D is normally about information usually kept hidden.

      1. It can be something about which you're ashamed.

      2. It can be something for which you'd be punished in some way.

   [Knowing what self-disclosure is, we can now look at its potential rewards.]

Generally the title, thesis, and general and specific purposes of the speech are prefaced to the outline. When the outline is an assignment that is to be handed in, additional information may be requested.

Note the general format for the outline: the headings (introduction, body, and conclusion) are clearly labeled and the sections are separated visually.

Notice that the introduction serves the three functions discussed in the text: it gains attention (by these extreme confessions); establishes an S-A-T connection (by noting that all of us, speaker and audience, have had this experience); and orients the audience (by identifying the three major ideas of the speech).

Note how the indenting helps you to see clearly the relationship that one item bears to another. For example, in Introduction I, the outline format helps you to see that A, B, and C are explanations (amplification and support) for I.

These brief statements are designed to get attention and perhaps a laugh or two, but also to introduce the nature of the topic.

Here the speaker seeks to establish a speaker-audience-topic connection.

Here the speaker orients the audience and explains the three parts of the speech. The use of guide phrases (first, second, third) helps the audience fix clearly in mind the major divisions of the speech.

This transition cues the audience that the speaker will consider the first of the major parts of the speech. Notice that transitions are inserted between all major parts of the speech. Although they may seem too numerous in this abbreviated outline, they'll be appreciated by your audience because the transitions will help them follow and understand your speech.

Notice the parallel structure throughout the outline. For example, note that II and III in the body are phrased in similar style. Although this may seem unnecessarily redundant, it will help your audience follow your speech more closely and will also help you in logically structuring your thoughts.

Note that the references are integrated throughout the outline just as they would be in a term paper. In the actual speech, the speaker might say something like: "Communication theorist Sandra Petronio presents evidence to show that. . . ."

These examples would naturally be recounted in greater detail in the actual speech. One of the values of outlining these examples is that you'll be able to see at a glance how many you have and how much time you have available to devote to each example. Examples, especially personal ones, have a way of growing beyond their importance to the speech.

This transition helps the audience see that the speaker is finished discussing what self-disclosure is and will now consider the potential rewards.

# Learning aids help you internalize the concepts and study for exams.

## Summary/Essential Concepts and Skills

Each chapter ends with a series of summary statements, called **Essentials,** designed to help you review the key concepts of the chapter. The major headings of the chapter are repeated in the summary to further clarify the chapter contents. You may find it helpful to look at these summary statements before reading the chapter to get an overview of what's covered. Then, after you finish reading the chapter, you can return to these statements as chapter refreshers.

## Essential Terms

Because knowing the specialized vocabulary of a discipline will help you think about and talk about the material more effectively, a list of key terms and the pages on which they are introduced is presented at the end of each chapter. Key terms also appear in the glossary at the end of the text.

## Public Speaking Exercises

Each chapter ends with two **Public Speaking Exercises** to help you work actively with the concepts and skills discussed in the text. A wide variety of additional exercises are available on MySpeechLab (access code required) are discussed on pages xxvi and xxvii.

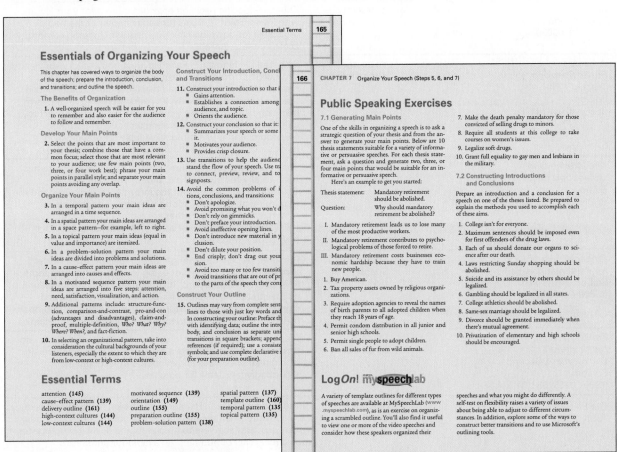

# Resources in Print and Online

| NAME OF SUPPLEMENT | PRINT | ONLINE | INSTRUCTOR OR STUDENT SUPPLEMENT | DESCRIPTION |
|---|---|---|---|---|
| Instructor's Resource Manual (ISBN: 0205030831) | ✓ | ✓ | Instructor Supplement | Prepared by Marianne S. Eggleston, the Instructor's Manual portion includes a wealth of resources for each chapter that can be used for developing your course and planning your lectures. There are chapter summaries, learning outcomes, and annotated Instructional Outlines that match the PowerPoint™ presentation package. Discussion Questions, designed to increase student engagement, can also be used for assignments, essay questions, or as review questions for an exam (sample answers are provided). In addition, there are activities and handouts. The Test Bank contains approximately 350 multiple-choice, true false, short answer, matching and essay questions organized by chapter. Each question is referenced by difficulty and page. (Available for download at www.pearsonhighered.com/irc; access code required.) |
| MyTest (ISBN: 0205030874) | | ✓ | Instructor Supplement | This flexible, online test generating software includes all questions found in the Test Bank, allowing instructors to create their own personalized exams. Instructors can also edit any of the existing test questions and even add new questions. Other special features of this program include random generation of test questions, creation of alternate versions of the same test, scrambling of question sequence, and test preview before printing. (Available at www.pearsonmytest.com; access code required.) |
| PowerPoint™ Presentation Package (ISBN: 020503084X) | | ✓ | Instructor Supplement | This text-specific package provides a basis for your lecture with PowerPoint™ slides for each chapter of the book. (Available for download at www.pearsonhighered.com/irc; access code required.) |
| A Guide for New Public Speaking Teachers, Fifth Edition (ISBN: 0205828108) | ✓ | ✓ | Instructor Supplement | Prepared by Jennifer L. Fairchild, Eastern Kentucky University and Calvin L. Troup, Duquesne University, this guide helps new teachers prepare for and teach the introductory public speaking course effectively. It covers preparing for the term, planning and structuring your course, evaluating speeches, utilizing the textbook, integrating technology into the classroom, and much more. (Available for download at www.pearsonhighered.com/irc; access code required.) |
| The Interviewing Guidebook, Second Edition (ISBN: 0205730515) | ✓ | ✓ | Student Supplement | This 112-page book on interviewing by Joseph DeVito has been totally revised and expanded. The *Interviewing Guidebook* discusses both the informative interview and the employment interview, along with the various types of résumés and the letters that are a part of the job interview (available for purchase or as an optional package with a new book purchase). |
| Preparing Visual Aids for Presentations, Fifth Edition (ISBN: 020561115X) | ✓ | | Student Supplement | Prepared by Dan Cavanaugh, this 32-page visual booklet provides a host of ideas for using today's multimedia tools to improve presentations, including suggestions for planning a presentation, guidelines for designing visual aids, and storyboarding, and a walkthrough that shows how to prepare a visual display using PowerPoint™ (available for purchase). |
| Public Speaking in the Multicultural Environment, Second Edition (ISBN: 0205265111) | ✓ | | Student Supplement | Prepared by Devorah A. Lieberman, Portland State University, this booklet helps students learn to analyze cultural diversity within their audiences and adapt their presentations accordingly (available for purchase). |
| The Speech Outline (ISBN: 032108702X) | ✓ | | Student Supplement | Prepared by Reeze L. Hanson and Sharon Condon of Haskell Indian Nations University, this workbook includes activities, exercises, and answers to help students develop and master the critical skill of outlining (available for purchase). |

*(Continued)*

## Resources in Print and Online (*Continued*)

| NAME OF SUPPLEMENT | PRINT | ONLINE | INSTRUCTOR OR STUDENT SUPPLEMENT | DESCRIPTION |
|---|---|---|---|---|
| *Multicultural Activities Workbook* (ISBN: 0205546528) | ✓ | | Student Supplement | By Marlene C. Cohen and Susan L. Richardson of Prince George's Community College, this workbook is filled with hands-on activities that help broaden the content of speech classes to reflect the diverse cultural backgrounds. The checklists, surveys, and writing assignments all help students succeed in speech communication by offering experiences that address a variety of learning styles (available for purchase). |
| *Speech Preparation Workbook* (ISBN: 013559569X) | ✓ | | Student Supplement | Prepared by Jennifer Dreyer and Gregory H. Patton of San Diego State University, this workbook takes students through the stages of speech creation—from audience analysis to writing the speech—and includes guidelines, tips, and easy to fill-in pages (available for purchase). |
| Study Card for Public Speaking (ISBN: 0205441262) | ✓ | | Student Supplement | Colorful, affordable, and packed with useful information, the Pearson Study Cards make studying easier, more efficient, and more enjoyable. Course information is distilled down to the basics, helping students quickly master the fundamentals, review a subject for understanding, or prepare for an exam. Because they are laminated for durability, they can be kept for years to come and pulled out whenever students need a quick review (available for purchase). |
| Contemporary Classic Speeches DVD (ISBN: 0205405525) | ✓ | | Instructor Supplement | This exciting supplement includes over 120 minutes of video footage in an easy-to-use DVD format. Each speech is accompanied by a biographical and historical summary that helps students understand the context and motivation behind each speech. Speakers featured include Martin Luther King Jr., John F. Kennedy, Barbara Jordan, the Dalai Lama, and Christopher Reeve. Please contact your Pearson representative for details; some restrictions apply. |
| Public Speaking Video Library | ✓ | | Instructor Supplement | This collection contains a range of different types of speeches delivered on a multitude of topics, allowing you to choose the speeches best suited for your students. Please contact your Pearson representative for details and a complete list of videos and their contents to choose which would be most useful in your class. Samples from most of our public speaking videos are available on www.mycoursetoolbox.com. Some restrictions apply. |
| Public Speaking Study Site | | ✓ | Student Supplement | This open access student Web resource features practice tests, learning objectives, and Web links organized around the major topics typically covered in the Introduction to Public Speaking course (available at www.abpublicspeaking.com). |
| VideoLab CD-ROM (ISBN: 0205561616) | ✓ | | Student Supplement | This interactive study tool for students can be used independently or in class. It provides digital video of student speeches that can be viewed in conjunction with corresponding outlines, manuscripts, note cards, and instructor critiques. Following each speech there are a series of drills to help students analyze content and delivery (available for purchase). |
| MySpeechLab | | ✓ | Instructor & Student Supplement | MySpeechLab is a state-of-the-art, interactive and instructive solution for public speaking courses. Designed to be used as a supplement to a traditional lecture course or to completely administer an online course, MySpeechLab combines a Pearson eText, MySearchLab™, MediaShare, multimedia, video clips, activities, research support, tests and quizzes to completely engage students. MySpeechLab can be packaged with your text or is available for purchase at www.myspeechlab.com (access code required). See next page for more details. |

# Save time and improve results with myspeechlab

Designed to amplify a traditional course in numerous ways or to administer a course online, **MySpeechLab** combines pedagogy and assessment with an array of multimedia activities—videos, speech preparation tools, assessments, research support, multiple newsfeeds—to make learning more effective for all types of students. Now featuring more resources, including a video upload tool, this new release of **MySpeechLab** is visually richer and even more interactive than the previous version—a leap forward in design with more tools and features to enrich learning and aid students in classroom success. (For more information or to take a tour, please go to **www.myspeechlab.com**; (access code required).)

## Teaching and Learning Tools

**NEW VERSION! Pearson eText:** Identical in content and design to the printed text, a Pearson eText provides students access to their text whenever and wherever they need it. In addition to contextually placed multimedia features in every chapter, our new Pearson eText allows students to take notes and highlight, just like a traditional book.

**Videos and Video Quizzes:** Interactive videos provide students with the opportunity to watch and evaluate sample speeches, both student and professional. Many videos are annotated with critical thinking questions or include short, assignable quizzes that report to the instructor's gradebook. Professional speeches include classic and contemporary speeches, as well as video segments from communication experts.

**MyOutline:** MyOutline offers step-by-step guidance for writing an effective outline, along with tips and explanations to help students better understand the elements of an outline and how all the pieces fit together. Outlines that students create can be downloaded to their computer, emailed as an attachment, or saved in the tool for future editing. Instructors can either select from several templates based on our texts, or they can create their own outline template for students to use.

**Topic Selector:** This interactive tool helps students get started generating ideas and then narrowing down topics. Our Topic Selector is question based, rather than drilldown, in order to help students really learn the process of selecting their topic. Once they have determined their topic, students are directed to credible online sources for guidance with the research process.

**Self-Assessments:** Online self-assessments, including the PRCA-24 and the PRPSA, allow students to assess and confirm their comfort level with speaking publicly. Instructors can use these tools to show learning over the duration of the course via MyPersonalityProfile, Pearson's online self-assessment library and analysis tool. MyPersonalityProfile enables instructors to assign self-assessments at the beginning and end of the course so students can compare their results and see where they've improved.

**Student Study Plan:** Pre- and post-tests for each chapter test students on their knowledge of the material in the course. The tests generate a customized study plan for further assessment and focus students on areas in which they need to improve using links to the textbook, as well as the top media items that can assist in improving their results.

**Speech Evaluation Tools:** Instructors have access to a host of Speech Evaluation Tools to use in the classroom, including a Speech Evaluation Rubric that can be customized to individual needs. An additional assortment of evaluation forms and guides for students and instructors offer further options and ideas for assessing presentations.

**Building Speaking Confidence Center:** In this special section of MySpeechLab, students will find self-assessments, strategies, video, audio, and activities that provide additional guidance and tips for overcoming their speech apprehension—all in one convenient location.

**ABC News RSS feed:** MySpeechLab provides an online feed from ABC news, updated hourly, to help students choose and research their speech topics.

## Cutting-Edge Technology

**MediaShare:** With our exciting, cutting-edge video upload tool, students are able to upload speeches for their instructor and classmates to watch (whether face-to-face or online) and provide online feedback and comments at time-stamped intervals. Media Share also includes a completely customizable grading rubric for instructors, which allows grades to be imported into most learning management systems. Structured much like a social networking site, MediaShare can help promote a sense of community among students.

**AmericanRhetoric.com partnership:** Through an exclusive partnership with AmericanRhetoric.com, MySpeechLab incorporates many great speeches of our time (without linking out to another site and without advertisements or commercials!). Many speeches are also accompanied by assessment questions that ask students to evaluate specific elements of those speeches.

**Audio Chapter Summaries:** Every chapter includes an audio chapter summary for online streaming use, perfect for students reviewing material before a test or instructors reviewing material before class.

## Online Administration

No matter what course management system you use—or if you do not use one at all, but still wish to easily capture your students' grade and track their performance—Pearson has a **MySpeechLab** option to suit your needs. Contact one of Pearson's Technology Specialists for more information and assistance.

A **MySpeechLab** access code is no additional cost when packaged with selected Pearson Communication texts. To get started, contact your local Pearson Publisher's Representative at **www.pearsonhighered.com/replocator**.

## Acknowledgments

I want to thank the many people who contributed to the development of the text you now hold. Thank you Karon Bowers, editor-in-chief; Carol Alper, development editor; Angela G. Mallowes, associate development editor; Megan Higginbotham, media producer; Megan Sweeney, editorial assistant; Blair Tuckman, marketing manager; Raegan Heerema, production manager; Tim Herzog and Tiffany Turner, photo researchers; Karen Stocz, copy editor; and Tom Conville, project manager. All helped tremendously at all stages of the development and production of this book. I am in their debt.

I want to thank the reviewers who shared their experiences and insights with me. Their suggestions were most helpful and most appreciated. Thank you,

Audrey L. Mosley, St. Phillip's College

Elaine Vander Clute, Wor-Wic Community College

Erin Heather Fox, Central Michigan University

Donata Nelson, Rockingham Community College

Andie Karras, The Art Institute–Hollywood

I also want to again thank reviewers of previous editions whose comments I continue to turn to with each revision. Thank you,

Bruce Ardinger, Columbus State College

Robert Arend, Miramar College

Valerie Belew, Nashville State

Ellen R. Cohn, University of Pittsburgh

John R. Foster, Northwestern State University

Fred Garbowitz, Grand Rapids Community College

Victoria Leonard, College of the Canyons

Ken Sherwood, Los Angeles City College

Anita Tate, Weatherford College

Chérie C. White, Muskingum Area Technical College

Emma Gray, Portland State University

Audra L. McMullen, Towson University

Kimberly Kilpatrick, University of Texas, El Paso

Amanda Brown, University of Wisconsin, Stout

Robert W. Wawee, The University of Houston–Downtown

Joseph A. DeVito
jadevito@earthlink.net
http://tcbdevito.blogspot.com
www.pearsonhighered.com/devito

1

# Introducing Public Speaking

## WHY READ THIS CHAPTER?

**Because it introduces one of the most practical and empowering subjects you will study in your entire college career and will help you to:**

- understand some of the many benefits you'll get from studying public speaking

- understand the elements involved in this unique kind of communication

- understand the nature of plagiarism and how to avoid it

- manage your fear of public speaking by mastering techniques to help you feel more comfortable in front of an audience

*Life is a series of steps.*

—RALPH RANSOM

Public speaking is one of the essential skills you'll need to function effectively in today's society. The higher up you go in the world's hierarchy—say, from intern, to junior analyst, to manager, to CEO—the more important public speaking becomes. This text explains these essential skills; the skills you'll need to prepare and present effective public speeches. And, as you'll see throughout this text, these skills will also prove useful to you in a variety of other situations as well.

Although public speaking principles were probably developed soon after our species began to talk, it was in ancient Greece and Rome that our Western tradition of public speaking got its start. This Greco-Roman tradition has been enriched by the experiments, surveys, field studies, and historical studies that have been done since classical times and that continue to be done today.

Contemporary public speaking—the kind discussed in this text—builds on this classical heritage with its emphasis on substance, ethical responsibilities of the speaker, and the strategies of organization, but also incorporates insights from the humanities, the social and behavioral sciences, and computer science and information technology. Likewise, perspectives from different cultures are being integrated into our present study of public speaking.

This brief introductory chapter discusses the benefits you'll derive from studying public speaking, the essential elements of every speech, plagiarism (what it is and how to avoid it), and—what is probably your number one concern—how to manage the very normal fear of speaking in public.

# The Benefits of Public Speaking

Fair questions to ask of any course or textbook are "What will I get out of this?" and "How will the effort and time I put into this class and this textbook benefit me?" Here are just a few of the benefits you'll derive from this text and from your course work in public speaking.

## Improved Public Speaking Abilities

At the most obvious level, you'll become a more accomplished and more effective public speaker. Speakers aren't born; they're made. Through instruction, exposure to different speeches, experience with diverse audiences, feedback on your own speeches, and individual learning experiences, you can become a more effective speaker. Regardless of your present level of competence, you can improve through proper training—hence, this course and this book.

At the end of this course you'll be a more competent, confident, and effective public speaker. You'll also be a more effective listener—more open, yet more critical; more empathic, yet more discriminating. And you'll emerge a more competent and discerning critic of public communication. You'll learn to organize and explain complex concepts and processes clearly and effectively to a wide variety of listeners. You'll learn to support an argument with all the available means of persuasion and to present a persuasive appeal to audiences of varied types.

As a leader (and in many ways you can look at this course as training in leadership skills) you'll need the skills of effective communication to help preserve a free and open society. As a speaker who wants your message understood and accepted, as a listener who needs to evaluate and critically analyze ideas and arguments before making decisions, and as a critic who needs to evaluate and judge the thousands of public communications you hear every day, you will draw on the skills you'll learn in this course.

## Increased Personal and Social Abilities

In your study of public speaking you'll also learn a variety of personal and social competencies. Perhaps one of the most important is to manage your fear of communication situations in general and of public speaking in particular. You may not eliminate your fear entirely, but you'll be able to manage it so that it works for you rather than against you.

You'll also develop greater self-confidence in presenting yourself and your ideas to others—competencies that are consistently ranked high in lists of what employers look for in hiring and promoting (Morealle & Pearson, 2005).

As you master the skills of public speaking you'll grow in power; you'll become more effective in influencing the thinking and behavior of others. At the same time, power enables you to empower others, whether as organizational manager, political leader, older sibling, or member of any of hundreds of groups.

## Enhanced Academic and Career Skills

As you learn public speaking, you'll also learn a wide variety of academic and career skills, many of which are largely communication skills (as you can tell from reading the employment ads, especially for middle-management positions in just about any field you can name). For example, you will learn to:

- conduct research efficiently and effectively, using the latest and the best techniques available
- critically analyze and evaluate arguments and evidence from any and all sources
- understand human motivation and make effective use of your insights in persuasive encounters
- develop an effective communication style (whether for conversation or for that important job interview) that you feel comfortable with
- give and respond appropriately to criticism, to increase your insight into your own strengths and weaknesses, and to provide useful feedback to others
- communicate your competence, character, and charisma so as to make yourself believable

Given that these benefits will permeate all aspects of your personal, social, and professional lives, it would be wise to make a commitment to put a major effort into this course. This public speaking course is a bit different from all your other courses— it aims not only to provide you with knowledge and

**PUBLIC SPEAKING CHOICE POINT: Public Speaking**
Robin is teaching a course in public speaking and wants to explain the importance of public speaking. Assuming she was teaching your specific class, what are some of the things Robin might say to convince your class of the significance and value of public speaking skills?

understanding of the topics of public speaking (ethics, persuasion, strategic argument, critical analysis, and more), but also with the skills for success that will make a difference everyday of your life.

## The Essential Elements of Public Speaking

In public speaking, a **speaker** presents a relatively continuous message to a relatively large audience in a unique context. Figure 1.1 presents a visualization of the public speaking process and Public Speaking Exercise 1.1, "A Model of Public Speaking," on page 19 invites you to create your own.

Like all communication, public speaking is a transactional process; a process whose elements are interdependent (Watzlawick, 1978; Watzlawick, Beavin, & Jackson, 1967). In other words, each element in the public speaking process depends on and interacts with all other elements. For example, the way in which you organize a speech will depend on such factors as your speech topic, your audience, the purpose you hope to achieve, and a host of other variables—all of which are explained in the remainder of this chapter and in the chapters to follow.

Let's now consider the essential elements of public speaking: speaker, audience, message, noise, context, channel, and ethics.

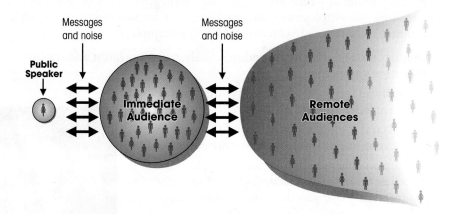

**FIGURE 1.1**
**The Basic Elements of Public Speaking**
This diagram is designed to illustrate the interplay of elements in the public speaking process and to emphasize that there are a variety of audiences of public speaking: (1) the immediate audience that hears the speaker as it is spoken, whether in person, on television, over the Internet, or even via cell phone, and (2) the remote audiences that get the material secondhand; for example, they read the speech, read about the speech, or hear from those who heard the speech or from those who heard about the speech from immediate audience members or from those who heard about the speech from those who heard about the speech. As you can appreciate, the immediate audience is finite (limited to the number of people who heard the speech first hand) but the remote audience is potentially infinite (and hence is indicated with a parabola).

## Speaker

In conversation the speaker's role occurs in short spurts: Pat says something to which Chris replies to which Pat responds and so on. In public speaking you deliver a relatively long speech and usually are not interrupted. As the public speaker you're the center of the transaction: You and your speech are the reason for the gathering.

In this course, your role of speaker is a bit different than it will be later in life. Here you're in a learning environment where you're expected to make mistakes as well as to profit from feedback from others (and to give constructive feedback to others). Outside of the classroom, your role as public speaker will be largely to inform others about something (as a teacher, a health care provider, or an engineer, for example) and to influence others (as a lawyer arguing for a client, as a parent addressing the PTA, or as a sales representative closing the deal, for example).

## Audience

In conversation the "audience" is often one listener or perhaps a few. The audience in public speaking is relatively "large," ranging from groups of perhaps 10 or 12 to hundreds of thousands, even millions.

As illustrated in Figure 1.1, there is more than one audience. Recognizing that both immediate and remote audiences exist is crucial to understanding the influence of public speaking throughout history as well as in any specific public speaking situation you might name. Abraham Lincoln's Gettysburg Address was presented to a relatively small audience, but it had influence far beyond that audience and that specific time. The same is true of many speeches; for example, Martin Luther King Jr.'s "I have a dream" speech was presented to thousands, but influenced millions. The same is true, though on a smaller scale, with all speeches, including those you'll present in this class. When you address 20 or 30 students in class, that's 20 or 30 people who might relay your message or arguments to others and these people may continue the process. As you grow in influence and in public speaking competence, so will your influence on both immediate and remote audiences.

In some public speaking situations, you may know your audience quite well—this class, for example, or when you are addressing work colleagues. In other situations, however, you will not know your audience quite so well and will have to analyze them to discover what they already know (so you don't repeat old news), to learn what their attitudes are (so you don't waste time persuading them of something they already believe), and so on.

But public speaking is more than the art of adjusting messages to listeners; it also incorporates active involvement by the listeners. The listener plays a role in encouraging or discouraging the speaker, in offering constructive criticism, in evaluating public messages, and in performing a wide variety of other functions. Because listening and criticism are so important (and so often neglected), they are covered in detail in Chapter 2.

## Message

**Messages** conveyed in public speaking include both verbal and nonverbal signals. In both conversation and public speaking, your message has a purpose.

For example, in conversation you might want to tell a friend about what happened at a recent basketball game. In this case your purpose would be to inform. Or you might want to convince a coworker to switch vacation schedules with you. Here your purpose would be to persuade. And in public speaking, too, you communicate with a purpose.

Generally in conversation you don't give any real thought to how you're going to organize your message. In public speaking, however, organization is crucial because it adds clarity to your message and therefore makes it easier for listeners to understand and to remember what you say.

In conversation you vary your language on the basis of the person with whom you're speaking, the topic you're talking about, and where you are. When talking with children, for example, you might use easier words and shorter sentences than you would with classmates. In public speaking you also adjust your language to your audience, the topic, and the situation.

In conversation the messages you send are essentially composed at the moment of utterance; you don't research them. In public speaking it's very different. Research is essential to the public speech and to any subject you might study.

In conversation you normally don't think of how you'd deliver or present your message; you don't concern yourself with how to stand or gesture or how to raise or lower your vocal volume. In public speaking, however, the situation is different. Because public speaking is a relatively new experience and you'll probably feel uncomfortable and self-conscious at first, you may wonder what to do with your hands or whether you should move about. With time and experience you'll find that your presentation will follow naturally from what you're saying, just as it does in conversation. Perhaps the best advice at this point is to view public speaking as "enlarged conversation" and not to worry about delivery just yet. In your early efforts it's better to concentrate on content; as you gain confidence, you can direct your attention to refining and polishing your presentation skills.

## Noise

**Noise** is anything that distorts the message and prevents the listeners from receiving your message as you intended it to be received. It's revealing to distinguish noise from "signal." In this context the term *signal* refers to information that is useful to you; information that you want. Noise, on the other hand, is what you find useless; it's what you do not want. So, for example, an e-mail list or electronic newsgroup that contained lots of useful information would be high on signal and low on noise; if it contained lots of useless information, it would be high on noise and low on signal. Spam is high on noise and low on signal, as is static on the radio, television, or telephone. Noise may be physical (others talking loudly, cars honking, illegible handwriting, "garbage" on your computer screen), physiological (hearing or visual impairment, articulation disorders), psychological (preconceived ideas, wandering thoughts), or semantic (misunderstood meanings).

Public speaking involves visual as well as spoken messages, so it's important to realize that noise also may be visual. Sunglasses that concealed the nonverbal messages from your eyes would be considered noise, as would dark print on a dark background in your slides.

# RESEARCH LINK

## Beginning Steps in Public Speaking Research

As a preface to the more specific Research Link boxes that follow, the nature of research will be covered here as well as some suggestions on researching efficiently or time management.

### The Nature of Research

Research is a systematic search for information; it's an investigation of the relevant information on a topic; it's an inquiry into what is known or thought about a subject. Research is undertaken, almost always, to discover an answer to one of several types of questions (www.webs.uidaho,edu/info_literacy/modules/module2/2_1.htm).

1. **Research for specifics such as facts, examples, illustrations, statistics, or definitions.** Here your question is simple: How is socialism defined? What is the population of Japan? What is the average salary for accountants? This type of research is the easiest and creates little difficulties. When you know something about the topic, you'll also learn where to search for the types of information you're looking for. You'll make use of this type of research in all your speeches as you search for supporting materials (see pp. 54–55).

2. **Research to discover what is known.** Here your question is "how"—how might you describe some person, object, event, or process. Or you seek to discover how a term or theory is defined and the differences and similarities among terms and systems. Or you might want to discover how to do something or how something operates. These types of research are at the heart of informative speech making. Notice, however, that you'll also make use of research for specific supporting materials.

3. **Research to support a position.** Here your questions can revolve around a variety of issues. For example, you might conduct research to discover which explanation or theory or position is the closest to being true—Are the parents guilty of child negligence? Do gay men and women make effective military personnel? Another type of question focuses on what is just or moral or right—Can bullfighting ever be morally justified? What procedures will be most humane? Still another type of question focuses on the policies that should or should not be adopted—Should medical marijuana be made legal? What should the government's policy be on immigration? These types of research questions are at the heart of persuasive speech making. To answer these kinds of questions, however, you'll also need to conduct the types of research discussed in 1 and 2.

### Time Management

Because a great deal of your time—in this course and in numerous others—will be spent on research, learn to use your research time efficiently. Here are a few suggestions:

- **Multitask.** Combine your research tasks and do them simultaneously. For example, when going to the library or logging on to the Internet, have more than one task in mind. If you know the topics of your next few speeches, do the research for both at the same time.

- **Watch detours.** Detours are often excellent learning experiences and are not necessarily detrimental. For purposes of time management, however, it will help if you keep your purpose clearly in mind—even to the point of writing it down—as you surf the Web or lurk among chat groups.

- **Consult your librarian.** Librarians are experts in the very research issues that may be giving you trouble. They'll be able to help you access biographical material, indexes of current articles, materials in specialized collections at other libraries, and a wide variety of computerized databases.

- **Organize your materials as you collect them.** Organize hard copy materials by topic in loose-leaf notebooks or manila folders. For electronic materials, use the organizational functions of your word processing program to create general and sub-folders as you need them. You can also scan your hard copy materials, recording citation information, to create a complete electronic research file. Alternatively you can use a specialized computer program, such as Microsoft's OneNote, to create and organize your materials and keep track of the source citations.

The next Research Link, "Interviewing for Information," appears on page 25. Also visit MySearchLab (see Figure 1.2 on page 8).

**FIGURE 1.2**

**MySearchLab**

As you read the various research links throughout the text also visit MySearchLab; it's specifically designed to help you learn the skills for effective and efficient researching.

All public speaking situations involve noise. You won't be able to totally eliminate noise, but you can try to reduce its effects. Making your language more precise, organizing your thoughts more logically, and reinforcing your ideas with visual aids are some ways to combat the influence of noise.

## Context

The speaker and his or her listeners operate in a physical, sociopsychological, temporal, and cultural **context**. The context influences you as the speaker, the audience, the speech, and the effects of the speech. The **physical context** is the actual place in which you give your speech (the room, hallway, park, or auditorium). A presentation in a small intimate room needs to be very different from an address in a sports arena.

The **sociopsychological context** includes, for example, the relationship between speaker and audience: Is a supervisor speaking to workers, or a worker speaking to supervisors? A principal addressing teachers, or a parent addressing principals? This sociopsychological context also includes the audience's attitudes toward and knowledge of you and your subject. A speech endeavoring to influence a supportive audience will employ very different strategies than would a speech delivered to a hostile audience.

The **temporal context** includes factors such as the time of day and, more importantly, where your speech fits into the sequence of events. For example, does your speech follow another presentation that has taken an opposing position? Is your speech the sixth in a series exploring the same topic?

The **cultural context** has to do with the beliefs, lifestyles, values, and behaviors that the speaker and the audience bring with them and that bear on the topic and purpose of the speech. **Culture** is passed down from one generation to the next through communication rather than through genes. Thus, the term *culture* does not refer to genetic traits such as color of skin or shape of eyes. Culture does include beliefs in a supreme being, attitudes toward family, and the values people place on friendship or money.

**PUBLIC SPEAKING CHOICE POINT: Cultural Insensitivity**

Ted is giving a speech critical of bullfighting, something he sees as animal cruelty. A significant part of the audience, however, celebrate this as a part of their culture. What options does Ted have for remaining true to his convictions and yet not insult audience members?

Even though culture is not synonymous with race or nationality, members of a particular race are often enculturated into a similar set of beliefs, attitudes, and values. Similarly, members living in the same country are often taught similar beliefs, attitudes, and values. Thus, we often speak of "Hispanic culture" or "African American culture." But, lest we be guilty of stereotyping, we need to recognize that within any large culture—especially a culture based on race or nationality—there will be enormous differences. The Pennsylvania farmer may in many ways be closer to the Chinese farmer than to the Philadelphia lawyer. Further, as an individual born into a particular race and nationality, you don't necessarily have to adopt the attitudes, beliefs, and values that may be dominant among the people of your race and nationality.

In a similar way, **gender** can be considered a cultural variable—largely because cultures teach boys and girls different attitudes, beliefs, values, and ways of communicating and relating to one another. In other words, you act like a man or a woman in part because of what your culture has taught you about how men and women should act. This does not, of course, deny that biological differences also play a role in the differences between male and female behavior. In fact, research continues to uncover biological roots of behavior once thought entirely learned, such as happiness and shyness.

There are lots of reasons for the cultural emphasis you'll find in this book (and probably in all your textbooks). Most prevalent, perhaps, are the vast demographic changes taking place throughout the United States. Whereas at one time the United States was largely a country populated by Europeans, it's now a country greatly influenced by enormous numbers of new citizens from South and Central America, Africa, and Asia. And the same is true on college and university campuses throughout the nation. With these changes come different communication customs and the need to understand and adapt to these new ways of looking at communication in general and public speaking in particular.

The principles for communicating information and for persuasion differ from one culture to another. For example, appealing to "competitive spirit" and "financial gain" may prove effective with Wall Street executives but ineffective with people who are more comfortable with socialist or communist economic systems and beliefs. The importance of culture is further explored in Public Speaking Exercise 1.2 "Cultural Beliefs and Your Audience" on page 19.

## Channel

The **channel** is the medium that carries message signals from sender to receiver. Both auditory and visual channels are significant in public speaking. Through the auditory channel you send spoken messages—your words and your sentences. Through the visual channel—eye contact (or the lack of it), body movement, hand and facial gestures, and clothing—you send visual messages. Increasingly, public speaking is mediated; public speeches are frequently delivered in a television studio and heard by millions in their own living rooms or caught on camera and put up on YouTube. Similarly, speeches may be digitally recorded and made available day and night to millions of Internet users. Politicians and business leaders currently post their speeches on websites, blogs, and newsgroups. As video and sound capabilities become more universal, the use of mediated channels is likely to increase in frequency. Advances in technology seem to move computer-mediated communication in the direction of duplicating as many of the elements of face-to-face interaction as possible.

## Ethics

Because your speech will have an effect on your audience, you have an obligation to consider **ethics**—issues of right and wrong, or the moral implication of your message. When you develop your topic, present your research, create persuasive appeals, and do any of the other tasks related to public speaking there are ethical issues to be considered (Bok, 1978; Jaksa & Pritchard, 1994; Johannesen, 1996; Thompson, 2000). You also have ethical obligations in your roles as listener and as critic.

In thinking about the ethics of public speaking and about the many ethical issues raised throughout this text, you can take the position that ethics is objective or that it's subjective. In an objective view you'd claim that the morality of an act—say, a communication message—is absolute and exists apart from the values or beliefs of any individual or culture. This objective view holds that there are standards that apply to all people in all situations at all times. If lying, advertising falsely, using illegally obtained evidence, and revealing secrets, for example, are considered unethical, then they'll be considered unethical regardless of the circumstances surrounding them or of the values and beliefs of the culture in which they occur.

In a subjective view you'd claim that the morality of an act depends on the culture's values and beliefs as well as on the particular circumstances. Thus, from a subjective position you would claim that the end might justify the means—a good result can justify the use of unethical means to achieve that result. For example, you might argue that lying is wrong to win votes or sell cigarettes, but that lying can be ethical if the end result is positive (such as trying to make someone who is unattractive feel better by telling them they look great, or telling critically ill patients that they'll feel better soon). Perhaps the major ethical issue in the public speaking classroom is that of plagiarism which is covered in depth below.

Because of the central importance of ethics in public speaking, each chapter contains an Ethical Choice Point box in which a brief scenario of an ethical dilemma is presented and you're asked to consider your ethical options.

Now that we've considered the essential elements of public speaking, let's turn to two persistent problems in public speaking and put these to rest. The first is plagiarism and the second is what is probably your major concern: fear, or what's called "communication apprehension."

# Plagiarism

One of the most difficult tasks in a public speaking course—and actually, in every course—is that of plagiarism. Very often plagiarism is committed because of a lack of understanding of proper citation. This section aims to clarify what plagiarism is, why it's unacceptable, and how you can avoid even the suggestion of plagiarism.

## What Is Plagiarism?

The word **plagiarism** refers to the process of passing off the work (ideas, words, illustrations) of others as your own. Understand that plagiarism is not the act of using another's ideas—we all do that. It is using another's ideas without acknowledging that they are the ideas of this other person; it is passing off the ideas as if they were yours.

Plagiarism exists on a continuum, ranging from representing as your own an entire term paper or speech written by someone else (this is often called "direct plagiarism") to using a quotation or research finding without properly citing the author (this is often called "misattribution plagiarism"). Plagiarism also can include getting help from a friend without acknowledging this assistance.

A related issue is "fair use" which, according to the Stanford University Libraries (**http://fairuse.stanford.edu**) grants permission to use copyright material for purposes of review, criticism, or commenting. Unfortunately, "fair use" has not been defined in specific terms; it merely says that the material used must in some way be of value to those reading or listening to it and that there is a limit on the amount of copyrighted information you can present under your name even if you acknowledge your source. It would be unethical under the "fair use standard" to deliver a speech in which you took three-quarters from another source even if you credit the person, especially when it's an ambiguous credit line like "some of this material I got from Professor Smith's lecture." The best guide in public speaking seems to be to make it very clear to your audience not only your sources, but exactly what you are using from others, for example, "This first argument was originally presented by . . ."

In some cultures—especially collectivist cultures (cultures that emphasize the group and mutual cooperation, such as Korea, Japan, and China)—teamwork is strongly encouraged. Students are encouraged to help other students with their work. In the United States and in many other individualist cultures (cultures that emphasize individuality and competitiveness), teamwork without acknowledgment is considered plagiarism.

## Why Is Plagiarism Unacceptable?

In U.S. colleges and universities, plagiarism is a serious violation of the rules of academic honesty and can bring serious penalties, sometimes even expulsion. And it's interesting to note that instructors are mobilizing and are educating themselves in techniques for detecting plagiarism. Further, as with all crimes, ignorance of the law is not an acceptable defense against charges of plagiarism. This last point is especially important, because many people plagiarize through a lack of information as to what does and what does not constitute plagiarism.

Here are just a few reasons why plagiarism is wrong.

- Plagiarism is a violation of another's intellectual property rights. Much as it would be unfair to take another person's watch without permission, it's unfair to take another person's ideas without acknowledging that you did it.
- You're in college to develop your own ideas and your own ways of expressing them; plagiarism defeats this fundamental purpose.
- Evaluations (everything from grades in school to promotions in the workplace) assume that what you present as your work is in fact your work.

## How Can You Avoid Plagiarism?

Here are a few guidelines to help you avoid plagiarism.

Let's start with the easy part. You do not have to, and should not, cite sources for common knowledge—information that is readily available in numerous sources and is not likely to be disputed. For example, the population of Thailand, the amendments to the U.S. Constitution, the actions of the United Nations, or the way the heart pumps blood all are widely available knowledge, and you would not cite the almanac or the political science text from which you got this information. On the other hand, if you were talking about the attitudes of people from Thailand or the reasons the constitutional amendments were adopted, then you would need to cite your sources because this information is not common knowledge and may well be disputed.

For information that is not common knowledge, you need to acknowledge your source. Four simple rules will help you avoid even the suggestion of plagiarism:

1. Acknowledge the source of any ideas you present that are not your own. If you learned of an idea in your history course, then cite the history instructor or the textbook. If you read an idea in an article, then cite the article.
2. Acknowledge the words of another. It's obvious what to do when you're quoting another person exactly; then of course, you need to cite the person you're quoting. You also should cite the

**PUBLIC SPEAKING CHOICE POINT: Plagiarism**

Zoe, an art major, is scheduled to give her first informative speech tomorrow. She has chosen to speak about the ways public art can benefit the entire community. She has collected an array of opinions from experts on the subject and wants to incorporate them into her speech, but does not want to plagiarize in the process. What advice can you give her?

person even when you paraphrase his or her words because you are still using the other person's ideas. It is not always clear when paraphrases need to be credited, so some of the plagiarism websites established by different universities include exercises and extended examples; see, for example, Indiana University's site at **www.indiana.edu/~istd/examples.html** or Purdue University's at **http://owl.english.purdue.edu/owl/resource/589/04/**.

3. Acknowledge help from others. If your roommate gave you examples or ideas or helped you style your speech, acknowledge the help. But you don't need to acknowledge the assistance of, say, a librarian who helped you find a book or website.

4. When in doubt as to whether you should cite a source or how you might best do it, ask your instructor.

**ETHICAL CHOICE POINT**

Plagiarism Detection

You hear a speech in class that you've seen on the Internet—a clear case of plagiarism. The instructor didn't realize it and gave the speech an A and thereby upset the expectations for all the speeches to be heard in class and screwed up the curve. You don't want to be a rat and get the student in trouble—the consequences of which could range from failing the speech assignment, failing the entire course, or being brought up on charges of plagiarism. At the same time you don't want yourself and the other students to be penalized because your speech and those of the other students are unlikely to be as good as this plagiarized speech. ➤*What are some ethical options you have for dealing with this problem?*

# Managing Your Apprehension

Most people would agree that public speaking can be a scary experience. After all, you're the center of attention of 20 or 30 people and you're being evaluated. Your fear is normal. Fortunately, this fear is also something that can be managed and made to work for you rather than against you. So, let's deal with this fear of public speaking, what is called **communication apprehension,** and explain what it is and how you can manage it.

## The Nature of Communication Apprehension

Apprehension in public speaking is normal; everyone experiences some degree of fear in the relatively formal public speaking situation. After all, in public speaking you're the sole focus of attention and are usually being evaluated for your performance. Experiencing nervousness or anxiety is a natural reaction. You are definitely not alone in these feelings.

### Trait and State Apprehension

Some people have a general communication apprehension that shows itself in all communication situations. These people suffer from **trait apprehension**—a general fear of communication, regardless of the specific situation. Their fear appears in conversations, small group settings, and public speaking situations. Not surprisingly, if you have high trait apprehension, you're also more likely to experience embarrassment in a variety of social situations (Withers & Vernon, 2006). Similarly, high apprehensives are likely to have problems in the work environment; for example, they may perform badly in employment interviews and may contribute few ideas on the job (Butler, 2005).

Other people experience communication apprehension in only certain communication situations. These people suffer from **state apprehension**—a fear that is specific to a given communication situation. For example, a speaker may fear public speaking but have no difficulty in talking with two or three other people. Or a speaker may fear job interviews but have no fear of public speaking. State apprehension is extremely common. Most people experience it for some situations; not surprisingly, it is public speaking that most people fear.

## Apprehension Exists on a Continuum

Communication apprehension exists on a continuum. Some people are so apprehensive that they're unable to function effectively in any communication situation and will try to avoid communication as much as possible. Other people are so mildly apprehensive that they appear to experience no fear at all; they're the ones who actively seek out communication opportunities. Most of us are between these extremes.

Contrary to popular belief, apprehension is not necessarily harmful. In fact, apprehension can work for you. Fear can energize you. It may motivate you to work a little harder—to produce a speech that will be better than it might have been had you not been fearful. Further, the audience cannot see the apprehension that you may be experiencing. Even though you may think that the audience can hear your heart beat faster, they can't. They can't see your knees tremble. They can't sense your dry throat—at least not most of the time.

You may wish to pause here and take the self-test "How Apprehensive Are You in Public Speaking?" to measure your own level of fear of public speaking.

# TEST YOURSELF

## How Apprehensive Are You in Public Speaking?

This questionnaire consists of six statements concerning your feelings about public speaking. Indicate the degree to which each statement applies to you by marking whether you (1) strongly agree, (2) agree, (3) are undecided, (4) disagree, or (5) strongly disagree with each statement. There are no right or wrong answers. Don't be concerned that some of the statements are similar to others. Work quickly; just record your first impression.

_____ **1.** I have no fear of giving a speech.

_____ **2.** Certain parts of my body feel very tense and rigid while giving a speech.

_____ **3.** I feel relaxed while giving a speech.

_____ **4.** My thoughts become confused and jumbled when I am giving a speech.

_____ **5.** I face the prospect of giving a speech with confidence.

_____ **6.** While giving a speech, I get so nervous that I forget facts I really know.

➤ **HOW DID YOU DO?** To obtain your public speaking apprehension score, begin with the number 18 (selected so that you won't wind up with negative numbers) and add to it the scores for items 1, 3, and 5. Then, from this total, subtract the scores from items 2, 4, and 6. A score above 18 shows some degree of apprehension. Most people score above 18, so if you scored relatively high, you're among the vast majority of people.

➤ **WHAT WILL YOU DO?** As you read the suggestions for reducing apprehension in the text, consider what you can do to incorporate these into your own public speaking experiences. Consider how these suggestions might be useful in reducing apprehension more generally—for example, in social situations and in small groups and meetings.

*Source:* McCroskey, J. C. (2006). *An introduction to rhetorical communication* (9th ed.). Boston: Allyn & Bacon. Reprinted by permission of the author.

Here are several ways you can deal with and manage your own public speaking apprehension: (1) reverse the factors that cause apprehension, (2) restructure your thinking, (3) practice performance visualization, and (4) desensitize yourself (Richmond & McCroskey, 1998; Bodie, 2010). The same techniques will also help you manage apprehensiveness in social and work situations.

## Reverse the Factors That Cause Apprehension

If you can reverse or at least lessen the factors that cause apprehension, you'll be able to reduce your apprehension significantly. The following suggestions are based on research identifying the major factors contributing to your fear in public speaking (Beatty, 1988; Richmond & McCroskey, 1998; Bodie, 2010).

- **Reduce the newness of public speaking by gaining experience.** New and different situations such as public speaking are likely to make anyone anxious, so try to reduce their newness and differentness. One way to do this is to get as much public speaking experience as you can. Experience will show you that the feelings of accomplishment you gain from public speaking are rewarding and will outweigh any initial anxiety. Try also to familiarize yourself with the public speaking context. For example, try to rehearse in the room in which you'll give your speech.

- **Reduce your self-focus by visualizing public speaking as conversation.** When you're the center of attention, as you are in public speaking, you may feel especially conspicuous, and this often increases anxiety. It may help, therefore, to think of public speaking as another type of conversation (some theorists call it "enlarged conversation"). Or, if you're comfortable talking in groups, visualize your audience as a small group.

- **Reduce your perceived differentness from the audience by stressing similarity.** When you feel similar to (rather than different from) your audience, your anxiety should lessen. This is especially important when your audience consists of people from cultures different from your own (Stephan & Stephan, 1992): In such cases you're likely to feel fewer similarities with your listeners and experience greater anxiety (Gudykunst & Nishida, 1984; Gudykunst, Yang, & Nishida, 1985). So with all audiences, but especially with multicultural groups, stress similarities such as shared attitudes, values, or beliefs. This tactic will make you feel more at one with your listeners and therefore more confident as a speaker.

- **Reduce your fear of failure by thoroughly preparing and practicing.** Much of the fear you experience is a fear of failure. Adequate and even extra preparation will lessen the possibility of failure and the accompanying apprehension (Smith & Frymier, 2006). Because apprehension is greatest during the beginning of the speech, try memorizing the first few sentences of your speech. If there are complicated facts or figures, be sure to write them out and plan to read them. This way you won't have to worry about forgetting them completely.

- **Reduce your anxiety by moving about and breathing deeply.** Physical activity—including movements of the whole body as well as small movements of the hands, face, and head—lessens apprehension. Using a visual aid, for example, will temporarily divert attention from you and will allow you to get rid of your excess energy as you move to display it. Also, try breathing deeply a few times before getting up to speak. You'll feel your body relax, and this will help you overcome your initial fear of walking to the front of the room.

- **Avoid chemicals as tension relievers.** Unless prescribed by a physician, avoid any chemical means for reducing apprehension. Tranquilizers, marijuana, or artificial stimulants are likely to create problems rather than reduce them. And, of course, alcohol does nothing to reduce public speaking apprehension (Himle, Abelson, & Haghightgou, 1999). These chemicals can impair your ability to remember the parts of your speech, to accurately read audience feedback, and to regulate the timing of your speech.

**PUBLIC SPEAKING CHOICE POINT: Apprehension**
This is Harry's first experience with public speaking, and he's very nervous. He's afraid he'll forget his speech or stumble somehow, so he's wondering if it would be a good idea to alert the audience to his nervousness. What are Harry's options in this situation? What would you advise Harry to do if his audience were your public speaking class?

## Restructure Your Thinking

**Cognitive restructuring** is a proven technique for reducing a great number of fears and stresses (Ellis, 1988; Beck, 1988; Nordahl & Wells, 2007). The general idea behind this technique is that the way you think about a situation influences the way you react to the situation. If you can change the way you think about a situation (reframe it, restructure it, reappraise it) you'll be able to change your reactions to the situation. So if you think that public speaking will produce stress (fear, apprehension, anxiety), then reappraising it as less threatening will reduce the stress, fear, apprehension, and anxiety.

Much public speaking apprehension is based on unrealistic thinking, on thinking that is self-defeating. For example, you may think that you're a poor speaker or that you're boring or that the audience won't like you or that you have to be perfect. Instead of thinking in terms of these unrealistic and self-defeating assumptions, substitute realistic ones, especially when tackling new things like public speaking.

Positive and supportive thoughts will help you restructure your thinking. Remind yourself of your successes, strengths, and virtues. Concentrate on your potential, not on your limitations. Use **self-affirmations** such as "I'm friendly and can communicate this in my speeches," "I can learn the techniques for controlling my fear," "I'm a competent person and have the potential to be an effective speaker," "I can make mistakes and can learn from them."

## Practice Performance Visualization

A variation of cognitive restructuring is **performance visualization**, a technique designed specifically to reduce the outward signs of apprehension and also to reduce the negative thinking that often creates anxiety (Ayres, 2005).

First, develop a positive attitude and a positive self-perception. Visualize yourself in the role of an effective public speaker. Visualize yourself walking to the front of the room—fully and totally confident, fully in control of the situation. The audience is in rapt attention and, as you finish, bursts into wild applause. Throughout this visualization avoid all negative thoughts. As you visualize yourself as this effective speaker, take note of how you walk, look at your listeners, handle your notes, and respond to questions; also, think about how you feel about the public speaking experience.

Second, model your performance on that of an especially effective speaker. View a particularly competent public speaker on video; YouTube (**youtube.com**) or Video Surf (**videosurf.com**) make these easy to access and enjoyable to watch. As you view the video gradually shift yourself into the role of speaker; become this speaker you admire.

## Desensitize Yourself

**Systematic desensitization** is a technique for dealing with a variety of fears, including those involved in public speaking (Richmond & McCroskey, 1998; Wolpe, 1957; Dwyer, 2005). The general idea is to create a hierarchy of behaviors leading up to the desired but feared behavior (say, speaking before an audience). One specific hierarchy might look like this:

**5.** Giving a speech in class

**4.** Introducing another speaker to the class

**3.** Speaking in a group in front of the class

**2.** Answering a question in class

**1.** Asking a question in class

The main objective of this experience is to learn to relax, beginning with relatively easy tasks and progressing to the behavior you're apprehensive about—in this case giving a speech in class. You begin at the bottom of the hierarchy and rehearse the first behavior mentally over a period of days until you can clearly visualize asking a question in class without any uncomfortable anxiety. Once you can accomplish this, move to the second level. Here you visualize a somewhat more threatening behavior; say, answering a question. Once you can do this, move to the third level, and so on until you get to the desired behavior.

In creating your hierarchy, use small steps to help you get from one step to the next more easily. Each success will make the next step easier. You might then go on to engage in the actual behaviors after you have comfortably visualized them: ask a question, answer a question, and so on.

# Next Steps

In this chapter, four techniques were identified that you can use to manage your fear of public speaking. If you want to reduce your fear of public speaking, consider the specific steps you can take. If you continue to experience extremely high levels of apprehension, or if you're so fearful of the speaking situation that you simply cannot function, talk with your instructor. The next chapter continues this discussion of fundamentals, focusing on listening and criticism.

# Essentials of Introducing Public Speaking

This first chapter has looked at the nature of public speaking and at probably the most important obstacle to public speaking—namely, communication apprehension.

1. Public speaking is a transactional process in which (a) a speaker (b) addresses (c) a relatively large audience with (d) a relatively continuous message.

## The Benefits of Public Speaking

2. Among the benefits of studying public speaking are:
   - Improved public speaking abilities—as speaker, as listener, and as critic—which results in personal benefits as well as benefits to society.
   - Increased personal and social abilities.
   - Wider academic and career skills in organization, research, style, and the like.

## The Essential Elements of Public Speaking

3. The essential elements of public speaking are:
   - Speaker, the one who presents the speech.
   - Audience, the intended receivers of the speech; may be immediate or remote.
   - Message, the verbal and nonverbal signals.
   - Noise, the interference that distorts messages.
   - Context, the physical space, the sociopsychological atmosphere, the time, and the culture in which the speech is presented and of the audience.
   - Channel, the medium through which the signals pass from speaker to listener.
   - Ethics, the moral dimension of communication.

## Plagiarism

4. Plagiarism, the process of passing off the work (ideas, words, illustrations) of others as your own, is unacceptable, and should and can be avoided by knowing what should and what should not be cited.

## Managing Your Communication Apprehension

5. Communication apprehension, the fear of speaking, is often especially high in public speaking. In managing your fear of public speaking, try to:
   - Reverse the factors that contribute to apprehension by reducing newness, self-focus, perceived differentness with audience, fear

of failure by thoroughly preparing and practicing, and move about to eliminate some excess energy.

- Restructure your thinking.
- Practice performance visualization.
- Desensitize yourself.

# Essential Terms

Here are the essential terms used in this chapter and the pages on which they are introduced.

audience **(5)**
channel **(10)**
cognitive restructuring **(16)**
communication apprehension **(13)**
context **(8)**
culture **(9)**

ethics **(10)**
gender **(9)**
message **(5)**
noise **(6)**
performance visualization **(17)**
plagiarism **(11)**

presentation **(6)**
public speaking **(2)**
self-affirmation **(17)**
speaker **(4)**
state apprehension **(14)**
systematic desensitization **(17)**
trait apprehension **(15)**

# Public Speaking Exercises

These exercises, presented at the end of each chapter, are designed to stimulate you to think more actively about the concepts and skills covered in the chapter and to help you practice your developing public speaking skills.

## 1.1  A Model of Public Speaking

Construct your own model of public speaking and indicate how it differs from various other forms of communication, such as face-to-face conversation, e-mail, blogging, interviewing, and small group communication.

## 1.2  Cultural Beliefs and Your Audience

Evaluate each of the cultural beliefs listed below in terms of how effective each would be if used as a basic assumption by a speaker addressing your public speaking class. Use the following scale: A = the audience would accept this assumption and welcome a speaker with this point of view; B = some members would listen open-mindedly and others wouldn't; or C = the audience would reject this assumption and would not welcome a speaker with this point of view. What guidelines for speeches to be given to this class audience does this analysis suggest?

_____ 1. A return to religious values is the best hope for the world.

_____ 2. Embryonic stem cell research should be encouraged.

_____ 3. The invasion of Iraq was morally unjustified.

_____ 4. Winning is all-important; it's not how you play the game, it's whether or not you win that matters.

_____ 5. Keeping the United States militarily superior is the best way to preserve world peace.

_____ 6. Immigration to the United States should be significantly reduced.

_____ 7. Gay and lesbian relationships are equal in all ways to heterosexual relationships.

_____ 8. The strong and the rich are responsible for taking care of the weak and the poor.

_____ 9. Getting to heaven should be life's major goal.

_____ 10. Money is a positive good; the quest for financial success is a perfectly respectable (even a noble) goal.

# Log On! PEARSON my speech lab

## Introducing Public Speaking

Visit MySpeechLab (MSL) at myspeechlab.com. Under **Media Resources** you'll find a wealth of material to help you master the principles of public speaking under such headings as:

1. Explore (added explanations of concepts discussed in the text, some of which are interactive—asking you to respond to a series of prompts).

2. Quick Quizzes (tests for assessing your understanding of the concepts discussed in the text).

3. Author Choice (a variety of self-tests and additional explanations of public speaking concepts.

4. Visualize (diagrams or tables illustrating various concepts from this textbook and other communication texts, which are especially helpful since they offer the same material but present and organize it in different ways).

5. Watch (videos of actual speeches, mainly by college students much like yourself but also some professional speakers). Of special relevance to this chapter are the self-tests on shyness and willingness to communicate, an informative speech, and additional explanation of plagiarism and how to avoid it.

# 2 Listening and Criticism

## WHY READ THIS CHAPTER?

**Because it will enable you to become a more effective listener and critic of public speeches by helping you to:**

- improve your listening effectiveness in public speaking (or in any communication situation)

- express your evaluations in ways that will help speakers improve their skills and listen openly to the evaluations given by others

- listen and criticize with cultural awareness

- analyze public speaking effectiveness and apply the insights to your own speeches

*[E]very wrong attempt discarded is another step forward.*

—THOMAS A. EDISON

Listening, according to the International Listening Association, is "the process of receiving, constructing meaning from, and responding to spoken and/or nonverbal messages" (Emmert, 1994, cited in Brownell, 2006). Here we look at the nature of listening as it occurs in the context of public speaking, the influence of culture on listening, and some principles for listening more effectively.

Listening skills yield numerous benefits. Effective listening will help you increase the amount of information you learn and will decrease the time you need to learn it. It will help you distinguish logical from illogical appeals and thus decrease your chances of getting duped. And, not surprisingly, effective listening will help you become a better public speaker. When you listen effectively to other speakers, you'll see more clearly what works and what doesn't work (and why); this will help you identify the principles of public speaking to follow, along with the pitfalls to avoid.

## Listening in Public Speaking

**Listening** can be described as a series of five steps: receiving, understanding, remembering, evaluating, and responding. The process is represented in Figure 2.1.

### Receiving

Unlike listening, hearing begins and ends with the first stage: **receiving.** Hearing is something that just happens when you get within earshot of some auditory stimulus. Listening is quite different; it begins (but does not end) with receiving a speaker's messages. The messages a listener receives are both verbal

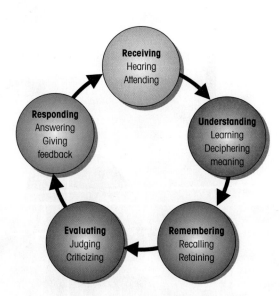

**FIGURE 2.1**
**The Process of Listening**
This five-step model draws on a variety of models that listening researchers have developed (Alessandra, 1986; Barker, 1990; Brownell, 2010).

and nonverbal; they consist of words as well as gestures, facial expressions, variations in volume and rate, and lots more, as we will see throughout this book.

At this stage of listening you recognize not only what is said but also what is not said. For example, you receive both the politician's summary of accomplishments in education as well as his or her omission of failed promises to improve health care programs.

Receiving messages is a highly selective process. You don't listen to all the available auditory stimuli. Rather, you selectively tune in to certain messages and tune out others. Generally, you listen most carefully to messages that you feel will prove of value to you or that you find particularly interesting. At the same time, you give less attention to messages that have less value or interest. Thus, you may listen carefully when your instructor tells you what will appear on the examination but may listen less carefully to an extended story or to routine announcements. To improve your receiving skills:

- Look at the speaker; make your mind follow your body and focus attention on the person speaking.
- Focus your attention on the speaker's verbal and nonverbal messages, on what is said and on what isn't said.
- Avoid attending to distractions in the environment.
- Focus your attention on what the speaker is saying rather than on any questions or objections you may have to what the speaker is saying.

## Understanding

**Understanding** a speaker means grasping not only the thoughts that are expressed but also the emotional tone that accompanies these thoughts; for example, the urgency or the joy or sorrow expressed in the message. To enhance understanding:

- Relate the new information the speaker is giving to what you already know.
- See the speaker's messages from the speaker's point of view; avoid judging the message until you fully understand it as the speaker intended.
- Rephrase (paraphrase) the speaker's ideas into your own words as you continue to listen.

## Remembering

Messages that you receive and understand need to be retained for at least some period of time. In public

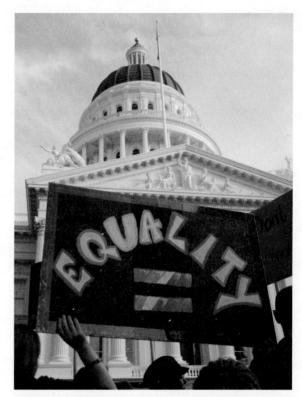

**PUBLIC SPEAKING CHOICE POINT: Self-Identification**
Claire is planning to give a speech in favor of gay marriage. Claire herself is heterosexual, and she wonders if she should identify her affectional orientation in the speech. If Claire were giving her speech to your class, what would you see as the advantages and disadvantages of including reference to her own affectional orientation? Would the advantages and disadvantages you identified be different if Claire were a lesbian? What would you advise Claire to do?

speaking situations you can enhance the process of **remembering** by taking notes or by taping the messages.

What you remember is actually not what was said, but what you think (or remember) was said. Memory for speech isn't reproductive; you don't simply reproduce in your memory what the speaker said. Rather, memory is reconstructive; you actually reconstruct the messages you hear into a system that seems to make sense to you. This is well illustrated in Public Speaking Exercise 2.1 "Do You Really Remember What You Hear?" on page 44.

In remembering:

- Identify the thesis or central idea and the main points.
- Summarize the message in a more easily retainable form, being careful not to ignore crucial details or important qualifications.
- Repeat names and key concepts to yourself.
- Identify the organizational pattern and use it (visualize it) to organize what the speaker is saying.

## Evaluating

**Evaluating** consists of judging the message and the speaker's credibility, truthfulness, or usefulness in some way. At this stage your own biases and prejudices become especially influential. They will affect what you single out for evaluation and what you'll just let pass. They will influence what you judge to be good and what you judge to be bad. In some situations evaluation is more in the nature of critical analysis—a topic explored in detail later in this chapter. When evaluating:

- Resist evaluation until you feel you understand (at least reasonably well) the speaker's point of view.
- Distinguish facts from inferences (see Chapter 8, "Word Your Speech," on p. 167), opinions, and personal interpretations that you're making as well as those made by the speaker.
- Identify any biases, self-interests, or prejudices that may lead the speaker to slant unfairly what he or she is presenting.
- Identify any biases that may lead you to remember what supports your attitudes and beliefs and to forget what contradicts them.

## Responding

**Responding** occurs in two phases: (1) nonverbal (and occasionally verbal) responses you make while the speaker is talking and (2) responses you make after the speaker has stopped talking. Responses made while the speaker is talking should support the speaker and show that you're listening. These include what nonverbal researchers call **backchannel cues**—gestures that let the speaker know that you're listening, such as nodding your head, smiling, and leaning forward (Burgoon, Guerrero, & Floyd, 2010).

Responses you make to the speaker after he or she has stopped talking are generally more elaborate and might include questions of clarification ("I wasn't

# RESEARCH LINK

→ **Interviewing for Information**

One research activity that you'll often find helpful is to interview people who have special information that you might use in your speech. For example, you might want to interview a veterinarian for information on proper nutrition for household pets; an eyewitness for information on living through a hurricane; or average people for their opinions on politics, religion, or any of a wide variety of topics.

Here are ten steps you might take to more effectively interview for information.

1. **Select the person you wish to interview.** You might, for example, look through your college catalog for an instructor teaching a course that involves your topic or visit blogs and look for people who have posted articles on your topic.

2. **Secure an appointment.** Phone the person or send an e-mail requesting an interview. State the purpose of your request and say that you hope to conduct a brief interview by phone or that you'd like to send this person a series of questions by e-mail.

3. **Select your topic areas.** Depending on the topic of your speech, the time you have available, and the areas of expertise that your interviewee has, you'll need to select the areas you want to talk about. Generally, it will be best to limit these to perhaps two or three.

4. **Create a list of what you want to say during the interview.** If this is a phone interview, you can keep the cheat sheet in front of you; if a face-to-face interview, review the cheat sheet immediately before the interview. On this cheat sheet write all the questions you want to ask in the order you want to ask them along with notes to yourself to thank the interviewer at the beginning and again at the end of the interview.

5. **Establish rapport with the interviewee.** Open the in-person, telephone, e-mail, or chat-group interview by thanking the person for making the time available and again stating your purpose. You might say something like: "I really appreciate your making time for this interview. As I mentioned, I'm preparing a speech on XYZ, and your experience in this area will help me a lot."

6. **Ask open-ended questions.** Generally, ask questions that provide the interviewee with room to discuss the issues you want to raise. Thus, asking, "Do you have formal training in the area of family therapy?" may elicit a simple yes or no. On the other hand, asking, "Can you tell me something of your background in this field?" is open-ended, allowing the interviewee to talk in some detail.

7. **Display effective interpersonal communication.** Generally, it will help to be open, positive, and flexible. Be open to the interviewee's ideas. Avoid challenging the person; after all, your aim is to get this person's perspective. Be positive about the interview and the interviewee. Be flexible and be ready to adjust your interview on the basis of the ongoing interaction.

8. **Ask for permission to tape or print the interview.** It's a good idea to keep an accurate record of the interview, so ask permission to tape the interview if it's in person or by telephone. Taping will provide you with a more accurate record of the interview than will handwritten notes. But always ask permission first. Similarly, if the interview is by e-mail or via chat group and you want to quote the interviewee's responses, ask permission first. An agreement to be interviewed does not include permission to print or distribute the interview or even parts of it.

9. **Close with an expression of appreciation.** In your expression of appreciation be specific and try to refer back to the conversation. For example, *I want to thank you for making time for me and for sharing those great stories about how you started your business; these will make wonderful examples in my speech.*

10. **Follow up with a thank-you note.** Even though you thank the person at the end of the interview, it's especially polite to follow up with a note later that day or the next day. Or perhaps you might send the person you interviewed a copy of your speech with a note of thanks.

The next Research Link, "Libraries," appears on page 55.

sure what you meant by reclassification"); expressions of agreement ("You're absolutely right on this, and I'll support your proposal when it comes up for a vote"); and expressions of disagreement ("I disagree that Japanese products are superior to those produced in the United States"). In responding:

- Use a variety of backchanneling cues to support the speaker. Using only one cue—for example, nodding constantly—will make it appear that you're not listening but are on automatic pilot.

- Support the speaker in your final responses by saying something positive.

- Own your own responses: State your thoughts and feelings as your own, and use I-messages. For example, say, "I think the new proposal will entail greater expense than you outlined" rather than "Everyone will object to the plan because it will cost too much."

## Guidelines for Listening

Effective listening is extremely important simply because you spend so much time listening. In fact, if you measured importance by the time you spend on an activity, listening would be your most important communication activity. Studies conducted from 1929 to 1980 showed that listening was the most often used form of communication (occupying about 45 to 53 percent of communication time), followed by speaking (about 16 to 30 percent), reading (about 16 to 17 percent), and writing (about 9 to 14 percent) (Wolvin & Coakley, 1996; Brownell, 2010). This was true of high school and college students as well as of adults from a wide variety of fields. With the widespread use of the Internet, these studies have become dated, and today their findings are of limited value. However, anecdotal evidence (certainly not conclusive in any way) suggests that listening is probably still the most used communication activity. Just think of how you spend your day; listening probably occupies a considerable amount of time. Listening is also important in your professional life; regardless of what profession you enter, you'll always need the skills of effective listening (Allen, 1997; Salopek, 1999; Brownell, 2006).

### Listen Actively

The first step in listening improvement is to recognize that it isn't a passive activity. You cannot listen without effort. Listening is a difficult process. In many ways it's more demanding than speaking. In speaking you control the situation; you can talk about what you like in the way you like. In listening, however, you have to follow the pace, the content, and the language of the speaker.

The best preparation for **active listening** is to act like an active listener: to focus your complete attention on the speaker (Perkins & Fogarty, 2006). Recall, for example, how your body almost automatically reacts to important news. You sit up straighter, cock your head toward the speaker, and remain relatively still and quiet. You do this almost reflexively, because this is how you listen most effectively. This isn't to say that you should be tense and uncomfortable, but only that your body should reflect your active mind. In listening actively:

- **Use your listening time wisely.** Think about what the speaker is saying, summarize the speaker's thoughts, formulate questions, draw connections between what the speaker says and what you already know. At the same time, avoid focusing on external issues—with what you did last Saturday or your plans for this evening.

- **Work at listening.** Listening is hard, so be prepared to participate actively. Avoid "the entertainment syndrome," the expectation that you'll be amused and entertained by a speaker (Floyd, 1985). Set aside distractions (cell phones, laptops, and headphones) so that your listening task will have less competition.

- **Assume there's value in what the speaker is saying.** Resist assuming that what you have to say is more valuable than the speaker's remarks.

- **Take notes if appropriate.** Taking notes may be helpful if you want to ask a question about a specific item of information or if you want to include a specific statement in your critical evaluation.

## Listen for Total Meaning

The meaning of a message isn't only in the words; it's also in the speaker's nonverbal behavior.

The meanings communicated in a speech will also depend on what the speaker does not say. The speaker on contemporary social problems who omits references to homeless people or to drug abuse communicates important messages by these very omissions. For example, listeners may infer that the speaker is poorly prepared, that the speaker's research was inadequate, or that the speaker is trying to fool the audience by not mentioning these issues. As a listener, therefore, be particularly sensitive to the meanings that significant omissions may communicate. As a speaker, recognize that most inferences that audiences draw

**PUBLIC SPEAKING CHOICE POINT: Active Listening**
Alex is taking a public speaking class that meets at 4 in the afternoon and he realizes that it will take some extra effort to encourage the class to listen to his speech. What are some of the things Alex can do to encourage the class to listen?

from omissions are negative and will reflect negatively on your credibility and on the total impact of your speech. In listening for total meaning:

- **Focus on both verbal and nonverbal messages.** Recognize both consistent and inconsistent "packages" of messages and take these cues as guides for drawing inferences about the meaning the speaker is trying to communicate. Ask questions when in doubt.
- **See the forest, then the trees.** Connect the specifics to the speaker's general theme rather than merely remembering isolated facts and figures.
- **Balance your attention between the surface and the underlying meanings.** Don't disregard the literal (surface) meaning of the speech in your attempt to uncover the more hidden (deeper) meanings.
- **Resist the temptation to filter out difficult or unpleasant messages.** You don't want to hear that something you believe is untrue or to be told that people you respect are behaving unethically, yet these are the very messages you need to listen to with great care. If you filter out this kind of information, you risk failing to correct misinformation. You risk losing new and important insights.

## Listen with Empathy

The word **empathy** refers to the process by which you are able to feel what others are feeling, to see the world as they see it, to walk in their shoes (Eisenberg & Strayer, 1987). Of course, you can never feel exactly what the speaker is feeling, but you can attempt to feel something of what he or she is feeling, to listen to the feelings as well as the thoughts.

Empathic listening is best viewed in two stages. First, there is the empathy that you feel for the speaker, which enables you to understand better the speaker's thoughts and feelings. Second, there are the empathic responses that you communicate back to the speaker to let the speaker know that you do indeed understand what he or she means and feels. Let's start with a few suggestions for feeling empathy for the speaker.

- **See the speaker's point of view.** Before you can understand what the speaker is saying, you have to see the message from the speaker's vantage point. Try putting yourself in the role of the speaker and looking at the topic from the his or her perspective.
- **Understand the speaker's thoughts and feelings.** Don't consider your listening task complete until you've understood what the speaker is feeling as well as thinking.
- **Avoid "offensive listening."** Offensive listening is the tendency to listen to bits and pieces of information that will enable you to attack the speaker or to find fault with something the speaker has said.
- **Don't distort messages because of the "friend-or-foe" factor.** In other words, avoid listening for positive statements about friends and negative statements about enemies. For example, if you dislike Fred, make the added effort to listen objectively to Fred's speeches or to comments that might reflect positively on Fred.

The second part of empathy—expressing your empathy back to the speaker—can best be accomplished in two steps corresponding to the two parts in true empathy: thinking empathy and feeling empathy (Bellafiore, 2005). In *thinking empathy* you express an understanding of what the person means. For example, when you paraphrase someone's comment, showing that you understand the meaning the person is trying to communicate, you're communicating *thinking empathy*. When you nod your head in approval of a speaker's argument, you're communicating *thinking empathy*. In communicating *feeling empathy,* you express your feeling of what the other person is feeling. When your facial expressions are appropriate to the tone of the speaker's talk, you're communicating *feeling empathy*. Often you'll respond with both thinking and feeling empathy in the same brief response; for example, *I can understand what it must be like living with a partner who is always depressed [thinking empathy]; you must get depressed yourself [feeling empathy]*.

## Listen with an Open Mind

Listening with an open mind is difficult. It isn't easy to listen to arguments attacking your cherished beliefs. Listening often stops when such remarks are made. Yet in these situations it's particularly important to continue listening openly and fairly. To listen with an open mind, try these suggestions.

- **Avoid prejudging.** Delay both positive and negative evaluation until you've fully understood the intention and the content of the message being communicated. Also avoid prejudging the speech as irrelevant or uninteresting. Give the speaker a chance.

- **Avoid filtering out difficult, unpleasant, or undesirable messages.** Avoid distorting messages through oversimplification or leveling—the tendency to eliminate details and to simplify complex messages to make them easier to remember.

- **Recognize your own biases.** A **bias,** prejudice, or partiality may interfere with accurate listening and cause you to distort message reception to fit your own prejudices and expectations. Biases may also lead to sharpening—an effect in which an item of information takes on increased importance because it seems to confirm your stereotypes or prejudices.

- **Avoid assimilation.** The tendency to reconstruct messages so they reflect your own attitudes, prejudices, needs, and values is known as **assimilation.** It is the tendency to hear relatively neutral messages ("Management plans to institute drastic changes in scheduling") as supporting your own attitudes and beliefs ("Management is going to screw up our schedules again").

A useful technique for ensuring effective listening is presented in Public Speaking Exercise 2.2, "Listening to New Ideas," on page 45.

## Listen Ethically

As a listener you share not only in the success or failure of any communication but also in the moral implications of the communication exchange.

**PUBLIC SPEAKING CHOICE POINT: Ethical Listening**

Simone is teaching a class in public speaking, and one of her students, a sincere and devout Iranian Muslim, gives a speech on "why women should be subservient to men." After the first two minutes of the speech, half the class walks out, returning 10 minutes later, after the speech is over. Simone decides to address this incident. What would you advise Simone to say?

Consequently, bear ethical issues in mind when listening as well as when speaking. Two major principles govern ethical listening:

- **Give the speaker an honest hearing.** Avoid prejudging the speaker before hearing her or him out. Try to put aside prejudices and preconceptions and to evaluate the speaker's message fairly. At the same time, try to empathize with the speaker. You don't have to agree with the speaker, but try to understand emotionally as well as intellectually what he or she means. Then accept or reject the speaker's ideas on the basis of the information offered—not on the basis of some bias or prejudice or incomplete understanding.

- **Give the speaker honest responses and feedback.** In a learning environment such as a public speaking class, listening ethically means giving frank and constructive criticism to help the speaker improve. It also means reflecting honestly on the questions speakers raise. Much as the listener has a right to expect an active speaker, the speaker has the right to expect a listener who will actively deal with, rather than just passively hear, the message of a speech.

When learning the art of public speaking, you can gain much insight from the criticism offered by others as well as from your own efforts to critique others' speeches. The following sections consider the nature of criticism in a learning environment, the influence of culture on criticism, and the standards and principles for evaluating a speech and for making criticism easier and more effective.

In addition to these guidelines, consider the specific situation of listening in the classroom. After all, if you're going to spend the time, you might as well spend it efficiently and effectively. Table 2.1 provides a few specific suggestions.

## Criticism in Public Speaking

Critics and criticism are essential parts of any art. The word *criticism* comes into English from the Latin *criticus*, which means "able to discern," and "able to judge." Speech **criticism,** therefore, is the process of evaluating a speech, of rendering a judgment of its value. Note that there is nothing inherently negative about criticism; criticism may be negative, but it also may be positive.

Perhaps the major value of criticism in the classroom is that it helps you improve your public speaking skills. Through the constructive criticism of others, you'll learn the principles of public speaking more effectively. You'll be shown what you do well; what you could improve; and, ideally, how to improve. As a listener-critic you'll also learn the principles of public speaking

**TABLE 2.1 Listening in the Classroom**

Oliver Wendell Holmes once said "It is the privilege of wisdom to listen." Nowhere is that more true than in the classroom where a large part of your listening takes place. As you read these, consider any additional suggestions that you might offer.

| GENERAL SUGGESTIONS | EXAMPLES |
|---|---|
| Prepare yourself to listen. | Sit up front where you can see your instructor and any visual aids clearly and comfortably. You listen with your eyes as well as your ears. |
| Avoid distractions. | Avoid mental daydreaming as well as physical distractions like your laptop, iPhone, or newspaper. |
| Pay special attention to the introduction; this will often contain a preview and will help you outline the lecture. | Listen for orienting remarks and for key words and phrases such as "another reason," "three major causes," and "first." Use these cues to help you outline the lecture. |
| Take notes in outline form. | Listen for headings and then use these as major headings in your outline. When the instructor says, for example, "there are four kinds of noise," you have your heading and you will have a numbered list of 4. |
| Assume that what is said is relevant. | It may eventually prove irrelevant (unfortunately) but if you listen with the assumption of irrelevancy, you'll never hear anything relevant. |
| Listen for understanding. | Avoid taking issue with what is said until you understand fully and then, of course, take issue if you wish. But, generally, don't rehearse in your own mind your arguments against, say, a particular position. When you do this, you run the risk of missing additional explanation or qualification. |

through assessing the speeches of others. Just as you learn when you teach, you also learn when you criticize.

When you give criticism—as you do in a public speaking class—you're telling the speaker that you've listened carefully and that you care enough about the speech and the speaker to offer suggestions for improvement.

Of course, criticism can be difficult—for the critic (whether student or instructor) as well as for the person criticized. As a critic, you may feel embarrassed or uncomfortable about offering evaluation. After all, you may think, "Who am I to criticize another person's speech; my own speech won't be any better." Or you may be reluctant to offend, fearing that your criticism may make the speaker feel uncomfortable. Or you may view criticism as a confrontation that will do more harm than good.

But reconsider this view. By offering criticism you're helping the speaker; you're giving the speaker another perspective that should prove useful in future speeches. When you offer criticism, you're not claiming to be a better speaker; you're simply offering another point of view. It's true that by offering criticism you're stating a position with which others may disagree. That's one of the things that will make this class and the study of public speaking exciting and challenging.

Criticism is also difficult to receive. After working on a speech for a week or two and dealing with the normal anxiety that comes with giving a speech the last thing you want is to stand in front of the class and hear others say what you did wrong. Public speaking is ego-involving, and it's normal to take criticism personally. But if you learn how to give and how to receive criticism, it will help you improve your public speaking skills. Constructive criticism also can serve as an important support mechanism for the developing public speaker, a way of patting the speaker on the back for all the positive effort.

# Guidelines for Criticism

A useful standard to use in evaluating a classroom speech is the speech's degree of conformity to the principles of the art. Using this standard, you'll evaluate a speech positively when it follows the principles of public speaking established by the critics, theorists, and practitioners of public speaking (as described throughout this text) and evaluate it negatively if it deviates from these principles. These principles include speaking on a subject that is worthwhile, relevant, and interesting to listeners; designing a speech for a specific audience; and constructing a speech that is based on sound research. A critical checklist for analyzing public speeches that is based on these principles is presented on the inside front cover of this book.

Before reading the specific suggestions for making critical evaluations a more effective part of the total learning process and avoiding some of the potentially negative aspects of criticism, take the following self-test which asks you to identify what's wrong with selected critical comments.

## TEST YOURSELF

### What's Wrong with These Critical Comments?

For the purposes of this exercise, assume that each of the following 10 comments represents the critic's complete criticism. What's wrong with each?

1. I loved the speech. It was great. Really great.
2. The introduction didn't gain my attention.
3. You weren't interested in your own topic. How do you expect us to be interested?
4. Nobody was able to understand you.
5. The speech was weak.
6. The speech didn't do anything for me.
7. Your position was unfair to those of us on athletic scholarships; we earned those scholarships.
8. I found four things wrong with your speech. First, . . .
9. You needed better research.
10. I liked the speech; we need more police on campus.

➤ **HOW DID YOU DO?** Before reading the following discussion, try to explain why each of these statements is ineffective. Visualize yourself as the speaker receiving such comments and ask yourself if these comments would help you in any way. If not, then they are probably not very effective critical evaluations.

➤ **WHAT WILL YOU DO?** To help you improve your criticism, try to restate the basic meaning of each of these comments but in a more constructive manner.

## Giving Criticism

Here are a few suggestions for giving criticism in the classroom.

### Stress the Positive

Egos are fragile, and public speaking is extremely personal. Speakers understand what Noel Coward meant when he said, "I love criticism just as long as it's unqualified praise." Part of your function as a critic is to strengthen the already positive aspects of someone's public speaking performance. Positive criticism is particularly important in itself, but it's almost essential as a preface to negative comments. There are always positive characteristics about any speech, and it's more productive to concentrate on these first. Thus, instead of saying (as in the self-test), "The speech didn't do anything for me," tell the speaker what you liked first, then bring up a weak point and suggest how it might be improved.

When criticizing a person's second or third speech, it's especially helpful if you can point out specific improvements ("You really held my attention in this speech," "I felt you were much more in control of the topic today than in your first speech").

Remember, too, that communication is irreversible. Once you say something, you can't take it back. Remember this when offering criticism—especially criticism that may be negative. If in doubt, err on the side of gentleness.

### Be Specific

Criticism is most effective when it's specific. General statements such as "I thought your delivery was bad," "I thought your examples were good," or, as in the self-test, "I loved the speech. . . . Really great" and "The speech was weak" are poorly expressed criticisms. These statements don't specify what the speaker might do to improve delivery or to capitalize on the examples used. When commenting on delivery, refer to such specifics as eye contact, vocal volume, or whatever else is of consequence. When commenting on the examples, tell the speaker why they were good. Were they realistic? Were they especially interesting? Were they presented dramatically?

When giving negative criticism, specify and justify—to the extent that you can—positive alternatives. Here's an example.

> I thought the way you introduced your statistics was vague. I wasn't sure where the statistics came from or how recent or reliable they were. It might have been better to say something like "The U.S. Census figures for 2000 show. . . ." That way we would know that the statistics were as recent as possible and the most reliable available.

### Be Objective

When criticizing a speech, transcend your own biases as best you can, unlike the self-test's example ("Your position was unfair. . .; we earned those scholarships").

See the speech as objectively as possible. Assume, for example, that you're strongly for a woman's right to an abortion and you encounter a speech diametrically opposed to your position. In this situation you'll need to take special care not to dismiss the speech because of your own biases. Examine the speech from the point of view of a detached critic. Evaluate, for example, the validity of the arguments and their suitability to the audience, the language, and the supporting materials. Conversely, take special care not to evaluate a speech positively because it presents a position you agree with, as in "I liked the speech; we need more police on campus."

## Be Constructive

Your primary goal in this learning laboratory class should be to provide the speaker with insight that will prove useful in future public speaking transactions. For example, saying that "The introduction didn't gain my attention" doesn't tell the speaker how he or she might have gained your attention. Instead, you might say, "The example about the computer crash would have more effectively gained my attention in the introduction."

Another way you can be constructive is to limit your criticism. Cataloging a speaker's weak points, as in "I found four things wrong with your speech," will overwhelm, not help, the speaker. If you're the sole critic, your criticism naturally will need to be more extensive. If you're one of many critics, limit your criticism to one or perhaps two points. In all cases, your guide should be the value your comments will have for the speaker.

## Focus on Behavior

Focus criticism on what the speaker said and did during the actual speech. Try to avoid the very natural tendency to read the mind of the speaker—to assume that you know why the speaker did one thing rather than another. Compare the critical comments presented in Table 2.2. Note that those in the first column, "Criticism as Attack," try to identify the reasons the speaker did as he or she did; they try to read the speaker's mind. At the same time, they blame the speaker for what happened. Those in the second column, "Criticism as Support," focus on the specific behavior. Note, too, that those in the first column

**TABLE 2.2 Criticism as Attack and as Support**
Comments in the first column will easily prompt defensiveness; comments in the second column are more likely to be responded to positively. As you read this table try to develop additional examples to illustrate these differences in critical expression.

| CRITICISM AS ATTACK | CRITICISM AS SUPPORT |
|---|---|
| "You weren't interested in your topic." | "I would have liked to see greater variety in your delivery. It would have made me feel that you were more interested." |
| "You should have put more time into the speech." | "I think it would have been more effective if you had looked at your notes less." |
| "You didn't care about your audience." | "I would have liked it if you had looked more directly at me while speaking." |

are likely to encourage defensiveness; you can almost hear the speaker saying, "I was so interested in the topic." Those in the second column are less likely to create defensiveness and are more likely to be appreciated as honest reflections of how the critic perceived the speech.

## Own Your Criticism

When giving criticism, own your comments; take responsibility for them. The best way to express this ownership is to use **I-messages** rather than **you-messages.** That is, instead of saying, "You needed better research," say, "I would have been more persuaded if you had used more recent research."

**Owning criticism** also means avoiding attributing what you found wrong to others. Instead of saying, "Nobody was able to understand you," say, "I had difficulty understanding you. It would have helped me if you had spoken more slowly." Remember that your criticism is important precisely because it's your perception of what the speaker did and what the speaker could have done more effectively. Speaking for the entire audience ("We couldn't hear you clearly" or "No one was convinced by your arguments") will not help the speaker, and it's likely to prove demoralizing.

Employing I-messages also will prevent you from using "should messages," a type of expression that almost invariably creates defensiveness and resentment. When you say, "You should have done this" or "You shouldn't have done that," you assume a superior position and imply that what you're saying is correct and that what the speaker did was incorrect. On the other hand, when you own your evaluations and use I-messages, you're giving your perceptions; it's then up to the speaker to accept or reject them.

## Recognize Your Ethical Obligations

Just as the speaker and listener have ethical obligations, so does the critic. Here are a few guidelines. First, the ethical critic *separates personal feelings about the speaker* from his or her evaluation of the speech. A liking for the speaker shouldn't lead you to give positive evaluations of the speech, nor should disliking the speaker lead you to give negative evaluations of the speech.

Second, the ethical critic *separates personal feelings about the issues* from an evaluation of the validity of the arguments. The ethical critic recognizes the validity of an argument even if it contradicts a deeply held belief; similarly, he or she recognizes the fallaciousness of an argument even if it supports a deeply held belief.

Third, the ethical critic *is culturally sensitive,* is aware of his or her own ethnocentrism, and doesn't negatively evaluate customs and forms of speech simply because they deviate from her or his own. Similarly, the ethical critic does not positively evaluate a speech just because it supports her or his own cultural beliefs and values. The ethical critic does not discriminate against or favor speakers simply because they're of a particular sex, race, nationality, religion, age group, or affectional orientation.

**ETHICAL CHOICE POINT**

Open Listening

You're listening to a speech advocating a position with which you strongly disagree. Your first impulse is to stop listening, lest your faith in your current beliefs gets shattered. At the same time, however, you want to give the speaker a fair and honest hearing; after all, you're in college and you should be able to listen logically to all opinions—not just to those with which you agree. ➤ *What are some of the things you can do to remain true to your own beliefs but also to follow the ethical principle of giving the speaker a fair hearing?*

## Responding to Criticism

At the same time that you need to express your criticism effectively, you'll also want to listen to criticism effectively. Here are some suggestions for making listening to criticism a less difficult and more productive experience. The following suggestions are appropriate in a learning environment such as a public speaking class, where criticism is used as a learning tool. In business and professional public speaking, in contrast, listeners don't offer suggestions for improvement; rather, they focus on the issues you raised.

### Accept the Critic's Viewpoint

Criticism reflects the listener's perception. Because of this the critic is always right. If the critic says that he or she wasn't convinced by your evidence, it won't help to identify the 10 or 12 research sources that you used in your speech; this critic was simply not convinced. Instead, consider why your evidence was not convincing. Perhaps you didn't make clear how the evidence was connected to your thesis or perhaps you raced through it too quickly. If you hear yourself saying, "But, I did...," then consider the possibility that you're not accepting the critic's point of view.

### Listen with an Open Mind

If you've already given your first speech, you know that public speaking is highly ego-involving. Because of this it may be tempting to block out criticism. After all, it's not easy to listen to criticism, especially in a fairly public place like a classroom filled with your peers. But if you do block out such criticism, you'll likely lose out on some useful suggestions for improvement. Realize too that you're in a learning environment—a kind of public speaking laboratory—and you're expected to make mistakes. And if this is your first exposure to public speaking, there's likely to be much room for improvement. So listen to criticism with an open mind, and let the critics know that you're really paying attention to what they have to say. In this way you'll encourage critics to share their perceptions more freely; in the process you'll gain greater insight into how you come across to an audience.

**PUBLIC SPEAKING CHOICE POINT: Noting an Error**
Bethany is giving her colleagues an overview of the sales results of the last quarter when Jeff notices an important error. What are Jeff's options for pointing out this error? What are some of the things he might say? What would be inappropriate?

### Separate Speech Criticism from Personal Criticism

Some speakers personalize the criticism to the point where they perceive a suggestion for improvement as a personal attack. Even when this perception is not conscious, it seems to influence the way in which criticism is taken. So recognize that when some aspect of your speech is criticized, your personality or your worth as an individual isn't being criticized or attacked. Listen to speech criticism with the same detachment that you'd use in listening to a biology instructor help you adjust the lens on the microscope or a computer expert tell you how to import photos into your blog.

## Seek Clarification

If you don't understand the criticism, ask for clarification. For example, if you're told that your specific purpose was too broad but it's unclear to you how you might narrow it, ask the critic to explain—being careful not to appear defensive or confrontational. Even when the criticism is favorable, if you don't understand it or it's not specific enough, ask for clarification. If a critic says, "Your introduction was great," you might want to say something like "Did it grab your attention?" or "Was it clear what I was going to cover in the speech?" In this way you encourage the critic to elaborate.

## Evaluate the Criticism

The suggestion to listen open-mindedly to criticism does not necessarily mean that you should do as critics say. Instead, evaluate what the critics suggest; perhaps even try out the suggestions (in your next rehearsal or in the actual speech); but then make your own decisions as to what criticisms you'll follow totally, what you'll modify and adapt, and what you'll reject.

# Listening, Criticism, and Culture

Culture influences all aspects of public speaking and listening and criticism are no exceptions. Here are some ways in which culture exerts this influence.

## Listening and Culture

Listening is difficult, partly because of the inevitable differences between the communication systems of speaker and listener. Because each person has had a unique set of experiences, each person's communication and meaning system is going to be different from the next person's system. When speaker and listener come from different cultures the differences and their effects are naturally much greater. Here are just a few areas where misunderstandings can occur.

### Language and Speech

Even when speaker and listener speak the same language, they speak it with different meanings and different accents. No two speakers speak exactly the same language. Every speaker speaks an idiolect—a unique variation of the language. Speakers of the same language will sometimes have different meanings for the same terms because they have had different experiences.

Speakers and listeners who have different native languages and who may have learned English as a second language will have even greater differences in meaning. Translations are never precise and never fully capture the meaning in the other language. If your meaning for *house* was learned in a culture in which

# PUBLIC SPEAKING SAMPLE ASSISTANT

## A Poorly Constructed Informative Speech

Throughout this text you'll find Public Speaking Sample Assistant boxes, which are designed to help you visualize the public speech as a whole. The annotations will help you explore important principles that you're likely to find helpful in your own speeches. The following speech and the one presented in Chapter 4 (pp. 78–79) are purposely designed to illustrate *in*effective speeches (no one really gives a speech this bad). Not surprisingly, research shows that we learn a great deal from negative examples (Hesketh & Neal, 2006; Goldstein, Martin, & Cialdini, 2008). All other speeches and outlines are presented as models of effectiveness.

You may find it useful to return to this speech at different points in the course; as the course progresses, your analysis will become more complete, more insightful, and more effective. After you have reviewed the speech and the comments on the right, offer a one or two minute critique of the speech.

| Speech | Problems and Correctives |
|---|---|
| **Topic/Title:**   The Falling Dollar | The title isn't bad; it gives listeners a general idea of the topic and arouses interest. |
| **Purpose:**   To inform my audience about the dollar | The purpose is not specific enough—it merely repeats what's in the title. This thesis is not helpful in guiding the speech preparation process. |
| **Thesis:**   The dollar falls. | A better phrasing might be: To inform my audience about some consequences of the dollar's decline in value. A thesis should be in statement form, for example: The decline in the U.S. dollar has significant consequences on our own wallets. |

### INTRODUCTION

Ok, I'm here. Whew! I'm not very good at public speaking—I only took this course because it's required—and I'm really nervous.

These comments are usually best avoided.

Lead with a strong, attention-getting opener.

Let's see [shuffles through notes, arranging them and mumbling, page 1, page 2,—ok, it's all here].

Things like this reveal a decided lack of preparation.

The speaker should have the notes arranged before getting up to speak and should have rehearsed with them in place.

This speech is about the dollar. I'm going to explain what happens when the dollar goes down.

Although this does announce the topic, it's weak and would fail to gain the attention of most audience members.

The speaker needs a strong opener to get the attention of the audience; also it might explain something of what "goes down" means.

This is a topic that's really important to everyone in this room so I hope you'll listen carefully.

Telling the audience they should pay attention is probably not the best idea.

Instead of just telling the audience that the topic is important, the speaker needs to explain why the audience should listen and why the topic is important to them, for example, it's going to cost them more when they buy something.

So, as I said, I'm going to talk about the dollar.

This is an insufficient orientation.

The speaker needs to tell the audience something more, perhaps identifying the main points to be considered.

### BODY

As the dollar goes down—say against the Japanese dollar or Europe's dollar—it becomes more expensive to buy stuff from Japan and Europe.

The speaker reveals a lack of knowledge and familiarity with the topic by not using the terms "yen" and "euro" for the currencies of Japan and Europe.

The speaker also needs to define the relationships among these currencies and state this in the speech. A simple graph might help. Parallel wording would also have helped; the speaker might have said "Japanese dollar and European dollar" (two adjectives) or "Japan's dollar or Europe's dollar" (two nouns) instead of an adjective and a noun.

So, if you're going to buy a new Sony television—that's what I really want a big flat screen television—it's going to be more expensive.

These 2 examples do nothing to explain why merchandise from Japan or Europe become more expensive as the dollar goes down.

The comment "that's what I . . ." is personal and not really related to explaining what happens when the dollar loses value compared to other world currencies.

The speaker might have said, "How many of you are planning to buy a new flat-screen TV? Well, if you're planning to buy a Sony, a Samsung, a . . ., you're going to be paying more. And the reason is the decline in the U.S. dollar. Let me explain how this works. . . ."

And if you're going to buy stuff from Germany or Italy, it's also going to be more expensive. Like pasta—but I guess that's made in this country too. But you know what I mean.

This kind of comment shows a lack of appropriate preparation and is likely to make the audience wonder why they're wasting their time when the speaker couldn't spend the time and energy necessary to come up with a really good example.

A list of popular German and Italian products that the audience uses (and the speaker would have to know something about the audience to select the most meaningful products) would have been appropriate here.

There are in fact no transitions to help the audience move with the speaker from one topic to another.

A transition is needed here that leads from the first main point to the next, something like "Not only is merchandise from Europe and Japan going to cost more, you're also going to be paying more for oil."

As the dollar goes down and oil prices go up—let's see if I got this right: Yes, as the value of the dollar goes down, the price of oil goes up.

Again, there is no explanation as to why oil prices go up as the dollar goes down. And the examples that follow don't help—they merely give examples of higher prices.

The speaker needs to explain why the prices are higher.

So, your gas and electric bill are going to be higher. And you know how expensive gas is. I last paid 3.29 a gallon—no, it was 3.19, no, no, 3.09 that's what it was. But that's still a lot.

Notice that there are no signposts that help the listeners follow the speech.

The speaker could have helped the audience understand the speech by using signposts such as, "the **first** change when the dollar goes down is" or "the **next** change," or "**another** example." Using words like these bold ones in these examples help the audience understand your progression of ideas.

Again, the speaker demonstrates a lack of preparation with the price of gas. The specific figures here and in most cases are less important than the implication of the numbers—the specific figures can be given, of course.

But, the important point is the expense and that is what the speaker needs to emphasize and not go on a detour of the exact price paid the last time at the pump.

A transition would help.

As the dollar goes down the price of merchandise made in this country goes down. So if you buy an American made television, the price will be cheaper. And if you buy an American car—instead of a car from Japan—the car will be less expensive.

The audience is probably asking itself, "Why does this happen?"

As the dollar goes down the price of raw materials—I'm not sure what that is, but I think it's like oil and metal—increases and so the price of American merchandize increases.

> The speaker should answer these questions that the audience is likely to ask. Again, parallel structure would help: "Japanese car" would have paralleled "American car" and made the sentence a lot clearer.

> On the surface, this point seems to contradict the previous examples.

> This speech could have profited greatly from some simple charts or graphs showing the value of the U.S. dollar versus the yen and the euro.

And here is the most important thing; all this contributes to making China's economy grow. China has almost 1 billion people and they live in an area smaller than the state of Texas.

> Here the speaker brings credibility into serious question. China has *more* than 1 billion people and is almost the size of the entire United States—only about 20,000 square miles smaller.

> A simple glance at an Almanac or a 3-minute Internet search would have provided accurate information and would not have detracted from the speaker's credibility as these incorrect statements do. Further, the speaker needs to explain the path or logic going from the weak dollar to China's economy. Where is the connection? And what does this mean to the audience's concerns?

## CONCLUSION

In summary, as I demonstrated, when the dollar goes down, lots of other things happen—like the price of oil and China's economy.

> Using the word "summary" is not a bad idea; it's a clear signal that the speaker is going to recap what was just said. However, this summary is far too brief.

> This speech needed a more detailed summary, perhaps itemizing the three or four things that happen when the value of the dollar goes down.

I got most of my information from my Economics 101 course—it's a good course; you should take it. Oh, and from a *New York Times* article—I don't have the date.

> This type of source and citation is certainly not enough. And of course, we wonder, where did the other information come from? And, whether Economics 101 is or is not a good course has nothing to do with the consequences of the falling dollar.

> An effective informative speech must be based on several varied and reliable sources with citations to these sources interwoven throughout the speech.

everyone lived in their own house with lots of land around it, then communicating your meaning for *house* with someone whose meaning was learned in a neighborhood of high-rise tenements is going to be difficult. Although you'll each hear the same word, the meanings you'll each develop will be drastically different. In adjusting your listening—especially when in an intercultural setting—understand that the speaker's meanings may be very different from yours even though you each know and speak the same language.

Another aspect of speech is the speaker's accent. In many classrooms throughout the United States, there will be a wide range of accents, both regional and foreign. People whose native language is tonal such as Chinese (in which differences in pitch signal important meaning differences), may speak English with variations in pitch that may seem unnatural to others. Those whose native language is Japanese may have trouble distinguishing *l* from *r*, as Japanese does not make this distinction. Regional accent differences may make it difficult for people from Mississippi and Maine, for example, to understand each other; words even may have different meanings in different regions, and this may make communication more difficult than if the speakers were from the same area.

## Nonverbal Differences

As you listen to other people, you also "listen" to their **nonverbal communication.** If their nonverbal messages are drastically different from what you expect on the basis of the verbal message, the nonverbals may be seen as a kind of noise or interference or they may be seen as contradictory messages.

Additionally, speakers from different cultures have different display rules— cultural rules that govern which nonverbal behaviors are appropriate and which are inappropriate in a public setting. Also, different cultures may give very different meanings to the same nonverbal gesture. For example, Americans consider direct eye contact an expression of honesty and forthrightness, but the Japanese often view this as a lack of respect. The Japanese will glance at the other person's face rarely and then only for very short periods (Axtell, 1990; Matsumoto, 2006). Among some Latin Americans and Native Americans, direct eye contact between, say, a teacher and a student is considered inappropriate, perhaps aggressive; appropriate student behavior is to avoid eye contact with the teacher.

## Ethnocentrism

How do you feel about your own culture versus those of others? For example, do you believe that other cultures are backward when compared to yours? Do you believe that other cultures would do well to become more like your culture? Do you believe that people would be happier if they lived in your culture than they would in another? Do you believe that people from other cultures are less trustworthy than people from your own (Neuliep, Chaudoir, & McCroskey, 2001)?

If you answer yes to these and similar questions, it's likely that you're ethnocentric in your thinking. **Ethnocentrism** is a "nearly universal syndrome of attitudes and behaviors" (Hammond & Axelrod, 2006). It is the tendency to evaluate the values, beliefs, and behaviors of your own culture as being more positive, logical, and natural than those of other cultures. The nonethnocentric, on the other hand, would see himself or herself and others as different but equal, with neither being inferior nor superior.

Ethnocentric listening occurs when you listen to members of other cultures and consider them to be lacking in knowledge or expertise because they are from another culture, or when you acknowledge members of your own culture as knowledgeable and expert simply because they are from your own culture. Similarly, you're listening ethnocentrically when you listen to ideas about other cultures and view these as inferior simply because they differ from those of your own culture, or when you view ideas of your own culture as superior simply because they are from your own culture.

Recognizing the tendency toward ethnocentrism is the first step in combating any excesses. In addition, try following the suggestions for effective listening offered in this chapter—especially when you're in an intercultural public speaking situation. Also, expose yourself to culturally different experiences, but resist the temptation to evaluate these through your own cultural filters. For many this will not be an easy experience; however, in light of the tremendous advantages to be gained through increased intercultural experiences, the effort seems well worth it.

### Gender and Listening

According to Deborah Tannen (1990) in her best-selling *You Just Don't Understand: Women and Men in Conversation,* women seek to build rapport and establish a closer relationship and so use listening to achieve these ends. Men, on the other hand, tend to play up their expertise, emphasize it, and use it to dominate the interaction. Women are apt to play down their expertise and are more interested in communicating supportiveness. Tannen argues that the goal of a man in conversation is to be accorded respect, so he seeks to show his knowledge and expertise. A woman, on the other hand, seeks to be liked, so she expresses agreement.

Men and women also show that they're listening in different ways (Hall, 2006). Women are more apt to give lots of listening cues, such as interjecting *yeah* or *uh-huh,* nodding in agreement, and smiling. A man is more likely to listen quietly without giving a lot of listening cues as feedback. Tannen (1990) argues, however, that men do listen less to women than women listen to men. The reason, says Tannen, is that listening places a person in an inferior position, whereas speaking places the speaker in a superior role.

As a result of these differences men may seem to assume a more combative posture while listening, as if getting ready to argue. They also may appear to ask questions that are more argumentative or that are designed to puncture holes in your position as a way to play up their own expertise. Women are more likely to ask supportive questions and perhaps to offer more positive criticism than men. Women also use more cues in listening in a public speaking context. They let the speaker see that they're listening. Men, on the other hand, seem to use fewer listening cues in a public speaking situation.

Men and women act this way to both men and women; their customary ways of communicating don't seem to change depending on whether the speaker is male or female. There's no evidence to show that these differences represent any negative motives—any conscious aim on the part of men to prove themselves superior or of women to ingratiate themselves. Rather, these differences in listening are largely the result of the ways in which men and women have been socialized.

## Criticism and Culture

There are vast cultural differences in what is considered proper when it comes to criticism. For example, criticism will be viewed very differently depending on whether members come from an **individualist culture** (which emphasizes the individual and places primary value on the individual's goals) or a **collectivist culture** (which emphasizes the group and places primary value on the group's goals).

Individual and collective tendencies are not mutually exclusive; this isn't an all-or-none cultural orientation but rather a matter of emphasis. For example, in basketball you may follow an individualist orientation and compete with other members of your team for most baskets or most valuable player award. However, in a game you will act with a collective orientation to benefit the entire group—in this case, to enable your team to win the game. In actual practice both individual and collective tendencies will help you and your team achieve your goals. At times, however, these tendencies may conflict; for example, do you shoot for the basket and try to raise your own individual score, or do you pass the ball to another player who is better positioned to score the basket and thus benefit your team?

Those who come from cultures that are highly individualist and competitive (the United States, Germany, and Sweden are examples) may find public criticism a normal part of the learning process. Those who come from cultures that are more collectivist and therefore emphasize the group rather than the individual (Japan, Mexico, and Korea are examples) are likely to find giving and receiving public criticism uncomfortable. Thus, people from individualist cultures may readily criticize speakers and are likely to expect the same "courtesy" from listeners. "After all" such a person might reason, "if I'm going to criticize your skills to help you improve, I expect you to help me in the same way." Persons from collectivist cultures, on the other hand, may feel that it's more important to be polite and courteous than to help someone learn a skill. Cultural rules that maintain peaceful relations among the Japanese (Midooka, 1990; Hendry, 1995; Watts, 2004) and norms of politeness among many Asian cultures (Fraser, 1990) may conflict with the classroom cultural norm calling for listeners to express criticism openly.

Collectivist cultures place a heavy emphasis on face-saving—on always allowing people to appear in a positive light (Hofstede, Hofstede, & Minkov, 2010). In these cultures people may prefer not to say anything negative in public. In fact they may even be reluctant to say anything positive, lest any omission be construed as negative. In cultures in which face-saving is especially important, communication rules such as the following tend to prevail:

- Don't express negative evaluation in public; instead, compliment the person.
- Don't prove someone wrong—especially in public; express agreement even if you know the person is wrong.
- Don't correct someone's errors; don't even acknowledge them.
- Don't ask difficult questions lest the person not know the answer and lose face or be embarrassed; generally, avoid asking questions.

The difficulties that these differences may cause can be lessened if they're discussed openly. Some people may become comfortable with public criticism once it's explained that the cultural norms of most public speaking classrooms include public criticism just as they incorporate informative and persuasive speaking and written outlines. Others may feel more comfortable offering written criticism as a substitute for oral and public criticism. Or perhaps private consultations can be arranged.

## Next Steps

This chapter focused on listening and criticism. A good next step is to consider your own listening and criticism tendencies and ask yourself how you might improve them. The next chapter provides an overview of the 10-step process for preparing and presenting effective public speeches.

# Essentials of Listening and Criticism

This chapter looked at listening and criticism and offered suggestions for making your listening and your criticism more effective.

## Listening in Public Speaking

1. Listening is a five-stage process: (1) receiving the speaker's verbal and nonverbal messages, (2) understanding the speaker's thoughts and emotions, (3) remembering and retaining the messages, (4) evaluating or judging the messages, and (5) responding or reacting to the messages.

## Guidelines for Listening

2. Among the principles for effective listening are these:
   - Listen actively.
   - Listen for total meaning.
   - Listen with empathy.
   - Listen with an open mind.
   - Listen ethically.

## Criticism in Public Speaking

3. Criticism is a process of judging and evaluating a work. Criticism can (1) identify strengths and weaknesses and thereby help you improve as a public speaker, (2) identify standards for evaluating all sorts of public speeches, and (3) show that the audience is listening and is concerned about the speaker's progress.

## Guidelines for Criticism

4. Among the principles for giving effective criticism are these:
   - Stress the positive.
   - Be specific.
   - Be objective.
   - Be constructive.
   - Focus on behavior.
   - Own your criticism.
   - Recognize your ethical obligations.

## Responding to Criticism

5. In listening to criticism:
   - Accept the critic's viewpoint.
   - Listen with an open mind.
   - Separate speech criticism from personal criticism.
   - Seek clarification.
   - Evaluate the criticism.

## Listening, Criticism, and Culture

6. Cultural differences in language and speech, nonverbal behavioral differences, ethnocentrism, and gender differences can create listening difficulties.

7. Cultural differences in criticism need to be considered. Cultures differ in their views of criticism and in the rules considered appropriate. For example, members of individualist cultures may find public criticism easier and more acceptable than people from collectivist cultures.

# Essential Terms

active listening **(26)**  
assimilation **(29)**  
backchannel cues **(24)**  
bias **(29)**  
collectivist culture **(42)**  
criticism **(30)**  
empathy **(28)**  
ethnocentrism **(41)**  
I-messages **(35)**  
individualist culture **(42)**  
listening **(22)**  
nonverbal communication **(41)**  
you-messages **(35)**

# Public Speaking Exercises

## 2.1 Do You Really Remember What You Hear?

When you remember a message, do you remember what was said, or do you remember what you think you heard? The commonsense response, of course, would be that you remember what was said. But before accepting this simple explanation, try to memorize the list of 12 words presented below, modeled on an idea from a research study (Glucksberg & Danks, 1975). Don't worry about the order of the words; only the number of words remembered counts. Take about 20 seconds to memorize as many words as possible. Then close the book and write down as many words as you can remember.

| | | |
|---|---|---|
| dining | table | milk |
| cafeteria | shopping | hungry |
| green beans | steak | having lunch |
| satisfied | knife | menu |

Don't read any farther until you've tried to memorize and reproduce the list of words.

If you're like most people, you not only remembered a good number of the words on the list but also "remembered" related words that weren't on the list, perhaps *eating*, *food*, or *meal*. What happens is that in remembering you don't simply reproduce the list; you reconstruct it. In this case you gave the list meaning, and part of that meaning included the word *eating* or some related word. In remembering speech, then, you reconstruct the messages you hear into a system that makes sense to you—but, in the process, often remember distorted versions of what was said.

## 2.2 Listening to New Ideas

Ideally, speeches communicate information that is new and potentially useful to you as a listener. A useful technique in listening to new ideas is PIP'N, a technique that derives from the insights of Carl Rogers (1970) on paraphrase as a means for ensuring understanding and from Edward deBono's (1976) PMI (plus, minus, interesting) technique for critical thinking. In analyzing new ideas with the PIP'N technique, you follow four steps:

**P = Paraphrase.** State in your own words what you think the other person is saying. Paraphrasing will help you understand and remember the idea.

**I = Interesting.** Consider why the idea is interesting.

**P = Positive.** Think about what's good about the idea; for example, might it solve a problem or improve a situation?

**N = Negative.** Think about any negatives that the idea might entail; for example, might it be expensive or difficult to implement?

Consider how you might use PIP'N to gain insight—into, say, the cultural emphasis you find in your college textbooks or in a particular required course, or into the PIP'N technique itself.

# LogOn! <sup>PEARSON</sup> myspeechlab

## Listening and Criticism

Visit MySpeechLab (www.myspeechlab.com) to explore further the topic of listening and criticism with a variety of exercises and speeches for analysis and criticism. An especially interesting feature is American Rhetoric Quizzes where you can watch a variety of speeches and, using the evaluation guides provided, analyze and criticize the speeches.

# 3

# Preparing and Presenting a Public Speech (Steps 1-10, in Brief)

## WHY READ THIS CHAPTER?

**Because it explains the steps you go through in preparing a public speech and will help you to:**

- take the mystery out of the public speaking process and enable you to see the entire process as a whole, as a manageable undertaking

- start giving speeches early in the semester after learning the 10 steps for public speaking preparation and presentation

*An intelligent plan is the first step to success.*

—BASIL S. WALSH

This chapter answers the FAQs you're likely to be wondering about by providing a brief overview of the public speaking process. By following the 10 steps outlined in this chapter and diagrammed in Figure 3.1, you'll be able to prepare and present an effective first speech almost immediately. The remainder of the text elaborates on these steps and will help you fine-tune your public speaking skills. But first we'll look at some issues to get you started.

# Getting Started with Public Speaking

Before we launch into the step-by-step process of public speaking, consider a few popular beliefs about public speaking and then ponder some helpful advice.

## Popular Beliefs about Public Speaking

Do you think each statement is true or false?

1. Good public speakers are born, not made.
2. The more speeches you give, the better you'll become at it.
3. It's best to memorize your speech, especially if you're fearful or apprehensive about speaking before an audience.
4. If you're a good writer, you'll be a good public speaker; a poor writer, a poor speaker.
5. The First Amendment allows the public speaker total freedom of expression.
6. Like a good novel, play, or essay, a good speech is relevant to all people at all times.

**FIGURE 3.1**

**The Steps in Preparing and Presenting a Public Speech**

This figure presents the 10 steps in a linear fashion. The process of constructing a public speech, however, doesn't always follow such a logical sequence. So you'll probably not progress simply from Step 1, to 2, to 3, through to 10. Instead, after selecting your topic, purpose, and thesis (Step 1) you may progress to Step 2 and analyze your audience. On the basis of this analysis, however, you may wish to go back and modify your purpose or thesis, or both. Similarly, after you research the topic (Step 3), you may want more information about your audience. You may, therefore, return to Step 2.

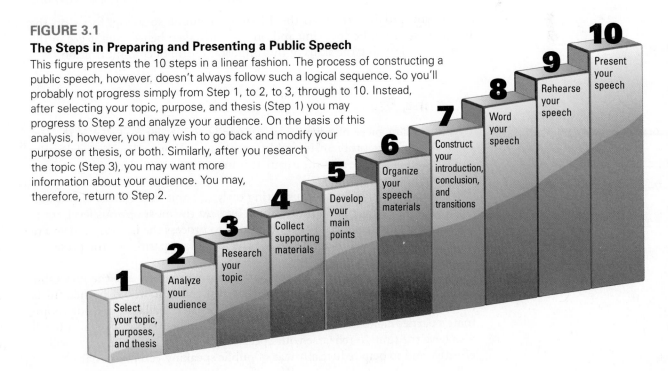

1. Select your topic, purposes, and thesis
2. Analyze your audience
3. Research your topic
4. Collect supporting materials
5. Develop your main points
6. Organize your speech materials
7. Construct your introduction, conclusion, and transitions
8. Word your speech
9. Rehearse your speech
10. Present your speech

All six of these statements are (generally) false and were written to highlight some of the myths about public speaking. As you'll see throughout this book, these assumptions can get in the way of your learning the skills of public speaking.

Briefly, here are the reasons each of these statements is more false than true:

1. **Effective public speaking is a learned skill.** To be sure, some people are born brighter or more extroverted—characteristics that do help in public speaking. But all people can improve their abilities and become effective public speakers.
2. **Practice is only helpful if you practice effective skills.** If you practice bad habits, you're likely to grow less effective rather than more effective; consequently, it's crucial to learn and follow the principles of effectiveness.
3. **Memorizing creates more problems than it solves.** This belief, if acted on, is likely to be detrimental. Memorizing your speech is one of the worst things you can do; there are easier and more effective ways to deal with fear.
4. **Speech is not the same as writing.** Although some communication skills apply to both writing and speaking, the two forms are more different than similar—in their focus on the audience, in their responsiveness to immediate feedback, and in their language.
5. **Speech is free but not totally.** Freedom of speech does not legalize slander, libel, defamation, or plagiarism. In addition, as the frequent examples of cultural incorrectness highlighted by the media illustrate, even when speech is not illegal, it can have serious negative consequences when used in culturally insensitive ways.
6. **Public speaking is (generally) time-bound.** Although there are exceptions (Lincoln's Gettysburg Address, Martin Luther King Jr.'s "I have a dream" speech), the most effective public speeches are those that are constructed for a specific time, for a specific audience, for a specific occasion.

As you progress through the 10 steps of public speaking, focus on the uniqueness of public speaking and on how mistaken beliefs might get in the way of your learning the skills of this important form of communication.

## Starting Early

One important piece of advice is warranted at this point and that is to start early. A common problem in public speaking is the tendency to delay the preparation of the speech. Substitute this unproductive tendency to procrastinate with a start-early ethic.

There are many benefits to starting early—a habit that will serve you well throughout your social and professional lives. At the most obvious level, starting early provides you with the time needed to process the information you're going to talk about and to get used to the idea of preparing for the presentation of your speech.

Starting early also provides you with the time to overcome the inevitable unanticipated roadblocks—a website that you thought would be helpful is now dead, the person you wanted to interview isn't available, or your roommate's parties make the weekends useless for working on your speech. You will also have the time to rehearse your speech to ensure that your delivery will be effective and to help reduce any fear of public speaking you might have.

Interestingly enough, starting early may enable you to avoid health problems often associated with procrastination—college students who procrastinate experience more colds and flu, more gastrointestinal problems, and more insomnia (Marano, 2003).

Here are several suggestions for overcoming the tendency to delay certain tasks. Supplement these with the excellent advice given on college websites such as the University of Buffalo at **http://ub-counseling.buffalo.edu/ stress** and California Polytechnic State University at **http://sas.calpoly.edu/asc/ ssl.html**.

1. **Think mindfully about the task.** Be mindful of the fact that delaying your preparation will only make it harder and is likely to increase your natural fear of public speaking. Make a commitment to starting early. Create a computer file for your speech, and collect information and file it for easy retrieval.
2. **Don't lie to yourself.** One popular lie is that we do better under pressure. With very few possible exceptions, this is simply not true (Marano, 2003). You do more poorly under pressure.
3. **Avoid distractions.** Distractions are all around us so beware of your tendency to seek these out. You don't need to redo your Facebook profile or clean your room before you can begin preparing your speech, for example. When you get the urge to do something else, become mindful of what you're really doing—making an excuse to delay the task at hand.
4. **Work in small units.** Fortunately, as already mentioned, this aid to overcoming procrastination is built into the 10-step public speaking system used here; each step is already a relatively small unit. Set aside 20 or 30 minutes (it's often best to start with small units of time) and see what you can do with Step 1. Then when you're farther along in the process, increase the time you spend on each step.

## The Public Speaking Class

Each class has somewhat different norms for what is, and what is not, appropriate or polite. And public speaking classes, which are more interactive, have even greater variation. Yet, amid this variation there are certain rules of politeness that are a customary part of the public speaking course experience. Here are some of them:

- **Give your speeches as assigned,** whether in a face-to-face or online. Lateness puts added pressure on the instructor, other students, and the class as a whole, often necessitating a rearrangement of the schedule— something no one enjoys. So, do whatever is within your power to follow the schedule.

- **Respect time limits.** Most public speaking syllabi are tight—speeches are scheduled so that everyone gets the same opportunities. But, that's only possible if everyone respects the time limits. So, when you rehearse your speech, give attention to time and, if necessary, revise the speech so that it fits into the time allotted.

- **Listen supportively to others.** Getting up and giving a speech to a class or sending a video or podcast online are not easy tasks. But, in a face-to-face class, if the audience acts positively toward the speaker, it can help put the speaker at ease. Supportiveness in an online environment will make it easier for the speaker's next efforts.

- **Give listening cues.** Make eye contact with the speaker and allow your positive feelings to be expressed in your facial expressions, posture, and head movements. Let the speaker see that you're listening. This too will help the speaker feel comfortable. In an online environment, participate as appropriate to the norms established for the class.

- **Avoid entering the room during a student presentation.** This is likely to increase the nervousness of the speaker. It also takes attention away from the speaker. At the same time, recognize that at conventions and many other speaking events, it's customary for audience members to enter and leave during presentations.

- **Give your full attention to the speaker**. Avoid playing games on your laptop, texting, or surfing during class and especially during a student's speech. Turn off your cell phone or at least put it on vibrate.

- **Offer constructive criticism.** The norm of most public speaking classrooms (whether on or offline) is that criticism is expected; it's a useful learning device for the speaker, the critic, and, in fact, for everyone in the course. Keep in mind the suggestions for giving and receiving criticism discussed in the previous chapter.

- **Come to class regularly.** Although class attendance is important in all courses, it's doubly important in the public speaking course. The reason is simply that speakers need audiences, audience feedback and criticism, and the interaction that only an audience can provide. In addition, you'll learn a great deal from observing the efforts of others.

# Step 1: Select Your Topic, Purposes, and Thesis

Your first step is to select your topic, your general and specific purposes, and your thesis (or main idea).

## Your Topic

The first step in preparing a speech is to select the **topic** (or subject) and the overall purpose you hope to achieve. Let's look first at the topic. For your classroom speeches—where the objective is to learn the skills of public speaking—there are thousands of suitable topics. Suggestions may be found everywhere and anywhere. Take a look at the Topic Generator on My Speech Lab (**www.myspeechlab .com**); it will provide you with lots of suggestions or simply search for "public speaking topics." Additional suggestions are provided on pages 65–72.

What makes a topic "suitable"? First, the topic of a public speech should be *worthwhile;* it should address an issue that has significant implications for the audience.

A topic should also be *appropriate* both to you as the speaker and to your audience. Try not to select a topic just because it will fulfill the requirements of an assignment. Instead, select a topic about which you know something and would like to learn more.

Topics should also be *culturally sensitive*. Culture plays an extremely important role in determining what people consider appropriate or worthwhile. For example, it would be considered inappropriate for an American businessperson in Pakistan to speak about politics or in Nigeria about religion or in Mexico about illegal aliens (Axtell, 2007).

Topics must also be *limited in scope*. A common problem for beginning speakers is that they attempt to cover too broad a topic in too little time: the Iraq War, the stock market, or abortion. Limit your topic so that you can cover some significant portion of it with some significant depth in the time you have available.

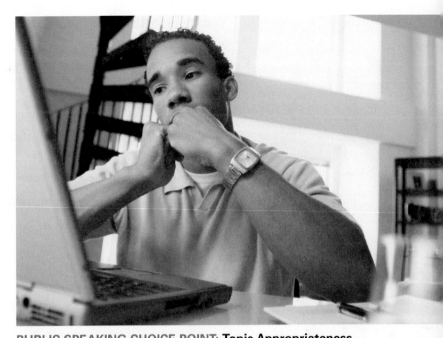

**PUBLIC SPEAKING CHOICE POINT: Topic Appropriateness**
Mac, a student in his 20s who is on the college basketball team, wants to give a speech on his hobby, flower arranging. But he wonders if this topic is going to seem inappropriate to him as a speaker; he also wonders, if he does decide to speak on this topic, whether he should say anything about the topic's appearing inappropriate. What are some of the options Mac has for dealing with this potential disconnect? What would you advise Mac to do?

## Your General Purpose

Once you have your general topic, consider your **general purpose.** Public speeches are generally designed to inform, to persuade, or to serve some ceremonial or special occasion function.

- The *informative speech* seeks to create understanding: to clarify, enlighten, correct misunderstandings, or demonstrate how something works.

- The *persuasive speech* seeks to influence attitudes or behaviors: to strengthen or change audience attitudes or to inspire listeners to take some specific action.

- The *special occasion speech,* containing elements of both information and persuasion, serves to introduce another speaker or a group of speakers, present a tribute, secure the goodwill of the listeners, or entertain the audience.

## Your Specific Purpose

Your speech also will have a **specific purpose.** For example, specific informative purposes might be to inform the audience about a proposed education budget or to describe the way a television pilot is audience tested. Specific persuasive purposes might be to persuade an audience to support a proposed budget or to influence them to vote for Smith. Specific purposes for special occasion speeches might include introducing a Nobel Prize for Nuclear Physics winner, celebrating Veterans Day, or giving a toast at a ceremony.

## Your Thesis

Your **thesis** or **central idea** is the one idea that you want your audience to remember after you've concluded your speech. This one central idea is your thesis. It's the essence of what you want your audience to get out of your speech. If your speech is informative then your thesis is the main idea that you want your audience to understand. For example:

> A newspaper company has three divisions.

If your speech is persuasive, then your thesis is the central idea that you want your audience to accept or believe. For example:

> We should adopt the new e-mail system.

The thesis is further explored in Public Speaking Exercise 3.1, "Theses," on page 63.

# Step 2: Analyze Your Audience

In public speaking your audience is central to your topic and purpose. In most cases, and especially in a public speaking class, you'll be thinking of both your audience and your topic at the same time; in fact, it's difficult to focus on one without also focusing on the other. Your success in informing or persuading an audience rests largely on **audience analysis**—the extent to which you know your listeners and the extent to which you've adapted your speech to them. Ask yourself, Who are they? What do they already know? What would they want to know more about? What special interests do they have? What opinions, attitudes, and beliefs do they have? Where do they stand on the issues you wish to address? What needs do they have?

For example, if you're going to speak on social security and health care for the elderly or on the importance of the job interview, it's obvious that the age of your listeners will influence how you develop your speech. Similarly, men and women often view topics differently. For example, if you plan to speak on caring for a newborn baby, you'd approach an audience of men very differently than an audience of women. With an audience of women, you could probably assume a much greater knowledge of the subject and a greater degree of comfort in dealing with it. With an audience of men, you might have to cover such elementary topics as the type of powder to use, how to test the temperature of a bottle, and the way to prepare a bottle of formula.

**PUBLIC SPEAKING CHOICE POINT: Audience Analysis**
Stella is planning to give a speech on the need for developing wind energy sources. She has no information about the audience's knowledge of wind energy or their political attitudes. What are some of the things Stella can do to learn about her audience to prepare for this speech?

# Step 3: Research Your Topic

If your speech is to be worthwhile and if both you and your audience are to profit from it, you'll need to research your topic. There are several values to be derived from **research**. The most obvious value is that it is through research you'll find examples, illustrations, and definitions to help you inform your listeners; testimony, statistics, and arguments to support your major ideas; personal anecdotes, quotations, and stories to help you bring your topics to life.

Another value to research in public speaking is that it helps you establish the truth of what you're saying—the more and better information you have, the more likely you are to come up with a compelling argument, and the more likely your listeners will believe you.

Research will also help you establish your credibility—your competence, your mastery over the material. If you're audience sees you as credible—as having done your research—the more likely are they to believe in you—even apart from any specific argument you might make.

And, as you likely know, research is required in almost all college courses; the techniques learned here are more than likely to help you in the wide variety of research tasks you'll undertake in school but also later in life—whether it's to investigate graduate or professional schools, a stock you want to invest in, or a company with which you'll be interviewing.

Here are a few suggestions to help you get started researching your speeches.

- **Develop your research questions and identify key terms.** What exactly do you need to find? Population statistics? Arguments for or against a particular position? Biographical information? Since you'll be conducting most if not all your research online, it will help to identify the key terms you want to search. Writing down both your research questions and your key terms will help guide your search and minimize detour distractions.

- **Examine what you know.** Think about your research question by first examining what you already know. For example, write down what you know about books, articles, or websites on the topic that you're familiar with; jot down names of people who might know something about the topic. Also consider what you know from your own personal experiences and observations. Once you are aware of what you know, you can start searching for what you don't know.

- **Begin with a general overview.** Continue your search by getting an authoritative but general overview of the topic. An encyclopedia article, book chapter, or magazine article will serve this purpose well. This general overview will help you see the topic as a whole and understand how its various parts fit together.

- **Consult increasingly specific sources.** Follow up the general overview with increasingly more detailed and specialized sources. Fortunately, many general articles contain references or links to direct this next stage of your search for more specific information.

■ **Keep an eye out for supporting materials.** When you come upon a great example, a little known statistic, or a great quotation save them to your speech file. Look too for audio and video clips, charts and graphs, and images that might prove useful.

Additional research principles are covered throughout the text in the Research Link boxes.

# Step 4: Collect Supporting Materials

Once you've identified your thesis, turn your attention to supporting each point. Tell the audience what it needs to know about the newspaper divisions. Convince the audience that the new e-mail system is easier to use, has a spell-checker feature, and provides useful options for organizing e-mails.

In the informative speech your **supporting materials** primarily amplify—describe, illustrate, define, exemplify—the various concepts you discuss. For example, you want the causes of inflation to come alive for the audience. You want your listeners to see and feel the drug problem, the crime rate, or the economic hardships of the people you're talking about. Supporting materials accomplish this. Presenting definitions, for example, helps the audience to understand specialized terms; definitions breathe life into concepts that may otherwise be too abstract or vague. Statistics (summary figures that explain various trends) are essential for certain topics. Presentation aids—charts, maps, actual objects, slides, films, and so on—enliven normally vague concepts. Because presentation aids have become so important in public speaking, you may want to include these in each of your speeches—they're easy to use and inexpensive to produce, help you maintain attention, and communicate information more efficiently and more effectively. If you start using them with your first speeches, you'll develop considerable facility by the end of the semester. The best way to do this is to read Chapter 6's section on presentation aids (pp. 114–120) immediately after you complete this chapter and to begin incorporating such aids into all your speeches.

In a persuasive speech your support is **proof**—material that offers evidence, argument, motivational appeal, and establishes your credibility. Proof helps you convince the audience to agree with you. Let's say, for example, that you want to persuade the audience to believe that the new e-mail system is easier to operate (your first main point, as noted above). To do this you need to give your audience good reasons for believing in its greater ease of operation. Your point might be supported this way:

The new e-mail system is easier to operate.

I. It's easier to install.

II. It's easier to configure to your personal preferences.

III. It makes it easier to save and delete messages.

# RESEARCH LINK → Libraries

Libraries are the major depositories of stored information and have evolved from a concentration on print sources to their current focus on computerized databases. Starting your research at the library (and with the librarian's assistance) is probably a wise move.

You'll likely go to one virtual or online library to access other virtual libraries or databases maintained by local and national governments, cultural institutions, and various corporations and organizations. Here are a few online libraries that you'll find especially helpful.

- **Quick Study**, the University of Minnesota's Library Research Guide (http://tutorial.lib.umn.edu), will help you learn how to find the materials you need and will answer many of your questions about research.

- For a list of **library catalogs** that will help you find the location of the material you need, try www.libdex.com/. By clicking on "library-type index" you'll get a list of categories of libraries; for example, government or medical or religious.

- The **largest library** in the United States is the Library of Congress, which houses millions of books, maps, multimedia, and manuscripts. Time spent at this library (begin with www.loc.gov) will be well invested. The home page will guide you to a wealth of information.

- Maintained by the National Archives and Records Administration, the **presidential libraries** may be accessed at www.archives.gov/.

- The **Virtual Library** is a collection of links to 14 subject areas; for example, agriculture, business and economics, computing, communication and media, and education. Visit this at www.vlib.org.

- If you're not satisfied with your own college library, visit other **college libraries;** those of the large state universities will prove extremely helpful. Take a look at the website for the University of Pennsylvania (www.library.upenn.edu/cgi-bin/res/sr.egi) or the University of Illinois (http://gateway.library.uiuc.edu), for example.

- The **Internet Public Library 2,** a merger of the Internet Public Library and the Librarians' Index (www.ipl.org) is actually not a library; it's a collection of links to a wide variety of materials. But it will function much like the reference desk at any of the world's best libraries.

Of course, you'll also need to go to a brick-and-mortar library because it houses materials that are not on the Web or that you want to access in print. Because each library functions differently, your best bet in learning about your own college library is to talk with the librarian about what the library has available, what kinds of training or tours it offers, and how materials can be most easily accessed.

The next Research Link, "Primary, Secondary, and Tertiary Sources," appears on page 75.

# Step 5: Develop Your Main Points

Once you have worded your thesis, identify its component ideas—the main ideas you want to use to clarify or support your thesis. We'll call these the **main points** of the speech. You can identify these main points by asking strategic questions of your thesis. These questions are used to help you generate your main points and would not normally appear in your outline or in the actual oral speech. For informative speeches the most helpful questions are "What?" and "How?" For example, for the thesis "A newspaper company has three divisions," you'd ask, "What are the divisions?" The answer to this question will yield your main points. Following one mass communication theorist (Rodman, 2001), the main points can be listed in the form of a brief outline like this:

Thesis: "A newspaper company has three divisions." (What are the divisions?)

I.  The publishing division makes major decisions for the entire paper.
II. The editorial division produces news and features.
III. The business division sells advertising and prints the paper.

For a persuasive speech, the question you'd ask of your thesis is often "Why?" For example, if your thesis is "We should adopt the new e-mail system," then the inevitable question is "Why should we adopt the new system?" Your answers to this question will identify the major parts of the speech, which might look like this:

Thesis: "We should adopt the new e-mail system." (Why should we adopt the new e-mail system?)

I.  The new system is easier to operate.
II. The new system enables you to check your spelling.
III. The new system provides more options for organizing messages.

# Step 6: Organize Your Speech Materials

The appropriate **organization** of your materials will help your audience understand and retain what you say. You might, for example, select a simple topical organization. This pattern involves dividing your topic into its logical subdivisions or subtopics. Each subtopic becomes a main point of your speech and each is treated about equally. You'd then organize the supporting materials under each of the appropriate points. The body of the speech, then, might look like this:

I. Main point I
   A.  Supporting material for I
   B.  Supporting material for I

II. Main point II
   A.  Supporting material for II
   B.  Supporting material for II
   C.  Supporting material for II

III. Main point III
   A.  Supporting material for III
   B.  Supporting material for III

# Step 7: Construct Your Introduction, Conclusion, and Transitions

The next items to consider are the introduction, conclusion, and transitions for your speech.

## Introduction

In your **introduction,** try to accomplish three goals.

■ **First, gain your listeners' attention.** A provocative statistic, a little-known fact, an interesting story, or a statement explaining the topic's significance will help secure this initial attention.

> For example, here is how one student, Elizabeth Hobbs from Truman State University, used a dramatic example to gain and focus the audience's attention on her and her speech (Schnoor, 2006):

> He was kidnapped in January 2004 while making a business trip to Macedonia. To be transported to a secret prison in Afghanistan, he was beaten, his underwear was forcibly removed and he was put into a diaper and chained spread eagle inside the plane. In Afghanistan, he was beaten, interrogated, and put into solitary confinement. To get out, he started a hunger strike, but after 37 days without food, a feeding tube was forced through his nose and into his stomach. Nearly five months later, he was released, with no explanation for his imprisonment. Does this sound like Chile under the Pinochet regime? Prisoner abuse in Uzbekistan? A Russian gulag? It wasn't. This is the story told by the *Houston Chronicle* on December 24, 2005 of a victim of America's War on Terror.

■ **Second, establish connections among yourself, the topic, and the audience.** Tell audience members why you're speaking on this topic. Tell them why you're concerned with the topic and why you're competent to address them. These are questions that most audiences will automatically ask themselves. Here's one example of how this might be done.

> You may be wondering why a twenty-five-year-old woman with no background in medicine or education is talking to you about AIDS education. I'm addressing you today as the mother of a child with AIDS, and I want to talk with you about my child's experience in school—and about every child's experience in school—your own children as well as mine.

■ **Third, orient your audience;** tell them what you're going to talk about.

> I'm going to explain the ways in which war movies have changed through the years. I'm going to discuss examples of movies depicting World War II, the Korean War, Vietnam, and Iraq.

At times, orientations are connected with the thesis of the speech. For example,

---

**ETHICAL CHOICE POINT**

**Using Research**

You recently read an excellent summary of research on aging and memory in a magazine article. The magazine is a particularly respectable publication, so it's reasonable to assume that this research is reliable. But you feel that citing the original research studies will give your speech greater persuasive appeal and will make you look more thorough in your research. You want to use research honestly but you wonder if this would just be a waste of time. ➤ *What are your ethical options in this case?* ➤ *What would you do if you were in this situation?*

here's how one student, Sarah Collins of Cameron University, oriented the audience by identifying the three points (problems, causes, and solutions) she would cover in her speech on fraudulent charities (Schnoor, 2006):

> By discussing the problems, causes, and solutions to fraudulent charities, we will provide a safe way to donate funds and ensure that our money isn't going to aid in the spread of hate messages.

## Conclusion

In your **conclusion,** you can do three things (though not all conclusions need all three).

- **First, summarize your ideas.** For example, you might restate your main points, summing up what you've told the audience.

  > Let's all support Grace Moore. She's our most effective negotiator. She's honest, and she knows what negotiation and our union are all about.

  Here is how one student, Kristen K. Gunderson from Murray State University, summarized her speech on tax reform, reiterating the three points she covered in her speech (Schnoor, 2006):

  > After analyzing the current U.S. tax system [first point], the flat tax trend that is working in Europe [second point] and finally, how Europe's trends could work for America [third point], it is certain that the U.S. can learn plenty from its neighbors across the Atlantic.

- **Second, motivate the audience.** For example, you might ask for a specific response (for instance, to volunteer at the local hospital), restate the importance of the issue for the audience, or suggest future actions your listeners might take (this function is most appropriate for persuasive speeches).

- **Third, wrap up your speech.** Develop a crisp ending that makes it clear to your audience that your speech is at an end.

  > I hope then that when you vote on Tuesday, you'll vote for Moore. She's our only real choice.

## Transitions

After you've completed the introduction and conclusion, review the entire speech for **transitions:** Make sure that the parts flow into one another and that the movement from one part to another (say, from the introduction to the first major proposition) will be clear to the audience. Transitional words, phrases, and sentences will help you achieve this smoothness of movement.

- Connect your introduction's orientation to your first major proposition:

  > *Let's now look at the first of these three elements*, the central processing unit, in detail. The CPU is the heart of the computer. It consists of . . .

- Connect each main point to the next:

  > . . . *But not only is* cigarette smoking dangerous to the smoker, *it's also* dangerous to the nonsmoker. Passive smoking is harmful to everyone. . . .

- Connect your last main point to your conclusion:

  > *As we saw*, there were three sources of evidence against the butler. He had a motive; he had no alibi; he had the opportunity.

## Step 8: Word Your Speech

Because your audience will hear your speech only once, make what you say instantly intelligible. Don't talk down to your audience; but do make your ideas, even complex ones, easy to understand in one hearing.

Use words that are simple rather than complex, concrete rather than abstract. Use personal and informal rather than impersonal and formal language. For example, use lots of pronouns (*I, me, you, our*) and contractions (*can't* rather than *cannot; I'll* rather than *I will*). Use simple and direct sentences. Say "Vote in the next election" instead of "It is important that everyone vote in the next election."

Perhaps the most important advice at this point is that you should not write out your speech word for word. This will only make you sound as if you're reading to your audience. You'll lose the conversational quality that is so important in public speaking. Instead, outline your speech and speak with your audience, using the outline to remind yourself of your main ideas and the order in which you want to present them.

Title your speech. Create a title that's relatively short (so it's easy to remember)—two, three, or four words are often best. Choose a title that will attract the attention and arouse the interest of the listeners and that has a clear relationship to the major purpose of your speech.

**PUBLIC SPEAKING CHOICE POINT: Speaking Style**
Danny is preparing to be a television salesman, following in the style of Danny Sullivan and Billy Mays. What are some of the things Danny can do to conform to the general norms of the class and yet not lose this opportunity to learn the style of speaking that he wants to make his profession?

## Step 9: Rehearse Your Speech

You've prepared your speech to deliver it to an audience, so your next step is **rehearsal,** or practice. Rehearse your speech, from start to finish, out loud, at least four times before presenting it in class. During these rehearsals, time your speech to make sure that you stay within the specified time limits. Practice any words or phrases you have difficulty with; consult a dictionary to clarify any doubts about pronunciation. Include in your outline any notes that you want to remember during the actual speech—notes to remind you to use a presentation aid, for example, or to read a quotation.

## Step 10: Present Your Speech

In your actual presentation, use your voice and bodily action to reinforce your message. Make it easy for your listeners to understand your speech. Any vocal or body movements that draw attention to themselves (and away from what you're saying) obviously should be avoided. Here are a few guidelines that will prove helpful.

# PUBLIC SPEAKING SAMPLE ASSISTANT

## A Speech of Introduction

The relatively brief speech of introduction illustrated here is a commonly used first assignment in public speaking classes. Its purpose is to give each person in the class an early and nonthreatening public speaking experience and at the same time give class members a chance to get to know each other. (A different type of speech of introduction is discussed in Chapter 12, "Speaking on Special Occasions.") In the speech presented here one student introduces another student to the class. The speech, although fairly complete and detailed, would take only about three minutes to present.

---

### INTRODUCTION
It's a real pleasure to introduce Joe Robinson to you. I want to tell you a little about Joe's background, his present situation, and his plans for the future.

In this introduction, the speaker accomplishes several interrelated purposes: to place the speech in a positive context, to explain the purpose of the speech and orient the audience, to tell them what the speech will cover, and to indicate that it will follow a time pattern—beginning with the past, moving to the present, and then ending with the proposed future. What other types of opening statements might be appropriate? In what other ways might you organize a speech of introduction?

### TRANSITION
Let's look first at Joe's past.

This transitional statement alerts listeners that the speaker is moving from the introduction to the first major part of what is called the "body" of the speech.

### BODY, FIRST MAIN POINT (THE PAST)
Joe comes to us from Arizona, where he lived and worked on a small ranch with his father and grandparents—mostly working with dairy cows. Working on a farm gave Joe a deep love and appreciation for animals, which he carries with him today and into his future plans.

Joe's mother died when he was three years old, so he lived with his father most of his life. When his father, an Air Force lieutenant, was transferred to Stewart Air Force Base here in the Hudson Valley, Joe thought it would be a great opportunity to join his father and continue his education.

Joe also wanted to stay with his father to make sure he eats right, doesn't get involved with the wrong crowd, and meets the right woman to settle down with.

The speaker here gives us information about Joe's past that makes us see him as a unique individual. We also learn something pretty significant about Joe: the fact that his mother died when he was very young. The speaker continues here to answer one of the questions that audience members probably have—namely, why this somewhat older person is in this class and in this college. If this were a longer speech, what else might the speaker cover here? What else would you want to know about Joe's past?

Here the speaker shows that Joe has a sense of humor in his identifying why he wanted to stay with his father, the very same things that a father would say about a son. Can you make this more humorous?

### TRANSITION
So Joe and his father journeyed from the dairy farm of Arizona to the Hudson Valley.

Here's a simple transition, alerting the audience that the speaker is moving from the first main point (the past) to the second (the present). In what other ways might you state such a transition?

### SECOND MAIN POINT (THE PRESENT)
Right now, with the money he saved while working on the ranch and with the help of a part-time job, Joe's here with us at Hudson Valley Community College.

Here the speaker goes into the present and gives Joe a very human dimension by identifying his fears and concerns about being in college and taking this course and by emphasizing his concern for animals. The speaker also explains some

Like many of us, Joe is a little apprehensive about college and worries that it's going to be a difficult and very different experience, especially at 28. Although an avid reader—mysteries and biographies are his favorites—Joe hasn't really studied, taken an exam, or written a term paper since high school, some 10 years ago. So he's a bit anxious but at the same time looking forward to the changes and the challenges of college life.

And again, like many of us, Joe's a bit apprehensive about taking a public speaking course.

Joe is currently working for a local animal shelter. He was especially drawn to this particular shelter because of their no-kill policy; lots of shelters will kill the animals they can't find adopted homes for, but this one sticks by its firm no-kill policy.

### TRANSITION

But it's not the past or the present that Joe focuses on, it's the future.

### THIRD MAIN POINT (THE FUTURE)

Joe is planning to complete his AB degree here at Hudson Valley Community and then move on to the State University at New Paltz, where he intends to major in communication with a focus on public relations.

His ideal job would be to work for an animal rights organization. He wants to help make people aware of the ways in which they can advance animal rights and stop so much of the cruelty to animals common throughout the world.

### TRANSITION, INTERNAL SUMMARY

Joe's traveled an interesting road from a dairy farm in Arizona to the Hudson Valley, and the path to New Paltz and public relations should be just as interesting.

### CONCLUSION

Having talked with Joe over the last few days, I'm sure he'll do well—he has lots of ideas, is determined to succeed, is open to new experiences, and enjoys interacting with people. I'd say that gives this interesting dairy farmer from Arizona a pretty good start as a student in this class, as a student at Hudson Valley Community, and as a soon-to-be public relations specialist.

commonalities between Joe and the rest of the audience (for example, feeling apprehension in a public speaking class is shared by nearly everyone). Some textbooks suggest that telling an audience that a speaker has apprehension about speaking is a bad idea. What do you think of this disclosure in this context?

This transition tells listeners that the speaker has finished talking about the past and present and is now moving on to the future.

The speaker moves to the future and identifies Joe's educational plans. Having a plan is one thing that everyone has in common, and Joe's plan is something that most in the class would want to know about. The speaker also covers Joe's career goals—again, something the audience is likely to be interested in. In this the speaker also reveals important aspects of Joe's interests and belief system—his concern for animals and his dedication to building his career around this abiding interest. What kinds of information might this speech of introduction give you about the attitudes and beliefs of its intended audience?

This transition (a kind of internal summary) tells you that the speaker has completed the three-part discussion (past, present, and future) and offers a basic summary of what has been discussed.

In this concluding comment the speaker appropriately expresses a positive attitude toward Joe and summarizes some of Joe's positive qualities. These qualities are then tied to the past–present–future organization of the speech. Although the speaker doesn't say "thank you"—which can get trite when 20 speakers in succession say this—it's clear that this is the end of the speech from the last sentence, which brings Joe into his future profession. How effective do you think this conclusion is? What other types of conclusions might the speaker have used in this speech?

1. When called on to speak, approach the front of the room with enthusiasm; even if, like most speakers, you feel nervous, show your desire to speak with your listeners.
2. When at the front of the room, don't begin immediately; instead, pause, engage your audience eye to eye for a few brief moments, and then begin to talk directly to the audience. Talk at a volume that people can hear easily without straining.
3. Throughout your speech, maintain eye contact with your entire audience; avoid concentrating on only a few members or looking out of the window or at the floor.

Public Speaking Exercise 3.2, "Preparing and Presenting a Speech," on page 63 will guide you through the 10-step process.

# Next Steps

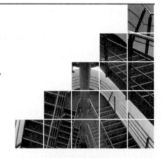

You should now have a general idea of the entire process—admittedly, in rough sketch form—to enable you to take some initial steps to preparing and presenting public speeches. The remaining chapters revisit these steps in depth and provide the kind of practical advice you need when making your public speaking choices. The next chapter focuses on Step 1 and will guide you in selecting your topic, purposes, and thesis.

# Essentials of Preparing and Presenting a Public Speech

This chapter identified and explained in brief the 10 steps to preparing and presenting a public speech.

## Getting Started with Public Speaking

1. Popular myths (such as effective speakers are born, not made or practice is always helpful) often get in the way of learning the principles of public speaking.
2. Starting early will give you the needed time to think about the issues and to deal with any unpredictable snags.
3. Follow the norms established for your class, whether on or offline.

## The 10 Steps for Public Speaking Preparation and Presentation

4. Select your topic, general and specific purposes, and your thesis (Step 1).

5. Analyze your audience: Seek to discover what is unique about your listeners and how you might adapt your speech to them (Step 2).
6. Research your topic so that you know as much as you possibly can, within your time limits (Step 3).
7. Collect your supporting materials (Step 4).
8. Develop your main points (Step 5).
9. Organize your speech materials into an easily comprehended pattern (Step 6).
10. Construct your introduction (to gain attention, establish a speaker–audience–topic connection, and orient the audience), conclusion (to summarize, motivate, and close), and transitions (to hold the parts together and make going from one part to another clear to your audience) (Step 7).
11. Word your speech, focusing on being as clear as possible (Step 8).

**12.** Rehearse your speech until you feel confident and comfortable with the material and with your audience interaction (Step 9).

**13.** Present your speech to your intended audience (Step 10).

## Essential Terms

audience analysis **(52)**          organization **(56)**          thesis **(52)**
conclusion **(58)**                 rehearsal **(59)**            topic **(50)**
general purpose **(51)**            research **(53)**             transition **(58)**
introduction **(57)**               specific purpose **(51)**
main points **(55)**                supporting materials **(54)**

## Public Speaking Exercises

### 3.1 Theses

For any one of the following theses (take whatever position you want), or develop your own thesis, construct a brief outline of a potential public speech—specifically, develop a specific purpose, note your research questions and key terms, identify the main points you'd cover in your speech, develop two or three types of supporting materials (make up your own examples for this exercise), and organize the speech into an introduction, body, and conclusion.

- Take a course in cultural anthropology [or in any subject you want].

- The war in Iraq is similar to the Vietnam War [or is not similar].

- Religion is too influential [or not influential enough] in the United States.

- Current drug laws that mandate life imprisonment for persons convicted three times for drug violations are excessive [or reasonable].

- Adoption by gay men and lesbians should be legal [or illegal] in all states.

### 3.2 Preparing and Presenting a Speech

Apply the 10 steps for public speaking preparation and presentation.

**1.** Select a topic, general and specific purpose, and thesis. If you need help with selecting a topic, see the "Dictionary of Topics" at www.myspeechlab.com for suggestions.

**2.** Analyze this class as your potential audience and identify ways that you can relate your topic to the interests and needs of your audience.

**3.** Research your topic.

**4.** Collect your supporting materials.

**5.** Develop your main points.

**6.** Organize the speech materials you have collected.

**7.** Construct your introduction and conclusion and insert transitions at appropriate places.

**8.** Word your speech for maximum clarity.

**9.** Rehearse your speech.

**10.** Present your speech to the class.

Try to secure some feedback on your speech, and think about what you might do differently in your next speech—how you might improve your speech and its presentation.

## LogOn! mySpeechlab

Log on to MySpeechLab (www.myspeechlab.com) for a complete annotated speech and videos of other speeches. You might also want to look at the topic generator, the outlining software, and the available research resources and databases (My Search Lab at www.mysearchlab.com).

# 4

# Select Your Topic, Purposes, and Thesis (Step 1)

## WHY READ THIS CHAPTER?

**Because it will enable you to develop a more effective speech by helping you to:**

- find a topic that is interesting to you and to your audience

- phrase a purpose statement that crystallizes what you hope to achieve in your speech and that will guide you as you prepare the speech

- formulate a thesis sentence, a statement of your central idea

*There is no one giant step that does it. It's a lot of little steps.*

—PETER A. COHEN

Now that you've learned the basic steps in public speaking preparation, the fundamentals of controlling apprehension, and the basics of listening and criticizing, you can now focus on the first step in the public speaking process—selecting a topic (and narrowing it down so that you can cover it in the allotted time), selecting a purpose, and framing your central idea or thesis.

# Your Topic

As you begin to think about public speaking (and especially about your own future speeches) perhaps the first question you have is "What do I speak about?" The answer to this question will change as your life situation changes; in the years ahead you'll most likely speak on topics that grow out of your job or your social or political activities. In the classroom, however, where your objective is to learn the skills of public speaking, there are literally thousands of subjects to talk about. Therefore, the question remains: "What do I speak about?" To answer this question, focus on three related questions: What makes a good topic? How do I find such a topic? and How do I focus or limit my topic?

## A Good Public Speaking Topic

A good public speaking topic is one that deals with matters of substance, is appropriate to you and the audience, and is culturally sensitive. These three characteristics suggest some guidelines for selecting a good topic, so let's consider each briefly.

### Substantive

The most important criterion of a good topic is that it should *deal with matters of substance*. So select a topic that is important enough to merit the time and attention of a group of intelligent people. Ask yourself: Would this topic engage the attention of my classmates? Would a reputable newspaper cover such a topic? Would students find this topic relevant to their social or professional lives?

### Appropriate

Select a topic that is *appropriate to you as the speaker*. For example, if you've never been incarcerated then a speech on what life is like in prison is probably not going to ring true to your audience. If you're known as someone with lots of money who is always spending, then giving a speech on how to scrape by on ten dollars a day is not likely to be well received. The best way to look at this criterion is to ask if—given what the audience already knows about you and what you'll tell them during your speech—your listeners will see you as a knowledgeable and believable spokesperson on this topic. If the answer is yes, then you have a topic appropriate to you as a speaker. If the answer is no, then it will probably be useful to continue your search for an appropriate topic. The next section focuses on this search.

Also, select a topic that is *appropriate to your audience in terms of their interests and needs.* Giving a speech on the usefulness of a computer to students in your class will be inappropriate simply because they already know about that. But that same topic may be quite appropriate if given at a senior center where most of the members do not own computers. Giving a speech advocating a specific religious belief may well prove insulting to members of the audience who don't share your religious beliefs. Yet that same speech may be very well received by members of a particular religious congregation. So always look to your audience when thinking about a topic, and try to gauge their reaction to it. After all, your audience is giving you their time and attention; selecting a topic that is responsive to their needs and interests seems only fair.

### Culturally Sensitive

A good topic is *culturally sensitive.* Select a topic that will not offend members of other cultures (who may even be in your audience). But also recognize that we live in a time when a person's degree of **cultural sensitivity** is taken as a sign of education and sophistication—attainments that can only help a speaker.

In many Arab, Asian, and African cultures, for example, discussing sex in an audience of both men and women would be considered obscene and offensive. In Scandinavian cultures, on the other hand, sex is discussed openly and without embarrassment or discomfort. Listed below are some taboos that intercultural experts recommend that Americans avoid when traveling abroad. These **taboo topics** change with the times, however, so what is true today may not be true tomorrow (Axtell, 2007; Allan & Burridge, 2007):

- In Spain avoid discussing family, religion, or jobs or making negative comments on bullfighting

- In the Caribbean avoid discussing race, local politics, or religion

- In Brazil avoid discussing politics or religion and avoid telling ethnic jokes

- In Japan avoid discussing World War II or bodily contact (patting someone on the back or putting your arm around someone's shoulders)

- In Mexico avoid talking about the Mexican-American War, illicit drugs, or illegal aliens.

- In many Muslim countries avoid talking about religion, politics, and sexuality, and avoid any references that can be interpreted as profane.

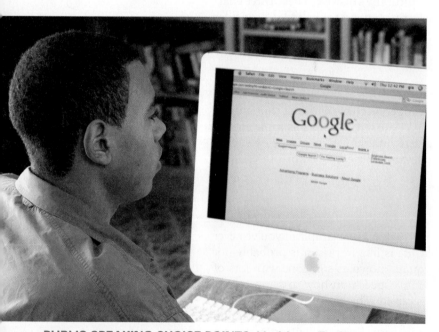

**PUBLIC SPEAKING CHOICE POINTS: Limiting a Topic**
Richard wants to give a speech on women's rights, but he can't seem to narrow the topic down to manageable proportions. Everything he comes across seems important and cries out for inclusion. What options does Richard have for limiting his topic? What would make a good topic?

# Finding Topics

Here are five ways to find topics: yourself, brainstorming, surveys, news items, and topic lists.

## Yourself

Perhaps your first step in thinking about appropriate speech topics is to look at **your interests.** What are you interested in? What engages your time and interest? If you were in a bookstore, what book topics would encourage you to flip through the books? What titles of magazine articles would interest you enough so that you would thumb through the magazine? What topics would encourage you actually to buy the magazine? What do you want to learn more about? In short, think about your own interests; they may be similar to your audience's. If you plan a speech on a topic that you're interested in and want to learn more about, you'll enjoy and profit from the entire experience a great deal more. The research that you do for your speech, for example, will be more meaningful; the facts you uncover will be more interesting. At the same time, your enthusiasm for your topic is likely to make your delivery more exciting, less anxiety-provoking, and more engaging to the audience. All around, you win by selecting a topic in which you're especially interested or to which you have a special connection.

At the same time that you consider your interests, consider *your experiences.* Have you been a part of well-known events or lived in different places? Do you have special talents? Are you knowledgeable about odd or different topics? What are your hobbies? If you're a philatelist, a speech on unique stamps or the value of some stamps or the way in which stamps are printed might prove interesting. If you're a spelunker, perhaps a speech on caves, how they form, and what they mean to the ecology might prove interesting.

## Brainstorming

Another useful method for finding a topic is **brainstorming**, a technique designed to enable you to generate lots of topics in a relatively short time (DeVito, 1996; Osborn, 1957). You begin with your "problem," which in this case is "What will I talk about?" You then record any and all ideas that occur to you. Allow your mind to free-associate. Don't censor yourself; instead, allow your ideas to flow as freely as possible. Record all your thoughts, regardless of how silly or inappropriate they may seem. Write them down or record them on tape. Try to generate as many ideas as possible. The more ideas you think of, the better your chances of finding a suitable topic in your list. After you've generated a sizable list—it should take you no longer than five minutes—read over the list or replay the tape. Do any of the topics on your list suggest other topics? If so, write these down as well. Can you combine or extend your ideas? Which ideas seem workable? Suggestions for practicing brainstorming are provided in Public Speaking Exercise 4.1, "Brainstorming for Topics" on page 83.

## Surveys

Look at some of the national and regional issues that are identified by polls or research organizations. For example, one political website (**www.ontheissues.org/issues.htm**) identifies such issues as abortion, budget and economy, civil rights, crime, drugs, education, families and children, gun control, homeland security, immigration, and infrastructure. The Rand Corporation (**www.rand.org/pubs**)

reports such issues as Obama's health reform bill, intellectual property rights, air pollution, drug use, employment among military spouses, risk management, health care quality, and patient protection. And *Issues in Science and Technology* (**www.issues .org**) identifies such major topics as climate, competitiveness, education, energy, environment, foreign policy, national security, public health, and transportation.

Survey data are now easier than ever to obtain because many of the larger poll results are available on the Internet. For example, the Gallup Organization maintains a website at **www.gallup.com** that includes national and international surveys on political, social, consumer, and other issues speakers often talk about. The Polling Report website also will prove useful; it provides a wealth of polling data on issues in fields such as political science, business, journalism, health, and social science (**www.pollingreport.com**). Other sources are search directories where you can examine the major directory topics and any subdivisions of those you'd care to pursue—a process that's explained later in this chapter. Many search engines and browsers provide lists of "hot topics," which are often useful starting points. These are exactly the topics that people are talking about and therefore often make excellent subjects for speeches.

Or you can conduct a survey yourself. Roam through the nonfiction section of your bookstore (online, if you prefer—for example, at Amazon, **www .amazon.com**, Barnes and Noble, **www.bn.com**, or Borders, **www.borders.com**) and you'll quickly develop a list of the topics book buyers consider important. A glance at your newspaper's best-seller list will give you an even quicker overview.

## News Items

Other useful starting points are newspapers and newsmagazines. Here you'll find the important international and domestic issues, the financial issues, and the social issues all conveniently packaged in one place. The editorial page and the letters to the editor also are useful indicators of what people are concerned about.

Newsmagazines such as *Time* and *Newsweek* and financial magazines such as *Forbes, Money,* and *Fortune* (in print or online) will provide a wealth of suggestions. Similarly, news shows such as *20/20, 60 Minutes,* and *Meet the Press* and even the ubiquitous talk shows (and their corresponding websites) often identify the very issues that people are concerned with and on which there are conflicting points of view.

## Topic Lists

One of the easiest ways of examining and selecting a potential topic is to look at some of the topic lists that are available. For example, the interactive topic selector on MSL (available at **www.myspeechlab.com**) lists hundreds of appropriate topics for informative and persuasive speeches (see Figure 4.1). A variety of educational and commercial websites contain **topic generators,** similar to that on MSL, where you can repeatedly press a button and view a wide variety of topics. For example, WritingFix (**www.writingfix.com**) helps you with topics for writing (which can often, though not always, be adapted for public speaking). And McMaster eBusiness Research Center (**http://merc.mcmaster.ca/mclaren/ebiztopics.html**) maintains a topic generator for business topics. There are also useful topic lists that have been compiled by various communication and English instructors. For example, the University of Hawaii maintains a website, Topic Selection Helper, which lists hundreds of topics (**www.hawaii.edu/mauispeech/html/infotopichelp.html**). Similarly, Cincinnati State Technical and Community College has lists for informative and persuasive speeches at **http://faculty.cinstate.cc.oh.us/gesellsc/publicspeaking/topics.html**.

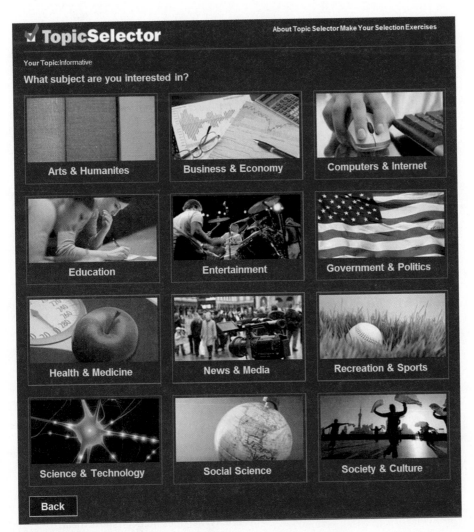

**FIGURE 4.1**
**MySpeechLab's (**www.myspeechlab.com**) Topic Generator**
With this topic selector, you'll find topics suitable for information and persuasive speeches.
Reprinted with permission from Pearson Education.

There is another class of website that will sell you speeches and term papers for a fee. When searching for topics you're likely to run across these sites. Avoid these websites. Many colleges now have software to identify plagiarism, so it's easy to get caught; considering that the consequences are often severe, it's not worth going that route. Another reason for not using these sites and services is that by letting others do your work for you, you'll never learn the very skills that you'll need later in life.

## Limiting Topics

Probably the major error beginning speakers make is to try to cover a huge topic in too short a period of time. The inevitable result is that such speakers cannot cover anything in depth—they touch on everything superficially. To be suitable for a public speech, a topic must be limited in scope; it must be narrowed down to fit the time restrictions and yet permit some depth of coverage.

Another reason to narrow your topic is that it will help you focus your collecting of research materials. If your topic is too broad, you'll be forced to review a lot more research material than you're going to need. On the other hand, if you narrow your topic, you can search for information more efficiently. Here are three methods for narrowing and limiting your topic: topoi, tree diagrams, and search directories.

## Topoi, the System of Topics

**Topoi**, the system of topics, is a technique that comes from the classical rhetorics of ancient Greece and Rome but today is used more widely as a stimulus to creative thinking (DeVito, 1996). When using the method of topoi, you ask yourself a series of questions about your general subject. The process will help you see divisions of your general topic on which you might want to focus.

### TABLE 4.1   Topoi, the System of Topics

These questions should enable you to use general topics to generate more specific ideas for your speeches. You'll be amazed at how many topics you'll be able to find. Your problem will quickly change from "What can I speak on?" to "Which one of these should I speak on?" Here's an example on the topic of homelessness.

| GENERAL QUESTIONS | SUBJECT-SPECIFIC QUESTIONS |
| --- | --- |
| **Who?** Who is he or she, or who are they? Who is responsible? To whom was it done? | Who are the homeless? Who is the typical homeless person? Who is responsible for the increase in homelessness? Who cares for the homeless? |
| **What?** What is it? What effects does it have? What is it like? What is it different from? What are some examples? | What does it mean to be homeless? What does homelessness do to the people themselves? What does homelessness do to the society in general? What does homelessness mean to you and me? |
| **Why?** Why does it happen? Why does it not happen? | Why is there homelessness? Why are there so many homeless people? Why did this happen? Why does it happen in the larger cities more than in smaller towns? Why is it more prevalent in some countries than in others? |
| **When?** When did it happen? When will it occur? When will it end? | When did homelessness become so prevalent? When does it occur in the life of a person? |
| **Where?** Where did it come from? Where is it going? Where is it now? | Where is homelessness most prevalent? Where is there an absence of homelessness? |
| **How?** How does it work? How is it used? How do you do it? How do you operate it? How is it organized? | How does someone become homeless? How can we help the homeless? How can we prevent others from becoming homeless? |
| **So?** What does it mean? What is important about it? Why should I be concerned with this? Who cares? | Why is homelessness such an important social problem? Why must we be concerned with homelessness? How does all this affect me? |

Table 4.1 provides an example; the column on the left contains seven general questions (Who? What? Why? When? Where? How? and So?) and a series of subquestions (which will vary depending on your topic). The right column illustrates how some of the questions on the left might suggest specific aspects of the general subject of "homelessness."

## Tree Diagrams

**Tree diagrams** help you to divide your topic repeatedly into its significant parts. Starting with the general topic, you divide it into its parts. Then you take one of these parts and divide it into its subparts. You continue with this dividing process until the topic seems manageable—until you believe you can reasonably cover it in some depth in the time allotted.

Figure 4.2 illustrates a tree diagram that begins with the topic of mass communication. Take the topic of television programs as the first general topic area. Television programs, without some limitation, would take a lifetime to cover adequately. So you might divide this topic into such subtopics as comedy, children's programs, educational programs, news, movies, reality programs, soap operas, game shows, and sports. You might then take one of these topics, say comedy, and divide it into subtopics. Perhaps you might consider it on a time basis and divide television comedy into its significant time periods: pre-1960, 1961–1999, 2000 to the present. Or you might focus on situation comedies. Here you might examine a topic such as women in situation comedies,

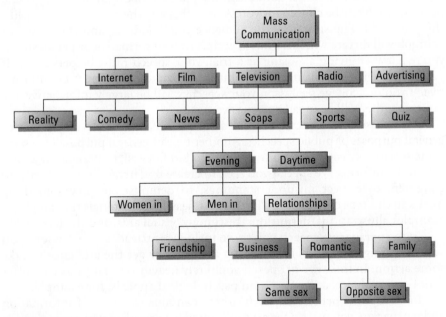

## FIGURE 4.2

### A Tree Diagram for Limiting Speech Topics

How would you draw a tree diagram for limiting topics beginning with such general subjects as immigration, education, sports, transportation, or politics? An alternative method for limiting topics with the "Fishbone Diagram" may be found at **www .myspeechlab.com**.

*Source:* DeVito, *The Elements of Public Speaking*, © 2000. Reproduced by permission of Pearson Education, Inc.

race relations in situation comedies, or family relationships in situation comedies. The resulting topics are at least beginning to look manageable.

### Search Directories

A more technologically sophisticated way of both selecting and limiting your topic is to let a **search directory** (such as Yahoo! or Google) do some of the work for you. A search directory is a nested list of topics. You go from the general to the specific by selecting a topic, and then a subdivision of that topic, and then a subdivision of that subdivision. Eventually you'll find your way to relatively specific areas and websites that will suggest topics that may be suitable for a classroom speech. Public Speaking Exercise 4.2, "Limiting Topics" on page 83 offers some suggestions for practicing limiting topics.

# Your Purposes

The overall purpose of your speech is the goal you want to achieve; it identifies the effect that you want your speech to have on your audience. In constructing your speech you'll first identify your general purpose and then your specific purpose.

## General Purpose

Since you're now in a course about learning public speaking skills, your general purpose will likely be chosen for you. And in this way the classroom is very like the real world. The situation, the audience you'll address, and the nature of your job will dictate whether your speech is to be informative or persuasive. If you're a lawyer giving a closing at a trial, your speech must be persuasive. If you're an engineer explaining new blueprints, your speech must be informative. If you're a college professor, your speeches will be largely informative; if a politician, they will be mostly persuasive.

As discussed in Chapter 2, *to inform* and *to persuade* are the two major types of general purposes of public speeches. Another type of general purpose is to serve some specific occasion function—to toast, to bid farewell, to present an award.

In the **informative speech** you seek to create understanding: to clarify, to enlighten, to correct misunderstandings, to demonstrate how something works. In this type of speech you'll rely most heavily on materials that amplify—examples, illustrations, definitions, testimony, visual aids, and the like.

In the **persuasive speech** you try to influence attitudes or behaviors; you seek to strengthen or change existing attitudes or get the audience to take some action. In this type of speech you'll rely heavily on materials that offer proof—on evidence, argument, and psychological appeals, for example.

In the **special occasion speech,** which contains elements of information and persuasion, you might, for example, introduce another speaker or a group of speakers, present a tribute, try to secure the goodwill of the listeners, toast your friends' anniversary, or "just" entertain your listeners.

## Specific Purpose

Once you have chosen your general purpose, develop your specific purpose by identifying more precisely what you aim to accomplish. For example, in an informative speech, your specific purpose will identify the information you want to convey to your audience. Here are a few possible specific purposes for a speech on the topic of stem cell research:

General purpose:     To inform.
Specific purposes:   To inform my audience of the differences between embryonic and adult stem cell research.
                     To inform my audience about two areas of stem cell research progress.
                     To inform my audience of the current federal regulations on funding stem cell research.

You may find it helpful to view your specific informative purpose in behavioral terms; identifying how you want the audience to demonstrate what they've learned from your speech. Here are a few examples:

- After listening to my speech, audience members should be able to describe the procedures for systematic desensitization.
- After listening to my speech, audience members should be able to define the three major differences between communism and capitalism.
- After listening to my speech, audience members should be able to demonstrate the three techniques of active listening.

In a persuasive speech, your specific purpose identifies what you want your audience to believe, to think, or perhaps to do. Here are a few examples:

General purpose:     To persuade.
Specific purposes:   To persuade listeners to use systematic desensitization to reduce their apprehension.
                     To persuade listeners to believe that capitalism is superior to communism.
                     To persuade listeners to use active listening more often.

As you formulate your specific purpose, follow these five guidelines: Use an infinitive phrase; focus the purpose in terms of its impact on your audience; limit it to one idea; limit it to what you can reasonably expect to achieve; and use specific terms.

## Use an Infinitive Phrase

Begin the statement of each specific purpose with your general purpose (to inform, to persuade) and elaborate on your general purpose. For example:

To inform my audience of the new registration procedures.
To persuade my audience to contribute a book for the library fund-raiser.
To introduce the main speaker of the day to my audience.

## Focus on the Audience

Right now your audience is your public speaking class. It may at first seem unnecessary to include reference to them in each specific purpose (as was done in the examples in the previous paragraph). Actually, referring to the audience is crucial because it keeps you focused on the people you want to inform or persuade; it's a reminder that everything you do in your speech needs to be directed by the purpose you want to achieve with this specific audience. Your speech purpose must be relevant to your audience. In your life and career, you'll probably address a variety of different audiences, and you need to keep each unique and distinct audience clearly in focus.

### Limit Your Specific Purpose to One Idea

Avoid the common pitfall of trying to accomplish too much in too short a time. For example:

> To persuade my audience of the prevalence of date rape in our community and that they should attend the dating seminars offered on campus.

This contains two specific purposes, not one. Select one or the other. Beware of any specific purpose that contains the word *and*; it's often a sign that you have more than one purpose.

### Limit Your Specific Purpose to What Is Reasonable

Limit your specific purpose to what you can reasonably develop and achieve in the allotted time. Specific purposes that are too broad are useless. Note how broad and overly general are such purposes as:

> To inform my audience about clothing design.
> To persuade my audience to improve their health.

You couldn't hope to cover such topics in one speech. It would be much more reasonable to have such purposes as:

> To inform my audience of the importance of color in clothing design.
> To persuade my audience to exercise three times a week.

### Use Specific Terms

Phrase your specific purpose with specific terms. The more precise your specific purpose, the more effectively it will guide you in the remaining steps of preparing your speech. Notice that the purposes used as examples of covering too much are also overly general and very unspecific ("clothing design" can mean hundreds of things as can "improve your health"). Instead of the overly general:

> To persuade my audience to help the homeless.

consider the more specific:

> To persuade my audience to donate a few hours a month to make phone calls for the Homeless Coalition.

## Your Thesis

Like your specific purpose, your **thesis** needs to be given special attention. This section defines the thesis and explains how you should word and use it in your preparation and in your actual speech.

# RESEARCH LINK

As you research your speeches, distinguish between primary, secondary, and tertiary source material whether your materials come from print or online.

**Primary sources** are first hand, contemporary accounts written or spoken by someone who has had direct experience with or witnessed a particular event. Also considered primary sources are reports of original research by the researcher himself or herself. Primary sources would include, for example, an original research study reported in an academic journal, a corporation's annual report, and an eyewitness report of an accident. With primary sources there is nothing (or very little) standing between the event (say, an accident) and the reporting of it (the eyewitness testimony).

**Secondary sources** are those that interpret, comment on, analyze, and/or summarize primary source material. Secondary source material would include, for example, a summary of research appearing in a popular magazine, a television news report on a corporation's earnings, and a report by someone who talked to someone who witnessed an accident. With secondary sources someone stands between the actual event and the report; for example, a science reporter reads the scientist's monograph (primary source), then writes up a summary for the popular press (secondary source).

Note that the same source material may be primary or secondary, depending on the use to which it is put. For example, a speech on Afghanistan by President Obama may be considered primary if, for example, your concern was with what Obama said or his speaking style or speeches on the war in Afghanistan. But, this same speech would be secondary source material if used as information on how the war is proceeding, what the Afghan people are thinking, or the morale of the soldiers.

**Tertiary sources** are a "distillation and collection of primary and secondary sources" (www.lib.umd.edu/guides/primary-sources.html). Tertiary source material would include articles in encyclopedias, almanacs, handbooks, and guidebooks. Also considered tertiary are statistical compilations such as movie attendance figures or Nielsen figures.

Your textbooks are in part secondary source material (they interpret and summarize the primary source material that appears in scholarly journals) and in part tertiary source material (they also make use of academic summaries of research and theories, i.e., secondary source material).

To complicate matters just a bit further the same article—in a scholarly journal, for instance—may contain primary (for example, the report of an experiment), secondary (for example, a review of previous research by others), and tertiary source materials (for example, statistics relevant to the subject of the research).

As a listener and speaker you'll hear and use all three types of source material. However, there are important differences that you should keep in mind. Secondary source material is usually less reliable than primary source material because it is a step removed from the actual facts or events. The writer of secondary material may have forgotten important parts, may be biased and so may have slanted the reporting to reflect his or her attitudes, or may have distorted the material because of a misreading of the data. On the other hand, the writer may have been able to express complicated scientific data in simple language—often making it easier for a non-scientist to understand than the original report would be. Tertiary material (say, an encyclopedia article) is usually an excellent starting place but your research needs to go beyond that and include secondary and perhaps primary source materials. When using or listening to secondary or tertiary sources, examine the information for any particular spin the writer may be giving the material. If possible, check the primary source material itself to see if anything was left out or if the conclusions are really warranted on the basis of the primary evidence.

The next Research Link, "Scholarly and Popular Journals" appears on page 94.

## What Is a Thesis?

As you'll recall from Chapter 2, your thesis is your central idea; it's the theme, the essence of your speech. It's your point of view; it's what you want the audience to get out of your speech. The thesis of Lincoln's Second Inaugural Address was that Northerners and Southerners should work together for the entire nation's welfare; the thesis of Martin Luther King Jr.'s "I have a dream" speech was that true equality is a right of African Americans and all people; and the thesis of political campaign speeches is generally something like: "Vote for me," or "I'm the better candidate," or "My opponent is the wrong choice."

In an informative speech your thesis states what you want your audience to learn. For example, a suitable thesis for an informative speech on jealousy might be "There are two main theories of jealousy." Notice that here, as in all informative speeches, the thesis is relatively neutral and objective.

In a persuasive speech your thesis states what you want your audience to believe or accept; it summarizes the claim you're making, the position you're taking. For example, let's say that you're planning to present a speech against using animals for experimentation. Your thesis statement might be something like "Animal experimentation should be banned." Here are a few additional examples of persuasive speech theses:

- We should all contribute to the Homeless Shelter Project.
- Everyone over 40 should get tested for colon cancer.
- Condoms should be distributed free of charge.

As you can see, these thesis statements identify what you want your audience to believe or do as a result of your speech—you want them to contribute to the homeless shelter, to believe that everyone over 40 should be tested for colon cancer, and to be convinced that condoms should be distributed without charge. Notice that in persuasive speeches the thesis statement puts forth a point of view, an opinion. The thesis is arguable; it's debatable.

## How Do Thesis and Specific Purpose Differ?

The thesis and the specific purpose are similar in that they are both guides to help you select and organize your speech materials. Because they both serve these similar goals, they are often confused. Let's consider some of the ways in which they're different.

First, the thesis and purpose differ in their form of expression. The specific purpose is worded as an infinitive phrase; for example, "To inform my audience of the provisions of the new education budget" or "To persuade my audience to vote in favor of the new education budget." The thesis, on the other hand, is phrased as a complete declarative sentence; for example, "The education budget must be increased."

Second, they differ in their focus. The specific purpose is audience-focused; it identifies the change you hope to achieve in your audience. For example, your specific purpose may be for the audience to gain information, to believe something, or to act in a certain way. The thesis, on the other hand, is message-focused. It identifies the main idea of your speech; it summarizes—it epitomizes—the content of your speech. It's the one idea that you want your audience to remember even if they forget everything else.

Third, the specific purpose and thesis differ in their concern for practical limitations. No matter how sweeping or ambitious the thesis, the specific purpose must take into consideration the time you have to speak and the attitudes of the audience toward you and your topic. The specific purpose, therefore, needs to be phrased with these practical limitations in mind. For example, the thesis might be that "Colleges are not educating students for today's world." The speech, however, might have any one of several different specific purposes: for example, (1) to persuade my audience that colleges must change to keep pace with today's world, (2) to persuade my audience to adapt the Illinois Educational Proposal, or (3) to persuade my audience to quit college. The thesis epitomizes the speech without regard to practical limitations of, say, time or current audience attitudes.

Here are two examples to clarify further the difference between purpose and thesis:

| | |
|---|---|
| General purpose: | To inform. |
| Specific purpose: | To inform my audience of three ways to save on their phone bills. |
| Thesis: | You can reduce your phone bills. |
| | |
| General purpose: | To persuade. |
| Specific purpose: | To persuade my audience to take a computer science course. |
| Thesis: | Computer science knowledge is essential. |

Especially in your early stages of mastering public speaking, formulate both the specific purpose and the thesis statement. With both of these as guides, you'll be able to construct a more coherent and more understandable speech.

## Wording and Using Your Thesis

Here are a few suggestions on how to word and use your thesis.

### Limit Your Thesis to One Central Idea

Be sure to limit your thesis statement to one and only one central idea. A statement such as "Animal experimentation should be banned, and companies engaging in it should be prosecuted" contains not one but two basic ideas. Whenever you see an *and* or a semicolon (;) in a thesis statement, it probably contains more than one idea.

### State Your Thesis as a Complete Declarative Sentence

In phrasing your thesis, word it as a complete declarative sentence; for example:

Hate speech corrupts.
Speak out against hate speech.
Support the college's new hate speech code.

This will help you focus your thinking, your collecting of materials, and your organizational pattern. Avoid stating your thesis as a question or a sentence fragment; these will not provide the clear and specific focus you need to use the thesis effectively.

### Use Your Thesis Statement to Generate Main Points

Within each thesis there is an essential question that allows you to explore and subdivide the thesis. Your objective here is to find this question and use it to help

# PUBLIC SPEAKING SAMPLE ASSISTANT

## A Poorly Constructed Persuasive Speech

This speech was written to illustrate both broad errors as well as some subtle errors that a beginning speaker might make in constructing a persuasive speech. First, read the entire speech without reading any of the "Problems/ Correctives." As you read the speech consider what errors are being demonstrated and how you might correct them. Then, after you've read the entire speech, reread each paragraph and combine your own analysis with the "Problems/Correctives" annotations.

| Speech | Problems/Correctives |
|---|---|
| **Title:** Prenups<br><br>**Topic:** Prenuptial agreements<br><br>**Purpose:** Prenuptials are bad.<br><br>**Thesis:** Why do we need pre-nuptial agreements? | This title sounds like an informative speech title and doesn't give the idea that a position will be argued. In addition, the topic, purpose, and thesis are not clearly focused or appropriately worded.<br><br>A more appropriate title might be something like "Prenups have got to go" or "The dangers of prenups." The topic would need to be narrowed by some qualification such as "The negative aspects of prenuptial agreements." The purpose should be stated as an infinitive phrase: to persuade my audience that prenuptial agreements should be declared illegal. The thesis needs to be stated as a declarative sentence: Prenuptial agreements should be declared illegal. |

### INTRODUCTION

You're probably not worried about prenuptial agreements yet. But, maybe you will be. At any rate, that's what my speech is on. I mean that prenuptial agreements should be made illegal.

This opening is weak and can easily turn off the audience. After all, if they're not worried about it now, why listen? The speaker could have made a case for the importance of this topic in the near future, however. It appears as if the speaker knows the topic's not important but will speak on it anyway.

A more effective introduction would have (1) captured the audience's attention—perhaps by citing some widely reported celebrity prenup; (2) provided a connection among the speaker-audience-topic—perhaps by noting the consequences one might suffer with a prenup; and (3) orient the audience as to what is to follow.

### BODY

Here, a transition would help. In fact, transitions should be inserted between the introduction and the body and between the body and the conclusion. Using transitions between the main points and signposts when introducing each main point would help.

The speaker might have said something like: "There are three main reasons why prenups should be banned."

Prenuptial agreements make marriage a temporary arrangement. If you have a prenuptial agreement, you can get out of a marriage real fast—and we know that's not a good thing. So if we didn't have prenups—that's short for prenuptial agreements—marriages would last longer.

This is the speaker's first argument but it isn't introduced in a way the audience will find easy to understand. Abbreviations should be introduced more smoothly.

A simple signpost like, "My first argument against prenups is. . . ." would make the audience see where the speaker is and get a visual image of the outline. To introduce the abbreviation that will be used throughout the speech, the speaker might have incorporated it into the first sentence—"Prenuptial agreements—for short, prenups—make a marriage. . . ."

Right now, most people don't have prenups and yet somewhere around 50 percent of marriages last. That would be equivalent to a baseball player batting 500. If we had prenups that number would go up—I mean down—I mean the number of marriages that last will go up if we had prenups, I mean if we didn't.

The fact that 50 percent of the marriages fail seems to be the more telling statistic, yet the speaker treats a 50 percent success rate as good—something the audience is likely to see very differently. And the baseball analogy seems weak at best. The speaker also betrays a lack of preparation in confusing *up* with *down*.

Poor people are going to be discriminated against. Poor people won't be able to marry rich people because rich people will want a prenup and if a poor person doesn't want a prenup they wouldn't get married.

This argument just doesn't seem logical and the speaker would have been better served by omitting this entirely.

For this argument to be useful in advancing the speaker's purpose, the speaker would have had to show that in fact poor people suffer in, say, divorce proceedings *because of* prenups.

These agreements are difficult to discuss. I mean, how do you tell someone you've told you love that you now want a prenup just in case the marriage gets screwed up? I guess you can say something like, "By the way, how about signing a prenup?"

This argument too doesn't seem important or logical. The fact that something is difficult to discuss doesn't mean you shouldn't discuss it; it merely means it's difficult to discuss. The speaker seems to be implying that if something is difficult to discuss it should be abandoned—clearly a poor communication strategy.

And they're expensive. I mean you need a lawyer and all. I don't know what a lawyer charges, but I'd guess it's a lot. So it's expensive and a young couple could use the money on other things.

This argument also seems weak simply because if there is enough money involved to warrant a prenup, there's probably enough money to hire a lawyer.

If the speaker wanted to make this argument, specific costs should have been cited.

I had a prenup two years ago. And when we got divorced, I got nothing. If we didn't have a prenup I'd be rich and I'd be at some private college instead of here.

Here the audience is likely thinking that there was a personal and emotional reason for arguing against prenups and not any logical reasons. And yet, the audience is probably asking itself, what were the specifics of the prenup and how much money was involved.

The speaker probably should have disclosed this earlier in the speech and assured the audience that this personal experience led to a thorough study of the subject. And if a personal experience is going to be used—and there's no reason it shouldn't—then it needs to be discussed more fully and, at the least, answer the audience's obvious questions.

## CONCLUSION

My conclusions. So, you can see that prenups are not a good thing. Like they're unfair to poor people. And it creates a lot of stress for the couple, especially for the one who didn't want the prenup in the first place, like myself.

Using the word "conclusion" is not a bad idea, but it stands out like a heading in a textbook. This speech also needed a more detailed conclusion, reiterating the main points in the speech. This speaker also commits one of the common faults of conclusions, and that is to introduce new material—notice that we hadn't heard of the stress factor before.

The speaker might have said something like: "In conclusion, we can see there are three main arguments against prenups. First, . . ."

Any questions?

This seems too abrupt.

A good pause should preface this request for questions and perhaps a more inviting request could be offered, something like, "If anyone has any questions, I'd be happy to respond."

## ETHICAL CHOICE POINT

### Thesis Appropriateness

Visualize yourself as a public speaking instructor. Your students are getting ready to deliver their first round of speeches. You've asked them to submit their thesis statements to you so that you can make sure they're on the right track and offer whatever help may be needed. Among the theses you receive are the following:

1. You can cheat on your income tax with two great strategies.
2. Help revitalize the KKK.
3. Growing marijuana can be fun and profitable.
4. The Holocaust has been exaggerated.
5. You can create computer viruses in three easy steps.

You believe that in a democracy speakers should be free to speak on any side of an issue and so your first impulse is to approve all these theses. At the same time you don't want to create problems in the classroom (and possibly beyond) and divert attention from the purpose of the course—to teach the skills of public speaking. ➤ *What ethical choices do you have for dealing with these seemingly contradictory goals?*

you discover the major ideas or assertions or propositions that will support this thesis. For example, let's take a hypothetical proposed bill—call it the Hart Bill—and let's say your thesis is "The Hart Bill provides needed services for senior citizens." When the thesis is stated in this form, the obvious question suggested is "What are the needed services?" The answer to this question suggests the main parts of your speech; let's say, health, food, shelter, and recreational services. These four areas then become the four main points of your speech.

Some public speaking instructors and trainers advise speakers to include their main points in the statement of the thesis. If you did this, your thesis for the above speech would be "The Hart Bill provides needed health, food, shelter, and recreational services for senior citizens." You may find it helpful to use the briefer thesis statement for some speech topics and purposes and the more expanded thesis statement for others.

| | |
|---|---|
| General purpose: | To inform. |
| Specific purpose: | To inform my audience of the provisions of the Hart Bill. |
| Thesis: | The Hart Bill provides needed services for senior citizens. |

Or, if you were using an expanded thesis, it might be stated like this:

The Hart Bill provides needed health, food, shelter, and recreational services for senior citizens.

Regardless of whether you use the brief or the expanded thesis, an outline of the main points would look like this:

I. The Hart Bill provides needed health services.
II. The Hart Bill provides needed food services.
III. The Hart Bill provides needed shelter services.
IV. The Hart Bill provides needed recreational services.

The remainder of the speech would then be filled in with supporting materials. Under main point I, for example, you might identify several health services and explain how the Hart Bill would provide them. In outline form, this first main point of your speech might look something like this:

I. The Hart Bill provides needed health services.
   A. Neighborhood clinics will be established.
   B. Medical hotlines will be established.

In the completed speech, this first main point and its two subordinate statements might be spoken like this:

> The Hart Bill provides senior citizens with the health services they need so badly. Let me give you some examples of these necessary health services. One of the most important services will be the establishment of neighborhood health clinics. These clinics will help senior citizens get needed health advice and medical care right in their own neighborhoods.
>
> A second important health service will be the health hotlines. These phone numbers will be for the exclusive use of senior citizens. These hotlines will connect seniors with trained medical personnel who will be able to give advice and send emergency medical services to seniors as needed.

## Use Your Thesis to Suggest Organizational Patterns

Your thesis will provide you with useful guidelines in selecting the organization for your main points. For example, let's suppose your thesis is "We can improve our own college education." Your answer to the inherent question "What can we do?" will suggest a possible organizational pattern. If, for example, you identify the remedies in the order in which they should be taken, then a time-order pattern will be appropriate. If you itemize a number of possible solutions, all of which are of about equal importance, then a topical pattern will be appropriate. If your thesis is "The proposed fringe benefits package has both advantages and disadvantages," then your speech might logically be organized into two parts: advantages and disadvantages. These and other patterns are explained in detail in Chapter 7, "Organizing Your Speech."

## Use Your Thesis to Focus Audience Attention

Because the thesis sentence focuses the audience's attention on your central idea and reveals what you hope to achieve in your speech, you'll want to consider the options you have for stating your thesis. Here are a few guidelines that will help you make a strategically effective decision about how and when to present your thesis to your audience.

- In an informative speech, state your thesis early, clearly, and directly:
  - Immigration patterns are predicted to change drastically over the next 50 years.
  - Carpal tunnel syndrome can be corrected with surgery.
  - An iPhone can organize your life.

**PUBLIC SPEAKING CHOICE POINT: Statement of Thesis**

Miranda wants to give her speech in favor of allowing singles to adopt children. What choices does Miranda have for presenting her thesis? What advice would you give Miranda about presenting her thesis if she were facing an audience opposed to her position? What advice would you give if the audience was in favor of her position and she wanted to strengthen it?

- In a persuasive speech addressed to an audience already in agreement with you, state your thesis explicitly and early in your speech:

  Immigration laws should be changed.

  You can avoid carpal tunnel syndrome with rest and exercise.

  Organize your life electronically.

- In a persuasive speech addressed to an audience opposed to your position, give your evidence and arguments first and gradually move the audience into a more positive frame of mind before stating your thesis explicitly.

- When you are speaking to a relatively uneducated or uninformed audience, it is probably best to state your thesis explicitly. If the thesis is not explicit, the listeners may fail to grasp what your thesis is and therefore may be less likely to change their attitudes or behaviors.

- Recognize, too, that there are cultural differences in the way a thesis should be stated. In some Asian cultures, for example, making a point too directly or asking directly for audience compliance may be considered rude or insulting.

# Next Steps

With the information covered here and with your previous and future speeches in mind, consider how you might have selected and narrowed your topic, worded your purpose, and formulated your thesis more effectively. Keep your topic, purposes, and thesis in mind as you consider the ways to analyze and adapt your speech to your specific audience, step 2, and the subject of the next chapter.

# Essentials of Selecting Your Topic, Purposes, and Thesis

In this chapter we considered the speech topic and ways to find and limit it, general and specific speech purposes and how to phrase them, and speech theses and how to word and use them to best effect.

## Your Topic

1. Suitable speech topics are topics that are substantive, appropriate to you and your audience, and culturally sensitive.
2. Topics may be found through:
   - Yourself.
   - Brainstorming.
   - Surveys.
   - News items.
   - Topic lists.
3. Speech topics may be limited by:
   - Topoi, the system of topics.
   - Tree diagrams.
   - Search directories.

## Your Purposes

4. Speech purposes are both general (for example, to inform or to persuade) and specific (for example, to inform an audience of new health plan options). A specific purpose should be:
   - Worded as an infinitive phrase.
   - Focused on the audience.

- Limited to one idea.
- Limited to what you can reasonably accomplish.
- Phrased with precise terms.

### Your Thesis

5. The speech thesis is your central idea; the theme, the essence of your speech.

6. In wording and using your thesis:

- Limit your thesis to one central idea.
- State your thesis as a complete declarative sentence.
- Use your thesis statement to generate main ideas.
- Use your thesis to suggest organizational patterns.
- Use your thesis to focus audience attention.

## Essential Terms

brainstorming (67)
cultural sensitivity (66)
general purpose (72)
informative speech (72)
persuasive speech (72)

search directory (72)
special occasion speech (72)
specific purpose (72)
taboo topics (66)
thesis (74)

topic (66)
topic generators (68)
topoi (70)
tree diagrams (71)

## Public Speaking Exercises

### 4.1 Brainstorming for Topics

With a small group of students or with the entire class sitting in a circle, brainstorm for suitable speech topics. Be sure to appoint someone to write down all the contributions or use a recorder.

After this brainstorming session, consider:

1. Did any members give negative criticism (even nonverbally)?
2. Did any members hesitate to contribute really wild ideas? Why?
3. Was it necessary to re-stimulate the group members at any point? Did this help?
4. Did some useful speech topics emerge in the brainstorming session?

### 4.2 Limiting Topics

Listed below are a few overly general topics. Using one of the methods discussed in this chapter (or

any other method you're familiar with), limit each topic to a subject that would be reasonable for a 5- to 10-minute speech.

1. Dangerous sports
2. Race relationships
3. Parole
4. Censorship on the Internet
5. Ecological problems
6. Problems faced by college students
7. Morality
8. Health and fitness
9. Ethical issues in politics
10. Urban violence

## LogOn! myspeechlab

### Selecting Your Topic, Purpose, and Thesis

Visit MySpeechLab (www.myspeechlab.com) for Chapter 4. Here you'll find the topic generator to help you select an appropriate topic, speeches for

analysis, and lots of research guidance in My Search Lab. Watch one or two of the informative and persuasive speeches for appropriateness of topic, purpose, and thesis.

# 5 | Analyze and Adapt to Your Audience (Step 2)

## WHY READ THIS CHAPTER?

**Because it will enable you to tailor your speech to your specific audience by helping you to:**

- discover the demographics or sociology of your listeners (age, culture, gender, religion, for example) and their psychology (willingness to listen, attitudes toward your thesis, for example)

- adapt your speech to these specific listeners

- adapt to your audience during the actual speech

*When it is obvious that the goals cannot be reached, don't adjust the goals, adjust the action steps.*

—CONFUCIUS

Y ou can inform or persuade an audience only if you know who they are, what they know, and what they believe. Once you have this information you can begin to tailor your speech to these specific listeners. In this chapter we look at the nature of today's audiences, ways to analyze the sociology and psychology of the audience, and some suggestions for adapting to the audience during the actual speech.

# Audiences and Audience Analysis

The public speaking audience is best defined as a group of people with the common purpose of listening and responding to a speech. An audience can be of almost any size—five people listening to a street orator, 20 students in a classroom, thousands at a stadium listening to a political or religious speaker. Audience analysis is the process of discovering useful information about these listeners so as to tailor a speech to them.

## The Audience: Two Basic Characteristics

Among all the qualities that might be said to characterize today's audiences, two stand out: uniqueness (no audience is like any other audience) and diversity (audiences are never truly homogeneous). Let's look at each of these briefly.

### All Audiences Are Unique

Each public speaking audience you address is unique. Audiences are unique because people are different and unique as individuals; but even when you address the same persons repeatedly (as you will in this course and in various business and other situations), the individuals are not necessarily the same as they were the last time you addressed them. For example, audiences on September 10 and on September 12, 2001, may have been composed of the same people, but probably very few audience members were the same in attitudes and beliefs on those two different dates. Not only world events but also personal experiences (new relationships, children, graduation, new jobs) change us all to some extent and in some way.

### All Audiences Are Diverse

As important as uniqueness is the contemporary audience's diversity—in age, race, gender, religion, affectional orientation, nationality, economic situation, relationship status, occupation, political affiliation, attitudes, values, beliefs, and in hundreds of other ways. If you're in a typical college classroom in the United States, your classroom audience represents a

## ETHICAL CHOICE POINT

### Audience Interests

You've just been hired by an advertising agency to design a campaign to promote a cereal that's extremely high in sugar and trans fat—both of which you know are not healthy. The job, however, is a particularly good one, and should you succeed on this account, your future in advertising would be assured. Your problem is relatively simple: you don't want to promote unhealthy foods and yet you want the job and these goals are incompatible. ▶ *What are some of your ethical choices for dealing with this dilemma? What would you do?*

diverse group of people. Further, each subgroup within this diverse group is itself diverse. People of the same age will differ in race, gender, religion, and so on. And those of the same religion will differ from one another in age, nationality, politics, and so on. As you prepare to learn about your audience, keep this notion of diversity in mind. It will help you focus on your audience as a mix of unique individuals rather than a blend.

## Learning about Your Audience

You can seek out audience information in four general ways: observation, data collection, interviewing, and inference (Sprague & Stuart, 2008). Let's explore each.

### Observe

Think about your audience based on the way they present themselves physically. What can you infer about their economic status from their clothing and jewelry, for example? Might their clothing reveal any conservative or liberal leanings? Might clothing provide clues to attitudes on economics or politics? What do they do in their free time? Where do they live? What do they talk about? Are different cultures represented? Do your observations give you any clue as to what audience members' interests or concerns might be?

### Collect Data Systematically

Two major ways to collect data are polling sites and questionnaires. Polling sites enable you to discover what a wide range of people think about varied topics whereas questionnaires reveal what your specific audience (in this case, your class) thinks.

**Polling Sites.**   A good place to start with understanding what people think is to visit some of the numerous polling sites on the Internet. Here you'll find a variety of information on all sorts of attitudes and opinions on economics, business, politics, lifestyles, buying habits, and more; search for "opinion poll" or, if you have access, visit MySearchLab (www.MySearchLab.com) for lots of suggestions. One of the most extensive polling websites is the Gallup Organization's at www.gallup.com. Many newspapers maintain polls, one of the best of which is maintained by the Washington Post (www.washingtonpost.com). Another useful source is the Polling Report (www.pollingreport.com), which tracks trends in American public opinion.

Many universities conduct polls and make the results available on their websites. Some of the best include the Cornell Institute for Social and Economic Research's website, with hot links to a wide variety of polls and surveys, at www.ciser.cornell.edu/info/polls.shtml; Marist College's Institute for Public Opinion (www.maristpoll.marist.edu); Quinnipiac University's Polling Institute (www.quinnipiac.edu); and Fairleigh Dickenson University's Public Opinion Research Center (http://publicmind.fdu.edu).

**Audience Questionnaires.**   Another useful way to secure information about your audience is to use a questionnaire. Let's say you've taken a course in website design and are thinking about giving an informative speech on ways to design effective Web pages. One thing you'll need to know is how much your audience already knows about Web design. A questionnaire asking them about their experience with Web design can help you judge the level at which to approach the topic, the information that you can assume the audience already has, the terms you need to define, and so on. You might also want to find out how much experience the audience members have had with Web pages, either as users or as designers.

To help you answer these and other relevant questions, you might compose a questionnaire. If your class is set up as a listserv, or if members can communicate through some Web group (like BlackBoard or WebCT) or you all follow each other on Twitter (though the 140 character limit may pose problems), these questionnaires will be extremely easy to distribute. You can do it with one e-mail questionnaire sent to the listserv or one tweet. If your class is

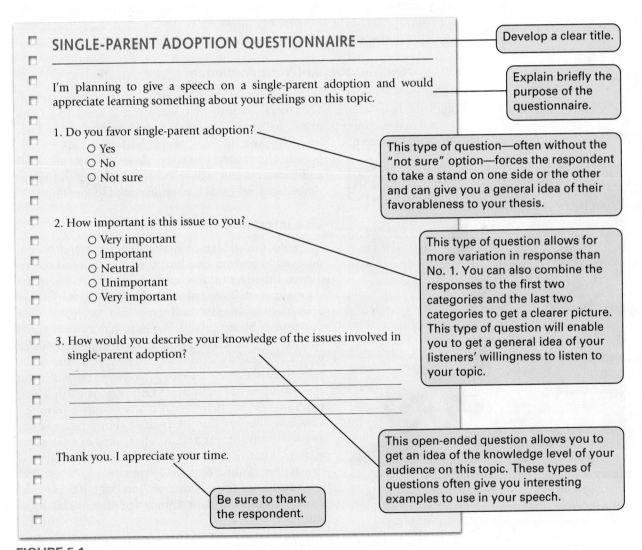

**SINGLE-PARENT ADOPTION QUESTIONNAIRE**

Develop a clear title.

I'm planning to give a speech on a single-parent adoption and would appreciate learning something about your feelings on this topic.

Explain briefly the purpose of the questionnaire.

1. Do you favor single-parent adoption?
   ○ Yes
   ○ No
   ○ Not sure

This type of question—often without the "not sure" option—forces the respondent to take a stand on one side or the other and can give you a general idea of their favorableness to your thesis.

2. How important is this issue to you?
   ○ Very important
   ○ Important
   ○ Neutral
   ○ Unimportant
   ○ Very important

This type of question allows for more variation in response than No. 1. You can also combine the responses to the first two categories and the last two categories to get a clearer picture. This type of question will enable you to get a general idea of your listeners' willingness to listen to your topic.

3. How would you describe your knowledge of the issues involved in single-parent adoption?

This open-ended question allows you to get an idea of the knowledge level of your audience on this topic. These types of questions often give you interesting examples to use in your speech.

Thank you. I appreciate your time.

Be sure to thank the respondent.

**FIGURE 5.1**

**Audience Questionnaire for a Persuasive Speech**
This sample questionnaire is built around the three audience psychology factors considered later in this chapter and illustrates three types of questions you might ask.

not electronically connected, you can distribute printed questionnaires before class begins or as students are leaving.

Audience questionnaires are even more useful as background for persuasive speeches. Let's say you plan to give a speech in favor of allowing single people to adopt children. To develop an effective speech, you need to know your audience's attitudes toward single-parent adoption. Are they in favor of this idea? Opposed to it? Do they have reservations? If so, what are they? Are audience members undecided? To answer such questions, you might use a questionnaire such as that presented in Figure 5.1 on page 87.

In constructing your questionnaire, keep it brief, express thanks to responders for filling it out, and include whatever background information the responders will need to fill out the form (for example, definitions of technical terms). Generally, it's best not to reveal your thesis in the questionnaire—after all, you're going to use this information to help formulate your thesis; besides, you may not want the audience to know your thesis before you give them some evidence and specific examples that support your position.

### Interview Members of Your Audience

In a classroom situation you can easily take the time to interview members of your audience in order to find out more about them. But if you're to speak to an audience you'll not meet prior to your speech, you might interview those who know the audience members better than you do. For example, you might talk with the person who invited you to speak and inquire about the audience's culture, age, gender, knowledge and educational levels, religious background, and so forth.

### Use Inference and Empathy

Use your knowledge of human behavior and human motivation and try to adopt the perspective of the audience. Intelligent inference and empathy will help you estimate your listeners' attitudes, beliefs, values, and even their thoughts and emotions on your topic (Sprague & Stuart, 2008). For example, let's say you're addressing your class on the need to eliminate (or expand) affirmative action. What might you infer about your audience—are they likely to be in favor of affirmative action or opposed to it? Can they be easily classified in terms of their liberal or conservative leanings? How informed are they likely to be about the topic and about the advantages and disadvantages of affirmative action? What feelings might they have about affirmative action? Public Speaking Exercise 5.1, "How Well Do You Know Your Audience?" on page 103 provides some issues to test your knowledge of your classroom audience.

Let's turn now to some of the ways in which audiences differ—sociologically and psychologically—and consider how you might analyze and adapt to the unique and diverse audiences you'll face.

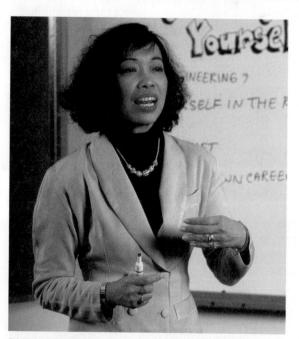

**PUBLIC SPEAKING CHOICE POINT: Analyzing an Audience**

Shirley, a professor of engineering, has been asked to speak about the engineering program in her college to a group of freshman who are undecided about their majors. What are some of the things Shirley would need to know about her audience? What are her options for learning this needed information?

# Analyze Audience Sociology

**Sociological audience analysis** includes consideration of six major sociological or demographic variables of audiences: (1) age, (2) gender, (3) affectional orientation, (4) educational levels, (5) religion and religiousness, and (6) cultural factors.

## Age

Different age groups have different attitudes and beliefs largely because they have had different experiences in different contexts and they have different futures. To complicate matters further, recognize that culture will also influence attitudes toward age. Among some Native Americans and Chinese, for example, there is great respect for the aged and elders are frequently asked for advice and guidance by the young. Among some groups in the United States—though certainly not all or even necessarily a majority—the aged are often ignored and devalued. In thinking about your next speech, consider how the age of your listeners might influence the topics you speak on and the way you develop, support, and word what you say.

Different age groups vary in their goals, interests, and day-to-day concerns that may be related to your topic and purpose. Consider, for example, how your class would respond to such topics as the following:

1. Achieving corporate success
2. Raising a family
3. Successful job interviewing

If your class is typical (say, with most members from 18 to 24 or so) they are likely to react somewhat like this:

1. Corporate success would be nice but I'm not at that point yet—I need to get my foot in the door first;
2. Raising a family is important but that's not on my mind and won't be for a few years at least;
3. Job interviewing is something relevant to me now and might help me achieve my immediate goals, like getting a job.

At the same time, recognize that topic (1) might be highly relevant to middle-management people; topic (2) might be interesting to new mothers and fathers; and topic (3) might be irrelevant and uninteresting to a group of people in their 80s.

Very often, the age of your audience will give you clues as to what they may and may not be interested in, what their goals are, what they feel they need and want. Show your audience how they can more effectively achieve their goals, and you'll have an interested and attentive group of listeners.

Different age groups will also differ in their knowledge of the topics and supporting materials you might discuss. For example, if you are using examples of musicians, people like Dizzy Gillespie or Hoagy Carmichael will have little meaning to people in their 20s but much meaning for those in their 60s or 70s, while their knowledge of Lady Gaga and Jay-Z will likely be reversed. Similarly, events that happened 10 or so years ago will mean a great deal to people in their 30s and older but a great deal less to those in their 20s. The favorite television shows for viewers between 18 and 49 (for the week of February 12–18, 2009) were *American Idol* (Tues and Wed), *House*, and *Grey's Anatomy*. But for those over 50 the top shows were *CSI*, *CSI: Miami*, and *NCIS*.

The most important implication here is that you need to adjust your speech to the age of the audience. Adjust your speech to appeal to your audience's current concerns and use supporting materials they can easily relate to from recent experience.

## Gender

Gender is one of the most difficult audience variables to analyze. The rapid social changes taking place today make it difficult to pin down the effects of gender. At one time researchers focused primarily on biological sex differences. Now, however, many researchers are focusing on psychological sex roles. When we focus on a psychological sex role, we consider a person feminine if that person has internalized those traits (attitudes and behaviors) that society considers feminine and rejected those traits society considers masculine. We consider a person masculine if that person has internalized those traits society considers masculine and rejected those traits society considers feminine. Thus, a biological woman may display masculine sex-role traits and behaviors, and a biological man may display feminine sex-role traits and behaviors (Pearson, West, & Turner, 1995).

Because of society's training, biological males generally internalize masculine traits and biological females generally internalize feminine traits. So there's probably great overlap between biological sex roles and psychological sex roles, even though they're not equivalent.

Although it's not possible to make generalizations about all men or all women, you may be able to make some assumptions about the men and women in your specific audience. At the same time that you want to take gender differences into consideration, realize the dangers of stereotyping.

Men and women often differ in the values they consider important and that are related to your topic and purpose. For example, research shows that men consider power, stimulation, achievement, self-direction, and hedonism more important than do women (Schwartz & Rubel, 2005). Traditionally, men have been found to place greater importance on theoretical, economic, and political values. Women have traditionally been found to place greater importance on aesthetic, social, and religious values. Of course, you're unlikely ever to find yourself speaking to an audience of all "traditional" men and "traditional" women. Rather, your audience is likely to be composed of men and women whose values overlap. Be careful not to assume that the women in your audience are religious simply because they're women and that the men, because they're men, are not; or that the men are interested in sports and the stock market but that the women are not.

Men and women may see your topic differently. Although both men and women may find the topic important, they may nevertheless view it from different perspectives. For example, men and women don't view such topics as abortion, date rape, performance anxiety, anorexia, equal pay for equal work, or exercise in the same way. So if you're giving a speech on date rape on campus, you need to make a special effort to relate the topic and your purpose to the attitudes, knowledge, and feelings that the men and the women in your audience bring with them.

Men and women often watch different television shows and see different movies. For example, a Pew Research Center study conducted in 2008 found that men and women watched different types of news shows (**http://pewresearch .org/pubs/722/men-women-follow-news**); men followed such news stories as the Super Bowl, U.S.–Iran tensions, Venezuela, and shipment of arms to Iraq more than women. Women, on the other hand, were more apt to follow news such as the tornadoes in the Midwest, recently kidnapped children, and flooding in parts of the country. Generally, men are more into news about sports, science and technology, and business and finance whereas women were more into news about religion, health, and culture and the arts. Take these differences into consideration when choosing your supporting materials.

## Affectional Orientation

The issue of affectional orientation has received enormous media attention within the last decade or so—especially when you compare today's coverage to the way the subject was treated 40 or 50 years ago. The *New York Times*, for example, now regularly features same-sex unions along with those of opposite-sex couples in their Sunday Styles section and gay and lesbian celebrities and fictional characters are common in the media. Despite these changes, because of the social climate, much of the gay and lesbian experience remains unreported and unknown. Yet you can be reasonably sure that in all your public speaking experiences, you will never address an audience that is totally heterosexual.

The affectional orientation of your audience members may influence the way they see your topic—especially if your topic is politics, the military's current policies on gay men and lesbians, taxes, marriage, or any of a host of other topics. Polls and frequent news items consistently report on attitudes among gay men and lesbians that differ from those of heterosexuals in significant ways. But don't assume that heterosexuals and homosexuals necessarily see things differently on every topic. There are differences but there are also many similarities.

Be especially careful that you don't come across stereotyping people according to their affectional orientation. While it's true that the media are portraying more gay and lesbian characters, most of them are stereotypical and these ultimately prove insulting to everyone. Be especially careful that you avoid stereotypical portrayals in your examples (the heterosexual male as boorish, the gay male as compulsively neat) or language that is not as inclusive as it might be. Especially with an educated audience, stereotypes are likely to destroy your credibility.

## Educational Levels

The interests and concerns of audience members may differ on the basis of their educational level. Generally, educated people are more concerned with issues outside their immediate field of operation. They're concerned with international affairs, economic issues, and the broader philosophical and sociological issues confronting the nation and the world. Educated groups recognize that these issues affect them in many ways. Uneducated people often don't see the connection. Therefore, when speaking to a less-educated audience, draw connections explicitly to relate such topics to their more immediate concerns.

The educational level of your listeners may also influence how critical the audience will be of your evidence and argument. More educated audiences will probably be less swayed by appeals to emotion and to authority (see Chapter 11). They'll be more skeptical of generalizations (as you should be of the generalizations put forth in this chapter). They'll question the validity of statistics and frequently will demand better substantiation of your propositions. Therefore, pay special attention to the logic of your evidence and arguments in addressing an educated audience.

Also consider the educational level of your listeners when you word your speech. You may need to use more common words and define more terms with an uneducated audience. Similarly, references to literature, specialized research, classical music, or Renaissance art may need to be limited or explained to those without an educational background but used freely with more educated listeners.

In all your adjustments on the basis of education and intelligence, be especially careful not to talk down to your listeners.

## Religion and Religiousness

Today there's great diversity among the religious backgrounds of audiences. And the attitudes of religions vary widely on numerous issues: abortion, same-sex marriage, women's rights, immigration, divorce, capital punishment, and war, for example. Attitudes also vary within religions; almost invariably there are conservative, liberal, and middle-of-the-road groups within each.

According to a 2006 Pew Research Center study, the clergy have addressed such issues as the following from the pulpit: hunger and poverty, abortion, the situation in Iraq, laws regarding homosexuals, the environment, evolution, the death penalty, stem cell research, and immigration. There seem few topics that religion does not address—despite the fact that almost half the population (46 percent) believes that religion should stay out of politics (Many Americans Uneasy with Mix of Religion and Politics, 2006).

Consider if members of your audience will see your topic and your thesis from the point of view of their religion. On a most obvious level, we know that views on such issues as birth control, abortion, and divorce are closely connected to religious affiliation. Similarly, attitudes about premarital sex, marriage, child rearing, money, cohabitation, responsibilities toward parents, and thousands of other issues are clearly influenced by religion. Religion is also important, however, in areas where its connection isn't so obvious. For example, religion influences people's ideas concerning such topics as obedience to authority; responsibility to government; and the usefulness of such qualities as honesty, guilt, and happiness.

Be especially careful of appearing insensitive to the religious beliefs of any segment of your audience. Even people who claim total alienation from the religion in which they were raised may still have strong emotional (though perhaps unconscious) ties to that religion which may influence attitudes and beliefs. When dealing with any religious beliefs (and particularly when disagreeing with them), recognize that you're likely to meet stiff opposition. Proceed slowly and inductively. Present your evidence and argument before expressing your disagreement.

Realize also that members of any religion may deviate from many of the official teachings of their religion. Don't assume that the rank-and-file members of a faith necessarily accept religious leaders' opinions or pronouncements. Official statements by religious leaders often take more conservative positions than those of laypeople.

## Cultural Factors

Nationality, race, and cultural identity are crucial in audience analysis. Largely because of different training and experiences, members of different cultures develop different interests, values, and goals.

The use of cultural information about your audience to help you select the right motivational appeals may be effective only in certain situations. For example, researchers have found that appeals to self-interest have greater influence on audiences from individualist cultures (the United States, Australia, Canada, Denmark, and Sweden, for example) than on audiences from collectivist cultures (Guatemala, Venezuela, Indonesia, Pakistan, and China, for example). And appeals to other-interests are more influential on audiences of collectivist cultures than on people from individualist cultures (Han & Shavitt, 1994; Dillard & Marshall, 2003). Thus, using an audience's cultural information to select appeals works best when you speak to audiences that are almost exclusively from one cultural orientation and when all or almost all members of that audience subscribe to the specific values you are addressing.

Consider if the attitudes and beliefs held by different cultures are relevant to your topic and purpose. Find out what these are. For example, the degree to which listeners are loyal to family members, feel responsibility for the aged, and believe in the value of education will vary from one culture to another. Build your appeals around your audience's attitudes and beliefs.

Consider too if the cultures differ in their expectations of the speaker. Members of some cultures—for example, many Asian cultures—expect speakers to be humble and to avoid self-praise and self-commendation. With these groups, if you appear too confident or mention your accomplishments and credits too directly or too often, you run the risk of appearing forward, arrogant, or pushy. On the other hand, if you are addressing an American audience, the humbleness and avoidance of self-praise may work against you, and you'll be perceived as less competent than you otherwise might be.

Speakers who fail to demonstrate an understanding of cultural differences will be distrusted. For example, speakers, especially those who are seen to be outsiders, who imply that all African Americans are athletic and all lesbians are masculine will quickly lose credibility. Many African Americans are poor athletes, and many lesbians are extremely feminine. Once again, avoid any implication that you're stereotyping audience members (or the groups to which they belong). It's sure to work against achieving your purpose.

## Other Audience Factors

No list of audience characteristics can possibly be complete, and the list presented here is no exception. You'll need another category—"other factors"—to identify any additional characteristics that might be significant to your particular audience. Here are a few categories and questions you might want to ask.

- **Occupation and income.** Is your audience's level of job security and occupational pride related to your topic, purpose, or examples? Will people from different economic levels have different preferences for immediate or long-range goals?

- **Relational status.** Will singles be interested in hearing about the problems of selecting preschools? Will those in long-term relationships be interested in the depression many people who are not in close relation-ships experience during the holidays?

- **Special interests.** What special interests do the audience members have? What occupies their leisure time? How can you integrate these interests into your examples and illustrations or use them as you select quotations?

- **Political beliefs.** Will audience members' political affiliations influence how they view your topic or purpose? Are they politically liberal? Conserv-ative? Might this influence how you develop your speech?

- **Organizational memberships.** Might audience members' affiliations give you cues as to their other beliefs and values? Might you use references to these organizations in your speech, perhaps as examples or illustra-tions?

## Context Characteristics

In addition to analyzing specific listeners, think about **context factors**—aspects of the specific context in which you'll speak. In this class, the context will likely remain the same for all your speeches. Yet outside of this learning laboratory, the context will exert significant influence and needs to be considered.

- **Number of listeners.** Generally, the larger the audience, the more formal the speech presentation should be. With a small audience, you may be more casual and informal. In a large audience you'll have a wider variety of religions, a greater range of occupations and income levels, and so on. All the variables noted earlier will be intensified in a large audience. Therefore, you'll need supporting materials that will appeal to all members.

- **Physical environment.** Consider the physical environment—indoors or outdoors, room or auditorium, sitting or standing audience—which will obviously influence your speech presentation. Also, consider the equipment

## RESEARCH LINK

### Scholarly and Popular Journals

Throughout your research you'll use both schol-arly journals and popular magazines, each for different purposes. If you want scientifically reli-able information, then the scholarly journals are what you need to look at, though they'll prove difficult to read—especially if they're outside your area of ex-pertise. If you want more popular material in easy to understand language, then you'd consult popular mag-azines. The type of information you're seeking will de-termine which types of publications you'd consult. If you wanted to read the original research studies on, say, emotional contagion, then you'd consult scholarly journals; if you wanted to get a broad and general overview of the nature of emotional contagion, then an

article written in a popular magazine might prove more useful. If you want information on Madonna's latest concert, then a popular maga-zine would likely have what you wanted. If you wanted information on Madonna and feminist theory, then a scholarly journal might be more helpful.

Some publications are not so easy to classify. For example, *Psychology Today* would normally be con-sidered a popular magazine and yet it often contains scholarly articles by academic researchers. *National Geographic* is both a scholarly publication and a popu-lar magazine. With this caveat in mind, here is a chart comparing these two types of publications on a vari-ety of criteria.

| | **SCHOLARLY JOURNALS** | **POPULAR MAGAZINES** |
|---|---|---|
| **Purpose** | ■ To advance research, to stimulate research and theory building<br>■ To communicate specialized knowledge, research findings | ■ To entertain and inform people about general issues and concerns<br>■ To communicate general interest knowledge, to summarize and popularize more specialized knowledge |
| **Types of Articles** | Original scientific research studies; critical analyses; usually written in the jargon of the particular field, making it difficult for outsiders to understand | Personality profiles; news summaries; usually written in easy to understand, fast-paced prose |
| **Article Authors** | Professors, researchers, scientists, graduate students | Professional writers, journalists, and some academics |
| **Hardcopy and Online Accessibility** | Available by subscription, usually fairly expensive; online access available for a fee that libraries, publishers, or individuals pay for | Available by subscription, usually fairly inexpensive and at newsstands and bookstores; online copies are often free |
| **Review Process** | Often blind review by peers (ideally the reviewers do not know the author when they review the article) | Varies greatly from a review board to a general editor |
| **Reliability** | Probably the most reliable types of articles available | Varies greatly depending on the magazine |
| **Readers** | Academics, scientists, researchers, undergraduate and graduate students | The general reading public or those interested in specific areas, for example, photography, finance, movies, or sports |
| **Design and Appearance** | Scholarly looking, one-color, little variation in typeface, seldom containing photos (with obvious exceptions as in art and architecture journals); few advertisements, perhaps of other scholarly journals or books | Glossy, colorful, varied fonts, lots of photos, advertisements for all sorts of products |
| **Examples of Journals and Magazines** | *Communication Monographs, Journal of Personality and Social Psychology, New England Journal of Medicine* | *People, Us, Time, Newsweek, Business Week, Reader's Digest, Forbes* |
| **Examples of articles** | ■ Attachment and relational satisfaction: the mediating effect of emotional communication<br>■ Managing self-uncertainty through group identification<br>■ The interface between academic education and the professional training of accountants<br>■ The conceptualization and measurement of interpersonal communication satisfaction | ■ How to ace your interview<br>■ Tiger Wood's caddy: I would have blown the whistle<br>■ What exactly is the fight over health care<br>■ Procrastination: 5 strategies to get started<br>■ Create a comfy cottage-style living room |
| **Publication Schedule** | Usually quarterly; articles are often published 9–12 months after they are accepted (a process that itself can take 6 months or more) for publication. As a result most articles do not address immediate concerns or very recent issues | Usually weekly or monthly; articles are likely to be published within days of the happenings they report |

The next Research Link, "General Reference Works," appears on page 111. →

that is available. Is there a whiteboard, flip chart, or transparency projector? Is there a slide projector and screen? Is there a computer with a projector for showing PowerPoint slides? Are markers available? If at all possible, rehearse in the room you'll be speaking in with the same equipment that you'll have when you deliver your speech.

- **Occasion.** Consider the occasion for your speech. When you give a speech as a class assignment, for example, you'll probably be operating under a number of restrictions—time limitations, the type of general purpose you can use, the types of supporting materials, and various other matters. The same will be true of your speeches outside the classroom; you'll be operating under various requirements and expectations. If you're invited to speak to a group, find out what they expect of you, how long you'd be expected to speak, how many will be in the audience, if there'll be a question-and-answer session, and so on.

- **Time of day.** Consider the time of your speech. If your speech is to be given in an early morning class, say around 8 a.m., then take into consideration that some of your listeners will still be half asleep. Express your appreciation for their attendance; compliment their attention. If necessary, wake them up with your voice, gestures, attention-gaining materials, visual aids, and the like. If your speech is in the evening, when most of your listeners are anxious to get home, recognize this fact as well.

## Analyze Audience Psychology

**Psychological audience analysis** considers audience members along such dimensions as willing-to-unwilling, favorable-to-unfavorable, and knowledgeable-to-unknowledgeable.

## How Willing Is Your Audience?

Audiences gather with varying degrees of willingness to hear a speaker. Some are anxious to hear the speaker and may even have paid a substantial admission price. The "lecture circuit," for example, is a most lucrative aspect of public life. But whereas some audiences are willing to pay to hear a speaker, others don't seem to care one way or the other. Some audiences need to be persuaded to listen (or at least to sit still during the speech). Still other audiences gather because they have to. For example, negotiations on a union contract may require members to attend meetings where officers give speeches, just as students are required to attend class.

Your immediate concern, of course, is with the willingness of your fellow students to listen to your speeches. How willing are they? If they're a willing group, then you have few problems. If they're an unwilling group, all is not lost; you just have to work a little harder in adapting your speech. Here are a few suggestions to help change your listeners from unwilling to willing.

- **Get their interest and attention as early in your speech as possible.** Then maintain this attention throughout your speech by using little-known facts, humor, quotations, startling statistics, examples, narratives, audiovisual aids, and the like.

- **Reward the audience for their attendance and attention.** Do this in advance of your main arguments. Let the audience know you're aware they're making a sacrifice in coming to hear you speak. Tell them you appreciate it. One student, giving a speech close to midterm time, said simply:

> I know how easy it is to cut classes during midterm time to finish the unread chapters and do everything else you have to do. So I especially appreciate your being here this morning. What I have to say, however, will interest you . . .

- **Relate your topic and supporting materials directly to your audience's needs and wants.** Show the audience how they can save time, make more money, solve their problems, or become more popular. If you fail to address your listeners' needs and wants, then your audience has good reason for not listening.

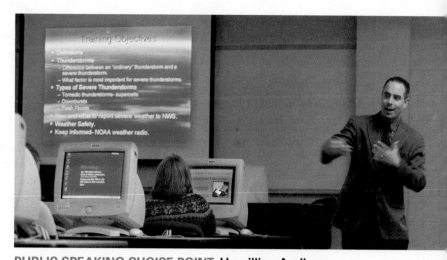

**PUBLIC SPEAKING CHOICE POINT: Unwilling Audience**
Ted is scheduled to give a speech on careers in computer technology to a group of high school students who have been forced to attend this Saturday career day. The audience definitely qualifies as unwilling. What are some of Ted's options in dealing with this type of audience?

## How Favorable Is Your Audience?

Audiences vary in the degree to which they're favorable or unfavorable toward your thesis or point of view. And even within the same audience, of course, you're likely to have some who agree with you, others who disagree, and perhaps still others who are undecided. If you hope to change an audience's attitudes, beliefs, or values and ultimately their behaviors, you must understand their current attitudes, beliefs, and values and how these might influence the way they view your speech and especially your thesis. In estimating this possible influence, you'll find it helpful to ask some of the following questions about their attitudes, beliefs, and values.

What **attitudes** (tendencies to respond for or against an object, person, or position) do your listeners have that might influence their response to your thesis? If your audience has a favorable attitude toward conservation, then they'll likely be more favorable toward speeches on the need to reduce pollution, to drive smaller cars, and to recycle. On the other hand, they might not favor proposals for reducing fines for companies guilty of pollution or a speech on the benefits of owning larger SUVs. How might you use the listeners' current attitudes to adapt your speech to them? For example, if you know their attitudes and your thesis is consistent with them, you might mention your attitudinal similarity.

What **beliefs** (convictions in the existence or truth of something) do your listeners have that will impact on your speech? If they believe in God and in a specific religion, then they will likely respond well to religious examples, will respect testimony from religious leaders, and will likely believe what the religion teaches. At the same time, they're likely to resist ideas that go against their religious beliefs. Capital punishment, abortion, and same-sex marriage are just some of the topics about which the listeners' religious beliefs will influence their responses. How can you use the beliefs of the audience in adapting your speech to them?

What **values** (the worth a person puts on something or some action) does your audience have, and how might these impact on your topic? For example, if your listeners value equality and cultural diversity, they're likely to favor interracial adoption and fewer restrictions on immigration than would those who do not value cultural diversity. How can you use the values of your listeners to adapt your speech to them? For example, if people value financial success, they'll likely be interested in hearing speeches on the stock market, foreign currency, and the stories of successful entrepreneurs. Further, audiences respond favorably to topics that promise financial rewards or that teach skills that will prove financially beneficial.

Of course, when you face an audience whose attitudes, beliefs, and values are consistent with your thesis, your adaptation task is going to be relatively easy. But when you face an audience whose attitudes, beliefs, and values are contrary to your thesis, adapting your speech becomes much more difficult. Here are a few suggestions for dealing with the unfavorably disposed audience.

- **Clear up any possible misapprehensions.** Often disagreement is caused by a lack of understanding. If you feel this is the case, then your first task is to clear this up. For example, if the audience is hostile to the new team approach you are advocating because they wrongly think it will result in a reduction in their autonomy, then explain it to them very directly, saying something like:

  I realize that many people oppose this new team approach because they feel it will reduce their own autonomy and control. Well, it won't; as a matter of fact, with this approach, each person will actually gain greater control, greater power, greater autonomy.

- **Build on commonalities.** Emphasize not the differences between you and your listeners but the similarities. Stress what you and the audience share as people, as interested citizens, as fellow students. Theorist and critic Kenneth Burke (1950) argued that we achieve persuasion through identification with the audience. Identification involves emphasizing similarities between speaker and audience. When audience members see common ground between themselves and you, they become more favorable both to you and to your speech.

  For example, a former student who returns to her high school to speak about the importance of preparing early for college might identify with her audience by saying something like this:

  It wasn't very long ago that I sat in this auditorium and had to listen to speakers talk about college. And I remember wanting to be somewhere else, anywhere else. But, I'm glad I listened because it helped me tremendously and I hope I'll be able to help you in the same way I was helped.

- **Organize your speech inductively.** Try to build your speech from areas of agreement, through areas of slight disagreement, up to the point where major differences exist between the audience's attitudes and your own position. Let's say, for example, that you represent management and you wish to persuade employees to accept a particular wage offer. You might begin with such areas of agreement as the mutual desire for improved working conditions or for long-term economic growth. Once areas of agreement are established, it's easier to bring up differences such as, perhaps, the need to delay salary increases until next year. In any disagreement or conflict, there are still areas of agreement; emphasize these before considering areas of disagreement.

■ **Strive for small gains.** Don't use a five-minute speech to try to convince a pro-life group to contribute money for the new abortion clinic or a pro-choice group to vote against liberalizing abortion laws. Be content to get your listeners to see some validity in your position and to listen fairly. About-face changes take a long time to achieve. Attempting to exert too much persuasion or asking for too much change can result only in failure or resentment.

■ **Acknowledge the differences explicitly.** If it's clear to the audience that they and you are at opposite ends of the issue, it may be helpful to acknowledge this very directly. Show the audience that you understand and respect their position but that you'd like them to consider a different way of looking at things. Say something like:

> I know you don't all agree that elementary school teachers should have to take tests every several years to maintain their certification. Some teachers are going to lose their certification, and that isn't pleasant. And we all feel sorry that this will happen. What isn't widely known, however, is that the vast majority of teachers will actually benefit from this proposal. And I'd like an opportunity to sketch out the benefits that many of us will enjoy as a result of this new testing procedure.

## How Knowledgeable Is Your Audience?

Listeners differ greatly in the knowledge they have. Some listeners will be quite knowledgeable about your topic; others will be almost totally ignorant. Mixed audiences are the most difficult ones.

If you're unaware of the audience's knowledge level, you won't know what to assume and what to explain. You won't know how much information will overload the channels or how much will bore the audience to sleep. Perhaps you want to show that their previous knowledge is now inadequate. Perhaps you want to demonstrate a new slant to old issues. Or perhaps you want to show that what you have to say will not repeat but instead will build on the already extensive knowledge of the audience. However you accomplish this, you need to make the audience see that what you have to

**PUBLIC SPEAKING CHOICE POINT: Audience Attitudes**
Denny is planning to give a persuasive speech to your class urging listeners to support the National Rifle Association in its efforts to fight gun control. Assuming that the audience is evenly divided (half pro gun control and half against it), what are some of Denny's options for dealing with the unfavorable half of his audience? What are some of the things he can say by way of introduction?

say is new. Make them realize that you won't simply repeat what they already know.

Treat audiences that lack knowledge of the topic very carefully. Never confuse a lack of knowledge with a lack of ability to understand.

- **Don't talk down to your audience.** This is perhaps the greatest communication error that teachers make. Having taught a subject for years, they face, semester after semester, students who have no knowledge of the topic. As a result, many teachers tend to talk down to the students and, in the process, lose their audience.

- **Don't confuse a lack of knowledge with a lack of intelligence.** An audience may have no knowledge of your topic but be quite capable of following a clearly presented, logically developed argument. Try especially hard to use concrete examples, audiovisual aids, and simple language. Fill in background details as required. Avoid jargon and specialized terms that may not be clear to someone new to the subject. In sum, never overestimate your audience's knowledge, but never underestimate their intelligence.

- **Let your listeners know that you're aware of their knowledge and expertise.** Try to do this as early in the speech as possible. Emphasize that what you have to say will not be redundant. Tell them that you'll be presenting recent developments or new approaches. In short, let them know that they won't be wasting their time listening to your speech.

- **Emphasize your credibility, especially your competence in this general subject area** (see Chapter 11). Let your listeners know that you have earned the right to speak. Let them know that what you have to say is based on a firm grasp of the material.

Here, for example, Senator Christopher Dodd (2007) of Connecticut, addressing the Jesse Jackson Wall Street Summit, establishes his credibility:

> When Dr. King and President Kennedy asked young Americans to serve the cause of freedom and justice, I was among those who answered in the affirmative. I joined the Peace Corps as a young man. I lived and worked in a small village in the Dominican Republic. I worked side by side with people who had a different ethnic heritage, a different nationality, and a different language than me. I was very much in the minority. Yet, I was accepted into the community. We all brought different abilities and experiences to our common work. And together, we achieved significant things. We built a road, a school, and several homes.

Public Speaking Exercise 5.2, "Analyzing an Unknown Audience," on page 104 provides a group experience to practice drawing inferences about an audience from limited information.

## 2 Analyze and Adapt during the Speech

In addition to analyzing your audience and making adaptations in your speech before delivering it, devote attention to analysis and adaptation during the speech. This during-the-speech analysis is especially important when you know little about your audience or find yourself facing an audience very different from the one you expected. Here are a few suggestions.

## Focus on Listeners as Message Senders

As you're speaking, look at your audience. Remember that just as you're sending messages to your listeners, they're also sending messages to you. Pay attention to these messages; on the basis of what they tell you, make the necessary adjustments.

Remember that members of different cultures operate with different **display rules,** cultural rules that state what types of expressions are appropriate to reveal—and what expressions are inappropriate to reveal and should be kept hidden. Some display rules call for open and free expression of feelings and responses; these listeners will be easy to read. Other display rules call for little expression, and these listeners will be difficult to read.

You can make a wide variety of adjustments to each type of audience response. For example, if your audience shows signs of boredom, increase your volume, move closer to them, or tell them that what you're going to say will be of value to them. If your audience shows signs of disagreement or hostility, stress a similarity you have with them. If your audience looks puzzled or confused, pause for a moment and rephrase your ideas, provide necessary definitions, or insert an internal summary. If your audience seems impatient, say, for example, "my last argument..." instead of your originally planned "my third argument...."

## Use Answers to Your "What If" Questions

The more preparation you put into your speech, the better prepared you'll be to make on-the-spot adjustments and adaptations. For example, let's say you have been told that you're to explain the opportunities available to the nontraditional student at your college. You've been told that your audience will consist mainly of working women in their 30s and 40s who are just beginning college. As you prepare your speech with this audience in mind, ask yourself **"what if" questions**. For example:

- What if the audience has a large number of men?
- What if the audience consists of women much older than 40?
- What if the audience members also come with their spouses or their children?

Keeping such questions in mind will force you to consider possible answers as you prepare your speech. Use these answers to make on-the-spot adjustments.

## Address Audience Responses Directly

Another way of dealing with audience responses is to confront them directly. To people who are reacting negatively to your message, for example, you might say:

> Regardless of your present position, hear me out and see if this new way of doing things will not simplify your accounting procedures.

Or, to those who seem puzzled, you might say:

> This plan may seem confusing, but bear with me; it will become clear in a moment.

Or, to those who seem impatient, you might respond:

> I know this has been a long day, but give me just a few more minutes and you'll be able to save hours recording your accounts.

By responding to your listeners' reactions and feedback, you acknowledge their needs. You let them know that you hear them, that you're with them, and that you're responding to their very real concerns.

# Next Steps

Once your audience has been analyzed and you have a good idea of their attitudes, values, and beliefs, focus on conducting research (Step Three). Guidelines for this are provided in the Research Link boxes throughout the text. The next chapter, then, focuses on Step Four, collecting supporting materials and presentation aids.

# Essentials of Analyzing and Adapting to Your Audience

This chapter looked at the audience and particularly at how you can analyze your listeners and adapt your speeches to them.

## Audiences and Audience Analysis

1. In analyzing any audience, remember that all audiences are unique and all audiences are diverse.

2. In seeking information about your audience, consider the values of observation, collecting data (for example, with audience questionnaires), interviewing members, and using intelligent inference and empathy.

## Analyze Audience Sociology

3. In analyzing the sociology of your audience, consider especially the following characteristics:
   - Age
   - Gender (biological sex role and psychological sex role)
   - Affectional orientation
   - Educational levels
   - Religion and religiousness
   - Cultural factors

4. In addition, look into other relevant audience factors such as your audience's occupation and income status, relational status, special interests, and political attitudes and beliefs.

5. Consider the context factors such as the physical space, the number of listeners, and the format expected for the speech.

## Analyze Audience Psychology

6. In analyzing audience psychology consider your listeners' willingness, degree of favorableness toward your ideas, knowledge level, and degree of homogeneity.

7. In adapting to an unwilling audience:
   - Secure their attention as early as possible.
   - Reward the audience for their attendance and attention.
   - Relate your topic and supporting materials to the audience's needs and interests.

**8.** In adapting to an unfavorable audience:
- Clear up any possible misunderstandings.
- Build on the similarities you have with the audience.
- Build your speech from areas of agreement up to the major areas of difference.
- Strive for small gains.

**9.** In adapting to an unknowledgeable audience:
- Avoid talking down to your listeners (or to any audience).
- Avoid confusing a lack of knowledge with a lack of intelligence.

**10.** In adapting to a knowledgeable audience:
- Let your listeners know that you're aware of their expertise.
- Establish your credibility.

### Analyze and Adapt during the Speech

**11.** To help you adapt your speech during your presentation:
- Focus on audience members as message senders, not merely as message receivers.
- Use answers to your "what if" for on-the-spot adjustments.
- Address audience responses directly.

# Essential Terms

attitude **(97)**
belief **(97)**
context factors **(95)**
display rules **(101)**

psychological audience analysis **(96)**
sociological audience analysis **(89)**

value **(98)**
"what if" questions **(101)**

# Public Speaking Exercises

## 5.1 How Well Do You Know Your Audience?

Here are some statements of beliefs that members of your class may agree or disagree with—and which you might want to use as basic theses (propositions) in your in-class speeches. Try predicting how favorable or unfavorable you think your class members would be to each of these beliefs. Use a 10-point scale ranging from 1 (extremely unfavorable) through 5 (relatively neutral) to 10 (extremely favorable).

**1.** The welfare of the family must come first, even before your own.

**2.** Sex outside of marriage is wrong and sinful.

**3.** In a heterosexual relationship, a wife should submit graciously to the leadership of her husband.

**4.** Individual states should be allowed to fly the Confederate flag if they wish.

**5.** Intercultural relationships are OK in business but should be discouraged when it comes to intimate or romantic relationships; generally, the races should be kept "pure."

_____ **6.** Money is good; the quest for financial success is a perfectly respectable (even noble) one.

_____ **7.** Immigration into the United States should be curtailed, at least until current immigrants are assimilated.

_____ **8.** Parents who prevent their children from receiving the latest scientific cures because of a belief in faith healing should be prosecuted.

_____ **9.** Single people should be allowed to adopt children in the same way that couples do.

_____ **10.** Medicinal marijuana should be readily available.

_____ **11.** Physician-assisted suicide should be legalized.

_____ **12.** Male and female prostitution should be legalized and taxed like any other income producing occupation.

After you've indicated your predictions, discuss these with the class as a whole to get a better idea of how your audience thinks and ultimately how you can adapt your speeches given these attitudes and beliefs of your audience.

### 5.2 Analyzing an Unknown Audience

This experience should familiarize you with some of the essential steps in analyzing an audience on the basis of relatively little evidence and in predicting their attitudes on the basis of that analysis. The class should be broken up into small groups of five or six members. Each group will be given a different magazine (print or online); their task is to analyze the audience (i.e., the readers or subscribers) of that particular magazine in terms of the characteristics discussed in this chapter. The only information the groups will have about their audience is that they're avid and typical readers of the given magazine. Pay particular attention to the types of articles published in the magazine, the advertisements, the photographs or illustrations, the editorial statements, the price of the magazine, and so on. Magazines that differ widely from one another are most appropriate for this experience.

After all groups have analyzed their audiences, try to identify at least three favorable and three unfavorable attitudes that each audience probably holds on contemporary issues. On what basis do you make these predictions? If you had to address this audience and advocate a position with which it disagreed, what adaptations would you make? What strategies would you use to prepare and present this persuasive speech?

Each group should share with the rest of the class the results of their efforts, taking special care to point out not only their conclusions but also the evidence and reasoning they used in arriving at the conclusions.

# Log On! PEARSON myspeechlab

Visit MySpeechLab (www.myspeechlab.com) for additional insight into the public speaking audience and to learn how you can better adapt your speeches to specific audiences. See, for example, the activities for analyzing audiences (under Author Choice), the informative and persuasive speeches, and explore ways to analyze your audience and the public speaking setting.

# 6

# Collect Supporting Materials and Presentation Aids (Step 4)

## WHY READ THIS CHAPTER?

**Because it will contribute to your public speaking success by helping you to:**

- select supporting materials (such as examples and statistics) to make your speech come alive in the minds of the audience

- develop interesting and appropriate presentation aids, including PowerPoint presentations, to further inform and persuade

*The elevator to success is out of order. You'll have to use the stairs . . . one step at a time.*

—JOE GIRARD

This chapter focuses on Step 4 and begins by examining the various types of supporting materials and explaining how to use them most effectively: examples, analogies, definitions, narratives, testimony, and statistics. Next, it focuses on presentation aids and how to use them effectively.

## Supporting Materials

Supporting materials are a vital part of an effective public speech; they add concreteness, help maintain interest and attention, and provide vital information and persuasive appeal. In this section we cover examples, narration, testimony, and statistics. In the next section we consider a special kind of support, the presentation aid.

### Examples, Illustrations, and Narratives

Examples, illustrations, and narratives are specific instances that are explained in varying degrees of detail and will help greatly in helping the audience remember your speech.

#### Types of Examples, Illustrations, and Narratives

Generally, a relatively brief specific instance is referred to as an **example**; a longer and more detailed example is referred to as an **illustration;** and an example told in story-like form is referred to as a **narrative.** Examples (the shorthand "examples" will be used to refer to all three of these forms of support) may be distinguished on the basis of their being real or hypothetical.

The main value of examples is that they allow you to bring an abstract concept down to specifics. For example, to clarify what you mean by determination, you might provide a brief example, give an illustration from history, or narrate the story of any of the numerous great people who rose to prominence against the odds. In a speech on unfair sentencing practices, student Jillian Collum (2008) provided a particularly dramatic illustration. After stating that a man was sentenced to 55 years in prison under the federal mandatory minimum sentencing laws for selling marijuana, she said:

> The sentencing brief noted that if Angelos had provided weapons to a terrorist organization, hijacked an aircraft, committed second-degree murder, and raped a 10-year-old child he would have received a lower combined sentence than he got for selling about $1,000 worth of marijuana.

Here's another example of the effectiveness of a dramatic illustration, from a speech by Kyle Akerman, a student from the University of Texas at Austin (2010):

> Initially, a Human Rights Watch report on March 19, 2009 substantiates that there are reports of detainees being shackled, and denied basic medical procedures. The January 9, 2010 *New York Times* tells the story of Nery Romero, a 22-year-old detainee who repeatedly begged for treatment of unbearable pain, and was repeatedly denied. The Office of Professional Responsibility discovered falsified documents saying that Romero received medication. Falsification was easy to detect . . . because [he] died days before he supposedly received his last treatment. This article notes that there have been 107 deaths of this type since October of 2003.

## Guidelines for Using Examples, Illustrations, and Narratives

**Limit the length.** Keep in mind that the function of examples is to make your ideas vivid and easily understood; they are not ends in themselves. Make your examples only as long as necessary to ensure that your purpose is achieved.

**Stress relevancy.** Make sure your example is directly relevant to the proposition you want it to support, and make its relationship with your assertion explicit. Remember that although this relationship is clear to you (because you've constructed the speech), the audience is going to hear your speech only once. Show the audience exactly how your example relates to the assertion or concept you're explaining. Here for example, New York's Mayor Rudolph Giuliani, in his address to the United Nations after the World Trade Center attack of September 11, 2001, gave relevant examples to support his proposition that we are a land of immigrants and must continue to be so (**www.washingtonpost.com/wp-srv/nation/specials/attached/transcripts/giulianitext_100101.html**):

**ETHICAL CHOICE POINT**

Misleading Your Audience

For a speech on false arrests, you develop a hypothetical story about a college student who gets arrested and is held unlawfully in custody for several days. As you rehearse this story, you realize it would be a lot more convincing if the audience were allowed to think that the story was true and that the person was you. Actually, you wouldn't be saying that it was you or that it wasn't you; you'd just be allowing the audience to infer this from what you say. ➤ *What are your ethical choices to be both true and effective?*

> New York City was built by immigrants and it will remain the greatest city in the world so long as we continue to renew ourselves with and benefit from the energizing spirit from new people coming here to create a better future for themselves and their families. Come to Flushing, Queens, where immigrants from many lands have created a vibrant, vital commercial and residential community. Their children challenge and astonish us in our public school classrooms every day. Similarly, you can see growing and dynamic immigrant communities in every borough of our city: Russians in Brighton Beach, West Indians in Crown Heights, Dominicans in Washington Heights, the new wave of Irish in the Bronx, and Koreans in Willow Brook on Staten Island.

Distinguish between real and hypothetical examples. Don't try to foist a hypothetical example on the audience as a real one. If they recognize the deception, they'll resent your attempt to fool them. Let the audience know when you're using a real example and when you're using a hypothetical example.

| **Real examples** | **Hypothetical examples** |
|---|---|
| ■ A situation such as this occurred recently; it involved . . . | ■ We could easily imagine a situation such as . . . |
| ■ I have a friend who . . . | ■ I think an ideal friend would be someone who . . . |
| ■ An actual example of this was reported in the . . . | ■ A hypothetical example of this type of friendship would be like . . . |

Use a series of very brief examples to emphasize the widespread nature or significance of an issue or problem. Here, for example, U.S. Senator from

California Dianne Feinstein (2006) uses a series of examples to make the point that law enforcement officers are in danger from gang violence:

> Los Angeles Police Officer Ricardo Lizarraga. Killed while responding to a domestic violence call, by a man who drew a gun and shot him twice in the back. The suspect was a known member of the Rollin 20s Bloods.
> Merced Police Officer Stephan Gray. Officer Gray was shot and killed when a suspect (a gang member he had encountered before) fired two **bullets** into this chest.
> The list goes on:
> Los Angeles Sheriff's Deputy Jeffrey Ortiz.
> Burbank Police Officer Matthew Pavelka.
> California Highway Patrol Officer Thomas Steiner.
> And San Francisco Police Officer Isaac Espinoza.

## Analogies

**Analogies** are comparisons that are often extremely useful in making your ideas clear and vivid to your audience.

### Types of Analogies

Analogies may be of two types: figurative and literal. **Figurative analogies** compare items from different classes—for example, the flexibility afforded by a car with the freedom of a bird, a college degree with a passport to success, playing baseball with running a corporation. Figurative analogies are useful for illustrating possible similarities and provide vivid examples that are easily remembered.

**Literal analogies** compare items from the same class, such as two cars or two cities. For example, in a literal analogy you might argue (1) that two companies are similar—both are multinational, multibillion-dollar pharmaceutical companies, both have advertising budgets in the hundreds of millions of dollars, and so on; and (2) that therefore the advertising techniques that worked for one company will work for the other.

### Guidelines in Using Analogies

Analogies do not constitute evidence of the truth or falsity of an assertion. Avoid presenting analogies as proof and beware of speakers who do this; they may be doing this because there is no real evidence.

When using literal analogies, make sure that the cases compared (say, two corporations) are alike in essential respects. Or do they differ from each other in ways that might negate the comparison? For example, do the two companies differ in the location of their headquarters? Do they differ in the types of products they produce? Of course, not all differences make a (significant) difference so consider whether the differences are important or incidental.

## Definitions

A **definition** is a statement explaining the meaning of a term or concept; it explains what something is.

## Types of Definitions

Some of the most important ways in which you can define a term are by etymology, authority, negation, and specific examples.

**Definition by Etymology.**    One way to define a term is to trace its historical or linguistic development. In defining the word *communication,* for example, you might note that it comes from the Latin *communis,* meaning "common"; in "communicating" you seek to establish a commonness, a sharing, a similarity with another individual. And *woman* comes from the Anglo-Saxon *wifman,* which meant literally a "wife man," where the word *man* was applied to both sexes. Through phonetic change *wifman* became *woman.* Most larger dictionaries and, of course, etymological dictionaries will help you find useful etymological definitions.

Or you might define a term by noting not its linguistic etymology, but how it came to mean what it now means. For example, you might note that *spam,* meaning unwanted e-mail, comes from a Monty Python television skit in which every item on a menu contained the product Spam. And much as the diner was forced to get Spam, so the e-mail user gets spam, even when he or she wants something else.

**Definition by Authority.**    You can often clarify a term by explaining how a particular authority views it. You might, for example, define *lateral thinking* by authority and say that Edward deBono, who developed lateral thinking in 1966, has noted that "lateral thinking involves moving sideways to look at things in a different way. Instead of fixing on one particular approach and then working forward from that, the lateral thinker tries to find other approaches." Or you might use the authority of cynic and satirist Ambrose Bierce and define love as nothing but "a temporary insanity curable by marriage" and friendship as "a ship big enough to carry two in fair weather, but only one in foul."

**Definition by Negation.**    You also might define a term by noting what the term is not; that is, define it by negation. "A wife," you might say, "isn't a cook, a cleaning person, a babysitter, a seamstress, a sex partner. A wife is . . ." or "A teacher isn't someone who tells you what you should know but rather one who . . . ."

**Definition by Specific Examples.**    An example is not a definition, but it can serve defining functions; it can help clarify terms or phrases. Here, for example, Ohio Congressman Dennis Kucinich (2007) uses a series of specific examples to clarify what he means by "human rights" in a speech presented to the Wall Street Project Conference on January 8, 2007:

> We have a right to a job.
> We have a right to a living wage.
> We have a right to an education.
> We have a right to health care.
> We have a right to decent and affordable housing.
> We have a right to a secure pension.
> We have a right to air fit to breathe.
> We have a right to water fit to drink.
> We have a right to be free of the paralyzing fear of crime.

## Guidelines in Using Definitions

Use definitions when you wish to explain difficult or unfamiliar concepts or when you wish to make a concept more vivid or forceful. If the purpose of the definition is to clarify, then it must do just that. This would be too obvious to mention except for the fact that so many speakers, perhaps for want of something to say, define terms that don't need extended definitions. Some speakers use definitions that don't clarify and sometimes even complicate an already complex concept. Make sure your definitions define only what needs defining.

As you think of terms to define, or after you've selected a term, take a look at the OneLook Dictionary Search website at **www.onelook.com**. This website will enable you to search a wide variety of dictionaries at the same time. There are, of course, many other useful online dictionaries; search for "dictionary," "definitions," or "thesaurus" and you'll find a wealth of material for speeches of definition. Once you have the definition, make sure that you pronounce it correctly; defining a word you mispronounce is likely to severely damage your credibility. Fortunately, many online dictionaries include audios of the correct pronunciation.

## Testimony

**Testimony** is often a useful form of support, and involves using the opinions of others to clarify or support your assertions.

### Types of Testimony

Testimony is of two basic types: expert and eyewitness. In expert testimony, the speaker cites the opinions, beliefs, predictions, or values of some authority or expert. For example, you might want to state an economist's predictions concerning inflation and depression, or you might want to support your analysis by citing an art critic's evaluation of a painting or art movement. The faculty of your college or university is one of the best, if rarely used, sources of expert information for almost any speech topic. Regardless of what your topic is, a faculty member of some department likely knows a great deal about the subject. At the very least, faculty members will be able to direct you to appropriate sources. Experts in the community can serve similar functions. Local politicians, religious leaders, doctors, lawyers, museum directors, and the like often are suitable sources of information.

Beyond your college or university lies a world of experts—religious and business leaders, politicians, educators at other colleges and research institutes, medical personnel, researchers in almost any field imaginable. Ask yourself if your speech and your audience could profit from the insights of experts. If your answer is yes—and few topics could not so profit—then consider the steps suggested in the Research Link in Chapter 2 (p. 25) for interviewing such experts. Interviews can take place in person; by telephone; or, as is becoming increasingly popular, over the Internet, especially in e-mail or chat groups.

Of course, if 500 public speaking students all descend on the faculty or on the community, chaos can easily result. So going to these experts is often discouraged as a class assignment. But it's often a useful practice for speeches you'll give later in life.

The second type of testimony is that of the eyewitness to some event or situation. For example, you might cite the testimony of someone who saw an accident, of a person who spent two years in a maximum-security prison, or of a person who had a particular kind of operation.

### Guidelines in Using Testimony

Whether you use the testimony of a world-famous authority or draw on an eyewitness account, you need to establish your source's credibility—to demonstrate to the audience that your expert is in fact an authority or that your eyewitness is believable.

Stress the competence of the person. Whether the person is an expert or a witness, make sure the audience sees this person as competent. To cite the

# RESEARCH LINK

## General Reference Works

General reference works are tertiary sources and are excellent starting points for researching your topic.

### Encyclopedias

One of the best general reference works is the standard encyclopedia. Any good encyclopedia will give you a general overview of your subject and suggestions for additional reading. The most comprehensive and the most prestigious is the Encyclopædia Britannica, available in print, on CD-ROM, and online. A variety of other encyclopedias also are available in print, on CD-ROM, or online. One way to search for these is to visit Freeality.com (www.freeality.com/encyclop.htm) and search through the available general and specific encyclopedias.

Perhaps the most widely known online encyclopedia, and one that you'll find extremely useful, is Wikipedia (www.wikipedia.com). This encyclopedia is a bit different from those mentioned above. The articles in Wikipedia—some brief and some extremely long and detailed—are written by people who are not necessarily experts. Many of the articles are reviewed, updated, and corrected periodically. But, because this work doesn't have the authority of the more traditional encyclopedias, you'll need to check the facts and statistics—most of which you'll find easy to do because of the extensive hot links written into each article and the list of additional sources provided for most articles.

### Almanacs

Another excellent general reference work is the almanac. Like encyclopedias, almanacs are available in print (usually inexpensively) and online. Start with InfoPlease (www.infoplease.com) which contains a wide variety of hot links to similar works covering such categories as the World, U.S. History and Government, Biography, Sports, Business, Society and Culture, Health and Science, and Arts and Entertainment. Another useful source is the Internet Public Library's list of almanac resources at www.ipl.org/ref/RR/static/ref05.00.00.html.

### Biographical Materials

As a speaker you'll often need information about particular individuals. For example, in using expert testimony, it's helpful to stress your experts' qualifications, which you can easily learn about from even brief biographies. Or you may want to look up authors of books or articles to find out something about their education, their training, or their other writings. Or you may wish to discover if there have been critical evaluations of authors' work such as book reviews or articles about them or their writings. Knowing something about your sources enables you to more effectively evaluate their competence, convey their credibility to the audience, and answer audience questions about them.

One of the most enjoyable and useful biography sites is maintained by The Biography Channel (www.biography.com), which contains biographies of some 25,000 individuals from all walks of life. Two other useful sites which provide links to hundreds of biographical sources are http://www.ahisd.net/campuses/cambridge/library/biographies.htm and http://www.42explore2.com/biographies.htm.

### Statistical Information

A variety of organizations collect statistics but none as thoroughly as the government and its various agencies. Each government department (see Research Link, p. 134) publishes statistics and you can go to the specific department (for example, the Department of the Treasury) to get relevant statistics. An even easier way is to log on to FedStats (www.fedstats.gov). Here you'll find statistics from more than 100 U.S. federal agencies, including statistical profiles of each state, country, and city as well as statistics on crime, population, economics, mortality, and energy, along with comparisons with other countries.

The next Research Link, "The Government," appears on page 134.

predictions of a world-famous economist of whom your audience has never heard will mean little, so first explain the person's competence. To prepare the audience to accept what this person says, you might introduce the testimony by saying, for example:

> This prediction comes from the world's leading economist, who has successfully predicted all major financial trends over the past 20 years.

Here, for example, is how student Ashley Hatcher established the credibility of her testimony:

> As the 2005 book *The Structure of the Innate Mind* states, the answer may lie in Homicide Adaptation Theory, the conclusion of an unprecedented six-year study conducted by leading evolutionary psychologists David Buss and Joshua Duntley from the University of Texas.

Stress the unbiased nature of the testimony. If listeners perceive the testimony to be biased—whether or not it really is—it will have little effect. You want to check out the biases of a witness so that you may present accurate information. But you also want to make the audience see that the testimony is in fact unbiased. You might say something like this:

> Researchers and testers at Consumer Reports, none of whom have any vested interest in the products examined, found wide differences in car safety. Let's look at some of these findings. In the October 2011 issue, for example, . . .

Stress the recency of the testimony. When you say, for example, "General Bailey, who was interviewed last week in the *Washington Post*, noted that the United States has twice the military power of any other world power," you show your audience that your information is recent and up to date.

## Numerical Data

Numerical data are often essential and will help to support what you mean by, say, high tuition, reasonable wage, or appropriate executive compensation.

### Types of Numerical Data

Numerical data is of two basic types: raw numbers and statistics. **Raw numbers** are simply figures unmodified by any mathematical operation. For example, if you want to show that significant numbers of people now get their news from the Internet, you could give the total number of online users for each of the last 10 years and compare that with the numbers of newspaper readers and television news viewers in those same years. These data would then allow you to show that the number of people who get their news from the Internet is increasing, while the number of those getting the news from papers and television is declining.

**Statistics**, on the other hand, are summary figures that help you communicate the important characteristic of a complex set of numbers such as the **mean** (the average—the average grade on the test was 86), the **mode** (the most frequent score in an array—more students scored 85 than any other grade), **percentages** (the portion of a total, expressed as a portion of 100—96 percent of the students passed). For example, you might compare the percentage of a tuition increase at your school to the national average or to the rate of inflation. To illustrate the growth of instant messaging or social networking as a means of communication, you might note the percentage that usage has grown in each of the last five years.

Here is a good example of how President Barack Obama (2006) (then Senator from Illinois) used statistics in his speech to the 2006 Global Summit on AIDS and the Church.

> You know, AIDS is a story often told by numbers. Forty million infected with HIV. Nearly 4.5 million this year alone. Twelve million orphans in Africa. Eight thousand deaths and 6,000 new infections every single day. In some places, 90 percent of those with HIV do not know they have it. And we just learned that AIDS is set to become the third leading cause of death worldwide in the coming years. These are staggering, these numbers, and they help us understand the magnitude of this pandemic.

In a speech on auto safety, Meagan Hagensick of Wartburg College used numbers effectively to drive home the importance of seat belts (Schnoor, 2008):

> One fatality every 13 minutes. One injury every 10 seconds. One accident every 5 seconds. Six million crashes. 2.8 million injuries. 43,000 people killed each year. These numbers are not spawned from a deadly virus or new strain of bacteria; they are the result of avoidable human error.

## Guidelines for Using Numerical Data

In using numerical data of any kind, make sure the numbers are clear, remembering that your audience will hear the figures only once. Round off figures so they're easy to comprehend and retain. If your numbers are difficult to remember, reinforce your oral presentation with some type of presentation aid—perhaps a slide or a chart. Numbers presented without some kind of visual reinforcement are often difficult to grasp and remember.

Make explicit the meaning of the numbers you're using. For example, if you state that the average home health aide makes less than $30,000 a year, you need to compare this figure to the salaries of other workers and to your proposition that salaries need to be increased.

Use numbers in moderation. Most listeners' capacity for numerical data presented in a speech is limited, so use figures sparingly.

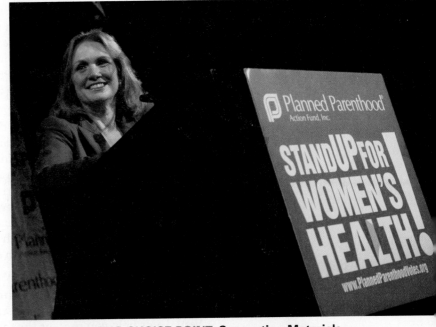

**PUBLIC SPEAKING CHOICE POINT: Supporting Materials**
Luanne is planning to give a speech on the lack of research on women's health issues and wants to show that it's a real problem needing a real solution. What kinds of supporting materials would help Luanne to establish the severity of the problem for, say, an audience of students from your college? How about for an audience consisting of the parents of students in your class?

Use only reliable and current numerical data and make sure that your audience is aware of their reliability and currency.

Public Speaking Exercise 6.1, "Supporting Materials," on page 128 provides some examples for practice in developing supporting materials.

# 4 Presentation Aids

As you plan your speech, consider using some kind of **presentation aid**—a visual or auditory means for clarifying ideas. Ask yourself how you can visually present what you want your audience to remember. For example, if you want your audience to see the growing impact of the sales tax, consider showing them a chart of rising sales tax over the last 10 years. If you want them to see that Brand A is superior to Brand X, consider showing them a comparison chart identifying the superiority of Brand A. Presentation aids are not added frills—they are integral parts of your speech. They will help you gain your listeners' attention and maintain their interest; they can add clarity, reinforce your message, and contribute to your credibility and confidence (Sojourner & Wogalter, 1998).

- **Presentation aids help you gain attention and maintain interest.** Americans today have grown up on multimedia entertainment. We are used to it and we enjoy it. It's not surprising, then, that we as members of an audience appreciate it when a speaker makes use of visuals or audio aids. We perk up when the speaker says, "I want you to look at this chart showing the employment picture for the next five years" or "Listen to the vocal range in this voice." Presentation aids provide variety in what we see and hear—something audiences will appreciate and respond to favorably.

- **Presentation aids add clarity.** Let's say you want to illustrate the projected growth in Internet usage. You might note that in the United States in 2002, 167 million people were Internet users; in 2004 it was 201 million; in 2007 it was 212 million; in 2009 it was 228 million. But such recitals get boring pretty fast. Further, the numbers you want the audience to appreciate are difficult to retain in memory, so by the time you get to the current figures, your listeners have already forgotten the previous figures. As a result, the very growth that you want your audience to see is likely to get lost. It would be much easier to communicate this kind of information in a bar graph.

- **Presentation aids reinforce your message.** Presentation aids help ensure that your listeners understand and remember what you've said. Visual aids help you present the same information in two different ways: verbally, as audience members hear you explain the aid, and visually, as they see the chart, map, or model. The same is true with audio aids. For example, you might discuss the range of vocal variety and at the same time provide recorded samples. This kind of one-two punch helps the audience understand your ideas more clearly and remember them more accurately.

- **Presentation aids contribute to credibility and confidence.** If you use appropriate and professional-looking presentation aids—something that will be covered later in this chapter—your listeners are likely to see you as a highly credible speaker; as someone who cares enough about both them and the topic to do this "extra" work. When listeners view you as credible and have confidence in you, they're more likely to listen carefully and to believe what you have to say.

- **Presentation aids help reduce apprehension.** When you have to concentrate on coordinating your speech with your presentation aids, you're less likely to focus on yourself—and self-focus often increases apprehension. In addition, the movement involved in using presentation aids relaxes many speakers, and with greater relaxation comes greater confidence.

## Types of Presentation Aids

Among the presentation aids you have available are the object itself, models of the object, graphs, word charts, maps, people, photographs, and illustrations.

### The Object Itself

As a general rule (to which there are many exceptions), the best presentation aid is the object itself. Bring it to your speech if you can. Notice that infomercials sell their products not only by talking about them, but by showing them to potential buyers. You see what George Foreman's Lean Mean Grilling Machine looks like and how it works. You see the jewelry, the clothing, or the new mop from a wide variety of angles and in varied settings.

### Models

**Models**—replicas of the actual object—are useful for a variety of purposes. For example, if you want to explain complex structures such as the human auditory or vocal mechanism, the brain, or the structure of DNA, a model will prove useful. Models help to clarify the relative sizes and positions of parts and how each part interacts with each other part.

### Graphs

Graphs are useful for showing differences over time, clarifying how a whole is divided into parts, and comparing different amounts or sizes. Figure 6.1 shows a variety of graphs that can be drawn freehand or generated with the graphics capabilities of any word-processing or **presentation software**. Keep your graphs as simple as possible. In a **pie graph,** for example, don't have more than five segments. Similarly, in a bar graph limit the number of items to five or fewer. As in the graphs shown in Figure 6.1, be sure you add the legend, the labels, and the numerical values you wish to emphasize.

### Word Charts

Word charts (which also can contain numbers and even graphics) are useful for identifying the key points in one of your propositions or in your entire speech—in the order in which you cover them, of course. Or you could use a word chart to identify the steps in a process—for example, the steps in programming TIVO, dealing with sexual harassment, or downloading the latest version of Firefox. Another use of charts is to show information you want your audience to write down. Emergency phone numbers, addresses, or titles of recommended books or websites are examples of the type of information that listeners will welcome in written form.

## Maps

If you want to illustrate the locations of geographic features such as cities, lakes, rivers, or mountain ranges, maps will obviously prove useful as presentation aids. But maps also can be used for illustrating population densities, immigration patterns, world literacy rates, varied economic conditions, the spread of diseases, and hundreds of other issues you may wish to examine in your

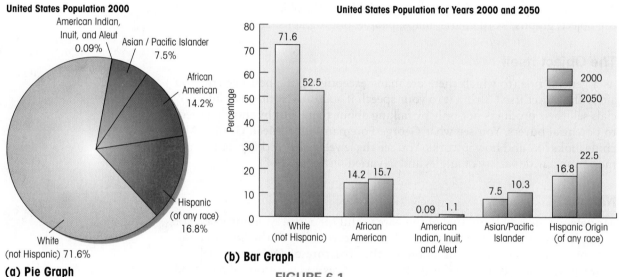

**(a) Pie Graph**

**(b) Bar Graph**

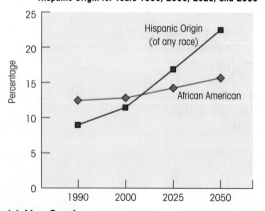

**(c) Line Graph**

**FIGURE 6.1**

**Assorted Graphs**

**The pie graph** (A) shows the cultural diversity in the population of the United States as recorded by the 2000 census. The pie graph is particularly helpful for showing relative proportions. However, the pie graph is useful only when the total equals 100 percent.

**The bar graph** (B) illustrates the population figures for 2000 (the same figures that appear in the pie graph) and projected figures for the year 2050. This graph enables you to see at a glance demographic changes that are predicted to occur by 2050.

**The line graph** (C) illustrates the percentages of African Americans and Hispanics for four different periods: the actual percentages as recorded in 1990 and 2000 and the projected percentages for the years 2025 and 2050. This graph not only enables you to see the changes over the years but also enables you to compare the relative changes of the two groups. Additional groups could have been added, but the graph would become increasingly difficult to read.

The figures for all graphs are taken from the Census Bureau website (www .census.gov).

speeches. A wide variety of maps may be downloaded from the Internet (most browsers have a *Maps* button) and then shown as slides or transparencies. Chances are you'll find a map on the Internet for exactly the purpose you need.

### People

If you want to demonstrate the muscles of the body, or different voice patterns, skin complexions, or hairstyles, consider using people as your aids. Aside from the obvious assistance they provide in demonstrating their muscles or vocal qualities, people help to secure and maintain the attention and interest of the audience.

### Photographs and Illustrations

Types of trees, styles of art, kinds of exercise machines, or the horrors of war—all can be made more meaningful with photographs and illustrations, which, ideally, you'll be able to project in a format large enough for everyone to see clearly. You'll also be able to point to specific parts of the photo as you explain the devastation of war or the fine art of combining colors and textures. You can also convert the images to transparencies to use with a transparency projector, although you'll lose some of the detail that you would have in slides. Another way to use photographs and illustrations is to have them enlarged to a size large enough for the entire audience to see. Try to mount these on cardboard so they'll be easier to handle. Most copy shops provide this service—though the cost may be considerable, especially if you have several photos to convert and you need them in color. Nevertheless, this is an option that may prove useful in some situations. Passing pictures around the room is generally a bad idea. Listeners will wait for the pictures to circulate to them, will wonder what the pictures contain, and will miss a great deal of your speech in the interim.

Once you've decided on the type of presentation aid you'll use, you need to decide on the medium you'll use to present it. Acquire skill in using both low-tech (the whiteboard or **flip chart**) and high-tech (the computerized slide show) resources. In this way you'll be able to select your presentation aids from the wide array available, choosing on the basis of the message you want to communicate and the audience to whom you'll be speaking. A variety of media, with their major uses, and some suggestions for using them effectively are presented in Table 6.1 on page 118.

## Using Presentation Aids

Your presentation aids will be more effective if you follow a few simple guidelines.

**PUBLIC SPEAKING CHOICE POINT: Visual Aids**
Harry is giving a speech on the anthropological implications of a collection of dinosaur bones. What principles for speaking with visual aids can you offer Harry? What options does Harry have for using presentation aids?

## TABLE 6.1 The Media of Presentation Aids

Once you've decided on the type of presentation aid you'll use, you need to decide on the medium you'll use to present it. Acquire skill in using both low-tech (the whiteboard or flip chart) and high-tech (the computerized slide show) resources. In this way, you'll be able to select your presentation aids from the wide array available, choosing on the basis of the message you want to communicate and the audience to whom you'll be speaking.

| MEDIA | USES | SUGGESTIONS |
|---|---|---|
| **Whiteboards** | The whiteboard may be used to record key terms or names, important numerical data, or even the main points of your speech (in very abbreviated form). | ■ Don't use it when you can present the same information with a preplanned chart or model.<br>■ Maintain audience eye contact even when writing. |
| **Chartboards**<br>Large semi-rigid boards come in a variety of colors and sizes. | Chartboards are useful when you have one or two relatively simple graphs, a few word charts, or diagrams that you want to display during your speech. | ■ Be sure you have a way of holding them up, for example, bring masking tape or enlist the aid of an audience member.<br>■ Black lettering on a white board provides the best contrast and is the easiest for people to read. |
| **Flip Charts**<br>Large pads of paper (usually about 24 x 24 inches) mounted on a stand or easel. | Flip charts can be used to record a variety of information, for example, key concepts or main points. Writing these out before the speech saves you the time of writing them during the speech (as you're forced to do with a whiteboard. | ■ Be sure the print is legible to the back of the audience.<br>■ Keep the charts simple.<br>■ Make sure the pages are in order and that you can flip the pages without losing eye contact. |
| **Slides and Transparencies**<br>Slides and transparencies can be created with many of the popular computer programs (see "Computer-Assisted Presentations," p. 119). | Slides and transparencies are helpful in showing a series of visuals that may be of very different types; for example, photographs, illustrations, charts, or tables. | ■ Must be easily seen from all parts of the room.<br>■ Follow the general suggestions for using computer-assisted presentations (p. 119). |
| **Audios and Videos**<br>Basically, you have two options with videos: You can record a scene from a film or television show with your DVD recorder and show it at the appropriate time in your speech.<br>    You can create your own video. | Adds variety to your presentation and helps to maintain audience attention. An audio or video in a speech on advertising or violence on television would help make your speech especially vivid. | ■ Avoid using long excerpts that will divert attention from your message; just use enough video to help your listeners understand the point you're making.<br>■ Videos are best used in small doses. |
| **Handouts**<br>Handouts are printed materials that you distribute to the audience a variety of handouts can be easily prepared with many of the computer presentation packages that we'll consider later in this chapter. | Handouts help explain complex material, provide listeners with a record of your speech, and encourage listeners to take notes. | ■ Encourage your audience to listen to you when you want them to and to look at the handout when you want them to by simply telling them.<br>■ If you distribute your handouts at the end of the speech, encourage your audience to read it by including additional material. |

- **Know your aids intimately.** Be sure you know in what order your aids are to be presented and how you plan to introduce them. Know exactly what goes where and when. Do all your rehearsal with your presentation aids so that you'll be able to introduce and use them smoothly and effectively.

- **Test the presentation aids before giving your speech.** Be certain that aids can be seen easily from all parts of the room. Don't underestimate, for example, how large lettering must be to be seen by those in the back of the room.

- **Rehearse your speech with the presentation aids incorporated into the presentation.** Practice your actual movements with the aids you'll use. If you're going to use a chart, how will you use it? Will it stand by itself? Will you ask another student to hold it for you?

- **Integrate presentation aids into your speech seamlessly.** Just as a verbal example should flow naturally into the text and seem an integral part of the speech, so should the presentation aid. It should appear not as an afterthought but as an essential part of the speech.

- **Avoid talking to your aid.** Talk to your audience at all times. Know your aids so well that you can point to what you want without breaking eye contact with your audience.

- **Use your aid only when it's relevant.** Show each aid when you want the audience to concentrate on it and then remove it. If you don't remove it, the audience's attention may remain focused on the visual when you want them to focus on what you'll be saying next.

## Computer-Assisted Presentations

A variety of **presentation software** packages are available; Microsoft's Power-Point, Corel Presentations, and Lotus Freelance are among the most popular and are very similar in what they do and how they do it. The speech presented in the Public Speaking Sample Assistant on pages 120–121 illustrates what a set of slides might look like; the slides are built around the speech outline were constructed in PowerPoint. As you review this figure, try to visualize how you'd use a slide show to present your next speech.

Computer-assisted presentations possess all of the advantages of aids already noted (for example, maintaining interest and attention, adding clarity, and reinforcing your message). In addition, however, they have advantages all their own—so many in fact that you'll want to seriously consider using this technology in your speeches. They give your speech a professional, up-to-date look, and in the process add to your credibility. They show you're prepared and care about your topic and audience.

As you read the following material, which applies PowerPoint technology to public speaking, take one of the many PowerPoint tutorials available online. A tutorial may be on your own computer or may be available somewhere on your campus. If not, visit one of the excellent tutorials from different colleges that are available to everyone; for example, http://homepage.cs.uri.edu/tutorials/csc101/powerpoint/ppt.html (University of Rhode Island), http://oregonstate.edu/instruction/ed596/ppoint/pphome.htm (Oregon State), or http://www.education.umd.edu/blt/tcp/powerpoint.html (The University of Maryland).

# PUBLIC SPEAKING SAMPLE ASSISTANT

## A Slide-Show Speech

This PowerPoint speech is intended to illustrate the general structure of a slide-show speech and is derived from the speech in the Public Speaking Sample Assistant on pages 157–159; you may find it helpful to look ahead to that speech to consider how you might improve this purposely sparse slide show. This PowerPoint presentation is available online at MySpeechLab (www.myspeechlab.com). Copy it to your computer and try altering this basic outline as you learn more about PowerPoint or similar presentation software.

**Slide 1**

- I'm in love with my nephew
- My husband is not my baby's father
- I'm really a man

This first slide aims to gain attention with these provocative confessions. These three bullets would come up one at a time, with the speaker pausing for (hopefully) some laughter. After you review the entire list of slides, try inserting graphics where you think they'd be appropriate.

**Slide 2**

- Jerry and Maury
- You and me

This slide recalls the popular confessions heard on the *Jerry Springer Show* and *Maury* but also relates the process of self-disclosure to the speaker and the audience, establishing a speaker–audience–topic connection.

**Slide 3**

**Self-Disclosure**

This third slide introduces the topic of the speech, self-disclosure.

**Slide 4**

- Self-disclosure
- Rewards
- Risks

This slide orients the audience by identifying the three main ideas to be discussed in the speech: the nature of self-disclosure, its rewards, and its risks. As with slide number 1, these three bullets should come up one at a time to give the speaker a chance to elaborate on each item and to give the audience a chance to digest the information. This slide show does not contain transitions. If you think they might help, insert transitions.

**Slide 5**

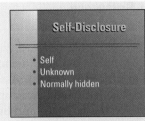

This fifth slide focuses on the first major idea: that self-disclosure is communication about the self, about something previously unknown, and about something that is normally kept hidden. Note here that very few words are used in the actual slide; the speaker will elaborate on each of these items in the actual speech. The words on slides are best thought of as tags you want the audience to hang on to as you explain each point.

**Slide 6**

This sixth slide focuses on the second main idea: that the rewards of self-disclosure include fuller self-knowledge, greater communication effectiveness, and improved health. The rewards should come up on the screen one at a time, rather than all together.

**Slide 7**

Slide 7 is the third main idea: that the risks of self-disclosure include possible personal, relationship, and professional problems. What types of graphics might make this slide more interesting and yet not take attention away from the main ideas?

**Slide 8**

This slide begins the conclusion and summarizes the three main points of the speech: the nature of self-disclosure, the rewards, and the risks.

**Slide 9**

While this slide, which contains only the words *Self-Disclosure*, is on screen, the speaker would likely motivate the audience to learn more about self-disclosure. Take a look at the conclusion of the speech from which this slide show was derived (pages 157–159) and create slides for the specific suggestions for learning more about self-disclosure.

**Slide 10**

This final slide closes the speech by repeating the theme of the speech; namely, that self-disclosure is both rewarding and risky and that these rewards and risks need to be weighed in any decision to self-disclose.

### Ways of Using Presentation Software

Presentation software enables you to produce a variety of aids. If you're speaking to a very small group, it may be possible to have your listeners gather around your computer as you speak. With larger audiences, however, you'll need a computer projector or LCD projection panel. Assuming you have a properly equipped computer in the classroom, you can copy your entire presentation to a CD-ROM or thumb drive, for example, and bring it with you the day of the speech.

Computer presentation software also enables you to print out a variety of materials: slides, slides with speaker's notes, slides with room for listener notes, and outlines of your speech. You can print out your complete set of slides to distribute to your listeners. Or you can print out a select portion of the slides, or even slides that you didn't have time to cover in your speech but which you'd like your audience to look at later. The most popular options are to print out two, three, or up to six slides per page. The two-slide option provides for easy readability and would be especially useful for slides of tables or graphs that you want to present to your listeners in an easy-to-read size. The three-slide option is probably the most widely used; it prints the three slides down the left side of the page with space for listeners to write notes on the right. This option is useful if you want to interact with your audience and you want them to take notes as you're speaking. Naturally, you'll distribute this handout before you begin your speech, during your introduction, or perhaps at that point when you want your listeners to begin taking notes. A sample three-slide printout with space for notes is provided in Figure 6.2. If you want to provide listeners with a complete set of slides, then the six-slide option may be the most appropriate. You can, of course, also print out any selection of slides you wish—perhaps only those slides that contain graphs, or only those slides that summarize your talk.

Another useful option is to print out your slides with your speaker's notes. That way you'll have your slides and any notes you may find useful—examples you want to use, statistics that would be difficult to memorize, quotations that you want to read to your audience, delivery notes, or anything that you care to record. The audience will see the slides but not your speaker's notes. It's generally best to record these notes in outline form, with key words rather than complete sentences. This will prevent you from falling into the trap of reading your speech. A sample printout showing a slide plus speaker's notes is provided in Figure 6.3 on page 124.

Another useful printout is the speech outline. Two outline options are generally available: the collapsed outline and the full outline. The collapsed outline contains only the slide titles and is useful if you want to give your audience a general outline of your talk. If you want your listeners to fill in the outline with the information you'll talk about, then you can distribute this collapsed outline at the beginning of your speech. The full outline option (slide titles plus bullets) is useful for providing listeners with a relatively complete record of your speech and also can be helpful if you cover a lot of technical information that listeners will have to refer to later. You might hand out a full outline, for example, if you are giving a speech on company health care or pension plans and you want to provide your listeners with detailed information on each option, or if you want to provide listeners with addresses and phone numbers. You would normally distribute a full outline not at the beginning but after your speech, because such a complete outline could lead your audience to read and not to listen.

**FIGURE 6.2**

**Slides with Space for Listeners' Notes**

This is an especially popular handout because it can be easily prepared and because it provides a neat combination of what you said and what listeners might be thinking.

You also can create overhead transparencies from your computer slides. You can make these on many printers and most copiers simply by just substituting transparency paper for regular paper.

## Suggestions for Designing Slides

Your slides will be more effective and easier to produce if you follow these few simple suggestions.

**Use the templates provided by your software.** Allow the design wizards to help you choose colors and typefaces. The templates are created by professional designers who are experts at blending colors, fonts, and designs into clear and appealing renderings.

**FIGURE 6.3**

**Slide and Speaker's Notes**

This example is from slide number 4, the orientation, in the self-disclosure slide-show speech on page 120.

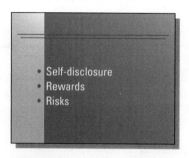

PAUSE!

SCAN AUDIENCE!

Today I'd like to discuss an extremely interesting and significant form of communication. It's called self-disclosure.

S-Disclosure can be greatly **rewarding**.

You might disclose your secret love and find that you too are your secret lover's secret lover.

S-Disclosure can also be **risky**.

You might disclose a mental or physical problem to your employer only to find yourself without a job.

Because the rewards and the risks are so high, we need to understand this unique form of communication. Before discussing the rewards and risks, we need to understand a little more about the nature of S-D.

PAUSE!

**Use consistent typeface, size, and color.** Give each item in your outline that has the same level head (for example, all your main points) the same typeface, size, and color throughout your presentation. This will help your listeners follow the organization of your speech. If you're using one of the pre-designed templates, this will be done for you.

**Be brief.** Your objective in designing these slides is to provide the audience with key words and ideas that will reinforce what you're saying in your speech; you don't want your audience to spend their time reading rather than listening. Generally, put one complete thought on a slide and don't try to put too many words on one slide.

**Use colors for contrast.** Remember that many people have difficulty distinguishing red from green; so if you want to distinguish ideas, it is probably best to avoid this color pairing. Similarly, if you're going to print out your slides in shades of gray, make sure the tones you choose provide clear contrasts. Also, be careful that you don't choose colors that recall holidays that have nothing to do with your speech—for example, red and green for Christmas or orange and black for Halloween. Remember, too, the cultural attitudes toward different colors; for example, among some Asian cultures, writing a person's name in red means that the person has died.

**Use only the visuals that you really need.** Presentation software packages make inserting visuals so easy that they sometimes encourage the user to include too many visuals. Most presentation packages provide a variety of graphic pictures, animated graphics, photos, and videos that are useful for a wide variety of speeches. With the help of a scanner, you can add your own visuals. Use visuals only when you have room on the slide and when the visual is directly related to your speech thesis and purpose. In deciding whether or not to include a visual, ask yourself if the inclusion of this graph or photo will advance the purpose of your speech. If it does, use it; if it doesn't, don't.

**Use charts and tables when appropriate.** Charts and tables are useful, as noted above, when you want to communicate complex information that would take too much text for one slide to explain. You have a tremendous variety of chart and graph types (for example, pie, bar, and cumulative charts) and tables to choose from. If you're using presentation software that's part of a suite, then you'll find it especially easy to import files from your word processor or spreadsheet. Also, consider the advantages of chart animation. Just as you can display bullets as you discuss each one, you can display the chart in parts so as to focus the audience's attention on exactly the part of the chart you want. You can achieve somewhat the same effect with transparencies by covering up the chart and gradually revealing the parts you want the audience to focus on.

**Anticipate questions.** If there's a question-and-answer period following your speech, consider preparing a few extra slides for responses to questions you anticipate being asked. Then, when someone asks you a predicted question, you can say: "I anticipated that someone might ask that question; it raises an important issue. The data are presented in this chart." You can then show the slide and explain it more fully. This is surely going the extra mile, but it can help make your speech a real standout.

**Use the spell-check.** You don't want professional-looking slides with misspellings; it can ruin your credibility and seriously damage the impact of your speech.

**Anticipate technical problems.** If you're planning to use a slide show, for example, consider what you'd do if the slide projector didn't arrive on time or the electricity didn't work. A useful backup procedure is to have transparencies and handouts ready just in case something goes wrong.

## Rehearsing with Presentation Programs

Presentation packages are especially helpful for rehearsing your speech and timing it precisely. As you rehearse, the computer program records the time you spend on each slide and will display that time under each slide; it will also record the presentation's total time. You can see these times at the bottom of each slide in a variety of views, but they won't appear in the printed handout, such as appears in Figure 6.3. You can use these times to program each slide so you can set it to run automatically. Or you can use the times to see if you're devoting the amount of time to each of your ideas that you want to. If you find in your rehearsal that your speech is too long, these times can help you see which parts may be taking up too much time and perhaps could be shortened.

Presentation software allows you to rehearse individually selected slides as many times as you want. But make sure that you go through the speech from beginning to end toward the end of your rehearsal period. Rehearse with this system as long as improvements result; when you find that rehearsal no

**PUBLIC SPEAKING CHOICE POINT: PowerPoint**
James is one of the admissions directors at his college and needs to present information to his audience of potential freshman and their parents about the career paths of recent graduates. There is a lot of information to present and he thinks a PowerPoint slide show would be helpful but he wants to avoid boring them to death. What advice can you offer him?

longer serves any useful purpose, then stop.

Another type of rehearsal is to check out the equipment available in the room you'll speak in and its compatibility with the presentation software you're using. If possible, rehearse with the very equipment you'll have available on the day you're speaking. In this way you can adjust to or remedy any incompatibilities or idiosyncrasies that are identified. Further, you'll discover how long it takes to warm up the slide projector or to load PowerPoint, so you won't have to use up your speaking time for these preparations.

A rehearsal of a somewhat different type is offered in Public Speaking Exercise 6.2, "Galileo and the Ghosts," on page 128. It will help you see your supporting materials (or any part or even all of your speech) from different perspectives.

## The Actual Presentation

During your actual presentation, you can control your slides with your mouse, advancing to the next one or going back to a previously shown slide. If you set the package to run automatically, programming each slide to be shown for its own particular amount of time, you won't be tied to the mouse—assuming you don't have a remote mouse. You can, of course, override the automatic programming by simply clicking your mouse either to advance or to go back to a slide that perhaps went by too quickly.

As with any presentation aid, make sure that you focus on the audience—don't allow the computer or the slides to get in the way of your immediate contact with the audience.

# Next Steps

Once you've collected your supporting materials, you'll want to develop your main points (Step 5), organize your speech materials (Step 6), and construct your introduction, conclusion, and transitions (Step 7). These three steps are covered in the next chapter.

# Essentials of Collecting Supporting Materials and Presentation Aids

This chapter focused on supporting materials, especially examples, analogies, definitions, narration, testimony, and statistics, and considered presentation aids at some length.

## Supporting Materials

1. Examples, illustrations, and narratives (specific instances) are explained in varying degrees of detail.

2. Analogies are comparisons of items from different classes (figurative analogy) or from similar classes (literal analogy).

3. Definitions are statements of the meaning of a term or concept. Terms may be defined by etymology, authority, negation, specific examples, or direct symbolization.

4. Testimony, the opinion of an expert or an eyewitness account, can lend authority or otherwise amplify assertions. To make testimony effective, stress the competence of the authority, the unbiased nature of the testimony, and the recency of the observation or opinion.

5. Statistics are figures that summarize the important characteristics of an otherwise complex set of numbers. Statistics are especially effective when they are clear, meaningful to the audience, connected to the idea they support, visually and verbally reinforced, and used in moderation.

## Presentation Aids

6. Common types of presentation aids are the actual object, models, graphs, word charts, maps, people, photos, and illustrations. Among the available media for presentation aids are the whiteboard, chartboards, flip charts, slide and transparency projections, audio and videotapes, and handouts.

7. When using presentation aids, know your aids intimately, test your aids before using them, don't talk to your presentation aid, and use the aid only when it's relevant.

8. Computer-assisted presentations offer a variety of advantages. Presentation software can provide great choice and flexibility; facilitate rehearsal and timing; facilitate the printing of handouts; and enable you to construct computer slide presentations, handouts, and transparencies.

9. In designing computer slides, consider using the templates provided. Aim for consistency in typeface, size, and color; seek brevity; and consider using color contrasts to emphasize your ideas. Use only the visuals you need; employ charts and tables effectively; consider preparing additional slides for anticipated questions; and use the spell-check.

10. Rehearse your speech with your presentation software, time your speech carefully, and make sure that you have all the needed equipment.

11. During the actual presentation, use your mouse to control the timing of slides, make sure that your slides don't interfere with your speaker–audience contact.

# Essential Terms

analogy **(108)**
bullets **(108)**
definition **(108)**
example **(106)**
figurative analogies **(108)**
flip chart **(117)**

illustration **(106)**
literal analogies **(108)**
mean **(112)**
mode **(113)**
models **(115)**
narrative **(106)**

percentages **(113)**
pie graph **(115)**
presentation aid **(114)**
presentation software **(115)**
statistics **(112)**
testimony **(110)**

# Public Speaking Exercises

## 6.1 Supporting Materials

Select one the following overly broad statements and support it, using at least three different types of supporting materials discussed in this chapter. Because the purpose of this exercise is to provide greater insight into supporting materials, you may, for this exercise, invent facts, figures, illustrations, examples, and the like.

1. Significant social contributions have been made by persons over 65.

2. The writer of this article is an authority.

3. Attitudes toward women in the workplace have changed over the last 20 years.

4. This college sounds ideal.

5. September 11, 2001, was a world-changing, life-changing event.

6. The athlete enjoyed a lavish lifestyle.

## 6.2 Galileo and the Ghosts

*Galileo and the Ghosts* is a technique for seeing a topic or problem through the eyes of a particular group of people and should prove useful at just about any stage of the public speaking preparation process (von Oech, 1990; Higgins, 1994; DeVito, 1996). In "ghost-thinking" (analogous to ghostwriting), you select a team of four to eight "people"—for example, historical figures like Galileo or Aristotle, fictional figures like Wonder Woman or James Bond, or persons from other cultures or of a different gender or affectional orientation. Selecting people who are very different from you and from one another will increase the chances that different perspectives will arise.

You then pose a question or problem (What supporting materials can I use? How can I make this example more powerful? In what ways might I present these statistics?) and ask yourself how each of these ghost-thinkers would answer your question or solve your problem, allowing yourself to listen to what each has to say. Of course, you're really listening to yourself—but to yourself acting in the role of another person. The technique forces you to step outside of your normal role and to consider the perspective of someone totally different from you. Try selecting a ghost-thinking team and asking your "team" for suggestions for finding, evaluating, and fine-tuning your supporting materials for your next speech.

## Log*On*! myspeechlab

Visit MySpeechLab (www.myspeechlab.com) for additional insight into supporting materials and explore some of the issues involved in using presentation aids. Especially helpful are the suggestions for using PowerPoint. Also watch the demonstration speech and look at the critique offered by a professor of public speaking.

# 7

# Organize Your Speech
# (Steps 5, 6, and 7)

## WHY READ THIS CHAPTER?

**Because it will enable you to organize your speech by helping you to:**

- organize your ideas so that your audience can more easily follow, understand, and remember what you say

- select an organizing pattern that best fits your topic, purpose, thesis, and audience

- construct effective introductions, conclusions, and transitions

- develop outlines that will help you rehearse and deliver your speech

*Champions know there are no shortcuts to the top. They climb the mountain one step at a time.*

—JUDI ADLER

In this chapter we first look at organizing the body of the speech, in which you set forth your main ideas. Once you've accomplished this, you can move on to develop your introduction, your conclusion, and the transitions that hold the pieces of the speech together. As you are developing these parts of the speech, you'll also be preparing outlines of your speech.

As you read this chapter, take a look at My Outline (**www.myspeechlab .com**, Figure 7.1). This program will help ensure that you're including all essential parts of the speech in an organized, easily recognizable pattern.

# The Benefits of Organization

Organizing your speech will yield several significant benefits.

- **Organizing will help guide the speech preparation process.** As you develop your organization, you'll be able to see the speech more clearly and as a whole (even in a preliminary and unfinished form). This will help you to see what needs further development, what needs paring down, or what should be rearranged or repositioned.

- **Organizing will help your audience understand your speech.** Because your audience will hear your speech only once, it must be instantly clear to them. They can't (as when you re-read a paragraph you didn't quite

**FIGURE 7.1**

**MyOutline**

This outlining website is one of the many online resources available at My Speech Lab (**www.myspeechlab.com**).

Reprinted with permission from Pearson Education.

understand) re-hear what was just said. Whether your aim is to inform or to persuade, your audience will be better able to follow your thinking if you present it in an organized pattern. If your listeners can visualize the pattern or outline you're following, it will be easier for them to understand your speech and to see, for instance, how an example supports a main point or how two arguments are related to your thesis.

- **Organizing will help your audience remember your speech.** People simply remember organized material better than unorganized material. And, if you want your audience to remember your speech, help them by presenting them with information in an easily identifiable and memorable organizational pattern.

- **Organizing will help establish your credibility.** Everything you do and say reflects on your credibility (the extent to which the audience believes you) and organization is no exception. When you present an effectively organized speech, you say in effect that you put work into this and that you're concerned with the audience understanding and remembering your speech. Your audience is more likely to see you as a competent person and as someone who is truly concerned with achieving your purpose.

# Develop Your Main Points (Step 5)

Begin organizing your speech by selecting and wording your main points. Let's look first at how you can select and word your main points and then at how you can logically arrange them.

## Select Your Main Points

Chapter 4's discussion of the thesis showed how you can develop your main points or propositions by asking strategic questions. To see how this works in detail, imagine that you're giving a speech to a group of high school students on the values of a college education. Your thesis is: "A college education is valuable." You then ask, "Why is it valuable?" From this question you generate your main points. Your first step may be to brainstorm this question and generate as many answers as possible without evaluating them. You may come up with answers such as the following:

1. It helps you get a good job.
2. It increases your earning potential.
3. It gives you greater job mobility.
4. It helps you secure more creative work.
5. It helps you to appreciate the arts more fully.
6. It helps you to understand an extremely complex world.
7. It helps you understand different cultures.
8. It allows you to avoid taking a regular job for a few years.
9. It helps you meet lots of people and make new friends.
10. It helps you increase your personal effectiveness.

There are, of course, other possibilities, but for purposes of illustration, these 10 potential main points will suffice. But not all 10 are equally valuable or relevant to your audience, so you should look over the list to see how to make it shorter and more meaningful. Try the following suggestions.

## Limit the Number of Main Points

For your class speeches, which will generally range from 5 to 15 minutes, use two, three, or four main points. Too many main points will result in a speech that's confusing, contains too much information, and proves difficult to remember. So we need to pare down the list from ten to perhaps three.

First, eliminate those points that seem least important to your thesis. On this basis you might want to eliminate number 8, as this seems least consistent with your intended emphasis on the positive values of college.

Second, combine those points that have a common focus. Notice, for example, that the first four points all center on the values of college in terms of jobs. You might, therefore, consider grouping these four items into one proposition:

A college education helps you get a good job.

This point might become a main point, which you could develop by defining what you mean by a "good job." This main point or proposition and its elaboration might look like this:

I. A college education helps you get a good job.
  A. College graduates earn higher salaries.
  B. College graduates enter more creative jobs.
  C. College graduates have greater job mobility.

Note that A, B, and C are all aspects or subdivisions of a "good job."

## Focus on Your Audience

Select those points that are most relevant or interesting to your audience. On this basis you might eliminate numbers 5 and 7, on the assumption that the audience will not see learning about the arts or different cultures as exciting or valuable at the present time. You also might decide that high school students would be more interested in increasing personal effectiveness, so you might select number 10 for inclusion as a second main point:

A college education increases your personal effectiveness.

Earlier you developed the subordinate points in your first proposition (the A, B, and C of I above) by defining more clearly what you meant by a "good job." Follow the same procedure here by defining what you mean by "personal effectiveness." It might look something like this:

I. A college education helps increase your personal effectiveness.
  A. A college education helps you improve your ability to communicate.
  B. A college education helps you acquire the skills for learning how to think.
  C. A college education helps you acquire coping skills.

Follow this same general procedure to develop the subheadings under A, B, and C. For example, point A might be divided into two major subheads:

A. A college education helps improve your ability to communicate.
   1. College improves your writing skills.
   2. College improves your speech skills.

Develop points B and C in essentially the same way, defining more clearly in B what you mean by "learning how to think" and in C what you mean by "coping skills."

## Word Your Main Points

Develop your main points so they're separate and discrete. Don't allow your main points to overlap each other. Each section labeled with a roman numeral should be a separate entity.

| **Not This** | **This** |
|---|---|
| I. Color and style are important in clothing selection | I. Color is important in clothing selection. |
| | II. Style is important in clothing selection. |

In addition, phrase your main points in parallel style; your main points should be phrased in similar grammatical structure with many of the same words. Julius Caesar's famous "I came, I saw, I conquered" is a good example of parallel style: Each statement is structured the same way, using the pronoun *I* plus a verb in the past tense. Phrase points labeled with roman numerals in parallel style. Likewise, phrase points labeled with capital letters and subordinate to the same Roman numeral (for example, A, B, and C under point I or A, B, and C under point II) in a similar style. Parallel styling will help the audience follow and remember your speech. Notice in the following that the first outline is more difficult to understand than the second, which is phrased in parallel style.

| **Not This** | **This** |
|---|---|
| The mass media serve four functions. | The mass media serve four functions. |
| I. The media entertain. | I. The media entertain. |
| II. The media function to inform their audiences. | II. The media inform. |
| III. Creating ties of union is a major media function. | III. The media create ties of union. |
| IV. The conferral of status is a function of all media. | IV. The media confer status. |

Public Speaking Exercise 7.1, "Generating Main Points," on page 166 provides some practice examples for generating main points from your thesis statement.

# RESEARCH LINK

## The Government

The various governments throughout the United States (federal, state, and municipal) publish an enormous amount of information that you're sure to find useful in speeches on almost any topic. One excellent starting point is Google's government search (www.google.com/unclesam). This engine covers all websites in the *.gov* domain. The amount of information you'll find, however, may at first be daunting. For example, if you searched for "publications," you'd find more than 27 million websites; 94 million for "education," and 125 million for "health." You'll definitely need to limit your search. One way to do this is of course to include additional terms (for example, health + drugs + teenagers) or use phrases in quotations ("teenage drug use"). Another useful way to learn about these sites is to take any of the many tutorials that are readily available; try, for example www.usa.gov/About/tutorials/index.shtml where you'll find tutorials that provide a general overview as well as more specific tutorials for completing government forms and finding government grants. You can also subscribe to receive e-mail updates on your favorite government sites.

Another way is to visit one or more of the 13 relevant departments of the federal government (these are the Departments of Agriculture, Commerce, Defense, Education, Energy, Health and Human Services, Housing and Urban Development, Interior, Justice, Labor, State, Treasury, and Transportation). All publish reports, pamphlets, books, and assorted documents dealing with their various concerns. Here are a few of the topics on which some of the departments have information that you'll find useful as you research your speeches.

- **Department of the Treasury** (www.ustreas.gov): taxes, property auctions, savings, economy, financial markets, international business, and money management.

- **Department of Housing and Urban Development** (www.hud.gov): home buying, selling, renting, and owning; fair housing, foreclosures, consumer information, FHA refunds, homelessness; and information for tenants, landlords, farm workers, senior citizens, and victims of discrimination.

- **Department of Defense** (www.defenselink.mil/): news releases, speech texts, military pay/benefits, casualty reports.

- **Department of Justice** (www.usdoj.gov): drugs and drug enforcement; Patriot Act information; trafficking in persons; inmate locator; Americans with Disabilities Act; sentencing statistics; and information from the Bureau of Alcohol, Tobacco, Firearms, and Explosives.

- **Department of Health and Human Services** (www.hhs.gov): aging, AIDS, disease, safety issues, food and drug information, disaster and emergency protection, families and children, disabilities, homelessness, and immigration.

- **Department of Education** (www.ed.gov): teaching resources in science, math, history, and language arts; innovations in education; reports on performance and accountability; "no child left behind" reports; at-risk and gifted students; Pell grant program; religious expression in schools.

- **Department of Labor** (www.dol.gov): pensions, unemployment, wages, insurance, and just about any topic even remotely related to labor.

- **The Department of Energy** (www.energy.gov) publishes materials on science and technology, energy efficiency, national security, and health and safety, as well as address issues currently in the news such as oil spills and ways to save money on energy.

- **The Department of the Interior** (www.interior.gov) is concerned with managing and sustaining America's water, wildlife, lands, and energy and publishes materials on these topics and others including those relating to Native Americans.

Other departments are equally prolific in their publishing of a wide range of information and are worth visiting. All of these departments can be followed on a variety of networks including Facebook and Twitter.

The next Research Link, "News Sources," appears on page 174.

# Organize Your Main Points (Step 6)

Once you've identified the main points you wish to include in your speech, organize them into a clearly identified organizational pattern. Here we consider some of the more useful patterns. Table 7.1 on page 136 identifies additional organizational patterns.

## Topical Pattern

When your topic conveniently divides itself into subdivisions, each of which is clear and approximately equal in importance, the **topical pattern** is useful. A speech on important cities of the world might be organized into a topical pattern, as might speeches on problems facing the college graduate, great works of literature, the world's major religions, and the like. For example, the topical pattern would be an obvious choice for organizing a speech on the powers of the government. The topic itself divides into three parts: legislative, executive, and judicial. Similarly, a talk on the major stock exchanges might follow a topical pattern; a sample outline might look like this:

### The Stock Exchanges

I. The New York Stock Exchange focuses on the largest companies.

II. The NASDAQ focuses largely on technology companies.

III. The American Stock Exchange focuses on the smaller companies.

Here is another example: a speech on ways to help people who have disabilities, in which each subtopic is treated about equally. The speaker is seeking to persuade the audience to devote some of their leisure time to helping people with disabilities, using the thesis "Leisure time can be well used to help people." Asking a strategic question of this thesis—"How can leisure time be spent helping people with disabilities?" or "What can we do to help people with disabilities?"—allows the speaker easily to identify the main points:

### Helping Others

I. Read for people with visual impairments.

  A. Read to students with visual impairments.

  B. Record a textbook for students with visual impairments.

II. Run errands for students with limited mobility.

III. Type for students who have manual difficulties.

## Temporal Pattern

With the **temporal pattern,** or time pattern, your speech is organized chronologically into two, three, or four major parts—beginning with the past and working up to the present or the future, or beginning with the present or the future and working back to the past. The temporal (sometimes called "chronological") pattern is especially appropriate for informative speeches in which you wish to describe events or processes that occur over time. It's also useful when you wish to tell a story, demonstrate how something works, or explain

**TABLE 7.1** **Additional Organizational Patterns**

The six patterns just considered are the most common and the most useful for organizing most public speeches. But there are other patterns that might be appropriate for different topics.

| ORGANIZATIONAL STRUCTURE | USES | POSSIBLE OUTLINES |
|---|---|---|
| In the **structure–function pattern** there are generally two main points, one for structure and one for function. | This pattern is useful in informative speeches in which you want to discuss how something is constructed (its structure) and what it does (its function). It might prove useful, for example, in a speech explaining what a business organization is and what it does, identifying the parts of a university and how they operate, or describing the nature of a living organism: its anatomy (its structures) and its physiology (its functions). | Thesis: To understand the brain you need to understand its structure and its function. <br> I. The brain consists of two main parts [explanation of structures] <br>    A. The cerebrum consists of . . . <br>    B. The cerebellum consists of . . . <br> II. The brain enables us to do a variety of things [explanations of functions] <br>    A. The cerebrum enables us to . . . <br>    B. The cerebellum enables us to . . . |
| In the **comparison-and-contrast pattern** your main points might be the main divisions of your topic | This pattern is often useful in informative speeches in which you want to analyze two different theories, proposals, departments, or products in terms of their similarities and differences. In this type of speech you would be concerned not only with explaining each theory or proposal but also with clarifying how they're similar and how they're different. | Thesis: Liberal and conservative political philosophies differ in important ways. <br> I. Government regulation. . . <br>    A. The liberal attitude is. . . <br>    B. The conservative attitude is . . . <br> II. Redistribution of income. . . <br>    A. Liberals view this . . . <br>    B. Conservatives view this . . . |
| In the **pro-and-con pattern**, sometimes called the **advantages–disadvantages pattern**, the speech has two main points—the advantages of Plan A and the disadvantages of Plan A (or Plan B). | This pattern is useful in informative speeches in which you want to explain objectively the advantages (the pros) and the disadvantages (the cons) of a plan, method, or product. Or you can use this pattern in a persuasive speech in which you want to show the superiority of Plan A (identifying its advantages) over Plan B (identifying its disadvantages). | Thesis: The proposals of the two health plans differ in co-payments, hospital benefits, and sick leave. <br> I. Co-payments . . . <br>    A. Plan A provides . . . <br>    B. Plan B provides. . . <br> II. Hospital benefits. . .. <br>    A. Plan A provides. . . <br>    B. Plan B provides. . . <br> III. Sick leave . . . <br>    A. Plan A provides. . . <br>    B. Plan B provides. . . |
| In the **claim-and-proof pattern** your thesis would essentially be your claim and then each main point would be support for your claim. | This pattern is especially useful in a persuasive speech in which you want to prove the truth or usefulness of a particular proposition. It's the pattern that you see frequently in trials, where the claim made by the prosecution is that the defendant is guilty and the proof is the varied evidence designed to show that the defendant had a motive, opportunity, and no alibi. | Thesis/Claim: The city must become proactive in dealing with the drug addicted. <br> I. Drug usage is increasing. [Proof No. 1] <br>    A. A particularly vivid example. . . <br>    B. Recent statistics. . . <br> II. Drug related crimes are increasing. [Proof No. 2] <br>    A. On-street crimes have increased. . . <br>    B. Business break-ins . . . |
| In the **multiple-definition pattern** each of your main points would consist of a different type of definition. | This pattern is useful for informative speeches in which you want to explain the nature of a concept. | Thesis: The nature of creative thinking is often misunderstood. <br> I. Creative thinking is not. . . [definition by negation] <br> II. According to Webster's dictionary. . . [dictionary definition] <br> III. Edward deBono defines . . . [a creative thinking theorist's view] <br> IV. A good example of creative thinking. . . [definition by example] |

**TABLE 7.1    Additional Organizational Patterns (*Continued*)**

| ORGANIZATIONAL STRUCTURE | USES | POSSIBLE OUTLINES |
|---|---|---|
| In the **who? what? why? where? when? pattern** your main points are explanations of who, what, why, where, and/or when. | This is the pattern traditionally used by journalists and is useful when you wish to report or explain an event; for example, a robbery, political coup, war, or trial. | Thesis: Understanding the Constitution is a first step toward responsible citizenship.<br>I. The Constitution is a document that sets forth . . . [answers the question What is the Constitution?]<br>II. The Constitution was needed because . . . [answers the question Why was it written?]<br>III. The Constitution was written at a time . . . [answers the question When was it written?]<br>IV. The Constitution was written by . . . [answers the question Who wrote it?] |
| In the **fiction–fact pattern** your main points would be the fiction and under these would be the facts. | This pattern may be useful in informative speeches when you wish to clarify misconceptions that people have about various things. In persuasive speeches this pattern might be used to defend or attack, whether a proposal, belief, or person. | Thesis: Three main misconceptions exist about the flu shot.<br>I. The first misconception is that you can get the flu from the flu shot.<br>  A. Studies show. . .<br>  B. The flu shot contains. . .<br>II. The second misconception is that antibiotics will help with the flu.<br>  A. Actually, antibiotics. . ..<br>  B. Viruses, such as the flu, however, . . .<br>III. The third misconception is that older people spread the flu.<br>  A. Actually, children. . .<br>  B. In studies done. . . . |

how to do something. Most historical topics lend themselves to organization by time. The events leading up to the Civil War, the steps toward a college education, or the history of writing would all be appropriate for temporal patterning. A speech on television scheduling might be organized in a temporal pattern, covering each of the four television periods in a time sequence beginning with the morning and ending with the evening—a pattern everyone would find easy to follow.

**Television Scheduling**

   I. Morning television gets people ready for their day.

   II. Daytime television keeps the homebound viewer company.

   III. Prime-time television appeals to everyone.

   IV. Late-night television appeals to adults.

## Spatial Pattern

Organizing your main points on the basis of space is useful when you wish to describe objects or places—progressing from top to bottom, from left to right, from inside to outside, or from east to west, for example. The structure of a place, an object, or even an animal is easily placed into a **spatial pattern.** You might describe the layout of a hospital, school, or skyscraper, or perhaps even the skeletal structure of a dinosaur, with a spatial pattern of organization. Here's an example of an outline describing the structure of the traditional textbook using a spatial pattern:

### The Textbook

I. The front matter contains the preface and the table of contents.

II. The text proper contains the chapters.

III. The back matter contains the glossary, bibliography, and index.

## Problem–Solution Pattern

The **problem–solution pattern** is especially useful in persuasive speeches, in which you want to convince the audience that a problem exists and that your solution would solve or lessen the problem. Let's say that you want to persuade your audience that jury awards for damages should be limited. A problem-solution pattern might be appropriate here. In the first part of your speech, you'd identify the problem(s) created by these large awards; in the second part you'd present the solution. A sample outline for such a speech might look something like this:

### Jury Awards

I. Jury awards for damages are out of control. **[the general problem]**

A. These awards increase insurance rates. **[a specific problem]**

B. These awards increase medical costs. **[a second specific problem]**

C. These awards place unfair burdens on business. **[a third specific problem]**

II. Jury awards need to be limited. **[the general solution]**

A. Greater evidence should be required before a case can be brought to trial. **[a specific solution]**

B. Part of the award should be turned over to the state. **[a second specific solution]**

C. Realistic estimates of financial damage must be used. **[a third specific solution]**

Here's another example to clarify the problem-solution organizational pattern. In this speech the speaker seeks to persuade the audience that cigarette advertising should be banned from all media. The thesis is that "Cigarette advertising should be abolished." Asking the strategic question "Why should it be abolished?" suggests the main points:

### Smoking

I. Cigarette smoking is a national problem.

A. Cigarette smoking causes lung cancer.

B. Cigarette smoking pollutes the air.

C. Cigarette smoking raises the cost of health care.

II. Cigarette smoking would be lessened if advertisements were prohibited.

A. Fewer people would start to smoke.

B. Smokers would smoke less.

In delivering such a speech, a speaker might begin like this:

I think we all realize that cigarette smoking is a national problem that affects each and every one of us. No one escapes the problems caused by cigarette smoking—not the smoker and not the nonsmoker. Cigarette smoking causes lung cancer. Cigarette smoking pollutes the air. And cigarette smoking raises the cost of health care for everyone.

Let's look first at the most publicized of all smoking problems: lung cancer. There can be no doubt—the scientific evidence is overwhelming—that cigarette smoking is a direct cause of lung cancer. Research conducted by the American Cancer Institute and by research institutes throughout the world all come to the same conclusion: cigarette smoking causes lung cancer. Consider some of the specific evidence. A recent study—reported in the January, 2011, issue of the . . . .

## Cause–Effect Pattern

The **cause–effect pattern** is useful in speeches when you want to show your audience the causal connection existing between two events or elements. Your speech divides into two major sections—causes and effects. For example, a speech on the reasons for highway accidents or birth defects might lend itself to a cause–effect pattern. Here you might first consider, say, the causes of highway accidents or birth defects and then some of the effects; for example, the number of deaths, the number of accidents, and so on.

In some cases you might want to place the effects first and then discuss the causes. Let's say you want to demonstrate the causes for an increase in gang violence. You might want to use an effect-to-cause pattern that might look something like this:

    I. Gang violence is increasing. **[general effect]**

       A. Gang violence is increasing among boys and girls. **[a specific effect]**

       B. Gang violence is increasing among younger people. **[a second specific effect]**

       C. Gang violence is increasing in the suburbs. **[a third specific effect]**

    II. Three factors contribute to the increase in gang violence. **[general causal statement]**

       A. Young people lack family guidance and discipline. **[a specific cause]**

       B. Young people have poor role models. **[a second specific cause]**

       C. Young people have few opportunities for recreation. **[a third specific cause]**

## The Motivated Sequence

The **motivated sequence** is another pattern for organizing a speech in such a way that your audience responds positively to your purpose (McKerrow, Gronbeck, Ehninger, & Monroe, 2007). This approach was developed by communication professor Alan H. Monroe in the 1930s, originally as a way to organize sales presentations. Now it's widely used in all sorts of oral and written communications. In fact, you'll probably find that you can analyze almost any persuasive message—from political speeches to television advertisements to Internet ribbon ads—in terms of the motivated sequence. The motivated sequence is especially appropriate for speeches designed to move listeners to action (to persuade the audience to do something). But you'll find it useful for informative speeches as well.

The organizational patterns we have considered so far divide speeches into three parts—introduction, body, and conclusion. The motivated sequence works a little differently; it organizes the speech into five parts or steps. Visualize the following: While walking down the street one day, a young boy with a shoe-shine box called out to a Wall Street–type executive:

> Hey, man. You look great. But your shoes are a mess. You don't want to walk into a meeting with mud on your shoes, do you? I can fix that for you. You'll look a lot better for that meeting if you have shined shoes. Sit right here and I'll polish them up.

In this brief "advertisement" the young boy executed all five steps of the motivated sequence:

> Hey, man. You look great. [**Step 1. Attention: Caught the attention of a passerby with a simple compliment.**]
>
> But your shoes are a mess. You don't want to walk into a meeting with mud on your shoes, do you? [**Step 2. Need: Demonstrated that the man had a problem and a need for change existed.**]
>
> I can fix that for you. [**Step 3. Satisfaction: Told the man that the problem could be corrected.**]
>
> You'll look a lot better for that meeting if you have shined shoes. [**Step 4. Visualization: Showed how things would be better if the problem were resolved.**]
>
> Sit right here and I'll polish them up. [**Step 5. Action: Told the man what he had to do to resolve the problem and satisfy the need.**]

Let's look at each of these steps in more detail and see how you might use each of them in actual speeches.

## Step 1: Gain Attention

In this step you gain the audience's undivided attention and get them to focus on you and your message. If you execute this step effectively, your audience should be anxious and ready to hear what you have to say. A variety of attention-getting devices are explained in the discussion of the introduction (pp. 145–147).

Regardless of what attention device you use, demonstrate your enthusiasm. Enthusiasm is highly contagious: If you show that you're enthusiastic, your attitude is likely to infect the audience, and they too will become involved and energized. Deliver your opening remarks with appropriate gestures, and vary bodily movement. Similarly, vary your voice so that it demonstrates your own involvement in the subject of your speech.

In phrasing your introductory remarks, involve the audience directly. Use *you* if appropriate, and use connecting pronouns—*us* and *we*—that show that you and your listeners are involved in this together.

For example, in a speech aiming to persuade your listeners to vote in favor of establishing a community youth center, you might gain attention by using a provocative question:

> If you could reduce juvenile crime by some 20 percent by just flipping a lever, would you do it?

Or you might make reference to specific audience members:

I know that several of you here have been the victims of juvenile vandalism. Thom, your drug store was broken into last month by three teenagers who said they did it because they were bored. And Loraine, your video rental shop's windows were broken by teenagers who, in a drunken spree, decided to have a rock fight. And. . . .

## Step 2: Establish the Need

In the second part of the motivated sequence, you demonstrate that there's a problem, that something is wrong, that a need exists. Your listeners should feel that they have something to learn (if you are making an informative speech) or that they have to change their attitudes or do something (if it's a persuasive speech). Here are some examples, first for informative speeches and second for persuasive speeches.

**State the problem or need.**    If you're giving an informative speech, the problem or need might be lack of information. For example, in an informative speech on how to gain access to your credit history, you might establish the need for information by saying, "You need access to your credit history because it's the best way to prevent yourself from being a victim of fraud," or, "Millions of people become victims of credit fraud because they don't have access to their own credit history," or, "You're more likely to become a victim of fraud if you don't regularly check your credit history."

If you're giving a persuasive speech, you might focus on your listeners' need to change their attitudes or their behaviors. For example, in a speech aiming to persuade your listeners to participate actively in the political process, you might establish the need by saying something like this: "You need to participate actively in the politics of your city if you want elected officials to address your needs and the needs of people like you." Or, in a speech on the need to establish a community youth center as a way of reducing juvenile crime, you might say, "Juvenile crime has been increasing dramatically in our community over the last several years. We need to do something about it."

**Show why this is really a problem.**    Make sure your audience understands that this problem affects them directly—that it is not simply some abstract problem that will not touch them personally. You also might support the existence of need with illustrations, statistics, testimony, and other forms of support we already explored in Chapter 6. Additionally, you might show your listeners how this need affects those values that motivate their behavior, such as their financial security, their career success, and their individual happiness (motivators that we'll examine in more detail in Chapter 11). In the speech on the youth center, you might say, "Federal crime statistics show that juvenile crime is likely to increase over the next several years, and it will happen in our community if we don't take a stand and do something about it *now*," or "Next year, your store, Jack, or yours, Shauna, may be broken into."

## Step 3: Satisfy the Need

In this step you present the "answer" or the "solution" that would eliminate the problem or satisfy the need that you demonstrated in Step 2. On the basis of this satisfaction step, your listeners should now believe that what you're informing them about or persuading them to do will effectively satisfy the need. So show here how the problem can be solved and why your solution will work.

**Show your listeners that your plan will satisfy the need or solve the problem.** Here you might say quite simply, "The best way to reduce credit card fraud is to check your credit history regularly," or, "Like our neighboring towns, we need to create a youth center for high school students to reduce juvenile crime and vandalism."

**Show why your solution will work.** You want your audience to understand that what you're asking them to believe or do will actually lead to resolving the problem or satisfying the need you identified in Step 2. So you might say something like: "Youth crime has been dramatically reduced in all of our neighboring towns since they established youth centers. The same will happen here."

This step is also a good place to answer any objections you anticipate from your listeners. For example, if you anticipate that audience members will object to the youth center for fear it would increase their taxes, you might address this now. For example, you might say, "A major portion of the financing will be secured from New York State grants, and local merchants have already agreed to contribute whatever additional financing is needed. So this youth center will impose absolutely no financial burden on anyone."

Notice that in an informative speech you could have stopped after the satisfaction step because you would have accomplished your goal of informing the audience about the youth centers and how they can effectively reduce juvenile crime. In a persuasive speech, on the other hand, you must continue at least as far as Step 4, visualization (if your purpose is limited to strengthening or changing attitudes or beliefs), or go on to Step 5, action (if your purpose is to get your listeners to do something).

## Step 4: Visualize the Need Satisfied

In this step of the motivated sequence, you take the audience beyond the present time and place and enable them to imagine, to visualize, the situation as it would be if the problem were eliminated (if the need were satisfied as you suggested in Step 3). Through this visualization you aim to intensify your listeners' feelings or beliefs. You can achieve this visualization with any one or combination of these basic strategies.

**Demonstrate the benefits that your listeners will receive if your ideas are put into operation.** You might, for example, point to the decrease in crime that accompanies the establishment of youth centers, or to the social and vocational skills that the students will learn there. Or you could visualize the need satisfied by returning to your introductory examples and say something like: "Wouldn't it have been great if Thom's drugstore had never been broken into and the time, energy, and expense that Thom had to go through could have been spent taking a well-deserved vacation? And Loraine, wouldn't it have been nice if your windows had never been broken? And. . . ."

**Demonstrate the negative effects that will occur if your plan is not put into operation.** Here you might argue, for example, that without such a youth center, juvenile crime will increase or students will fail to learn safe sex practices normally taught at these youth centers that are not currently taught at home or in the schools.

**Demonstrate the combined positive and negative effects.** You might combine both the demonstration of the positive effects that will result if your plan is put into operation and the negative effects that will result if your plan is denied. You might then say something like this: "Without a youth center teen crime is likely to increase, as the statistics from similar towns that I'll show will illustrate. But with such a center, juvenile crime is likely to decrease, and I'll also show you very recent and very dramatic statistics from towns just like ours that had the foresight to establish such centers."

## Step 5: Ask for Action

In this final step you tell the audience what they should do to ensure that the need (as demonstrated in Step 2) is satisfied (as described in Step 3). Here you want to move the audience in a particular direction; for example, to vote in favor of additional research funding for AIDS or against cigarette advertising, to attend the next student government meeting, or to contribute free time to the blind. In completing this step, consider two basic strategies.

**PUBLIC SPEAKING CHOICE POINT: Using the Motivated Sequence**

Gus wants to give a speech opposing a proposed youth center, arguing that the way to fight youth crime is by mandating harsher sentences for all youth crimes. He wants to use the motivated sequence pattern.

- How might he gain attention?
- How might he demonstrate the need to establish harsher sentences?
- How might he demonstrate that if harsher sentences are handed down, youth crime will be reduced, thus satisfying the need?
- How might he visualize what it will be like with harsher sentences for all youth crimes; that is, if the need is satisfied?

Gus wants to ask his audience to support harsher sentences for all youth crimes in a straw poll to be conducted next week.

- How might he phrase his action step?

**Tell the audience exactly what they must do.** Frequently, speakers use emotional appeals here (see Chapter 11). Or you might give your listeners guidelines for future action, saying something like this: "Proposition 14, establishing a youth center in the old post office building, is coming up for a vote next week. Vote *yes*, and urge your family members, your friends, and your work colleagues to also vote *yes*. It will make our town a better place for us all."

**Remind your listeners of the connections you've established throughout your speech.** Throughout your motivated sequence speech, you've established a series of important connections and relationships. Make sure your listeners remember them and see how the action you ask for here is related.

Make sure they see that the action you ask for will satisfy the need and enable them to live in a world (in a community, in our example of the youth center) that is a lot better than it would be otherwise.

**Stress specific advantages.**   Stress the specific advantages of the desired behaviors to your specific audience. In other words, don't ask your audience to engage in behaviors solely for abstract reasons. Give them concrete, specific reasons why they will benefit from the actions you want them to engage in. Instead of telling your listeners that they should devote time to reading to blind students because it's the right thing to do, show them how much they will enjoy the experience and how much they will personally benefit from it.

## Cultural Considerations in Organization

Cultural considerations are as important in organization as they are in all other aspects of public speaking. One factor that's especially important is whether the audience's culture is high-context or low-context (Hall & Hall, 1987). **High-context cultures** (Japanese, Arabic, Latin American, Thai, Korean, Apache, and Mexican are examples) are those in which much of the information in communication is in the context or in the person rather than in the actual spoken message. Both speaker and listener already know the information from, say, previous interactions, assumptions each makes about the other, or shared experiences. **Low-context cultures** (German, Swedish, Norwegian, and American are examples) are those in which most information is explicitly stated in the verbal message. In formal communications, the information would be in written form as well—as it is with mortgages, contracts, prenuptial agreements, or apartment leases.

Extending this distinction to speech organization, we can see that members of high-context cultures will probably prefer an organization in which the supporting materials are offered and the audience is allowed to infer the general principle or proposition themselves. Low-context culture members, on the other hand, will likely prefer an organization in which the proposition is clearly and directly stated and the supporting materials are clearly linked to the proposition.

Persons from the United States speaking in Japan, to take one well-researched example, need to be careful lest they make their point too obvious or too direct and thus inadvertently insult their audience. Speakers in Japan are expected to lead their listeners to the conclusion through example, illustration, and various other indirect means (Lustig & Koester, 2006). Persons from Japan speaking in the United States need to be careful lest their indirectness be perceived as unnecessarily vague, underhanded, or suggestive of an attempt to withhold information.

You might, for example, organize a speech on the need for random drug testing in the workplace somewhat differently depending on whether you are addressing a high-context or a low-context audience.

| High-Context Audience | Low-Context Audience |
|---|---|
| Implicitness and indirectness are preferred | Explicitness and directness are preferred |
| The main point is implicitly identified only after the evidence is presented | The main point is clearly stated at the outset, even before the evidence is presented |

Drugs in the workplace cause accidents. Drugs in the workplace contribute to the national drug problem. Drugs in the workplace increase costs for employers and consumers. These are some factors we need to think about as we consider the proposal to establish random workplace drug testing.

Random drug testing in the workplace is a must. It will reduce accidents. It will reduce the national drug problem. It will reduce costs. Let's examine each of these reasons why random drug testing in the workplace should become standard.

# Construct Your Introduction, Conclusion, and Transitions (Step 7)

Now that you have the body of your speech organized, devote your attention to the introduction, conclusion, and transitions that will hold the parts of your speech together.

As you read about introductions, conclusions, and transitions, also visit some websites containing speeches and examine the ways the speakers introduced, concluded, and tied the parts of their speeches together. Start with My Speech Lab (**www.myspeechlab.com**), History and Politics Out Loud (**www .hpol.org**), the History Channel (**www.historychannel.com/speeches**), or American Rhetoric (**www.americanrhetoric.com/speechbank.htm**). Many of these sites include audio and/or video material.

## Introductions

Together with your general appearance and your nonverbal messages, your introduction gives your listeners their first impression of you and your speech. And, as you know, first impressions are very resistant to change. Because of this, the introduction is an especially important part of the speech. It sets the tone for the rest of the speech; it tells your listeners what kind of a speech they'll hear.

Begin collecting suitable material for your introduction as you prepare the entire speech, but wait until all the other parts are completed before you put the pieces together. In this way you'll be better able to determine which elements should be included and which should be eliminated.

Your introduction may serve three functions: gain attention, establish a speaker–audience–topic connection, and orient the audience as to what is to follow. Gaining attention in your introduction is essential, establishing an S-A-T connection is almost always useful, and an orientation in some form is always needed. Let's look at how you can accomplish each of these functions.

### Function 1. Gain Attention

Your introduction should gain the **attention** of your audience and focus it on your speech topic. (And, of course, it should help you maintain that attention throughout your speech.) You can secure attention in numerous ways; here are just a few.

**Ask a Question.** Questions are effective because they're a change from the more common declarative statements, and listeners automatically pay attention to change. Rhetorical questions—questions to which you don't expect an answer—or polling type questions that ask the audience for a show of hands are especially helpful in focusing the audience's attention on your subject:

Do you want to succeed in college?

Do you want to meet the love of your life?

How many of you have suffered through a boring lecture?

How many of you intend to continue school after graduating from college?

**Refer to Recent Happenings.** Referring to a previous speech, a recent event, or a prominent person currently making news helps gain attention, because the audience is familiar with this and will pay attention to see how you're going to connect it to your speech topic.

Here is an especially good example by Caleb Graves (2010) from the University of Texas at Austin:

> On March 14, 2010, an American task force in Afghanistan successfully raided and apprehended a sizeable number of weapons stored by Taliban forces. *USA Today* of the same date reports though this effectively removed weapons from enemy hands, the task force soon realized the weapons should have never been there in the first place, considering they were supplied by the U.S. government. The article further substantiates that from the $330 million Americans spent on transports to Afghanistan in the past year, at least 13,000 weapons and 200,000 rounds of ammunition have gone missing, causing task force member Ken Feiereisen to worry that Americans are being killed by our very own weapons.

**Use an Example, Illustration, or Narrative.** Much as we are drawn to soap operas, so we are drawn to illustrations and stories about people, especially if they are dramatic or even startling. For further explanation refer back to the earlier discussion of this type of supporting material (pp. 106–108).

**Use a Quotation.** Quotations are useful because the audience is likely to pay attention to the brief and clever remarks of someone they have heard of or read about. Make sure that the quotation is directly relevant to your topic; if you have to explain its relevance, it probably isn't worth using. Quotations are easy to find; visit some of the quotations sites at **www.bartleby.com**, **www.yahoo .com/Reference/Quotations/** or **www.quotationspage.com**. You may find it helpful also to say something about the author of the quotation by consulting some of the biography sites mentioned in the Research Link on page 111.

**Cite a Little-Known Fact or Statistic.** These help pique an audience's attention. Headlines on unemployment statistics, crime in the schools, and political corruption sell newspapers because they gain attention. In a speech on the need for more severe punishments for hate speech, the speaker might cite a specific hate speech incident that the audience hadn't heard of yet or the statistic that violence inspired by hate speech tripled over the last six months.

**Use Humor.**    Humor is useful because it relaxes the audience and establishes a quick connection between speaker and listeners. In using humor make sure it's relevant to your topic, brief, tasteful, seemingly spontaneous, and appropriate to you as a speaker and to the audience.

## Function 2. Establish a Speaker–Audience–Topic Relationship

In addition to gaining attention, use your introduction to establish a connection among yourself as the speaker, the audience members, and your topic. Try to answer your listeners' inevitable question of why they should listen to you speak on this topic. You can establish an effective speaker–audience–topic (or S–A–T) relationship in any of numerous ways.

**Establish Your Credibility.**    The introduction is a particularly important time to establish your competence, character, and charisma (see Chapter 11). Here, for example, Ohio congressman and 2008 presidential hopeful Dennis Kucinich (2007) establishes his credibility by telling the audience of his background and accomplishments in a speech at the Tenth Annual Wall Street Project Conference on January 15, 2007:

> I am a product of the city. My parents never owned a home. I grew up in 21 different places by the time I was 17, including a few cars. I've learned about opportunities. I've learned that if you believe it you can conceive it.

**Refer to Others Present.**    Referring to others present not only will help you to gain attention; it also will help you to establish an effective speaker-audience-topic relationship. Use this technique sparingly and only when you know it will not embarrass any member to whom you refer. Be especially careful to avoid referring to a small group of friends; it might have the effect of making the others in the audience feel like outsiders. This technique is probably best used when there are several distinguished people in the audience and you want to point to their accomplishments which, ideally, will be closely related to your thesis.

**Express Your Pleasure or Interest in Speaking.**    In the following example Senator Christopher Dodd (2007) expresses his pleasure at speaking at Reverend Jesse Jackson's Tenth Annual Wall Street Summit.

> It's an honor for me to be invited to speak to you today at this, the 10th Anniversary of the Wall Street Economic Summit. Reverend Jackson, you should take enormous pride in the success of this event, and the growth of the Rainbow Push Wall Street Project. Your efforts over the years have helped millions more Americans achieve their dreams and aspirations.

**Compliment the Audience.**    Complimenting the audience is a commonly used technique to establish an S–A–T connection in much professional public speaking. In the classroom, however, this technique may seem awkward and obvious and so is probably best avoided. But it's important to realize

**PUBLIC SPEAKING CHOICE POINT: S–A–T Connection**
Hasan is giving an informative speech on ways to empower partnerships between rival departments in a large business organization. If the audience were your public speaking class, how might he establish a speaker–audience–topic connection?

that paying the audience an honest and sincere compliment (never overdoing it), not only will encourage your hearers to give you their attention but will help make them feel a part of your speech. In some cultures—Japan and Korea are good examples—the speaker is expected to compliment the audience, the beauty of the country, or its culture. It's one of the essential parts of the introduction. In this example, musician Billy Joel (1993) compliments his audience, the graduating class of the Berklee College of Music, directly and honestly:

> I am truly pleased that the road has twisted and turned its way up the East Coast to Boston. The Berklee College of Music represents the finest contemporary music school there is, and I am honored to be here with you this morning to celebrate.

**Express Similarities with the Audience.**   By stressing your own similarities with members of the audience, you create a bond with them and become an "insider" instead of an "outsider." Here Lester M. Crawford, Acting Commissioner of Food and Drugs, (2005) in a speech before the World Pharma IT Congress on June 6, 2005, established an S-A-T connection by expressing similarities:

> I think most people would be surprised to find the Commissioner of Food and Drugs at an IT conference. And certainly, I was asking myself just this question during most of this morning's presentations. However, I think it's significant to stress the importance of IT in the health care industry and that's why I'm pleased to be here today.*

---

*Reprinted with permission from Eastman & Eastman, on behalf of the author.

## Function 3. Orient the Audience

The introduction should orient the audience in some way as to what is to follow in the body of the speech. Preview for the audience what you're going to say. The **orientation** may be covered in a variety of ways.

**Give a General Idea of Your Subject.**   Orientation can consist simply of a statement of your topic. For example, you might say, "Tonight I'm going to discuss atomic waste" or "I want to talk with you about the problems our society has created for the aged." In a speech at the groundbreaking ceremony for the Dr. Martin Luther King Jr. National Memorial on November 13, 2006, President Barack Obama (then Senator from Illinois) (2006) gave a general idea of what he'd say in the main part of his speech:

> I have two daughters, ages five and eight. And when I see the plans for this memorial, I think about what it will [be] like when I first bring them here upon the memorial's completion. . . . And at some point, I know that one of my daughters will ask, perhaps my youngest, will ask, "Daddy, why is this monument here? What did this man do?" How might I answer them?

**Identify the Main Points You'll Cover.**   In your orientation you may want to identify very briefly the main points you'll cover.

**Give a Detailed Preview.**   Or you may wish to give a detailed preview of the main points of your speech, as in this example of an address by Microsoft founder Bill Gates (2004) at the United Nations Media Leaders Summit on January 15, 2004.

> I hope to do three things today: explain why I believe the media's role in increasing visibility for HIV/AIDS is so important, why I'm optimistic about the opportunities ahead, and what I believe is needed to stop this epidemic.

Here's how Christi Liu (2010), a student from the University of Texas at Austin, did it:

> So to better understand Witricity and its possibilities, we will first explore the phenomenon of wireless electricity, next plug in the uses of Witricity, and finally take a look at the shocking implications.

**Identify Your Goal.**   Here California Governor Arnold Schwarzenegger (2007) orients the audience by giving a general idea of the goal he hopes to achieve.

> Hello everybody. Thank you for being here. I believe that in Sacramento this year, we are going to make history. Using a comprehensive approach built on shared responsibility where everyone does their part we will fix California's broken health care system and create a model that the rest of the nation can follow. I know everyone has been eager to hear exactly what we are proposing.

**PUBLIC SPEAKING CHOICE POINT: Formulating an Effective Introduction**
Alice plans to give an informative speech outlining the changes that are taking place in health care. She knows that some members of her audience are not interested in the topic and she fears they may tune her out immediately. What options does Alice have for introducing her speech and securing the attention and interest of all audience members? What might she say?

# Conclusions

Your conclusion is especially important because it's often the part of the speech that the audience remembers most clearly. Your conclusion may serve three major functions: to summarize, motivate, and provide closure. A summary of the speech is useful to the listener in nearly any circumstance. Motivation is appropriate in many persuasive speeches and in some informative speeches. Providing closure in any speech is essential.

## Function 1. Summarize

You can summarize your speech in a variety of ways.

**Restate Your Thesis or Purpose.**   In the restatement type of summary, you recap the essential thrust of your speech by repeating your thesis or perhaps the goals you hoped to achieve.

Here is how Aviva Pinchas (2010), a student from the University of Texas at Austin, accomplished this:

> In 2008, Congress passed the ADA Amendments Act in the hopes of righting decades of judicial wrongs against disabled employees. While this law has not lived up to its potential, we have the power to ensure that, someday soon, it will. After looking at the causes for the law's failure, the effects of these court rulings, and then ways to combat a biased court system, it is clear that the job of protecting disabled workers lies not in the hands of lawyers or politicians but our own—to stand up and declare that this difficult economic time will not deter us from protecting America's most vulnerable workers.

**Restate the Importance of the Topic.**   Another method for concluding is to tell the audience again why your topic or thesis is so important. In the following example, Linse Christensen of Northern State University, in a speech on automobile safety, restated the importance of the topic by recalling a particularly dramatic example of why precautions need to be taken (Schnoor, 2008, p. 68).

> Andrew Clemens will forever remember the little sister, his best friend, Adrianna, who died as a result of being backed over by their father right in front of his own house.

**Restate Your Main Points.**   In this type of summary you restate your thesis and the main points you used to support it. In her conclusion, Christi Liu (2010) restates her main point like this:

> After looking at how wireless electricity works, what devices we no longer need to plug in, and the implications of Witricity, it is clear that our relationship with electricity is about to heat up, and within the next few years we could all be charging our devices with a little bit of magic.

## Function 2. Motivate

A second function of the conclusion—most appropriate in persuasive speeches—is to motivate your audience to do what you want them to do. In your conclusion you have the opportunity to give the audience one final push in the direction you wish them to take. Whether it's to buy stock, vote a particular way, or change an attitude, you can use the conclusion for a final motivation, a final appeal. Below are three excellent ways to motivate.

**Ask for a Specific Response.**   Specify what you want the audience to do after listening to your speech.

In a speech on bridge safety, Sarah Hoppes of Ohio University asks for a specific response (Schnoor, 2008, p. 54):

> I have prepared a handout that lists the web addresses for you to research bridge safety in your area. To get you started, and to protect you on the way home, I have included the location of three bridges in the greater Madison area you should avoid at all costs.

**Reiterate the Importance of the Issue.**   In a speech designed to strengthen attitudes, it may prove of value to restate the importance of the issue to the audience and to the community at large. For example, Alberto Mora (2006), in accepting the 2006 John F. Kennedy Profile in Courage award on May 26, 2006, restates why it's so important to address the issue of cruelty and torture.

> We should care because the issues raised by a policy of cruelty are too fundamental to be left unaddressed, unanswered, or ambiguous. We should care because a tolerance of cruelty will corrode our values and our rights and degrade the world in which we live. It will corrupt our heritage, cheapen the value of the soldiers upon whose past and present sacrifices our freedoms depend, and debase the legacy we will leave to our sons and daughters.*

**Provide Directions for Future Action.**   Another type of motivational conclusion is to spell out the action you wish the audience to take. Here's an example from a speech by Corey Reutlinger (2010), from Hastings College:

> Before doing this speech, I didn't think much about my carbon footprint when I traveled to Denver three years ago. But now, after looking at the causes, the effects, and the solutions to the Essential Air Service program, I realize I should've considered a more economic and eco-friendly option. As you think about your plans to future AFA's, NFA's, Phi Rho Pi's, NPDA's, or any other national tournament, consider driving or choosing a larger airline so that in the future we can continue to fly the friendly skies.

## Function 3. Provide Closure

The third function of your conclusion is to provide closure. Often your summary will accomplish this, but in some instances it will prove insufficient. End your speech with a conclusion that is crisp and definite. Make the audience aware that you have definitely and clearly ended. Some kind of wrap-up, some sort of final statement, is helpful in providing this feeling of closure. Here are three ways you can achieve closure.

**Refer to Subsequent Events.**   You can achieve closure by looking ahead to events that will take place either that day or soon afterwards. Notice how

---

*Source: Alberto Mora/Kennedy Library Foundation.

**PUBLIC SPEAKING CHOICE POINT: Concluding the Commencement Speech**
Graduates and their friends and families are usually ready to be off celebrating rather than listening to an overly long speech. How can speakers use the last few minutes to ensure that their message was heard?

effectively U.S. Secretary of State Madeleine K. Albright (1998) uses this method in a speech on NATO.

> Our task is to make clear what our alliance will do and what our partnership will mean in a Europe truly whole and free, and in a world that looks to us for principles and purposeful leadership for peace, for prosperity, and for freedom. In this spirit, I look forward to our discussion today and to our work together in the months and years to come.

**Refer Back to the Introduction.** It's sometimes useful to connect your conclusion with your introduction. One student, Jaime Garcia (2010), from the University of Texas at Austin, accomplished this neatly. In the introduction he said:

> American skier Lindsey Vonn cemented her place as America's latest sweetheart by becoming the first U.S. woman to win an Olympic gold medal in downhill skiing. Vonn's outstanding performance is in large part due to her incredible talent, her drive, and her hard work—evidenced by three consecutive world cup wins— but unbeknownst to many, she also had a technological leg up on her Olympic opponents in the form of piezoelectric fibres.

Then in the conclusion he referred back to the incident:

> This February, Lindsey Vonn may have captured the hearts of ski fans everywhere—but piezoelectric materials may soon allow all of us to capture energy everywhere and convert it to electricity. After examining the process behind piezoelectric technology, viewing its current uses, and finally discussing its potential future applications, it is clear that this technology may appear to bend the rules of physics and nature. But whichever way you bend it, you can't break the fact that piezoelectric technology could be the most powerful discovery to ever light up our world.

**Thank the Audience.** Speakers frequently conclude their speeches by thanking the audience for their attention or for their invitation to the speaker to address them. In almost all cases, the "thank you" should be brief—A simple "thank you" or "I appreciate your attention" is all that's usually necessary.

Public Speaking Exercise 7.2, "Constructing Introductions and Conclusions," on page 166 provides opportunities to practice developing these crucial parts of your speech.

## Transitions

Remember that your audience will hear your speech just once. They must understand it as you speak it, or your message will be lost. As discussed in Chapter 3, transitions help listeners understand your speech more effectively and efficiently.

**Transitions** are words, phrases, or sentences that help your listeners follow the development of your thoughts and arguments and get an idea of where you are in your speech.

You can think of transitions as serving four functions: to connect, to preview, to review, and to signal where the speaker is in the speech. All of these functions work to provide coherence to your speech and to make it easier for the audience to follow your train of thought.

### Connectives

Use connective transitions to connect the major parts of your speech. Use transitions in at least the following places:

- between the introduction and the body of the speech
- between the body and the conclusion
- between the main points in the body of the speech

You might say, for example, *Now that we have a general idea of . . . we can examine it in more detail.* This helps the listener see that you've finished your introduction and are moving into the first main point. Or you might say, *Not only are prison sentences too long, they are often incorrect.* This would help the listener see that you've concluded your argument about prison sentences and are now going to illustrate that sentences are often incorrect. Other common phrases useful as connective transitions include: *In contrast to . . . consider also . . ., Not only . . . but also . . ., In addition to . . . we also need to look at . . .,* and *Not only should we . . . but we should also . . . .* These transitions are generally indicated in your outline in square brackets.

### Previews

Preview transitions help the audience get a general idea of where you're going. For example, you might want to signal the part of your speech you're approaching and say something like, *By way of introduction . . .,* or *In conclusion . . .* or *Now, let's discuss why we are here today . . .,* or *So, what's the solution? What should we do?*

At other times, you might want to announce the start of a major proposition or piece of evidence and say something like, *An even more compelling argument . . .,* or *A closely related problem . . .,* or *My next point . . .,* or *If you want further evidence, just look at . . .*

### Reviews

It often helps to provide periodic reviews (sometimes called internal summaries), especially if your speech is long or complex. This review transition is a statement that reviews in brief what you've already said. It's a statement that usually recaps some major subdivision of your speech. Incorporate internal summaries into your speech—perhaps working them into the transitions connecting your main points. Notice how the internal summary presented below reminds listeners of what they've just heard and previews what they'll hear next.

Inadequate recreational facilities, poor schooling, and a lack of adequate role models seem to be the major problems facing our youngsters. Each of these, however, can be remedied and even eliminated. Here's what we can do.

### Signposts

Signpost transitions are individual words that tell listeners where you are in your speech and would include such terms as

> First, . . .
>
> A second argument . . .
>
> Next, consider . . .
>
> Thus, . . .
>
> Therefore, . . . ,
>
> So, as you can see . . .
>
> It follows, then, that . . .

## Common Faults in Introductions, Conclusions, and Transitions

In addition to understanding the principles of effective pubic speaking, it often helps to become aware of common mistakes. Here, then, are some of the common mistakes you'll want to avoid.

**In your introduction:**

- Don't apologize (generally). In the United States and western Europe, an apology may be seen as an excuse and so is to be avoided. In certain other cultures (those of Japan, China, and Korea are good examples), however, speakers are expected to begin with an apology. It's a way of complimenting the audience.

- Avoid promising something you won't deliver. The speaker who promises to tell you how to make a fortune in the stock market or how to be the most popular person on campus (and fails to deliver such insight) quickly loses credibility.

- Avoid gimmicks that gain attention but are irrelevant to the speech or inconsistent with your treatment of the topic. For example, slamming a book on the desk or telling a joke that bears no relation to your speech may accomplish the limited goal of gaining attention, but quickly the audience will see that they've been fooled and they'll resent it.

- Don't introduce your speech with ineffective statements such as "I'm really nervous, but here goes" or "Before I begin my talk, I want to say. . . ." These statements will make your audience uncomfortable and will encourage them to focus on your delivery rather than on your message.

**In your conclusion:**

- Don't introduce new material. Instead, use your conclusion to reinforce what you've already said and to summarize.

- Don't dilute your position. Avoid being critical of your own material or your presentation. Saying, for example, "The information I presented is probably dated but it was all I could find" or "I hope I wasn't too nervous" will detract from the credibility you've tried to establish.

■ Don't drag out your conclusion. End crisply.

**In your transitions:**

■ Avoid too many or too few transitions. Either extreme can cause problems. Use transitions to help your listeners, who will hear the speech only once, to understand the structure of your speech.

■ Avoid transitions that are out of proportion to the speech parts they connect. If you want to connect the two main points of your speech, you need something more than just "and" or "the next point." In contrast, if you want to connect two brief examples, then a simple "another example occurs when . . ." will do.

# Outlining the Speech

The **outline** is a blueprint for your speech; it lays out the elements of the speech and their relationship to one another. With this outline in front of you, you can see at a glance all the elements of organization considered here—the introduction and conclusion, the transitions, the main points and their relationship to the thesis and purpose, and the adequacy of the supporting materials. Like a blueprint for a building, the outline enables you to spot weaknesses that might otherwise go undetected.

Begin outlining at the time you start constructing your speech. Don't wait until you've collected all your material, but begin outlining as you're collecting material, organizing it, and styling it. In this way you'll take the best advantage of one of the major functions of an outline—to tell you where change is needed.

## Constructing the Outline

After you've completed your research and have mapped out an organizational plan for your speech, put this plan (this blueprint) on paper. That is, construct what is called a **preparation outline** of your speech, using the following guidelines.

### Preface the Outline with Identifying Data

Before you begin the outline proper, identify the general and specific purposes as well as your thesis. You also may want to include a working title—a title that you may change as you continue to polish and perfect your speech. This prefatory material should look something like this:

**What Do Media Do?**

| | |
|---|---|
| General purpose: | To inform. |
| Specific purpose: | To inform my audience of four functions of the media. |
| Thesis: | The media serve four functions. |

These identifying notes are not part of your speech proper. They're not, for example, mentioned in your oral presentation. Rather, they're guides to the preparation of the speech and the outline. They're like road signs to keep you going in the right direction and to signal when you've gone off course.

## Outline the Introduction, Body, and Conclusion as Separate Units

The introduction, body, and conclusion of the speech, although intimately connected, should be labeled separately and should be kept distinct in your outline. Like the identifying data above, these labels are not spoken to the audience but are further guides to your preparation.

By keeping the introduction, body, and conclusion as separate units, you'll be able to see at a glance if they do, in fact, serve the functions you want them to serve. You'll be able to see where there are problems and where repair is necessary. At the same time, make sure that you examine and see the speech as a whole—in which the introduction leads to the body and the conclusion summarizes your main points and brings your speech to a close.

## Insert Transitions

Insert [using square brackets] transitions between the introduction and the body, between the body and the conclusion, among the main points of the body, and wherever else you think they might be useful.

## Append a List of References

Some instructors require that you append a list of references to the written preparation outline of each of your speeches. If this is requested, then place the list at the end of the outline or on a separate page. Some instructors require that only sources cited in the speech be included in the list of references, whereas others require that the full list of sources consulted be provided (those mentioned in the speech as well as those not mentioned).

Whatever the specific requirements in your course, remember that source citations will prove most effective with your audience if you carefully integrate them into the speech. It will count for little if you consult the latest works by the greatest authorities but never mention this to your audience. So, when appropriate, weave into your speech the source material you've consulted. In your outline, refer to the source material by the author's name, date, and page in parentheses; then provide the complete citation in your list of references.

In your actual speech it might prove more effective to include the source with your statement. It might be phrased something like this:

> Sheena Lyenar, in her 2010 *The Art of Choosing,* argues that to be able to make choices, we need to first evaluate all the possible options.

## Use a Consistent Set of Symbols

The following is the standard, accepted sequence of symbols for outlining.

I.
   A.
      1.
         a.
            (1)
               (a)

# PUBLIC SPEAKING SAMPLE ASSISTANT

## A Preparation Outline with Annotations
### (Topical Organization)

**Self-Disclosure**

General purpose:   To inform.

Specific purpose:   To inform my audience of the advantages and disadvantages of self-disclosing.

Thesis:   Self-disclosure has advantages and disadvantages.

### INTRODUCTION

I. We've all heard them:

   A. I'm in love with my nephew.

   B. My husband is not my baby's father.

   C. I'm really a woman.

II. We've all disclosed.

   A. Sometimes it was positive, sometimes negative, but always significant.

   B. Knowing the potential consequences will help us make better decisions.

III. We look at this important form of communication in three parts:

   A. First, we look at the nature of self-disclosure.

   B. Second, we look at the potential rewards.

   C. Third, we look at the potential risks.

   [Let's look first at the nature of this type of communication.]

### BODY

I. Self-disclosure is a form of communication (Petronio, 2000; Erber & Erber, 2011).

   A. S-D is about the self.

      1. It can be about what you did.

      2. It can be about what you think.

   B. S-D is new information.

   C. S-D is normally about information usually kept hidden.

      1. It can be something about which you're ashamed.

      2. It can be something for which you'd be punished in some way.

   [Knowing what self-disclosure is, we can now look at its potential rewards.]

---

Generally the title, thesis, and general and specific purposes of the speech are prefaced to the outline. When the outline is an assignment that is to be handed in, additional information may be requested.

Note the general format for the outline: the headings (introduction, body, and conclusion) are clearly labeled and the sections are separated visually.

Notice that the introduction serves the three functions discussed in the text: it gains attention (by these extreme confessions); establishes an S–A–T connection (by noting that all of us, speaker and audience, have had this experience); and orients the audience (by identifying the three major ideas of the speech).

Note how the indenting helps you to see clearly the relationship that one item bears to another. For example, in Introduction I, the outline format helps you to see that A, B, and C are explanations (amplification and support) for I.

These brief statements are designed to get attention and perhaps a laugh or two, but also to introduce the nature of the topic.

Here the speaker seeks to establish a speaker–audience–topic connection.

Here the speaker orients the audience and explains the three parts of the speech. The use of guide phrases (first, second, third) helps the audience fix clearly in mind the major divisions of the speech.

This transition cues the audience that the speaker will consider the first of the major parts of the speech. Notice that transitions are inserted between all major parts of the speech. Although they may seem too numerous in this abbreviated outline, they'll be appreciated by your audience because the transitions will help them follow and understand your speech.

Notice the parallel structure throughout the outline. For example, note that II and III in the body are phrased in similar style. Although this may seem unnecessarily redundant, it will help your audience follow your speech more closely and will also help you in logically structuring your thoughts.

Note that the references are integrated throughout the outline just as they would be in a term paper. In the actual speech, the speaker might say something like: "Communication theorist Sandra Petronio presents evidence to show that. . . ."

These examples would naturally be recounted in greater detail in the actual speech. One of the values of outlining these examples is that you'll be able to see at a glance how many you have and how much time you have available to devote to each example. Examples, especially personal ones, have a way of growing beyond their importance to the speech.

This transition helps the audience see that the speaker is finished discussing what self-disclosure is and will now consider the potential rewards.

II. Self-disclosure has three potential rewards.

    A. It gives us self-knowledge.

    B. It increases communication effectiveness (Schmidt & Cornelius, 1987).

    C. It improves physiological health (Sheese, Brown, & Graziano, 2004).

    [Although these benefits are substantial, there are also risks.]

III. Self-disclosure has three potential risks.

    A. It can involve personal risks.

        1. This happened to a close friend.

        2. This also happened with well-known celebrities.

    B. It can involve relationship risks (Petronio, 2000).

        1. This happens on *Jerry Springer* five times a week.

        2. It also happened to me.

    C. It can involve professional risks (Korda, 1975; Fesko, 2001).

        1. This occurred recently at work.

        2. There are also lots of political examples.

    [Let me summarize this brief excursion into self-disclosure.]

### CONCLUSION

I. Self-disclosure is a type of communication.

    A. It's about the self, concerns something new, and something that you usually keep hidden.

    B. Self-disclosure can lead to increased self-knowledge, better communication, and improved health.

    C. Self-disclosure can also create risks to your personal, relational, and professional lives.

Note that each statement in the outline is a complete sentence. You can easily convert this outline into a phrase or keyword outline for use in delivery (see Public Speaking Sample Assistant, p. 160). The full sentences, however, will help you see more clearly relationships among items.

This transition connects what was just discussed to what will be discussed next.

As you see, transitions are inserted between all major parts of the speech. Although they may seem too numerous in this abbreviated outline, they'll be appreciated by your audience as useful aids that help them follow your speech.

This first part of the conclusion summarizes the major parts of the speech. The longer the speech, the more extensive the summary should be.

Notice that the Introduction's III A, B, and C correspond to the Body's I, II, and III, and to the Conclusion's I A, B, and C. This pattern will help you emphasize the major ideas in your speech—first in the orientation, second in the body of the speech, and third in the conclusion's summary.

Begin the introduction, the body, and the conclusion with roman numeral I. Treat each of the three major parts as a complete unit.

| Not This | This |
| --- | --- |
| Introduction | Introduction |
| I. | I. |
| II. | II. |
| Body | Body |
| III. | I. |
| IV. | II. |
| V. | III. |
| Conclusion | Conclusion |
| VI. | I. |
| VII | II. |

II. Self-disclosure is not only an interesting type of communication; it's also vital.

   A. You may want to explore this further by simply typing "self-disclosure" in your favorite search engine.

   B. If you want a more scholarly presentation, take a look at Sandra Petronio's *Balancing the Secrets of Private Disclosures* in the library or online.

III. The bottom line, of course: should you self-disclose?

   A. Yes.

   B. No.

   C. Maybe.

*This step, in which the speaker motivates the listeners to continue learning about self-disclosure, is optional in informative speeches. In persuasive speeches, you'd use this step to encourage listeners to act on your purpose—to vote, to donate time, to give blood, and so on.*

*This step provides closure; it makes it clear that the speech is finished. It also serves to encourage reflection on the part of the audience as to their own self-disclosing communication.*

### REFERENCES

Erber, R., & Erber, M. W. (2011). *Intimate relationships: Issues, theories, and research*, 2nd ed. Boston: Allyn & Bacon.

Fresko, S. L. (2001). Disclosure of HIV status in the workplace. *Health and Social Work 25*, 235–244.

Korda, M. (1975). *Power! How to get it, how to use it*. New York: Ballantine.

Petronio, S. (Ed.). (2000). *Balancing the secrets of private disclosures*. Mahwah, NJ: Erlbaum.

Schmidt, T. O., & Cornelius, R. R. (1987). Self-disclosure in everyday life. *Journal of Social and Personal Relationships, 4*, 365–373.

Sheese, B. E., Brown, E. L, & Graziano, W. G. (2004). Emotional expression in cyberspace: Searching for moderators of the Pennebaker disclosure effect via e-mail. *Health Psychology, 23* (September), 457–464.

*This reference list includes only the sources cited in the speech.*

### Use Complete Declarative Sentences

Phrase your ideas in the outline in complete declarative sentences rather than as questions or as phrases. This will further assist you in examining the essential relationships. It's much easier, for example, to see if one item of information supports another if both are phrased in the declarative mode. If one is a question and one is a statement, this will be more difficult.

## Sample Outlines

Now that the principles of outlining and organization are clear, here are some specific examples to illustrate how these principles are used in specific outlines. The accompanying Public Speaking Sample Assistant boxes present a variety of outlines.

# PUBLIC SPEAKING SAMPLE ASSISTANT

## Preparation Outline with Annotations
## (Motivated Sequence Organization)

This outline illustrates how you might construct an outline and a speech using the motivated sequence. To model the five steps in the motivated sequence, we'll return to the example given earlier in the chapter—the establishment of a youth center as a means of combating juvenile crime. In a longer speech, if you wanted to persuade an audience to establish a youth center, you might want to select two or three general arguments rather than limiting yourself to the one argument about reducing juvenile crime.

---

### The Youth Center

General purpose:   To persuade.

Specific purpose:   To persuade my listeners to vote in favor of Proposition 14 establishing a community youth center.

Thesis:   A youth center will reduce juvenile crime.

I. If you could reduce juvenile crime by some 20 percent by just flipping a lever, would you do it?

   A. Thom's drug store was broken into by teenagers.

   B. Loraine's video store windows were broken by teenagers.

II. Juvenile crime is on the rise.

   A. The overall number of crimes has increased.

      1. In 2001 there were 32 juvenile crimes.

      2. In 2004 there were 47 such crimes.

      3. In 2010 there were 63 such crimes.

**I. Attention step**

The speaker asks a question to gain attention and follows it with specific examples that audience members have experienced. The question and examples focus on one issue: the need to reduce juvenile crime. If the speech were a broader one that included other reasons for the center, then these would be previewed here as well.

**II. Need step**

The speaker states the need directly and clearly and shows that a problem exists. The speaker then demonstrates that the rise in crime is significant both in absolute numbers and in the severity of the crimes. To increase the listeners' ability to understand these figures, it would help if these figures were written on a whiteboard, on a prepared chart, or on Power-

## Preparation Outlines

The preparation outline is the main outline that you construct and—in most learning environments—turn in to your instructor. It is a detailed blueprint for your speech. Two preparation outlines are presented in the accompanying Public Speaking Sample Assistant boxes: a preparation outline following a topical organization starts on page 157 and a preparation outline following a motivated sequence pattern is above.

## Template Outlines

A **template outline,** like the templates you use for writing letters, résumés, greeting cards, or business cards, is a pre-established format into which you insert your specific information. A sample template outline for a speech using a topical organization pattern is presented in the Public Speaking Sample Assistant box on page 162. Note that in this template outline there are three main points (I, II, and III in the body). These correspond to the III A, B, and C of the

B. The number of serious crimes also has increased.

1. In 2010 there were 30 misdemeanors and 2 felonies.

2. In 2010 there were 35 misdemeanors and 28 felonies.

III. A youth center will help reduce juvenile crime.

A. Three of our neighboring towns reduced juvenile crime after establishing a youth center.

1. In Marlboro there was a 20 percent decline in overall juvenile crime.

2. In both Highland and Ellenville the number of serious crimes declined 25 percent.

B. The youth center will not increase our tax burden.

1. New York State grants will pay for most of the expenses.

2. Local merchants have agreed to pay any remaining expenses.

IV. Juvenile crime will decrease as a result of the youth center.

A. If we follow the example of our neighbors, our juvenile crime rates are likely to decrease by 20 to 25 percent.

B. Thom's store would not have been broken into.

C. Loraine's windows would not have been broken.

V. Vote *yes* on Proposition 14.

A. In next week's election, you'll be asked to vote on Proposition 14, establishing a youth center.

B. Vote *yes* if you want to help reduce juvenile crime.

C. Urge your family members, your friends, and your work colleagues also to vote *yes*.

Point slides. In a longer speech, other needs might also be identified in this step; for example, the need to offer teenagers a place where they can learn useful vocational and social skills.

III. Satisfaction step

In this step the speaker shows the listeners that the proposal to establish a youth center has great benefits and no significant drawbacks.

The speaker argues that the youth center will satisfy the need to reduce juvenile crime by showing statistics from neighboring towns. The speaker also answers the objection and removes any doubts about increased taxes. If the speaker had reason to believe that listeners might have other possible objections, those objections, too, should be answered in this step.

IV. Visualization step

Here the speaker visualizes what the town would be like if the youth center were established, using both the statistics developed earlier and the personal examples introduced at the beginning of the speech.

V. Action step

In this step the speaker asks listeners to take specific actions—to vote in favor of the youth center and to urge others to do the same. The speaker also reiterates the main theme of the speech; namely, that the youth center will help reduce juvenile crime.

---

introduction (in which you'd orient the audience), and to the I A, B, and C of the conclusion (in which you'd summarize your main points). The transitions are signaled by square brackets. As you review this outline, the faintly printed watermarks will remind you of the functions of each outline item. A variety of other template outlines are provided at **www.myspeechlab.com**.

## Delivery Outlines

After you construct your preparation outline, you can begin to construct your **delivery outline,** an outline consisting of key words or phrases that will assist you in delivering the speech. Resist the temptation to use your preparation outline to deliver the speech. If

**ETHICAL CHOICE POINT**

### Constructing an Outline

You have a speech due next week, and you're having trouble constructing your outline. But your friend, who is great at developing outlines, offers to help you write it. You could really use the help; also, in the process you figure you'll learn something about outlining. And besides, you'll fill in the outline, type it up, and present the speech. ➤*What are some of your ethical choices for getting a decent outline and yet not being dishonest?*

## PUBLIC SPEAKING SAMPLE ASSISTANT

### A Template Outline (Topical Organization)

Here's a template outline—a kind of template for structuring a speech. This particular outline would be appropriate for a speech using a topical organization pattern. Note that in this skeletal outline there are three main points (I, II, and III in the body). These correspond to the II A, B, and C in the introduction (where you'd summarize your main points). The transitions are signaled by square brackets. As you review this outline, the faintly printed watermarks will remind you of the functions of each outline item.

---

### Template Outline

General purpose:

your general aim (to inform, to persuade, to entertain)

Specific purpose:

what you hope to achieve from this speech

Thesis:

your main assertion; the core of your speech

#### INTRODUCTION

I. gain attention

II. establish speaker–audience–topic connection

III. orient audience

    A. first main point; same as I in body

    B. second main point; same as II in body

    C. third main point; same as III in body

[Transition:]

connect the introduction to the body

#### BODY

I. first main point

    A. support for I (the first main point)

---

you do use your preparation outline, you'll tend to read from it instead of presenting an extemporaneous speech in which you attend to and respond to audience feedback.

Instead, construct a brief delivery outline that will assist rather than hinder your delivery of the speech. A sample delivery outline based on the full-sentence preparation outline presented earlier on page 157 is presented in the Public Speaking Sample Assistant box.

Note first that the outline is brief enough so that you'll be able to use it effectively without losing eye contact with the audience. The outline uses abbreviations (for example, S-D for self-disclosure) and phrases rather than complete sentences. This helps to keep the outline brief and also helps you to scan your message more quickly.

B. further support for I

[Transition:]
connect the first main point to the second

II. second main point

  A. support for II (the second main point)

  B. further support for II

[Transition:]
connect the second main point to the third

III. third main point

  A. support for III

  B. further support for III

[Transition:]
connect the third main point (or all main points) to the conclusion

### CONCLUSION

I. summary

  A. first main point; same as I in body

  B. second main point; same as II in body

  C. third main point; same as III in body

II. motivation

III. closure

### REFERENCES

1. 
2. 
3. 

At the same time, however, the delivery outline is detailed enough to include all essential parts of your speech, including transitions. Be careful that you don't omit essential parts even if you're convinced that you couldn't possibly forget them. Normal apprehension may cause you to do exactly that.

This outline contains delivery notes specifically tailored to your own needs; for example, pause suggestions and guides to using visual aids.

The delivery outline is clearly divided into an introduction, body, and conclusion and uses the same numbering system as the preparation outline.

Rehearse with your delivery outline, not with your full-sentence preparation outline. This suggestion is simply a specific application of the general rule: Make rehearsals as close to the real thing as possible.

# PUBLIC SPEAKING SAMPLE ASSISTANT

## A Phrase/Key-Word Delivery Outline

### Self-Disclosure

PAUSE!

LOOK OVER THE AUDIENCE!

#### INTRODUCTION

I. We've heard them:
   A. "I'm in love with my nephew."
   B. "My husband is not my baby's father."
   C. "I'm really a woman."

II. We've all S-D
   A. sometimes 1, 2, significant
   B. consequences = better decisions

III. 3 parts: (WRITE ON BOARD)
   A. nature of S-D
   B. rewards
   C. risks

[1st = type of communication]

PAUSE, STEP FORWARD

#### BODY

I. S-D: communication
   A. about self
   B. new
   C. hidden information

[knowing what self-disclosure is, now rewards]

II. 3 rewards
   A. self-knowledge

   B. communication effectiveness
   C. physiological health

[benefits substantial, there are also risks]

PAUSE!

III. 3 risks
   A. personal
   B. relationship
   C. professional

[summarize: S-D]

#### CONCLUSION

I. S-D = communication
   A. about self, new, and usually hidden
   B. rewards: increased self-knowledge, better communication, and improved health
   C. risks: personal, relational, and professional

II. S-D not only interesting, it's vital
   A. explore further "S-D" into www
   B. scholarly: Sandra Petronio's *Boundaries*

III. Should you S-D?
   A. yes
   B. no
   C. maybe

PAUSE!

Any Questions?

# Next Steps

Once your speech is well organized—your main points are clear and well supported, your introduction and conclusion are developed to accomplish the goals you want, and the transitions are sufficient to hold the pieces of the speech together and provide signposts for the listeners—you can begin to devote attention to how you're going to word your speech (Step 8) to which the next chapter is addressed.

# Essentials of Organizing Your Speech

This chapter has covered ways to organize the body of the speech; prepare the introduction, conclusion, and transitions; and outline the speech.

## The Benefits of Organization

1. A well-organized speech will be easier for you to remember and also easier for the audience to follow and remember.

## Develop Your Main Points

2. Select the points that are most important to your thesis; combine those that have a common focus; select those that are most relevant to your audience; use few main points (two, three, or four work best); phrase your main points in parallel style; and separate your main points avoiding any overlap.

## Organize Your Main Points

3. In a temporal pattern your main ideas are arranged in a time sequence.

4. In a spatial pattern your main ideas are arranged in a space pattern—for example, left to right.

5. In a topical pattern your main ideas (equal in value and importance) are itemized.

6. In a problem–solution pattern your main ideas are divided into problems and solutions.

7. In a cause–effect pattern your main ideas are arranged into causes and effects.

8. In a motivated sequence pattern your main ideas are arranged into five steps: attention, need, satisfaction, visualization, and action.

9. Additional patterns include: structure-function, comparison-and-contrast, pro-and-con (advantages and disadvantages), claim-and-proof, multiple-definition, *Who? What? Why? Where? When?*, and fact-fiction.

10. In selecting an organizational pattern, take into consideration the cultural backgrounds of your listeners, especially the extent to which they are from low-context or high-context cultures.

## Construct Your Introduction, Conclusion, and Transitions

11. Construct your introduction so that it:
    - Gains attention.
    - Establishes a connection among speaker, audience, and topic.
    - Orients the audience.

12. Construct your conclusion so that it:
    - Summarizes your speech or some aspect of it.
    - Motivates your audience.
    - Provides crisp closure.

13. Use transitions to help the audience understand the flow of your speech. Use transitions to connect, preview, review, and to provide signposts.

14. Avoid the common problems of introductions, conclusions, and transitions:
    - Don't apologize.
    - Avoid promising what you won't deliver.
    - Don't rely on gimmicks.
    - Don't preface your introduction.
    - Avoid ineffective opening lines.
    - Don't introduce new material in your conclusion.
    - Don't dilute your position.
    - End crisply; don't drag out your conclusion.
    - Avoid too many or too few transitions
    - Avoid transitions that are out of proportion to the parts of the speech they connect.

## Construct Your Outline

15. Outlines may vary from complete sentence outlines to those with just key words and phrases. In constructing your outline: Preface the outline with identifying data; outline the introduction, body, and conclusion as separate units; insert transitions in square brackets; append a list of references (if required); use a consistent set of symbols; and use complete declarative sentences (for your preparation outline).

# Essential Terms

attention **(145)**
cause–effect pattern **(139)**
delivery outline **(161)**
high-context cultures **(144)**
low-context cultures **(144)**

motivated sequence **(139)**
orientation **(149)**
outline **(155)**
preparation outline **(155)**
problem–solution pattern **(138)**

spatial pattern **(137)**
template outline **(160)**
temporal pattern **(135)**
topical pattern **(135)**

# Public Speaking Exercises

## 7.1 Generating Main Points

One of the skills in organizing a speech is to ask a strategic question of your thesis and from the answer to generate your main points. Below are 10 thesis statements suitable for a variety of informative or persuasive speeches. For each thesis statement, ask a question and generate two, three, or four main points that would be suitable for an informative or persuasive speech.

Here's an example to get you started:

Thesis statement:     Mandatory retirement should be abolished.

Question:     Why should mandatory retirement be abolished?

I. Mandatory retirement leads us to lose many of the most productive workers.

II. Mandatory retirement contributes to psychological problems of those forced to retire.

III. Mandatory retirement costs businesses economic hardship because they have to train new people.

1. Buy American.
2. Tax property assets owned by religious organizations.
3. Require adoption agencies to reveal the names of birth parents to all adopted children when they reach 18 years of age.
4. Permit condom distribution in all junior and senior high schools.
5. Permit single people to adopt children.
6. Ban all sales of fur from wild animals.

7. Make the death penalty mandatory for those convicted of selling drugs to minors.
8. Require all students at this college to take courses on women's issues.
9. Legalize soft drugs.
10. Grant full equality to gay men and lesbians in the military.

## 7.2 Constructing Introductions and Conclusions

Prepare an introduction and a conclusion for a speech on one of the theses listed. Be prepared to explain the methods you used to accomplish each of these aims.

1. College isn't for everyone.
2. Maximum sentences should be imposed even for first offenders of the drug laws.
3. Each of us should donate our organs to science after our death.
4. Laws restricting Sunday shopping should be abolished.
5. Suicide and its assistance by others should be legalized.
6. Gambling should be legalized in all states.
7. College athletics should be abolished.
8. Same-sex marriage should be legalized.
9. Divorce should be granted immediately when there's mutual agreement.
10. Privatization of elementary and high schools should be encouraged.

# Log*On!* PEARSON myspeechlab

A variety of template outlines for different types of speeches are available at MySpeechLab (www.myspeechlab.com), as is an exercise on organizing a scrambled outline. You'll also find it useful to view one or more of the video speeches and consider how these speakers organized their speeches and what you might do differently. A self-test on flexibility raises a variety of issues about being able to adjust to different circumstances. In addition, explore some of the ways to construct better transitions and to use Microsoft's outlining tools.

# 8

# Word Your Speech (Step 8)

## WHY READ THIS CHAPTER?

**Because it will enable you to word your speech for greatest effectiveness by helping you to**

- select words that will communicate your thoughts clearly, vividly, appropriately, and in a personal style
- phrase your sentences so that they are clear and memorable

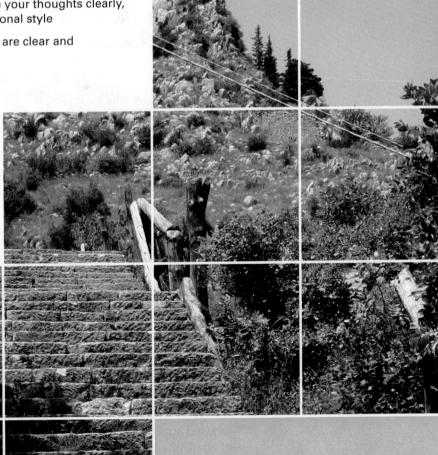

*One may walk over the highest mountain one step at a time.*

—JOHN WANAMAKER

Your success as a public speaker depends heavily on the way you express your ideas: on the words you select and the way you phrase your sentences. This chapter will focus on this crucial process of wording your speech, first explaining how language works and then suggesting ways to word and phrase your ideas for maximum impact and effectiveness.

# How Language Works

Your use of language will greatly influence your ability to inform and persuade an audience. Five qualities of language are especially important: directness, abstraction, objectivity, orality, and accuracy. In connection with this section, visit some of the online grammar guides to clarify anything about which you may not be sure. Among the many excellent sites are the grammar guides of Library Spot (**www.libraryspot.com**) and the University of Chicago (**http://writing-program.uchicago.edu**).

## Language Varies in Directness

Consider the following sentences:

| **Indirect** | **Direct** |
| --- | --- |
| We should all vote for Halliwell in the next election. | Vote for Halliwell in the next election. |
| It should be apparent that we should abandon the present system. | Abandon the present system. |
| Many people would like to go Xanadu. | How many of you want to go to Xanadu? |

Note that the direct sentences address the audience. The indirect sentences are more distant. Indirect sentences address only an abstract, unidentified mass of people. The sentences might as well address just anyone. In contrast, when you use direct sentences, you address your specific and clearly defined listeners.

Direct language is explicit and forthright. To achieve **directness,** use active rather than passive sentences; say, "The professor invented the serum" rather than "The serum was invented by the professor." Use personal pronouns and personal references. Refer to your audience as "you" rather than "the audience" or "my listeners."

The preference for directness will vary considerably with the culture of the speaker and the audience. Many Asian and Latin American cultures, for example, stress the values of indirectness, largely because indirectness enables a person to avoid appearing criticized or contradicted and thereby losing face. In most of the United States, however, you're taught that directness is the preferred style. "Be up-front" and "tell it like it is" are commonly heard communication guidelines. Many Asian Americans and Latin Americans may, in fact, experience a conflict between the recommendation of style manuals to be direct and the cultural recommendation to be indirect.

## Language Varies in Abstraction

Consider the following list of terms:

- entertainment
- film
- American film
- recent American film
- *Avatar*

At the top is the general or abstract term *entertainment*. Note that *entertainment* includes all the other items on the list plus various other items—television, novels, drama, comics, and so on. *Film* is more specific and concrete. It includes all of the items below it as well as various other items, such as Indian film or Russian film. The term excludes, however, all entertainment that is not film. *American film* is again more specific than *film* and excludes all films that are not American. *Recent American film* further limits *American film* to a time period. *Avatar* specifies concretely the one item to which reference is made. Choose words from a wide range of levels of **abstraction.** At times a general term may suit your needs best; at other times a more concrete, specific term may serve better. Generally, the specific term is the better choice.

The more general term—in this case, *entertainment*—conjures up numerous different images. One person in the audience may focus on television, another on music, another on comic books, and still another on radio. To some, *film* may bring to mind the early silent films. To others, it brings to mind postwar Italian films. To still others, it recalls Disney's animated cartoons. So as you get more specific and less abstract, you more effectively guide the images that come to your listeners' minds. Specific rather than abstract language will aid you in both your informative and persuasive goals.

## Language Varies in Objectivity

One way to explain how language varies in **objectivity**—in the degree to which it is factual and unemotional—is to introduce two new terms: **denotation** and **connotation.** The *denotative meaning* of a term is its objective meaning. This is the meaning that you'd find in a dictionary. This meaning points to specific references. Thus, the denotation of the word *book* is, for example, the actual book—a collection of pages bound together between two covers. The denotative meaning of *dog* is a four-legged canine; the denotative meaning of *kiss* is, according to the *Random House Dictionary*, "to touch or press with the lips slightly pursed in token of greeting, affection, reverence, etc."

*Connotative meaning*, however, is different. The connotative meaning is your affective, or emotional, meaning for the term. The word *book* may signify boredom or excitement. It may recall the novel you have to read or perhaps this textbook that you're reading right now. Connotatively, *dog* may mean friendliness, warmth, and affection. *Kiss* may, connotatively, mean warmth, good feeling, and happiness.

Seldom do listeners misunderstand the denotative meaning of a term. When you use a term with which the audience isn't familiar, you define it and thus make sure that the term is understood. Differences in connotative meanings, however, pose difficulties. For example, you may, use the term *neighbor*, intending to communicate security and friendliness. To some of your listeners, however, the term may connote unwanted intrusions, sneakiness, and nosiness. Notice that both you and your listeners would surely agree that denotatively *neighbor* means a person who lives near another person. What you and they disagree on—and what then leads to misunderstanding—is the connotation of the term.

Cultural differences add to the complexity and difficulty of accurately communicating meaning. The word *dog* will obviously mean one thing to a person from the United States, where *dog* signifies a "beloved pet," and quite another thing to a person from a culture where *dog* signifies "eating delicacy." *Beef* to a person from Kansas or Texas (where cattle provide much of the state's wealth) will mean something very different than *beef* does to a person from India (where the cow is a sacred animal).

As a speaker, consider the audience's evaluation of key terms before using them in your speech. When you're part of the audience, as in a public speaking class, you probably have a good idea of the meanings members have for various terms. When you address an audience very different from yourself, however, this prior investigation becomes crucial.

Good examples of the distinction between denotation and connotation can be seen in those language practices that seem, on the surface, to be denotative but are actually connotative: weasel words, euphemisms, and jargon.

**Weasel words** are words whose meanings are slippery and difficult to pin down (Pei, 1956; Hayakawa & Hayakawa, 1990). For example, a commercial claiming that Medicine M works "better than Brand X" doesn't specify how much better or in what respect Medicine M performs better. It's quite possible that it performs better in one respect but less effectively according to nine other measures. Other weasel words are *help, virtually, as much as, like* (as in "it will make you feel like new"), and *more economical*. Ask yourself, Exactly what is being claimed? For example, "What does 'may reduce cholesterol' mean? What exactly is being asserted?"

**Euphemisms** make the negative and unpleasant appear positive and appealing, as when a company calls the firing of 200 workers "downsizing" or "reallocation of resources." Often euphemisms take the form of inflated language designed to make the mundane seem extraordinary, the common seem exotic ("the vacation of a lifetime," "unsurpassed vistas"). When things sound too good to be true, they probably are.

**Jargon,** the specialized language of a particular group or profession (for example, the lingo of the computer hacker), becomes doublespeak when used with people who aren't members of the group and who don't know this specialized language. Jargon often intimidates, and that's one reason it's often used to confuse others and to put them in disadvantaged positions.

## ETHICAL CHOICE POINT

### Can You Sidestep Opposing Arguments?

You're giving a speech on homelessness and you want your listeners to contribute to the new homeless shelter that your community is building. In your research you discover that (1) the most recent statistics on the number of homeless people in your community are about 20 years old and (2) although many community leaders are in favor of building this halfway house, a sizable number object. You want to present the research accurately but at the same time you wonder if you have to identify opposing arguments or point out problems with your research. ➤*What are your ethical options for presenting an effective speech but without distorting data or misleading the audience?*

## Language Varies in Orality

**Orality** refers to the degree to which a communication style resembles that of informal conversation as opposed to the more formal style of writing. You don't speak as you write, nor should you. The main reason why spoken and written language should differ is that the listener hears a speech only once; therefore, speech must be *instantly intelligible*. The reader can reread an essay or look up an unfamiliar word; the reader can spend as much time as he or she wishes with the written page. The listener, however, must move at the pace set by the speaker. The reader may reread a sentence or paragraph if there's a temporary attention lapse; the listener doesn't have this option.

Generally, spoken language, or **oral style,** uses shorter, simpler, and more familiar words than does written language. Also, there's more qualification in speech than in writing. For example, when speaking you probably make greater use of such expressions as *although, however, perhaps,* and the like. When writing, you probably edit these out.

Spoken language has a greater number of self-reference terms (terms that refer to the speaker herself or himself): *I, me, our, us,* and *you*. Spoken language also has a greater number of "allness" terms such as *all, none, every, always, never*. When you write, you're probably more careful to edit out such allness terms, realizing that such terms are usually not very descriptive of reality.

Spoken language has more pseudo-quantifying terms (for example, *many, much, very, lots*) and terms that include the speaker as part of the observation (for example, "it seems to me that . . ." or "as I see it . . ."). Further, speech contains more verbs and adverbs; writing contains more nouns and adjectives.

## Language Varies in Accuracy

Language can reflect reality faithfully or unfaithfully. It can describe reality (as science tells us it exists) with great accuracy or with serious distortion. For example, we can use language to describe the many degrees that exist in, say, wealth, or we can describe wealth inaccurately in terms of two values, rich and poor. We can discuss the ways in which the accuracy of language may vary in terms of the five thinking errors central to the area of language study known as General Semantics (DeVito, 1974; Hayakawa & Hayakawa, 1990; Korzybski, 1933)—now so much a part of critical thinking instruction (Johnson, 1991). These five errors are polarization, fact–inference confusion, allness, static evaluation, and indiscrimination.

### Polarization

The term **polarization** refers to the tendency to look at the world in terms of opposites and to describe it in terms of extremes—good or bad, positive or negative, healthy or sick, intelligent or stupid, rich or poor, and so on. Polarization is often referred to as the "fallacy of either/or." So destructive is either/or thinking that the American Psychiatric Association identifies it as one of the major behavior characteristics of "borderline personality disorder"—a psychological disorder that lies between neurosis and psychosis and is characterized by unstable interpersonal relationships and confusion about identity.

Most people, events, and objects exist somewhere between the extremes of good and bad, health and sickness, intelligence and stupidity, wealth and poverty. Yet among all of us there's a strong tendency to view only the extremes and to categorize people, objects, and events in terms of these polar opposites.

Problems arise when polarization is used in inappropriate situations; for example, "The politician is either for us or against us." Note that these two options don't include all possibilities. The politician may be for us in some things and against us in other things, or may be neutral. Beware of speakers who imply and believe that two extreme classes include all possible classes—for example, that an individual must be pro–rebel forces or anti–rebel forces, with no other alternatives.

### Fact–Inference Confusion

Before reading about facts and inferences, take the following self-test.

## TEST YOURSELF

### Can You Distinguish Facts from Inferences?

Carefully read the following report and the observations based on it. Indicate whether you think the observations are true, false, or doubtful on the basis of the information presented in the report. Write *T* if the observation is definitely true, *F* if the observation is definitely false, and *?* if the observation may be either true or false. Judge each observation in order. Don't reread the observations after you've indicated your judgment, and don't change any of your answers.

*A well-liked college instructor had just completed making up the final examinations and had turned off the lights in the office. Just then a tall, broad figure with dark glasses appeared and demanded the examination. The professor opened the drawer. Everything in the drawer was picked up and the individual ran down the corridor. The dean was notified immediately.*

_____ **1.** The thief was tall and broad and wore dark glasses.

_____ **2.** The professor turned off the lights.

_____ **3.** A tall figure demanded the examination.

_____ **4.** The examination was picked up by someone.

_____ **5.** The examination was picked up by the professor.

_____ **6.** A tall, broad figure appeared after the professor turned off the lights in the office.

_____ **7.** The man who opened the drawer was the professor.

_____ **8.** The professor ran down the corridor.

_____ **9.** The drawer was never actually opened.

_____ **10.** Three persons are referred to in this report.

➤ **HOW DID YOU DO?** Number 3 is true, number 9 is false, and all the rest are "?" Review your answers by referring back to the story. To get you started, consider: Is there necessarily a thief? Might the dean have demanded to see the instructor's examination (statement 1)? Did the examination have to be in the drawer (statements 4 and 5)? How do you know it was the professor who turned off the lights (statement 6)? Need the professor have been a man (statement 7)? Do the instructor and the professor have to be the same person (statement 10)?

➤**WHAT WILL YOU DO?** There is, of course, nothing wrong with making inferences. When you hear inferential statements, however, treat them as inferences and not as facts. Be mindful of the possibility that such statements may prove to be wrong. As you read this next section, try to formulate specific guidelines that will help you distinguish facts from inferences.

In form or structure, facts and inferences are similar and can't be distinguished by any grammatical analysis. For example, you can say, "This proposal contains 17 pages" as well as "This proposal contains the seeds of its own self-destruction." Both sentences look similar in form, yet they're very different types of statements. You can observe the 17 pages, but how do you observe "the seeds of its own self-destruction"? Obviously, this isn't a descriptive but an inferential statement—a statement you make on the basis not only of what you observe, but on what you conclude.

In evaluating research, in presenting your information and arguments, and in listening to the speeches of others, beware of **fact–inference confusion;** be sure to distinguish between what is factual from what is inferential. Of course, there's nothing wrong with making inferences; the problem arises when you assume that an inference is a fact and treat it and behave as if it were a fact.

## Allness

Because the world is infinitely complex, we can never know all or say all about anything—at least we can't logically say all about anything. Beware of speakers who fall into the error of **allness**—who present information as if it's all that there is or as if it's all you need to know to make up your mind, as in, "There's only one way to save social security," "Never let financial considerations get in the way of romance," and "Always be polite."

"To be conscious that you are ignorant," said Benjamin Disraeli, famed British Prime Minister, "is a great step toward knowledge." This is an excellent expression of the non-allness attitude. If, as a critical listener, you recognize that there's more to learn, more to see, and more to hear, you'll treat what the speaker says as part of the total picture, not the whole, or the final word.

## Static Evaluation

Often when you form an abstraction of something or someone—when you formulate a verbal statement about an event or person—that statement remains static and unchanging. But the object or person to whom it refers has changed. Everything is in a constant state of change.

To avoid the error of **static evaluation,** respond to the statements of speakers as if they contain a tag that identifies the time frame to which they refer. Visualize each such statement as containing a date. Look at that date and ask yourself if the statement is still true today. Thus, when a speaker says that 10 percent of the population now lives at or below the poverty level, ask yourself about the date to which that statement applies. When were the statistics compiled? Does the poverty level determined at that time adequately reflect current conditions?

## Indiscrimination

Nature seems to abhor sameness at least as much as vacuums. Nowhere in the universe can you find two things that are identical. Everything is unique.

Language, however, provides you with common nouns (such as *teacher, student, friend, enemy, war, politician,* and *liberal*) that lead you to focus on similarities. Such nouns lead you to group all teachers together, all students together, all politicians together. These words divert attention away from the uniqueness of each individual, each object, and each event. **Indiscrimination,** then, is a thinking error that occurs when you focus on classes of individuals, objects, or events rather than on the unique individual, object, or event.

Of course, there's nothing wrong with classifying. No one would argue that classifying is unhealthy or immoral. On the contrary, it's an extremely useful method of dealing with any complex matter. Classifying helps us to deal with complexity. It puts order into our thinking. The problem arises from applying some evaluative label to that class, and then using that label as an "adequate" map for each individual in the group. Put differently, indiscrimination is a denial of uniqueness.

# RESEARCH LINK    ↳ News Sources

Often you'll want to read reports on scientific breakthroughs, political speeches, congressional actions, obituaries, financial news, international developments, United Nations actions, or any of a host of other topics. Or you may wish to select the time of a particular event and learn something about what else was going on in the world at that particular time. For this type of information you may want to consult one or more of the many news sources. Especially relevant are newspaper indexes, newspaper and newsmagazine websites, news wire services, and broadcast news networks.

■ **Newspaper indexes.** One way to start a newspaper search is to consult a newspaper index, such as www.all-links.com, www.newspapers.com, www.newslink.org, and www.newspaperlinks.com. At sites like these you'll find hot links to thousands of national and local newspapers.

■ **Newspaper and newsmagazine websites.** Most newspapers and magazines maintain their own websites from which you can access current and past issues. Here are a few to get you started: www.latimes.com (*Los Angeles Times*), www.usatoday.com (*USA Today*), www.wsj.com (*Wall Street Journal*), www.nytimes.com (the *New York Times*), and www.washingtonpost.com (the *Washington Post*).

■ **News wire services.** Four wire services should prove helpful. The Associated Press can be accessed at www.ap.org, Reuters at www.reuters.com, United Press International at www.upi.com, and PR Newswire at www.prnewswire.com. The advantage of getting your information from a news wire service is that it's more complete than you'd find in a newspaper; newspapers often must cut copy to fit space requirements and in some cases may put a politically or socially motivated spin on the news.

■ **News networks online.** All of the television news stations maintain extremely useful websites. Here are some of the most useful: Access CNN at www.cnn.com, ESPN at www.espn.go.com, ABC News at www.abcnews.com, CBS News at www.cbsnews.com, or MSNBC News at www.msnbc.com/news.

As you read these news sources, you'll find it helpful to compare the news available on one of the major newspapers' websites (for example, the *Washington Post* site or the *New York Times* site) with the news presented by a wire service such as the Associated Press or Reuters. Which seems the more reliable? The more complete? The more impartial?

The next Research Link, "The Web," appears on page 199.

Beware, therefore, of speakers who group large numbers of unique individuals under the same label. Beware of speakers who tell you that "Democrats are . . .," that "Catholics believe . . . ." that "Mexicans will . . ." Ask yourself, which Democrats, how many Catholics, which Mexicans, and so on.

# Choosing Words

Carefully choose the words you use in your public speeches. Choose words to achieve clarity, vividness, appropriateness, and a personal style.

## Clarity

**Clarity** in speaking style should be your primary goal. Here are some guidelines to help you make your speech clear.

### Be Economical

Don't waste words. Two of the most important ways to achieve economy are to avoid redundancies and to avoid meaningless words. Notice the redundancies in the following expressions. By removing the italicized terms you eliminate unnecessary words. You thus move closer to a more economical and clearer style.

| | |
|---|---|
| at 9 a.m. *in the morning* | *over*exaggerate |
| we *first* began the discussion | you, *members of the audience* |
| the full *and complete* report | *clearly* unambiguous |
| I *myself personally* | approximately 10 inches *or so* |
| blue *in color* | cash *money* |

### Use Specific Terms and Numbers

Picture these items:

- bracelet
- gold bracelet
- gold bracelet with a diamond clasp
- braided gold bracelet with a diamond clasp

Notice that as we get more and more specific, we get a clearer and more detailed picture. Be specific. Don't say *dog* when you want your listeners to picture a St. Bernard. Don't say *car* when you want them to picture a limousine. Don't say *television program* when you want them to think of *CSI: Los Angeles*.

The same is true of numbers. Don't say "earned a good salary" if you mean "earned $90,000 a year." Don't say "tuition will go up" when you mean "tuition will increase 32 percent." Don't say "the defense budget was enormous" when you mean "the defense budget was $100 billion."

### Use Signpost Phrases

Listening to a public speech is difficult work. Assist your listeners by using **signpost phrases** to help them see that you're moving from one idea to another, a suggestion made earlier in the discussion of transitions (p. 153). Use phrases such as "now that we have seen how . . ., let us consider how . . ." and "my next argument. . . ." Terms such as *first, second, and also, although*, and *however* will help your audience follow your line of thinking.

Signpost phrases are especially useful when your listeners aren't native speakers of the language you're speaking. And, of course, signpost phrases will also prove valuable if you're speaking in a language that you have not fully mastered. The phrases will help compensate for the lack of language and speech similarity between speaker and audience.

### Use Short, Familiar Terms

Generally, favor the short word over the long one. Favor the familiar word over the unfamiliar word. Favor the more commonly used term over the rarely used term. Say *harmless* rather than *innocuous, clarify* rather than *elucidate, use* rather than *utilize, find out* rather than *ascertain*.

### Use Repetition and Restatement

Repetition and restatement will help listeners follow what you're saying and will make your speech clearer and more easily understood. These are not the same as redundancy, which involves using unnecessary words that don't communicate any information. **Repetition** means repeating something in exactly the same way, usually at different points in your speech. This will help your listeners better remember the idea and remind them of how it's connected with what you're now saying. **Restatement** means rephrasing an idea or statement in different words. This is especially helpful when the idea is new or even moderately complex. Expressing the same idea in two different ways helps clarify the concept.

Another type of restatement is the internal summary. Internal summaries—periodic summary statements or reviews of subsections of your speech—help listeners appreciate the speech as a progression of ideas and show them how one idea leads to another. Be careful not to overuse these techniques, however; you don't want to bore the audience by repeating material that doesn't need to be repeated.

### Avoid Clichés

**Clichés** are phrases that have lost their novelty and part of their meaning through overuse. Avoid all clichés, which call attention to themselves because of their overuse. A few examples are:

| | |
|---|---|
| tell it like it is | for all intents and purposes |
| free as a bird | it goes without saying |
| in the pink | few and far between |
| no sooner said than done | no news is good news |
| tried and true | mind over matter |

### Distinguish between Commonly Confused Words

Many words, because they sound alike or are used in similar situations, are commonly confused. Underline the word in parentheses that you would use in each sentence.

1. He (accepted, excepted) the award and thanked everyone (accept, except) the producer.
2. The professor (affected, effected) her students greatly and will now (affect, effect) a complete curriculum overhaul.
3. Are you deciding (between, among) red and green or (between, among) red, green, and blue?
4. I (can, may) scale the mountain but I (can, may) not reveal its hidden path.
5. The table was (cheap, inexpensive) but has great style whereas the chairs cost a fortune but look (cheap, inexpensive).
6. The explorer's dream was to (discover, invent) uncharted lands but also to (discover, invent) computer programs.
7. She was (explicit, implicit) in her detailed description of the crime but made only (explicit, implicit) observations concerning the perpetrator.
8. He was evasive and only (implied, inferred) that he'd seek a divorce. You can easily (imply, infer) his reasons.
9. The wedding was (tasteful, tasty) and the food really (tasteful, tasty).
10. The student seemed (disinterested, uninterested) in the test while, in assigning grades, the teacher was always (disinterested, uninterested).

Here are the principles that govern correct usage in these examples. (1) Use *accept* to mean "to receive" and *except* to mean "with the exclusion of." (2) Use *to affect* to mean "to have an effect or to influence," and *to effect* to mean "to produce a result." (3) Use *between* when referring to two items and *among* when referring to more than two items. (4) Use *can* to refer to ability and *may* to refer to permission. (5) Use *cheap* to refer to something that is inferior and *inexpensive* to describe something that costs little. (6) Use *discover* to refer to the act of finding something out or to learn something previously unknown, and use *invent* to refer to the act of creating something new. (7) Use *explicit* to mean specific and *implicit* to describe something that's indicated but not openly stated. (8) Use *to imply* to mean "to state indirectly" and to *infer* to mean "to draw a conclusion." (9) Use *tasteful* to refer to good style and *tasty* to refer to something that is good to eat. (10) Use *uninterested* to refer to a lack of interest, and use *disinterested* to mean objective or unbiased.

## Carefully Assess Idioms

**Idioms** are expressions that are unique to a specific language (or regional dialect) and you cannot deduce their meaning from their individual words. So for example, you cannot infer the meaning of "kick the bucket" or "doesn't have a leg to stand on" from analyzing the individual words. Once you learn that "kick the bucket" means "die," the connection seems logical enough; but it's not a connection that you would have thought of merely by examining the words *kick* and *bucket*. Similarly, once you learn that "he doesn't have a leg to stand on" means "he doesn't have a reasonable argument" you can appreciate the idea behind the idiom—that is, that a position lacking reasonable arguments will collapse much as would a table (or a person) without legs.

The positive side of idioms is that they give your speech a casual and informal style; they make your speech sound like a speech and not like a written essay. The negative side of idioms is that they create problems for listeners who are not native speakers of your language. Many will simply not understand the meaning of your idioms. This problem is important, both because audiences are becoming increasingly intercultural and because the number of idioms we use is extremely high. If you're not convinced of this, read through any of the speeches in this text, especially in an intercultural group, and underline all idioms. You will no doubt find that you underline a great deal more than you would have suspected.

## Vividness

Select words to make your ideas vivid and come alive in the minds of your listeners (Frey & Eagly, 1993; Meade, 2000). You want your listeners to see as well as hear your thoughts.

### Use Active Verbs

Favor verbs that communicate activity rather than passivity. The verb *to be*, in all its forms—*is, are, was, were, will be*—is relatively inactive. Try using verbs of action instead. Rather than saying, "The teacher was in the middle of the crowd," say, "The teacher stood in the middle of the crowd." Instead of saying, "The report was on the president's desk for three days," try, "The report sat (or slept) on the president's desk for three days." Instead of saying, "Management will be here tomorrow," consider "Management will descend on us tomorrow" or "Management jets in tomorrow."

### Use Strong Verbs

The verb is the strongest part of your sentence. Instead of saying "He walked through the forest," consider such terms as *wandered, prowled, rambled,* or *roamed.* Consider whether one of these might not better suit your intended meaning. Consult a thesaurus for any verb you suspect might be weak. A good guide to identifying weak verbs is to look at your use of adverbs. If you use lots of adverbs, you may be using them to strengthen weak verbs. Consider cutting out the adverbs and substituting stronger verbs. Instead of *walked quickly* consider *ran, sped,* or *flew*; instead of *spoke softly* consider *whispered* or *murmured.*

### Use Figures of Speech

**Figures of speech** are stylistic devices that have been a part of rhetoric since ancient times. Figures of speech help achieve vividness, in addition to making your speech more memorable and giving it a polished, well-crafted sound (Borchardt, 2006). But be careful not to overdo the use of figures of speech. If you do, your speech is likely to sound overly prepared and not as spontaneous as it should. With this caveat, here are some figures that you may wish to incorporate into your public speeches.

- **Alliteration:** the repetition of the same initial sound in two or more words as in "fifty famous flavors" or "the cool, calculating leader" or "the characteristics of credibility are competence, character, and charisma."
- **Hyperbole:** the use of extreme exaggeration, as in "He cried like a faucet" or "I'm so hungry I could eat a whale."
- **Irony:** the use of a word or sentence whose literal meaning is the opposite of that which is intended; for example, a teacher handing back failing examinations might say, "So pleased to see how hard you all studied."

- **Metaphor:** an implied comparison between two unlike things, as in "She's a lion when she wakes up" or "He's a real bulldozer" or as Shakespeare said in Hamlet, "I will speak daggers but use none." References to the legs of a table, the mouth of a river, and the arms of destiny also are metaphors, though we seldom think of them as such.

- **Simile:** like metaphor, compares two unlike objects but uses the words *like* or *as*; for example, "The manager is as gentle as a lamb," "Pat went through the problems like a high-speed drill," "Chris always acts like a weasel."

- **Synecdoche:** using a part of an object to stand for the whole object, as in "all hands were on deck," in which hands stands for "sailors" or "crew members"; or "green thumb" for "expert gardener."

- **Metonymy:** the substitution of a name for a title with which it's closely associated, as in "City Hall issued the following news release," in which City Hall stands for "the mayor" or "the city council."

- **Antithesis:** the presentation of contrary or polar opposite ideas in parallel form, as in "My loves are many, my enemies are few" or in Charles Dickens's opening to *A Tale of Two Cities*: "It was the best of times, it was the worst of times," or John F. Kennedy's "Ask not what your country can do for you; ask what you can do for your country."

- **Personification:** the attribution of human characteristics to inanimate objects—"This room cries out for activity" or "My car is tired."

- **Rhetorical questions:** questions that are used to make a statement or to produce a desired effect rather than secure an answer—"Do you want to be popular?" "Do you want to get well?"

- **Oxymoron:** a term or phrase that combines two normally opposite qualities: bittersweet, the silent roar, poverty-stricken millionaires, the ignorant genius, or a war for peace.

Public Speaking Exercise 8.1, "Creating Figures of Speech," on page 190 provides some suggestions for developing creative figures of speech.

## Use Imagery

Appeal to the senses through visual, auditory, and tactile **imagery.** Make us see, hear, and feel what you're talking about.

**Visual Imagery.** In describing people or objects, create images your listeners can see. When appropriate, describe such visual qualities as height, weight, color, size, shape, length, and contour. Let your audience see the sweat pouring down the faces of the coal miners; let them see the short, overweight executive in a pinstriped suit smoking a cigar. Here Stephanie Kaplan (Reynolds & Schnoor, 1991), a student from the University of Wisconsin, uses visual imagery to describe the AIDS Quilt:

> The Names Project is quite simply a quilt. It's larger than 10 football fields, and composed of over 9,000 unique 3-feet-by-6-feet panels each bearing a name of an individual who has died of AIDS. The panels have been made in homes across the country by the friends, lovers, and families of AIDS victims.

**Auditory Imagery.** Appeal to our sense of hearing by using terms that describe sounds. Let your listeners hear the car screeching, the wind whistling,

**PUBLIC SPEAKING CHOICE POINT: Speaking Style**
Rochelle is asked to give a presentation on the library's new and complex online services to a group of faculty members. What kinds of advice would you give Rochelle concerning her speaking style? For example, should she strive for a personal or an impersonal style? Should she signal immediacy or distance? Would your advice differ if Rochelle's audience were a freshman communication class instead of faculty members?

the bells chiming, the angry professor roaring.

**Tactile Imagery.**   Use terms referring to temperature, texture, and touch to create tactile imagery. Let your listeners feel the cool water running over their bodies and the punch of the fighter; let them feel the smooth skin of the newborn baby.

## Appropriateness

Use language that is appropriate to you as the speaker. Also, use language that is appropriate to your audience, the occasion, and the speech topic. Here are some general guidelines to help you achieve this quality.

### Speak on the Appropriate Level of Formality

The most effective public speaking style is (usually but not always) less formal than the written essay but more formal than conversation. One way to achieve an informal style—if this seems the appropriate style on the basis of your audience analysis—is to use contractions. Say *don't* instead of *do not*, *I'll* instead of *I shall*, and *wouldn't* instead of *would not*. Contractions give a public speech the sound and rhythm of conversation—a quality that most listeners react to favorably.

Use personal pronouns rather than impersonal expressions. Say, "I found" instead of "it became evident," or "I will present three arguments" instead of "there are three arguments."

Do remember, as noted elsewhere, that the expected and desirable level of formality will vary greatly from one culture to another and from one situation to another. Part of the art of using language effectively is to be able to adjust your speaking style to the unique situation.

### Avoid Unfamiliar Terms

Avoid using terms the audience doesn't know. Avoid foreign and technical terms unless you're certain the audience is familiar with them. Similarly, avoid jargon (the technical vocabulary of a specialized field) unless you're sure the meanings are clear to your listeners. Some acronyms (NATO, UN, NOW, and CORE) are probably familiar to most audiences; most, however, are not. When you wish to use any of these types of expressions, fully explain their meaning to the audience.

### Avoid Slang

Avoid **slang** or other expressions that risk offending audience members, embarrassing them, or making them feel you have little respect for them. Although your listeners may themselves use such expressions, they often resent their use by public speakers. So avoid any words or examples that may be considered "off-color."

## Avoid Racist, Sexist, Ageist, and Heterosexist Terms

Avoid referring to culturally different groups with terms that carry negative connotations; be careful not to portray groups in stereotypical and negative ways.

- **Avoid racist language or any expressions that can be considered disparaging to members of a particular ethnic group.** Using unintentionally **racist language**—qualifying someone with a racial identifier that is neither relevant nor necessary—is perhaps the most frequent mistake speakers make. For example, referring to a "Chicano professor" or an "African American mathematician" can imply that you're pointing to the rareness of Hispanics' being professors or of African Americans' being mathematicians.

- **Use nonsexist language. Sexist language** is language that's derogatory to one gender (usually women). To avoid it, use gender-neutral terminology. Use *human* instead of *man* to include both sexes; use *she* and *he* instead of *he;* use *police officer* instead of *policeman* and *firefighter* instead of *fireman*. Avoid sex-role stereotyping; for example, avoid making the hypothetical elementary school teacher female and the college professor male. Avoid referring to doctors as male and nurses as female. Avoid noting the gender of a professional with terms such as "lady lawyer" or "male nurse." When you're referring to a specific lawyer or nurse, the person's gender will become clear when you use the appropriate pronoun.

- **Avoid ageist expressions or language that discriminates against people because of age.** Avoid **ageist language**, language that insults older people such as "old-timer," "little old lady," or "over the hill." As with racism, ageism also can creep in when you qualify or describe the abilities of an older person. For example, when you refer to a "quick-witted 75-year-old" or a "responsible teenager," you're indicating that those qualities are unusual in people in those age groups. You're saying that quick-wittedness and being 75 years old do not normally go together and that the fact that they do in this case merits special mention. You imply the same abnormality for the linking of "responsible" and "teenager."

- **Avoid heterosexist language, language that disparages gay men and lesbians.** As with racist language, **heterosexist language** can take the form of derogatory terms for lesbians and gay men as well as more subtle kinds of language usage. As with racist and sexist language, when you qualify a professional identifier—as in "gay athlete" or "lesbian doctor"—you're in effect stating that athletes or doctors are not normally gay or lesbian. Also, you're making the affectional orientation more important than it probably should be in the context of, as in the examples, sports or medicine.

Once brought to awareness, most people recognize the moral legitimacy of using language that is inclusive and refraining from using racist, sexist, ageist, or heterosexist words or phrases. There are also rhetorical reasons for avoiding such language:

**PUBLIC SPEAKING CHOICE POINT: Offensive Language**

Michael wants to illustrate the negative effects of racist language by using these derogatory terms throughout his speech—to further drive home the point of the pain they can cause. If Michael were addressing your class, what options would he have for making his point and yet not offending anyone?

- It's likely to offend a significant part of your audience.

- It's likely to draw attention to itself and away from what you're saying.

- It's likely to reflect negatively on your own credibility.

## Avoid Language that Disparages People with Disabilities

In addition to being sensitive to cultural differences, develop sensitivity to those in your audience who may have one or more disabilities. Scan your audience for any listeners who may have difficulty in hearing or seeing you. Don't identify them or in any way call attention to them, but keep their needs in mind as you present your speech. Here are just a few suggestions for such a situation; these hints would be helpful with any audience but are especially significant when your listeners have sight or hearing disabilities.

- If there are people in the audience who are blind or partially sighted, explain your visual aids in a bit more detail. For example, instead of saying, "As you can see from the graph, we're in good shape," consider saying, "As you can see from this graph, which shows a 40 percent increase in sales, we're in good shape." If you're using handouts, be especially sure to explain fully what their purpose is, and make it a point to reiterate the information on them. If you're writing on the whiteboard, say aloud what you're writing.

- If you notice persons with hearing deficits, be sure to maintain an adequate volume (loudness) and to speak distinctly. Be especially careful not to drop your voice at the ends of sentences. If you see your audience leaning forward or struggling to hear you, increase your volume.

- Use normal vocabulary, and don't avoid topics that you would speak on to (for example) an audience of all sighted people with good hearing. Don't avoid terms such as *see, hear, look, listen,* or even *blind* or *deaf.* Don't avoid illustrating your speech with an example from a television show or a song.

- Try to eliminate as much "noise" as you can. For example, audible noise might include the sounds of voices in nearby hallways or other classrooms; visual noise might take the form of sun washing out the colors on your slides. Sometimes something as simple as closing the door or pulling the shades is all that's necessary to make your speech more understandable.

- In talking about people with disabilities, use language that emphasizes the person rather than the disability. Refer to "persons with disabilities" rather than "disabled persons." If your speech topic requires you to discuss people with a specific disability, be sure you have done adequate research on the terms preferred by that population. For example, many people born with *achondroplastic dwarfism* prefer to be referred to as "little people." In general, people with disabilities are able in most respects; in only some situations does the specific disability come into play.

And, of course, persons with disabilities have responsibilities too. So if you have hearing problems, take a seat close to the front of the room. If you hear better in one ear than the other, be sure to position yourself on the proper side of the room. If you have vision problems, be sure to bring your glasses and to sit as close to the front as possible.

## Avoid Ethnic Expressions (Generally)

**Ethnic expressions** are words and phrases that are peculiar to a particular ethnic or language group. At times these expressions are known only by members of the ethnic group; at other times they are known more widely but still recognized as ethnic expressions.

When you are speaking to a multicultural audience, it's generally best to avoid ethnic expressions unless they're integral to your speech and you explain them. Such expressions often seem exclusionist—that is, they highlight the connection between the speaker and the members of that particular ethnic group and the lack of connection between the speaker and all others who are not members of that ethnic group. And, of course, ethnic expressions should never be used if you're not a member of the ethnic group.

If, on the other hand, you're speaking to an audience from one ethnic group and you're also a member of that group, then such expressions are fine. Politicians who run in districts in which they and the voters are of the same national origin or language community will frequently use ethnic terms or even phrases in the native language of the audience. In these cases ethnic expressions may well prove effective; they are part of the common language of speaker and audience and will help to stress your similarities with the audience.

## Use Preferred Cultural Identifiers

One useful way to avoid racism, sexism, ageism, and heterosexism is to examine the **cultural identifiers** to use (and not to use) in talking about members of different cultures. As always, when in doubt, find out. The preferences and many of the specific examples identified here are drawn largely from the findings of the Task Force on Bias-Free Language of the Association of American University Presses (Schwartz, 1995). Although not everyone necessarily agrees with these recommendations; they're presented here—in the words of the Task Force—"to encourage sensitivity to usages that may be imprecise, misleading, and needlessly offensive" (Schwartz, 1995, p. ix). They're not presented so that you can "catch" someone being "politically incorrect" or label someone "culturally insensitive." More recent discussions support these suggestions (for example, Goshgarian, 2009; UC Davis, A Guide to Bias Free Communication, http://ccc.ucdavis.edu/bias_free_communication.pdf).

**Race and Nationality.** Generally, most African Americans prefer *African American* to *black* (Hecht, Collier, & Ribeau, 1993), though *black* is often used with *white* and is used in a variety of other contexts (for example, Department of Black and Puerto Rican Studies, the *Journal of Black History*, and Black History Month). The terms *negro* and *colored*, although used in the names of some organizations (for example, the United Negro College Fund and the National

Association for the Advancement of Colored People), are not used outside of these contexts.

*White* is generally used to refer to those whose roots are in European cultures and usually does not include Hispanics. Analogous to *African American* is the term *European American*. Few "European Americans," however, want to be called that; most prefer their national origins emphasized, as in, for example, *German American* or *Greek American*. This preference may well change as Europe moves into a more cohesive and united entity. *People of color*—a literary-sounding term that may be appropriate in public speaking, but may seem awkward in most conversations—is preferred to *nonwhite*, which implies that whiteness is the norm and non-whiteness is a deviation from that norm. The same is true of the term *non-Christian*.

Generally, *Hispanic* is used to refer to anyone who identifies himself or herself as belonging to a Spanish-speaking culture. *Latina* (female) and *Latino* (male) refer to people with roots in Latin American countries such as the Dominican Republic, Nicaragua, or Guatemala. *Hispanic American* refers to U.S. residents whose ancestry is culturally Spanish and includes people of Mexican, Caribbean, and Central and South American origins. But in emphasizing a Spanish heritage, the term is really inadequate, because large numbers in the Caribbean and in South America have French or Portuguese roots. *Chicana* (female) and *Chicano* (male) refer to those with roots in Mexico, though it often connotes a nationalist attitude (Jandt, 2006) and is considered offensive by many Mexican Americans. *Mexican American* is preferred. Similarly, equating "illegal immigrants" with Mexicans, rather than recognizing the term as applying to citizens of any other country who enter the United States illegally, is naturally offensive and should be avoided.

*Inuk* (the plural is *Inuit*) was officially adopted at the Inuit Circumpolar Conference to refer to the indigenous peoples of Alaska, northern Canada, Greenland, and eastern Siberia. This term is preferred to *Eskimo* (a term the U.S. Census Bureau uses), which was applied to the indigenous peoples of Alaska by Europeans and derives from a term that means "raw meat eaters" (Maggio, 1997).

*Indian* technically should refer only to someone from India; it is incorrectly used when applied to citizens of other Asian countries or to the indigenous peoples of North America. *American Indian* or *Native American* is preferred, even though many Native Americans refer to themselves as "Indians" and "Indian people." The term *native American* (with a lowercase *n*) is most often used to refer to persons born in the United States. Although the term technically could refer to anyone born in North or South America, people outside the United States generally prefer more specific designations such as *Argentinean*, *Cuban*, or *Canadian*. The term *native* refers to a person born in a particular place and is distinguished from *stranger* or *foreigner*; it's not used to mean "someone having a less developed culture."

When history was being written with a European perspective, Europe was taken as the focal point and the rest of the world was defined in terms of its location from Europe. Thus, Asia became "the East" or "the Orient" and Asians became *Orientals*—a term that is today considered inappropriate or "Eurocentric." Thus, people from Asia are *Asians*, just as people from Africa are *Africans* and people from Europe are *Europeans*.

**Religon.** *Muslim* is the preferred form (rather than the older *Moslem*) to refer to a person who adheres to the religious teachings of Islam. *Quran* (rather than *Koran*) is the preferred term for the scriptures of Islam. The terms *Mohammedan* or *Mohammedanism* are not considered appropriate; they imply worship of Muhammad, the prophet, "considered by Muslims to be a blasphemy against the absolute oneness of God" (Maggio, 1997, p. 277). *Jewish people* is generally preferred to *Jews*; and *Jewess* (a Jewish female) is considered derogatory. *Jew* should be used only as a noun and is never correctly used as a verb or an adjective (Maggio, 1997).

**Gender.** Generally, the term *girl* should be used only to refer to very young females and is equivalent to *boy*. Neither term should be used for people older than, say, 13 or 14. *Girl* is never used to refer to a grown woman, nor is *boy* used to refer to persons in blue-collar positions, as it once was. *Lady* is negatively evaluated by many because it connotes the stereotype of the prim and proper woman. *Woman* or *young woman* is preferred.

**Age.** *Older person* is preferred to *elder, elderly, senior,* or *senior citizen* (which technically refers to someone older than 65). Usually, however, terms designating age are unnecessary. There are times, of course, when you'll need to refer to a person's age group, but most of the time it isn't—in much the same way that racial or affectional orientation terms are usually irrelevant.

**Affectional Orientation.** Generally, *gay* is the preferred term to refer to a man who has an affectional preference for other men and *lesbian* is the preferred term for a woman who has an affectional preference for other women. (*Lesbian* means "homosexual woman," so the phrase "lesbian woman" is redundant.) *Homosexual* refers to both gay men and lesbians but more often to a sexual orientation to members of one's own sex. *Gay* and *lesbian* refer to a lifestyle and not just to sexual orientation. *Gay* as a noun, although widely used, may prove offensive in some contexts; for example, in the remark "We have two gays on the team." Although used within the gay community in an effort to remove the negative stigma through frequent usage, the term *queer*—as in "queer power" or "queer studies"—is often resented when used by outsiders. Because much scientific thinking holds that sexuality is not a matter of choice, the term *affectional orientation* is preferred to *sexual preference* or *sexual status* (which are also vague) (Rogers, 2001; Wright, 1999).

## Personal Style

Audiences favor speakers who speak in a **personal style** rather than in an impersonal way; they prefer speakers who speak with them rather than at them. Personal style sounds more like conversation than like lecturing and so the audience feels more comfortable "talking" rather than "being talked to."

### Use Personal Pronouns

Say *I* and *me* and *he* and *she* and *you*. Avoid such impersonal expressions as *one* (as in "One is led to believe . . .") or *this speaker*, or *listeners*. These expressions distance the audience and create barriers rather than bridges. Use personal pronouns in addressing the audience: Say *you* rather than *students*; say "you'll enjoy reading . . ." instead of "everyone will enjoy reading."

**PUBLIC SPEAKING CHOICE POINT: Language Differences**

Greg, an anthropology professor, is to give an address on the topic of violence in schools twice in one day: first to the junior class at the local high school and later that day to the Education Department of his college. What options does Greg have for tailoring his speech to his specific audience? Put differently, what are some of the ways these two speeches might differ? In what ways do you think they *should* differ?

## Use Questions

Ask the audience questions to involve them. In a small audience, you might even briefly entertain responses. In larger audiences, you might ask the question, pause to allow the audience time to consider their responses, and then move on. When you direct questions to your listeners, they feel a part of the public speaking transaction.

## Create Immediacy

**Immediacy** is a connectedness, a relatedness with one's listeners. Immediacy is the opposite of disconnected and separated. Here are some suggestions for creating immediacy through language.

- Use personal examples.
- Use terms that include both you and the audience; for example, *we* and *our*.
- Use specific names of audience members when appropriate.
- Express concern for the audience members.
- Reinforce or compliment the audience.

- Refer directly to commonalities between you and the audience, for example, "We are all children of immigrants" or "We all want to see our team in the playoffs."
- Refer to shared experiences and goals; for example, "We all want, we all need a more responsive PTA."
- Recognize audience feedback and refer to it in your speech. Say, for example, "I can see from your expressions that we're all anxious to get to our immediate problem."

Books about words abound on the Internet and will prove helpful in your choice of words. Visit the Internet Public Library (**www.ipl.org/ref**) or the Reference Desk (**www.refdesk.com**) and search for dictionaries, thesauruses, and related wordbooks.

# Phrasing Sentences

Give the same careful consideration that you give to words to your sentences as well. Here are some guidelines to help you make your sentences clear and persuasive.

## Use Powerful Sentences

Usually, in public speaking, you'd want to use a relatively powerful style—a style that is certain, definite, and persuasive. Perhaps the first step to achieving a powerful style of speech is to recognize the powerless forms that you may use now and may wish to lessen or eliminate (Molloy, 1981; Kleinke, 1986; Johnson, 1987; Dillard & Marshall, 2003; Lakoff, 1975; Timmerman, 2002). As you consider the powerless forms below, think of your own speech and how you can, should the occasion call for it, eliminate these forms to make it more powerful.

- **Hesitations.** Generally, hesitations (for example, "I, er, want to say that, ah, this one is, er, the best, you know, it's like") make you sound unprepared and uncertain.

- **Too many intensifiers.** When you use intensifiers too often, you weaken the forcefulness of your message. Intensifiers make your speech monotonous and don't allow you to stress what you do want to emphasize. When too many sentences contain words ending in –est, consider revising your sentences to stress only what you really want stressed.

- **Disqualifiers.** Statements such as "I didn't read the entire article, but . . . ." "I didn't actually see the accident, but . . . ." generally signal a lack of competence and a feeling of uncertainty. Qualify your statements as needed but just avoid unnecessary comments on your lack of preparedness or knowledge.

- **Tag questions.** When questions ask for agreement, they often contain a tag at the end that asks for agreement, for example, "That was a great movie, wasn't it?" "She's brilliant, don't you think?" These types of sentences often signal your need for agreement—and hence your own uncertainty. As a result they appear powerless—as if the power is in the person answering your question.

- **Self-critical statements.** Statements such as "I'm not very good at this." "This is my first public speech" may signal a lack of confidence and may make public and in fact highlight your own inadequacies.

- **Slang and vulgar language.** The reason that slang and vulgar language have little place in public speaking is that they signal low social class and hence little power.

As you read the remaining suggestions, you'll note that they too will make your sentences more powerful. Public Speaking Exercise 8.2, "Giving Life to Your Sentences," on page 190 offers some suggestions for making your sentences more effective.

## Use Short Sentences

Short sentences are more forceful and economical. They are easier to comprehend and they are easier to remember. Listeners don't have the time or the inclination to unravel long and complex sentences. Help them to listen more efficiently by using short rather than long sentences.

## Use Direct Sentences

Direct sentences are easier to understand. They are also more forceful. Instead of saying, "I want to tell you of the three main reasons why we should not adopt Program A," say "We should not adopt Program A. I'm going to focus on three main reasons."

## Use Active Sentences

Active sentences are easier to understand. They also make your speech seem livelier and more vivid. Instead of saying "The lower court's decision was reversed by the Supreme Court," say "The Supreme Court reversed the lower court's decision." Instead of saying "The proposal was favored by management," say "Management favored the proposal."

## Use Positive Sentences

Positive sentences are easier to comprehend and remember. Notice that the sentences under "This" are easier to understand that those under "Not this."

| Not This | This |
|---|---|
| The committee did not accept the proposal. | The committee rejected the proposal. |
| This committee does not work within the normal company hierarchy. | This committee works outside the normal company hierarchy. |

## Vary the Types of Sentences

The advice to use short, direct, active, and positive sentences is valid most of the time. Yet too many sentences of the same type or length will make your speech sound boring. Use variety while following (generally) the preceding advice. Here are a few special types of sentences that should prove useful, especially for adding variety, vividness, and forcefulness to your speech.

### Parallel Sentences

**Parallel sentences** convey ideas in parallel (similar, matching) style for ease of comprehension and memory. Note the parallelism in "This" and its absence in the "Not this" sentences.

| Not This | This |
|---|---|
| The professor prepared the lecture, the examination was graded, and she read the notices. | The professor prepared the lecture, graded the examination, and read the notices. |
| Love needs two people. Just one can create jealousy. | Love needs two people to flourish. Jealousy needs but one. |

### Antithetical Sentences

**Antithetical sentences** juxtapose contrasting ideas in parallel fashion. In his inaugural speech, President John F. Kennedy phrased one of his most often quoted lines in antithetical structure:

Ask not what your country can do for you; ask what you can do for your country.

## Periodic Sentences

In **periodic sentences** you reserve the key word until the end of the sentence. In fact, the sentence is not grammatically complete until you say this last word. For example, in "Looking longingly into his eyes, the old woman fainted," the sentence doesn't make sense until the last word is spoken.

# Next Steps

With your speech worded effectively, you're ready to begin the final two steps: rehearsing your speech (Step 9) and then presenting it (Step 10), topics of the next chapter.

# Essentials of Wording Your Speech

In this chapter we looked at how language works and at how you can use language to better achieve your public speaking goals.

### How Language Works

1. Language Varies in Directness.
2. Language Varies in Abstraction.
3. Language Varies in Objectivity.
4. Language Varies in Orality.
5. Language varies in accuracy and inaccuracy (including errors such as polarization, fact–inference confusion, allness, static evaluation, and indiscrimination).

### Choosing Words

6. Clarity: Be economical; be specific; use signpost phrases; use short, familiar terms; use repetition and restatement; avoid clichés; avoid misusing commonly confused words.
7. Vividness: Use active verbs; use strong verbs; use figures of speech; use imagery.

8. Appropriateness: Speak on the appropriate level of formality; avoid unfamiliar terms; avoid slang and vulgar terms; avoid racist, sexist, ageist, and heterosexist expressions; avoid ethnic expressions (generally); use preferred cultural identifiers.
9. Personal style: Use personal pronouns; ask questions; create immediacy.

### Phrasing Sentences

10. Use powerful sentences, avoiding hesitations, too many intensifiers, disqualifiers, tag questions, self-critical statements, and slang.
11. Use short rather than long sentences.
12. Use direct rather than indirect sentences.
13. Use active rather than passive sentences.
14. Use positive rather than negative sentences.
15. Vary the types and lengths of sentences, making use of parallel, antithetical, and periodic sentences.

# Essential Terms

| | | |
|---|---|---|
| abstraction **(169)** | figures of speech **(178)** | periodic sentences **(189)** |
| ageist language **(181)** | heterosexist language **(181)** | personal style **(185)** |
| alliteration **(178)** | hyperbole **(178)** | personification **(179)** |
| allness **(173)** | idioms **(177)** | polarization **(171)** |
| antithesis **(179)** | imagery **(179)** | racist language **(181)** |
| antithetical sentences **(188)** | immediacy **(186)** | repetition **(176)** |
| clarity **(175)** | indiscrimination **(174)** | restatement **(176)** |
| cliché **(176)** | irony **(178)** | rhetorical question **(179)** |
| connotation **(169)** | jargon **(170)** | sexist language **(181)** |
| cultural identifiers **(183)** | metaphor **(179)** | signpost phrases **(175)** |
| denotation **(169)** | metonymy **(179)** | simile **(179)** |
| directness **(168)** | objectivity **(169)** | slang **(180)** |
| ethnic expressions **(183)** | oral style **(171)** | static evaluation **(173)** |
| euphemism **(170)** | oxymoron **(179)** | synecdoche **(179)** |
| fact–inference confusion **(173)** | parallel sentences **(188)** | weasel words **(170)** |

# Public Speaking Exercises

## 8.1 Creating Figures of Speech

For each of the following concepts, develop a figure of speech (choose from among alliteration, hyperbole, irony, metaphor, simile, synecdoche, metonymy, antithesis, personification, rhetorical question, oxymoron, or other figures with which you're familiar):

1. a wonderful meal
2. the great speech
3. moderation is a virtue
4. he made a fortune
5. their love for each other is something else
6. the thief was big
7. the apartment was immaculate
8. she lived a good life
9. happiness is the only real goal
10. go green

## 8.2 Giving Life to Your Sentences

Here are some rather bland sentences. Improve each of them by making them clearer, more vivid, more appropriate, and more personal.

1. The teacher was discussing politics.
2. The player scored.
3. Only three of the previously mentioned people agreed.
4. The children each received presents.
5. I read the review of the movie.
6. The couple rented a great car.
7. The detective wasn't much help.
8. The animal approached the baby.
9. He walked up the steep hill.
10. They played games.
11. The cat climbed the fence.
12. The house is in the valley.

# Log *On!* PEARSON **my speech**lab

**MySpeechLab** (www.myspeechlab.com) for Chapter 8 offers a variety of aids for improving your use of language and style in public speaking. Additional guidelines for effective speech style are offered under Author Choice. Watch Martin Luther King Jr.'s "I have a dream" speech: In connection with this chapter's Research Link on News Sources, take a look at the *New York Times* Feed.

# 9

# Rehearse and Present Your Speech (Steps 9 and 10)

## WHY READ THIS CHAPTER?

**Because it will enable you to deliver your speech with effective voice and action by helping you to:**

- improve your public speaking delivery through systematic rehearsal
- use your voice (volume, rate, pitch, and pauses, for example) to your best advantage
- use nonverbal communication (eyes, face, body posture, gestures, and movements) to further your speech purpose

*Step by step and the thing is done.*

—CHARLES ATLAS

In this chapter, we'll focus on delivery skills that will help you achieve your speech purpose. After all, the best organized and researched speech, if delivered poorly, is not going to have the effect you want it to have. Let's start with considering some guidelines for rehearsing your speech.

# Rehearse Your Speech (Step 9)

Through rehearsal you can develop delivery skills that will help you achieve the purposes of your speech. Rehearsal also will enable you to time your speech and to see how the speech will flow as a whole. Additionally, rehearsal will help you test out your presentation aids, detect any technological problems, and resolve them. And, of course, through rehearsal you'll learn your speech, so you'll be more confident when you deliver it. This confidence will help to reduce your apprehension. The following procedures should assist you in achieving these goals.

## Rehearse the Speech as a Whole

Rehearse the speech from beginning to end. Don't rehearse the speech in parts. Rehearse it from getting out of your seat, through the introduction, body, and conclusion, to returning to your seat. Be sure to rehearse the speech with all the examples and illustrations (and audiovisual aids if any) included. This will enable you to connect the parts of the speech and to see how they interact with one another.

## Time the Speech

Time the speech during each rehearsal. Make any necessary adjustments on the basis of this timing. If you're using computer presentation software, you'll be able to time your speech very precisely. Such software will also enable you to time the individual parts of your speech so you can achieve the balance you want—for example, you might want to spend twice as much time on the solutions as on the problems, or you might want to balance the introduction and conclusion so that each constitutes about 10 percent of your speech.

## Approximate the Actual Speech Situation

Rehearse the speech under conditions as close as possible to those under which you'll deliver it. If possible, rehearse the speech in the same room where you'll present it. If this is impossible, try to simulate the actual conditions as closely as you can—in your living room or even in a bathroom. If possible, rehearse the speech in front of supportive listeners; one study found that students who practiced their speeches before an audience received higher grades than those who practiced without an audience (Smith & Frymier, 2006). It's always helpful (especially for your beginning speeches) if your listeners are supportive rather than critical—but merely having listeners present during your rehearsal will further simulate the conditions under which you'll eventually speak. Get together with two or three other students in an empty classroom where you can each serve as speaker and listener.

## Incorporate Changes and Delivery Notes

Don't interrupt your rehearsal to make notes or changes; if you do, you may never experience the entire speech from beginning to end. But do make any needed changes in the speech between rehearsals. While making these changes, note any words whose pronunciation or articulation you wish to check. Also, insert pause notations, "slow down" warnings, and other delivery suggestions into your outline.

If possible, record your speech (ideally on video) so you can hear exactly what your listeners will hear: your volume, rate, pitch, articulation and pronunciation, and pauses. You'll then be in a better position to improve these qualities.

## Rehearse Often

Rehearse the speech as often as seems necessary. Two useful guides: (1) Rehearse the speech at least three or four times; less than this is sure to be too little. And (2) rehearse the speech as long as your rehearsals continue to produce improvements in the speech or in your delivery.

## Undertake a Long-Term Delivery Improvement Program

To become a truly effective speaker, you may need to undertake a long-term delivery improvement program. Approach this project with a positive attitude: Tell yourself that you can do it and that you will do it.

- **Seek feedback.** Secure feedback from someone whose opinion and insight you respect. Your public speaking instructor may be a logical choice, but someone majoring in communication or working in a communication field might also be appropriate. Get an honest and thorough appraisal of both your voice and your bodily action.

- **See, hear, and feel the differences between effective and ineffective patterns.** For example, is your pitch too high or your volume too loud? A tape recorder will be very helpful. Learn to sense your rigid posture or your lack of arm and hand gestures. Once you've perceived these voice and/or body patterns, concentrate on learning more effective habits. Practice a few minutes each day. Avoid becoming too conscious of any source of ineffectiveness. Just try to increase your awareness and work on one problem at a time. Do not try to change all your patterns at once.

- **Seek additional feedback on the changes.** Make certain that listeners agree that the new patterns you're practicing really are more effective. Remember that you hear yourself through bone conduction as well as through air transmission. Others hear you only through air transmission. So what you hear and what others hear will be different.

- **For voice improvement, consult a book on voice and diction.** These will provide exercises for practice and additional information on the nature of volume, rate, pitch, and quality.

- **If difficulties persist, see a professional.** For voice problems, see a speech clinician. Most campuses have a speech clinic, and you can easily avail yourself of its services. For bodily action difficulties, talk with your public speaking instructor.

- **Seek professional help if you're psychologically uncomfortable with any aspect of your voice or bodily action.** It may be that all you have to do is to hear yourself or see yourself on a video—as others hear and see you—to convince yourself that you sound and look just fine. Regardless of what is causing this discomfort, however, if you're uncomfortable, do something about it. In a college community there's more assistance available to you at no cost than you'll ever be offered again. Make use of it.

With these rehearsal guidelines in mind, consider your actual presentation, beginning with defining what make for effective public speaking presentation.

# 10 Deliver Your Speech (Step 10)

This last step is the reason for all the others and will prove challenging, exciting, scary, difficult, and much more. Here we define the nature of effective presentation, the methods of presentation you might use, and ways to use your voice and bodily action to best advantage.

## What Is Effective Presentation?

Perhaps the most important characteristic of effective public speaking presentation is that it depends. What makes for effectiveness in one situation and with one speaker will not necessarily prove effective in another situation with a different speaker. And to complicate matters just a bit, audiences differ in what they consider effective delivery—some audiences expect and enjoy a lively entertaining style while others will prefer a more subtle, intellectualized presentation. Public Speaking Exercise 9.1, "Communicating Vocally but Nonverbally," on page 211 provides an interesting way to practice using your voice and bodily action to communicate more effectively.

You'll want to develop a presentation style that works for you while remaining flexible in adjusting that presentation style to the uniqueness of the specific public speaking situation. Nevertheless, amid these qualifications we can offer a few suggestions as to what constitutes effective presentation.

- **Comfortable.** Your presentation style should be comfortable to you. It should feel natural to you, and it should look natural to the audience. It should not appear phony or in any way unnatural.

- **Consistent.** Your presentation style should be consistent with all the other public speaking factors you've considered throughout your preparation. If your speech is on a humorous topic, then your presentation style is likely to be lighthearted. If your speech were on a more somber topic (such as the death penalty), then your presentation style would likely be fairly serious.

■ **Interesting.** Your presentation should add interest and some variety into your speech. Much like your language contributes to the interest of your speech, so does your delivery. If you stand motionless, it's not likely to prove terribly interesting. At the same time, you don't want to run around the room just to add interest which, in this case, would draw attention away from your speech.

■ **Contributes to the speech.** Your presentation style should contribute to your speech; it should add some degree of clarity to what you're saying. For example, moving a half step forward or to the side when introducing a main point might help reinforce your verbal transition. In addition, your presentation style—whatever that is—should not call attention to itself and away from the message of your speech. Your presentation style should reinforce your verbal message.

## Methods of Presentation

Public speakers vary greatly in their methods of presentation. Some speak off-the-cuff, with no apparent preparation (impromptu); others read their speeches from the printed text (manuscript). Some construct a detailed outline and create the speech itself at the moment of delivery (extemporaneous).

Still others memorize their speeches—a method that is not recommended. The major disadvantage of a **memorized speech** (actually more of an oral interpretation presentation than a public speech) is that you might forget your speech. In a memorized speech each sentence cues the recall of the following sentence. Thus, when you forget one sentence, you may forget the rest of the speech. Another disadvantage is that memorizing makes it virtually impossible to adjust to audience feedback. And if you're not going to adjust to feedback, you lose the main advantage of face-to-face contact.

Here we'll consider the impromptu, manuscript, and extemporaneous methods of presentation along with some general suggestions for using each method. These delivery suggestions—as you'll see—will also prove helpful in managing your apprehension. As you develop more control and comfort over your voice and bodily action in public speaking, you'll relax and feel more comfortable. These feelings will then help reduce your fear of public speaking.

### Speaking Impromptu

When you give an **impromptu speech,** you speak without any specific preparation or advance thinking. You and the topic meet for the first time, and immediately the speech begins. On some occasions you will not be able to avoid speaking impromptu. In a classroom, after someone has spoken, you may comment on the speech you just heard in a brief impromptu speech of evaluation. In asking or answering questions in an interview situation, you're giving impromptu speeches, albeit extremely short ones. At meetings you may find yourself speaking impromptu as you explain a proposal or defend a plan of action; these, too, are impromptu speeches. The ability to speak impromptu effectively depends on your general public speaking ability. The more proficient a speaker you are, the better you'll be able to function impromptu.

The impromptu experience provides excellent training in different aspects of public speaking, such as maintaining eye contact; responding to audience feedback; gesturing; organizing ideas; and developing examples, arguments, and appeals. The major disadvantage of speaking impromptu is that it does not permit attention to details of public speaking such as audience adaptation, research, and style.

When you are called upon to speak impromptu, the following suggestions should prove useful.

- Don't apologize. Everyone has difficulty speaking impromptu and there's no need to emphasize any problems you may have.

- Don't express verbally or nonverbally any displeasure or any negative responses to the experience, the topic, the audience, or even yourself. Approach the entire task with a positive attitude and a positive appearance. It will help make the experience more enjoyable both for you and for your audience.

- When you have to speak impromptu, jot down two or three subtopics that you'll cover and perhaps two or three bits of supporting material that you'll use in amplifying these two or three subtopics.

- Develop your conclusion. It will probably be best to use a simple summary conclusion in which you restate your main topic and the subtopics that you discussed.

- Develop an introduction. Here it will probably be best simply to identify your topic and orient the audience by telling them the two or three subtopics that you'll cover.

## Speaking from Manuscript

With a **manuscript speech**, you write out the entire speech exactly as you want it to be heard by your audience, and read it to the audience. Because the manuscript method allows you to control exactly what you'll say, it may be the logical method to use in, politics, for example, where an ambiguous phrase might prove insulting or belligerent and cause serious problems.

One of the major advantages of a manuscript speech is that you control the timing precisely. This is particularly important when you are delivering a speech that will be recorded (on television, for example). Also, there's no danger of forgetting an important point; everything is there for you on paper. Still another advantage is that the manuscript method allows you to use the exact wording you (or a team of speech writers) want. The most obvious disadvantage is that it's difficult to read a speech and sound natural and non-mechanical. Reading material from the printed page or a teleprompter with liveliness and naturalness is itself a skill that is difficult to achieve without considerable practice. Audiences don't like speakers to read their speeches. Also, reading a manuscript makes it difficult to respond to feedback from your listeners. And when the manuscript is on a stationary lectern, as it most often is, it's impossible for you to move around. You have to stay in one place. The speech controls your movement or, rather, your lack of movement.

When speaking from manuscript, consider the following suggestions.

- Write out your speech with an eye to oral presentation. Try to hear what your words will sound like as you write them down.

- Mark up your manuscript with delivery notes. Write in pause points—especially important in manuscript speaking because of the tendency to read quickly. Underline or boldface key terms that you want to stress.

- Be sure to maintain eye contact. Even though you're reading from manuscript, you are still delivering a speech and it should sound as natural and extemporaneous as possible. Rehearse your speech so that you can alternate looking at the manuscript with looking at the audience.

- Use large fonts that you'll be able to see easily without squinting or putting the manuscript up to your nose.

- Make page breaks coincide with natural breaks in the speech. Don't separate sentences or even main points on two different pages.

- Use only one side of the paper and number the pages clearly to reduce any chance of losing your place.

- Even when speaking from manuscript, memorize your first few opening lines and your last few closing lines. In this way you'll be able to maintain eye contact with the audience.

## Speaking Extemporaneously

An **extemporaneous speech** involves thorough preparation and a commitment to memory of the main ideas and their order (and, if you wish, your introduction and conclusion). There is, however, no commitment to exact wording for the remaining parts of the speech.

Extemporaneous delivery is useful in most speaking situations. Good college lecturers use the extemporaneous method. They prepare thoroughly and know what they want to say and in what order they want to say it, but they have given no commitment to exact wording.

One advantage of this method is that it allows you to respond easily to feedback. Should audience feedback suggest that a point needs clarification, for example, you can rephrase the idea or give an example. Extemporaneous delivery is the method that comes closest to conversation—a kind of "enlarged conversation." With this method you can move about and interact with the audience.

Here are a few guidelines for using the extemporaneous method—the method recommended for your classroom speeches and for most of the speeches you'll deliver throughout your life.

- Memorize the opening and closing lines; this will help you focus your complete attention on the audience and will put you more at ease. Similarly, memorize the main points and the order in which you'll cover them; this will free you from relying on your notes and will make you feel more in control of the speech and of the entire speech-making situation.

- Speak naturally. Listeners will enjoy your speech and believe you more if you speak as if you were conversing with a small group of people. Don't allow your delivery to call attention to itself. Your ultimate aim should be to deliver the speech so naturally that the audience won't even notice your delivery.

■ Use delivery to reinforce your message. All aspects of your delivery—your voice, bodily action, and general appearance, for example—should work together to make your ideas instantly intelligible to your audience.

■ Vary your delivery. Variety in voice and bodily action will help you maintain your listeners' attention. Vary your vocal volume and your rate of speaking. In a similar way, avoid standing in exactly the same position throughout the speech. Use your body to express your ideas, to communicate to the audience what is going on in your head.

■ Create immediacy with delivery. Make your listeners feel that you're talking directly and individually to each of them: Maintain appropriate eye contact with the audience members, talk directly to your audience and not to your notes or to your visual aids, smile when it's appropriate and consistent with your speech purpose, and maintain a physical closeness that reinforces a psychological closeness (don't stand behind the desk or lectern).

■ Be expressive. You can do this by allowing your facial muscles and your entire body to reflect and echo your inner involvement. Use gestures appropriately. Too few gestures may signal lack of involvement; too many may communicate uneasiness, awkwardness, or anxiety. Carefully read the feedback signals sent by your audience and respond to these signals with verbal, vocal, and bodily adjustments.

The remaining sections of this chapter will explain how you can use your voice and your bodily action to most effectively communicate your thoughts and feelings. In conjunction with reading about what makes for effective presentation, visit American Rhetoric at **www.americanrhetoric.com/speechbank .htm** for lots of links to Internet sites containing full text, audio, and video versions of public speeches. More general sites include YouTube (**www .youtube.com**) and Video Surf (**www.videosurf.com**). These sites as well as MySpeechLab (**www.myspeechlab.com**) will enable you to see effective delivery in action.

# Effective Vocal Delivery

You can achieve effective vocal delivery by mastering your volume, rate, pitch, articulation and pronunciation, and pauses. Let's look at each in turn.

## Volume

The word **volume** refers to the relative intensity of the voice. (The word *loudness* refers to the hearer's perception of that relative intensity.) In an adequately controlled voice, volume will vary according to several factors. For example, the distance between you and your listeners, the competing noise, and the emphasis you wish to give an idea will all influence your volume.

# RESEARCH LINK → The Web

It's convenient to think of the web as a three-part system consisting of the open, deep, and social web.

**The open web** (or visible or surface) consists of those materials that you'd be able to access with a simple search from most of your favorite search engines or directories. When you do a simple Google search, for example, you'd be accessing the open web.

**The deep web** (or invisible or hidden or deepnet)—estimated to be perhaps 50 times the size of the open web—contains that collection of documents that are not accessible through simple searches on general search engines or directions. These include databases of scholarly articles and academic research journals that are available only for a fee that your college library pays and that the publishers of textbooks that come with online research access. It also includes all those websites for which you need a password to enter. Images and video files would also be considered as residing on the deep web.

**The social web** (actually a part of the deep web but since it deals with a unique type of material, it's helpful to consider it as a separate category) consists of the millions of blogs, Facebook pages, tweets, newsgroups, and listservs. Blogs are extremely popular and often contain information that may be useful in public speaking. You can locate blogs easily with a variety of search engines (for example, www .blogsearch.google.com). Like websites, blogs (web logs) vary greatly in their usefulness to the public speaker. Some blogs are just personal ramblings (perhaps useful for examples or illustrations), some guide you to additional online materials (useful for locating information you might not have found otherwise), and some contain the thoughts and ideas of experts in a wide variety of fields. Generally, don't assume that anything on a blog is reliable and accurate; check first.

Clicking on "more" (on Bing, Google, or Yahoo!, for example) will provide searches for lots (but not all) deep web materials. This is changing and more and more of the deep web is being accessed through simple searches.

In most cases, searching the World Wide Web efficiently requires the use of search engines and subject directories, plus some knowledge of how these tools operate. A *search engine* is a program that searches a database or index of Internet sites for the specific words you submit. Search engines search an enormous number of websites but do not distinguish between reliable and unreliable information. A high school student's term paper may well be listed next to that of a world-famous scientist with no distinction between them. These search engines are easily accessed through your Internet browser.

Some search engines are *meta–search engines*; these search the databases of a variety of search engines at the same time. These programs are especially useful if you want a broad search and you have the time to sift through lots of websites. Some of the more popular meta-search engines include Ask at www.ask.com, Google at www.google.com, Dog Pile at www.dogpile.com, and Vivisimo at www .vivisimo.com. Other useful search engines (some of which also contain directories) include Yahoo! (www.yahoo.com), AltaVista (www.altavista.com), and Go (www.go.com).

In using search engines (and in searching many CD-ROM databases), you'll find it helpful to limit your search with *operators*—words and symbols that define relationships among the terms for which you're searching. Perhaps the most common are AND (or +), OR, NOT (or –), and quotation marks. Searching for *drugs AND violence* will limit your search to only those documents that contain both words—in any order. Searching for *drugs OR violence* will expand your search to all documents containing either word. And searching for *violence AND schools NOT elementary* will yield documents containing both *violence* and *schools* except those that contain the word *elementary*. Quotation marks around the phrase will yield only those sources that use the exact phrase; so, if you search for "drugs in New York City" it will identify primarily those sources in which that exact phrase appears. Be careful when using quotes; if you searched with only the example just given, you'd miss articles that do not use the exact phrase but which still deal with the topic you're researching.

Another way to limit your topic and refine your search is to use a search engine that limits its search to only certain types of websites. For example, if you want to search for publications of the U.S. government, it will prove more efficient to search with Google's government search (www.google.com/unclesam). With this search you'll retrieve only those websites that have a .gov domain. If you want to search for blogs you can use Google's blog search (www.blogsearch.google.com).

You can also search the web by setting up alerts. For example, you can go to Google Alerts (www.google.com/alerts) or Yahoo (http://alerts.yahoo.com) and enter your speech topic and the kind of search you want (whether news, Web, news and Web, for example) and how often you want to receive them. You'll then receive e-mail alerts with links to sites that include your speech topic.

A *directory* is a list of subjects or categories of Web links. You select the category you're most interested in, then a subcategory of that, then a subcategory of that, until you reach your specific topic. A directory doesn't cover everything; rather, the documents that it groups under its various categories are selected by the directory's staff members from those they deem to be especially worthwhile. Many search engines also provide directories, so you can use the method you prefer.

Learn about the search engines and directories that will help you find the information you need, and learn how to use them efficiently. Most search engines and directories work similarly, so you should be able to use essentially the same strategies with one that you use with another. However, each search engine and directory uses a somewhat different database; if you don't find what you want with one search engine or directory, try another.

The next Research Link, "Evaluating Internet Resources," appears on page 220.

Problems with volume are easy to identify in others, though difficult to recognize in ourselves. One obvious problem is a voice that is too soft. When speech is so soft that listeners have to strain to hear, they'll soon tire of expending so much energy. On the other hand, a voice that is too loud will prove disturbing because it intrudes on listeners' psychological space; it also may communicate aggressiveness and give others the impression that you are difficult to get along with.

The most common problems are too little volume variation and variation that falls into an easily predictable pattern. If the audience can predict volume changes, they'll focus on that pattern and not on what you're saying.

Fading away at the end of sentences is particularly disturbing. Some speakers begin sentences in an appropriate volume but end them at an extremely low volume. Be careful to avoid this tendency; when finishing sentences, make sure the audience is able to hear at an appropriate volume.

## Rate

Your speech **rate** is the speed at which you speak. About 150 words per minute seem to be the average for speaking as well as for reading aloud. The problems with rate are speaking too fast or too slow, speaking with too little variation, or speaking with too predictable a pattern. If you talk too fast, you deprive your listeners of time they need to understand and digest what you're saying; they may simply decide not to spend the energy needed to understand your speech. If your rate is too slow, your listeners' attention may wander to matters unrelated to your speech. Speak at a pace that engages the listeners and allows them time for reflection without boring them.

Use variations in rate to call attention to certain points and to add variety. For example, if you speak of the dull routine of an assembly line worker at a rapid and varied pace, or of the wonder of a circus with no variation in rate,

**PUBLIC SPEAKING CHOICE POINT: Speaking Volume**
After sitting through two rounds of speeches, Carmella wonders if the class wouldn't
be ready for a speech spoken at noticeably higher volume than normal—rather like
television commercials, which are played louder than the regular broadcast. What
would you advise Carmella to do?

you're surely misusing this important vocal dimension. Again, if you're interested in and conscious of what you're saying, your rate variations should flow
naturally and effectively.

## Pitch

**Pitch** is the relative highness or lowness of your voice as perceived by your listener. More technically, pitch results from the rate at which your vocal cords
vibrate. If they vibrate rapidly, listeners will perceive your voice as having a
high pitch. If they vibrate slowly, they'll perceive it as having a low pitch.

Pitch changes often signal changes in the meanings of many sentences.
The most obvious is the difference between a statement and a question. Thus,
the difference between the declarative sentence "So this is the proposal you
want me to support" and the question "So this is the proposal you want me to
support?" is inflection or pitch. This, of course, is obvious. But note that depending on where the inflectional change is placed, the meaning of the sentence changes drastically. Note also that all of the following questions contain
exactly the same words, but they each ask a different question when you emphasize different words:

- Is *this* the proposal you want me to support?
- Is this the proposal *you* want me to support?
- Is this the proposal you want *me* to support?
- Is this the proposal you want me to *support*?

The obvious problems with pitch are levels that are too high, too low, or too patterned. Neither of the first two problems is common in speakers with otherwise normal voices, and with practice you can correct a pitch pattern that is too predictable or monotonous. As you gain speaking experience, pitch changes will come naturally from the sense of what you're saying. Because each sentence is somewhat different from every other sentence, there should be a normal variation—a variation that results not from some predetermined pattern but rather from the meanings you wish to convey to the audience.

## Pauses

**Pauses** come in two basic types: filled and unfilled. Filled pauses are pauses in the stream of speech that you fill with vocalizations such as *er, um, ah, well,* and *you know.* Filled pauses are ineffective and will make you appear hesitant, unprepared, and unsure of yourself.

Unfilled pauses—silences interjected into the normally fluent stream of speech—can be effective in public speaking if used correctly. Here are just a few examples of places where unfilled pauses—silences of a second or two—should prove effective.

- **Pause before beginning your speech.** Don't start your speech as soon as you get to the front of the room; instead, position yourself so that you feel comfortable. Then scan the audience and begin your speech.

- **Pause at transitional points.** These pauses will help you signal that you're moving from one part of the speech to another or from one idea to another.

- **Pause at the end of an important assertion.** This will give the audience time to think about the significance of what you're saying.

- **Pause after asking a rhetorical question.** This will give your listeners time to think about how they'd answer the question.

- **Pause before an important idea.** This will help signal that what comes next is especially significant.

- **Pause before asking for questions.** If there's a question period following your speech and you're in charge of it, pause after you've completed your conclusion and ask the audience if they have any questions.

- **Pause after the last sentence of your conclusion** (if there's no period for questions and answers). Continue to maintain eye contact with the audience, and then walk, do not run, back to your seat. Once you are back in your seat, focus on the class activity taking place.

## Articulation

**Articulation** consists of the movements the speech organs make as they modify and interrupt the air stream you send from the lungs. Different movements of these speech organs (for example, the tongue, lips, teeth, palate, and vocal cords) produce different sounds. Our concern here is to identify the major problems in articulation.

The three major articulation problems are omission, substitution, and addition of sounds or syllables. These problems occur both in native speakers of English and in speakers whose first language is not English. Fortunately, they can be easily corrected with informed practice.

## Errors of Omission

Omitting sounds or even syllables is a major articulation problem—but one easily overcome with concentration and practice. Here are some examples.

| Not This | This |
|---|---|
| gov-a-ment | gov-ern-ment |
| hi-stry | hi-story |
| wanna | want to |
| studyin | studying |
| a-lum-num | a-lum-i-num |
| comp-ny | comp-a-ny |

## Errors of Substitution

Substituting an incorrect sound for the correct one is another easily corrected problem. Among the most common errors are substituting *d* for *t* and *d* for *th*.

| Not This | This |
|---|---|
| wader | waiter |
| dese | these |
| ax | ask |
| undoubtebly | undoubtedly |
| beder | better |
| ekcetera | etcetera |

## Errors of Addition

When there are errors of addition, sounds are added where they don't belong. Some examples include:

| Not This | This |
|---|---|
| acrost | across |
| athalete | athlete |
| Americer | America |
| idear | idea |
| filim | film |
| lore | law |

If you make any of these errors, you can easily correct them. First, become conscious of your own articulation patterns (and of any specific errors you may be making). Then listen carefully to the articulation of prominent speakers (for example, broadcasters), comparing their speech patterns with your own. Practice the correct patterns until they become part of your normal speech behavior.

**PUBLIC SPEAKING CHOICE POINT:**
**Mispronunciation**
In giving his speech Michael realizes that he mispronounced a key word twice and saw that some members of the audience noticed the mistake. What are some of Michael's options for dealing with this?

## Pronunciation

**Pronunciation** is the production of syllables or words according to some accepted standard, as identified in any good dictionary. Among the most widespread pronunciation problems are putting the **accent** (stress or emphasis) on the wrong syllable and pronouncing sounds that should remain silent. Both of these pronunciation problems may result from learning English as a second language. For example, a person may use the accent system of his or her first language to pronounce words in English that may have a different accent system. Similarly, in many languages, all letters that appear in a word are pronounced in speech, whereas in English some letters are silent.

### Errors of Accent

Here are some common examples of words accented incorrectly.

| Not This | This |
|---|---|
| New Orleáns | New Órleans |
| ínsurance | insúrance |
| orátor | órator |

### Errors of Pronouncing Silent Sounds

For some words correct pronunciation means not articulating certain sounds, as in the following examples.

| Not This | This |
|---|---|
| often | offen |
| homage | omage |
| Illinois | Illinoi |
| even-ing | eve-ning |

The best way to deal with pronunciation problems is to look up in a good, preferably audio, dictionary any words whose pronunciation you're not sure of. Make it a practice to look up words you hear others use that seem to be pronounced incorrectly as well as words that you wish to use yourself but are not sure how to pronounce. The numerous online audio-dictionaries make this checking process fun as well as useful. Public Speaking Exercise 9.2, "Checking Your Pronunciation," on page 211 identifies some frequently mispronounced terms that you may want to start with.

## Effective Bodily Action

You speak with your body as well as with your mouth. The total effect of the speech depends not only on what you say but also on the way you present it. It depends on your movements, gestures, and facial expressions as well as on your words. Here we'll consider some of the most essential aspects of bodily action: general appearance, eye contact, facial expression, posture, gestures, movement, proxemics, the use of notes, and handling questions.

## General Appearance

Public speaking is usually a more formal type of communication than most others, so you need to give some attention to your general appearance.

First, discover what the accepted and appropriate attire for the occasion is. For your classroom speeches, you'll probably be fine if you dress as you might for a conference with the dean or chair of your department. That is, try to dress perhaps one level above your everyday attire.

Second, dress comfortably but not too casually. Comfortable clothing will make you feel more at ease and will help you to be yourself. If you're in doubt as to how casual you should be, err on the side of formality; wear the tie, high heels, or dress.

Third, avoid excess in just about anything you can think of. Too much jewelry or especially wild colors are likely to call attention to your manner of dress instead of to what you're saying.

## Eye Contact

The most important single aspect of bodily communication is eye contact. The two major problems with eye contact are inappropriate eye contact and eye contact that does not cover the audience fairly. In much of the United States, listeners perceive speakers who don't maintain enough eye contact as distant, unconcerned, and less trustworthy than speakers who look directly at their audience. Consequently, it's generally best to maintain relatively focused eye contact with your audience. Use your eyes to communicate your concern for and interest in what you're saying and to convey your confidence and commitment. Avoid staring blankly through your audience or glancing over their heads, at the floor, or out the window. In other cultures—for example, in many Asian cultures—focused eye contact may prove embarrassing to audience members, so in such cultures, it's often best to scan the audience without locking eyes with specific listeners.

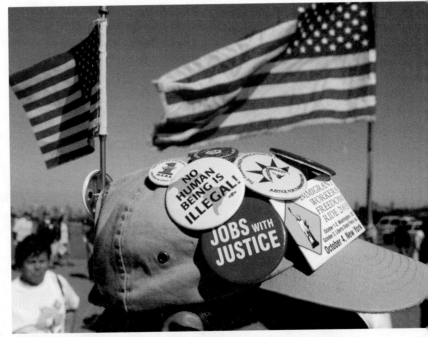

**PUBLIC SPEAKING CHOICE POINT: General Appearance**
J. T. has to give three speeches on the same topic—school hate speech codes—to (1) the faculty of an exclusive prep school, (2) your class, and (3) the city council. J. T. wonders how to dress for these presentations. Assuming J. T. has an unlimited wardrobe, what options does J. T. have for dressing for each audience? If you were an image consultant, what advice would you give J. T. for dressing in each of these three situations if J. T. were a woman? If J. T. were a man?

Involve all listeners in the public speaking transaction. Communicate equally with the members on the left and on the right, in both the back and the front. Eye contact will also enable you to secure audience feedback—to see if your listeners are interested or bored or puzzled. Use eye contact to gauge listeners' level of agreement and disagreement.

## Facial Expression

Facial expressions are especially important in communicating emotions—anger and fear, boredom and excitement, doubt and surprise. If you feel committed to and believe in your thesis, you'll probably display your meanings appropriately and effectively.

Nervousness and anxiety, however, may at times prevent you from relaxing enough so that your emotions come through. Fortunately, time and practice will allow you to relax, and the emotions you feel will reveal themselves appropriately and automatically.

Generally, members of one culture will be able to recognize the emotions displayed facially by members of other cultures. But there are differences in what each culture considers appropriate to display in public. Each culture has its own "display rules" (Ekman, Friesen, & Ellsworth, 1972). For example, Japanese Americans watching a stress-inducing film spontaneously displayed the same facial emotions as did other Americans when they thought they were unobserved. But when an observer was present, the Japanese Americans masked (tried to hide) their emotional expressions more than did the other Americans (Gudykunst & Kim, 1992).

## Posture

When delivering your speech, stand straight but not stiff. Try to communicate a command of the situation without communicating the discomfort that is actually quite common for beginning speakers.

Avoid the common mistakes of posture: Avoid putting your hands in your pockets or clasping them in front or behind your back; and avoid leaning on the desk, the lectern, or the whiteboard. With practice you'll come to feel more at ease and will communicate this by the way you stand before the audience.

## Gestures

Gestures in public speaking help illustrate your verbal messages. We gesture for this purpose regularly in conversation. For example, when saying "Come here," you probably move your head, hands, arms, and perhaps your entire body to motion the listener in your direction. Your body, as well as your verbal message, says "Come here."

Avoid using your hands to preen, however. For example, avoid fixing your hair or adjusting your clothing; don't fidget with your watch, ring, or jewelry. Effective bodily action is spontaneous and natural to you as the speaker, to your audience, and to your speech. If gestures seem planned or rehearsed, they'll appear phony and insincere. As a general rule, don't do anything with your hands that doesn't feel right for you; the audience will recognize it as unnatural. If you feel relaxed and comfortable with yourself and your audience, you'll generate natural bodily action without conscious or studied attention.

## Movement

In public speaking movement can often be of help. Movement keeps both you and the audience more alert. Even when speaking behind a lectern, you can give the illusion of movement. You can step back or forward or flex your upper body so it appears that you're moving more than you are.

If you're using a lectern, you may wish to signal transitions by stepping to the side or in front of it and then behind it again as you move from one point to another. Generally, however, it's best to avoid too much or too little movement around the lectern. Too much movement may make you appear ill at ease, fidgety, or nervous—which in turn will detract from your credibility. Too little movement may make you appear frightened or uninvolved, which also will work against your establishing credibility. For example, you may wish to lean over the lectern when, say, posing a question to your listeners or advancing a particularly important argument. But never lean on the lectern; never use it as support.

Avoid the three problems of movement: too little, too much, and too patterned. Speakers who move too little often appear strapped to the podium, afraid of the audience, or too uncommitted to involve themselves fully. With too much movement the audience begins to concentrate on the movement itself, wondering where the speaker will wind up next. With movement that is too patterned, the audience may become bored—too steady and predictable a rhythm quickly becomes tiring. The audience will often view the speaker as nonspontaneous and uninvolved.

Use whole-body movements to emphasize transitions and to emphasize the introduction of a new and important assumption, bit of evidence, or closely reasoned argument. Thus, when making a transition, you might take a step forward to signal that something new is coming.

## Proxemics

**Proxemics**, or the way you use space in communication, can be a crucial factor in public speaking. Consider the spaces between you and your listeners and among the listeners themselves. If you stand too close to your listeners, they may feel uncomfortable, as if their personal space is being violated. If you stand too far away from your audience, you may be perceived as uninvolved, uninterested, or uncomfortable.

Recognize too that there are often cultural differences in the expectations of where a speaker should stand. One useful rule to follow is to watch where your instructors and other speakers stand and adjust your own position accordingly. At the same time, keep your eyes on the audience for signs that you are standing too far away (perhaps you'll see them leaning toward you or with puzzled looks) or too close (they may literally lean back in their chairs). If you do notice such signs, just adjust your distance gradually without calling attention to the fact that you're changing the distance.

## Using Notes

For some speeches it may be helpful for you to use notes. As one public speaking consultant put it, "By using notes you are demonstrating that you 'plan your work and work your plan.' You are a well-organized speaker. You have more sense than to spend valuable time memorizing an entire presentation" (Fensholt, 2003, p. 66).

In Chapter 6, PowerPoint (pp. 119–126), and in Chapter 7, the delivery outline (pp. 161–163) were discussed as types of notes that will help you remember your speech and contain certain quotations or figures you want to recall exactly. Some speakers, however, prefer to use an abbreviated outline put on one piece of paper or one or a few index cards. To make the most effective use of such notes, keep in mind the following guidelines.

- **Keep your notes to a minimum.** The fewer notes you take with you, the better off you'll be. One reason so many speakers bring notes with them is that they want to avoid the face-to-face interaction required. With experience, however, you should find this face-to-face interaction the best part of the public speaking experience.

- **Resist the temptation to bring the entire speech outline with you.** You may rely on it too heavily and lose direct contact with the audience. Bring with you as much information as you absolutely need but never so much that it will interfere with your direct contact with the audience.

- **Use your notes with "open subtlety."** Don't make your notes more obvious than necessary. Don't gesture with your notes and thus make them more obvious than they need be. At the same time, don't try to hide them. Use them openly and honestly but gracefully, with "open subtlety." To do this effectively, you'll have to know your notes intimately. Rehearse at least twice with the same notes that you'll take with you to the speaker's stand.

- **Don't allow your notes to prevent directness.** When using your notes, pause to look at them. Then regain eye contact with the audience and continue your speech. Don't read from your notes; just take cues from them. The one exception to this is an extensive quotation or complex set of statistics that you have to read; read it and then, almost immediately, resume direct eye contact with the audience.

## Handling Questions

In many public speaking situations, a question-and-answer period will follow the speech, so be prepared to answer questions. Generally a question-and-answer session is helpful because the ensuing dialogue gives the speaker an opportunity to talk more about something he or she is interested in. In some cases, too,

### ETHICAL CHOICE POINT

**To Correct an Error, or Not?**

During a speech on HIV infection, you mention that the rate of HIV infection in women has increased by 10 percent over the last several years. You meant to say that the rate had decreased, but— probably because of nervousness—you said exactly the opposite of what you intended. Even though no one asks you about this during the question-and-answer session following your speech, you wonder if you should correct yourself. The problem, you feel, is that if you do correct yourself, the audience may question your entire speech; and this could undercut a message that you feel very strongly about. ➤*What are your ethical choices for presenting information accurately but also being persuasive in a case you believe in deeply?*

there seems an ethical obligation for the speaker to entertain questions; after all, if the audience sat through what the speaker wanted to say, the speaker should listen to what they want to say.

In most public speaking situations, the question-and-answer session focuses on the message of the speaker. In the public speaking classroom, the question-and-answer session may focus, in whole or in part, on the speech preparation, the effectiveness of organization, the style of language and delivery, the sufficiency of the evidence, and so on. In either case, here are ten suggestions for making this Q&A session more effective.

1. Probably the best way to prepare for this Q&A session is to anticipate questions you're likely to be asked and prepare answers to them as you're preparing your speech.

2. If you wish to encourage questions, preface the question period with some kind of encouraging statement; for example, "I know you've lots of questions—especially on how the new health program will work and how we'll finance it. I'll be happy to respond to your questions. Anyone?"

3. Maintain eye contact with the audience. Let the audience know that you're still speaking with them.

4. After you hear a question, pause to think about the question and about your answer. If you're not sure of what the question is asking you, seek clarification. There's no sense answering a question that wasn't asked. If you suspect that some members of the audience didn't hear the question, repeat it; then begin your answer.

5. You don't have to answer every question just because you're asked. If a question is too personal or you just don't want to get into that area, avoid responding by saying something like, "I'd like to stick to the matter at hand" or "That's a great question, but I really don't think this is the place to discuss that."

6. Control defensiveness. Don't assume that a question is a personal attack. Assume, instead, that the question is an attempt to secure more information or perhaps to challenge a position you've taken.

7. If appropriate, thank the questioner or note that it's a good question. This will encourage others also to ask questions. This can be overdone so be sure to avoid making this an automatic preface to each answer.

8. Don't bluff. If you're asked a question and you don't know the answer, say so. If appropriate, note that you'll try to find the answer and get back to the questioner.

9. Consider the usefulness of a persuasive answer. Question-and-answer sessions often give you opportunities to further advance your purpose by connecting the question and its answer with one or more of your major points: "I'm glad you asked about child care, because that's exactly the difference between the two proposals we're here to vote on. The plan I'm proposing. . . ."

10. Don't allow one person to dominate the Q&A session. Avoid getting into a debate with one person and neglecting your larger audience. Often there is an unstated rule that each questioner may also ask one follow-up question. If that is in effect, you'll want to follow it. Just be careful that this doesn't become a private dialogue.

# Next Steps

Now that we've covered the ten steps we can look at the types of speeches in greater depth. The next chapter examines the informative speech, explaining some principles for communicating information and the types and strategies for these speeches.

# Essentials of Rehearsing and Presenting Your Speech

In this chapter we looked at ways you can rehearse your speech and present it more effectively.

### Rehearse Your Speech

1. Follow these rehearsal guidelines: Rehearse the speech as a whole, time the speech, approximate the actual speech situation as best you can, incorporate changes and delivery notes, and rehearse often.

2. In addition, consider undertaking a long-term delivery program.

### Present Your Speech

3. Effective public speaking presentation is comfortable, consistent, maintains interest, and contributes to the overall effect of the speech.

4. Impromptu: speaking without preparation; useful in certain aspects of public speaking

5. Manuscript: reading from a written text; useful when exact timing and wording are essential.

6. Extemporaneous: speaking after thorough preparation and memorization of the main ideas; useful in most public speaking situations

### Effective Vocal Delivery

7. Volume: Avoid speech that is overly soft, loud, or unvaried, and be sure not to fade away at ends of sentences.

8. Rate: Avoid speaking too fast, too slowly, with too little variation, or in too predictable a pattern.

9. Pitch: Avoid a pitch that is overly high, low, or monotonous, or that falls into too predictable a pattern.

10. Pauses: Use pauses to signal transitions between parts of the speech, give the audience time to think, allow listeners to ponder rhetorical questions, and signal the approach of especially important ideas.

11. Articulation: Errors of articulation include omission, substitution, and addition.

12. Pronunciation: Errors of pronunciation include using the wrong accent and pronouncing silent sounds.

### Effective Bodily Action

13. Present an appropriate general appearance.

14. Maintain eye contact.

15. Allow facial expressions to convey thoughts and feelings.

16. Use posture to communicate command of the speech experience.

17. Dress comfortably and at an appropriate level of formality.

18. Gesture naturally.

19. Move around a bit.

20. Position yourself neither too close to nor too far from the audience.

21. Use a few notes, but use them with "open subtlety" so that they don't prevent your maintaining direct contact with your audience.

22. Treat the question and answer session as an extension of your speech, following the same general principles of effectiveness you followed in preparing and presenting your speech.

# Essential Terms

accent **(204)**
articulation **(202)**
extemporaneous speech **(197)**
impromptu speech **(195)**

manuscript speech **(196)**
memorized speech **(195)**
pauses **(202)**
pitch **(201)**

pronunciation **(204)**
proxemics **(207)**
rate **(200)**
volume **(198)**

# Public Speaking Exercises

## 9.1 Communicating Vocally but Nonverbally

This exercise is designed to give you practice in communicating effectively with your voice and body. In this exercise a speaker recites the alphabet and attempts to communicate with each letter one of the following emotions: anger, nervousness, fear, pride, happiness, sadness, jealousy, satisfaction, love, or sympathy. The speaker should first number the emotions in random order so that he or she will have a set order to follow that is not known to the audience, whose task it will be to guess the emotions expressed. As a variation, have the speaker go through the entire list of emotions twice: once facing the audience and employing any nonverbal signals desired, and once with his or her back to the audience and giving no nonverbal signals.

After the exercise is completed, consider some or all of the following questions:

1. What vocal cues help communicate the various emotions?

2. What bodily cues are useful in communicating these various emotions?

3. Are there gender display rules for effectively communicating some or all of these emotions? That is, are men and women expected to use different cues when communicating certain emotions?

## 9.2 Checking Your Pronunciation

Here are additional words that are often mispronounced. Consult a print or online dictionary (ideally, one with audio capabilities) and record the correct pronunciations here.

### Words Often Mispronounced

| | |
|---|---|
| abdomen | hierarchy |
| accessory | library |
| arctic | nausea |
| buffet | nuclear |
| cavalry | probably |
| clothes | prostate |
| costume | realtor |
| diagnosis | relevant |
| especially | repeat |
| espresso | salmon |
| February | sandwich |
| foliage | similar |
| forehead | strength |
| forte | substantive |
| herb | xenophobia |

Mispronouncing words in public speaking may significantly impact on your credibility. Feeling unsure of how to pronounce a word in your speech also is likely to contribute to your communication apprehension.

## LogOn! PEARSON myspeechlab

Visit MySpeechLab (**www.myspeechlab.com**) and work with some of the exercises; they will help you fine-tune your presentation style. Also take a look at some of the videos of sample speeches for both good and bad deliveries. Consider too the varied delivery suggestions, for example, dressing for speaking, demonstrating dynamism, and the general modes of delivery. Watch the video of an informative speech and/or read the annotated informative speech and the video of President Nixon's resignation speech. A variety of aids to help you explore in greater depth methods of delivery and physical delivery are provided here.

# 10

# Informing Your Audience

## WHY READ THIS CHAPTER?

**Because it will enable you to convey information to an audience by helping you to:**

- effectively inform an audience
- organize and develop speeches for describing (a person, object, event, or process), defining (a concept or theory), or demonstrating (how to do something or how something operates)

*The vision must be followed by the venture. It is not enough to stare up the steps—we must step up the stairs.*

—VANCE HAVNER

One of the important types of speeches you'll be called upon to deliver is the informative speech, the subject of this chapter. We'll first look at some key principles for communicating information and then we'll examine the varied types of informative speeches and see how you can develop each type most effectively.

As you read this chapter and the next two, take a look at SpeechFeed (http://myspeechfeed.wordpress.com) for a wide variety of current speeches (see Figure 10.1).

# Principles of Informative Speaking

To communicate information is to tell your listeners something they don't know, something new. In **informative speaking** you may inform your audience about a new way of looking at old things or an old way of looking at new things. You may discuss a theory not previously heard of or a familiar concept not fully understood. You may talk about events that the audience may be unaware of or explain happenings they may have misconceptions about. Regardless of what type of informative speech you intend to give, the following guidelines should help.

## Focus on Your Audience

Your audience will—to some extent—influence the information you'll present and how you'll present it. Consequently, it's wise to look to your audience as a first principle. So, let's say you want to give an informative speech on Microsoft's Windows 7. This will provide a good illustration of how the same topic can be pursued with different goals in mind.

- To an audience of dedicated Mac users, the information may be entirely new, so your goal will be to introduce a topic unknown to the audience.

- To an audience of dedicated Mac users who think there's little or no difference between the systems, you'll be clarifying misconceptions.

- To an audience of students using Vista you may wish to demonstrate how this new operating system is different. For example, you might explain the ways in which Windows 7 is superior to Vista.

As you can appreciate, each of these speeches would have to be somewhat different depending on the knowledge and experience of the audiences.

## Stress Relevance and Usefulness

Listeners remember information best when they see it as relevant and useful to their own needs or goals. Notice that as a listener you regularly demonstrate this principle of relevance and usefulness. For example, in class you may attend to and remember the stages in the development of language in children simply because you'll be tested on the information and you want to earn a high grade. Or you may remember a given piece of information because it will help you make a better impression in your job interview, make you a better

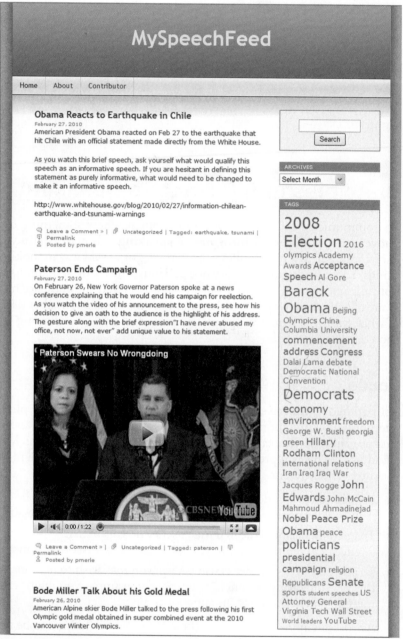

**FIGURE 10.1**

**Speech Feed**

This site provides a variety of videos of speeches currently in the news.

parent, or enable you to deal with relationship problems. Like you, listeners attend to information that will prove useful to them.

If you want the audience to listen to your speech, relate your information to their needs, wants, or goals. Throughout your speech, but especially in the beginning, make sure your audience knows that the information you're presenting is or will be relevant and useful to them now or in the immediate future. For example, you might say something like:

> We all want financial security. We all want to be able to buy those luxuries we read so much about in magazines and see every evening on television. Wouldn't it be nice to be able to buy a car without worrying about where you're going to get the down payment or how you'll be able to make the monthly payments? Actually, that is not an unrealistic goal, as I'll demonstrate in this speech. In fact, I'll show you several investment strategies that have enabled many people to increase their income by as much as 20 percent.

## Limit the Amount of Information

There's a limit to the amount of information that a listener can take in at one time. Resist the temptation to overload your listeners with information. Instead of enlarging the breadth of information you communicate, expand its depth. It's better to present two new items of information and explain these in depth with examples, illustrations, and descriptions than to present five items without this needed amplification. The speaker who attempts to discuss the physiological, psychological, social, and linguistic differences between men and women, for example, is clearly trying to cover too much and is going to be forced to cover these areas only superficially, with the result that little new information will be communicated. Even covering one of these areas completely is likely to prove difficult. Instead, select one subdivision of one area—say, language development or differences in language problems—and develop that in depth.

## Adjust the Level of Complexity

As you know from attending college classes, information can be presented in very simple or very complex form. Adjusting the level of complexity on which you communicate your information is crucial. This adjustment should depend on the wide variety of factors considered throughout this book: the level of knowledge your audience has, the time you have available, the purpose you hope to achieve, the topic on which you're speaking, and so on. If you simplify a topic too much, you risk boring or, even worse, insulting your audience. On the other hand, if your talk is too complex, you risk confusing your audience and failing to communicate your message.

Generally, beginning speakers err by being too complex and not realizing that a 5- or 10-minute speech isn't long enough to make an audience understand sophisticated concepts or complicated processes. At least in your beginning speeches, try to keep it simple rather than complex. Make sure the words you use are familiar to your audience; alternatively, explain and define any unfamiliar terms as you use them. For example, remember that jargon and technical vocabulary familiar to the computer hacker may not be familiar to the person who still uses a typewriter. Always see your topic from the point of view of the audience; ask yourself how much they know about your topic and its particular terminology.

## Relate New Information to Old

Listeners will learn information more easily and retain it longer when you relate it to what they already know. So relate the new to the old, the unfamiliar to the familiar, the unseen to the seen, the untasted to the tasted. Here, for example, Betsy Heffernan, a student from the University of Wisconsin (Reynolds & Schnoor, 1991), relates the problem of sewage to a familiar historical event.

> During our nation's struggle for independence, the citizens of Boston were hailed as heroes for dumping tea into Boston Harbor. But not to be outdone, many modern day Bostonians are also dumping things into the harbor: five thousand gallons of human waste every second. The New England Aquarium of Boston states that since 1900, Bostonians have dumped enough human sewage into the harbor to cover the entire state of Massachusetts chest deep in sludge. Unfortunately, Boston isn't alone. All over the country, bays, rivers, and lakes are literally becoming cesspools.

## Vary the Levels of Abstraction

You can talk about freedom of the press in the abstract by talking about the importance of getting information to the public, by referring to the Bill of Rights, and by relating a free press to the preservation of democracy. But you can also talk about freedom of the press on a low level of abstraction, a level that is specific and concrete; for example, you can describe how a local newspaper was prevented from running a story critical of the town council or how Lucy Rinaldo was fired from the *Accord Sentinel* after she wrote a story critical of the mayor.

Varying the **levels of abstraction**—combining high abstraction (the very general) and low abstraction (the very specific)—seems to work best. Too many generalizations without the specifics or too many specifics without the generalizations will prove less effective than the combination of abstract and specific.

Here, for example, is an excerpt from a speech on the homeless. Note that in the first paragraph we have a relatively abstract description of homelessness. In the second paragraph, we get into specifics. In the last paragraph the abstract and the concrete are connected.

> **[Here the speaker begins with relatively general or abstract statements.]** Homelessness is a serious problem for all metropolitan areas throughout the country. It's currently estimated that there are now more than 200,000 homeless in New York City alone. But what is this really about? Let me tell you what it's about.
>
> **[Here the speaker gets to specifics.]** It's about a young man. He must be about 25 or 30, although he looks a lot older. He lives in a cardboard box on the side of my apartment house. We call him Tom, although we really don't know his name. All his possessions are stored in this huge box. I think it was a box from a refrigerator. Actually, he doesn't have very much, and what he has easily fits in this box. There's a blanket my neighbor threw out, some plastic bottles Tom puts water in, and some Styrofoam containers he picked up from the garbage from Burger King. He uses these to store whatever food he finds.
>
> **[The conclusion combines the general and specific.]** What is homelessness about? It's about Tom and 200,000 other "Toms" in New York and thousands of others throughout the rest of the country. And not all of them even have boxes to live in.

## Make Your Speech Easy to Remember

The principles of public speaking (principles governing use of language, delivery, and supporting materials, for example) will all help your listeners remember your speech. If, for example, you stress interest and relevance—as already noted—the audience is more likely to remember what you say, because they will see it as important and relevant to their own lives. But here are a few extra suggestions.

- **Repeat the points you want the audience to remember.** Help your audience to remember what you want them to remember by repeating your most important points.

- **Use signposts.** Guide your audience's attention to your most memorable points by saying, for example, "the first point to remember is that ...," "the argument I want you to remember when you enter that voting booth is ...."

- **Use internal summary transitions.** Internal summary transitions will remind the audience of what you have said and how it relates to what is to follow. This kind of repetition will reinforce your message and help your listeners remember your main points.

- **Pattern your messages.** If the audience can see the logic of your speech, they'll be better able to organize what you say in their own minds. If they can see that you're following a temporal pattern or a spatial pattern, for example, it will be easier for them to retain more of what you say, because they'll have a framework into which they can fit what you say.

- **Focus audience attention.** The best way to focus the listeners' attention is to tell them to focus their attention. Simply say, "I want you to focus on three points that I will make in this speech. First, ..." or "What I want you to remember is this: ...."

Now that the principles of information speaking have been identified, let's consider the main types of informative speeches.

- **Speeches of description** are speeches in which you describe an object (the human heart) or person (a genius, artist, or Picasso) or describe an event (a hurricane) or process (adopting a child).

- **Speeches of definition** are speeches in which you define a term (linguistics), a system or theory (evolution), or similar and dissimilar terms (nature/nurture, communism/socialism).

- **Speeches of demonstration** are speeches in which you show how to do something (protecting yourself against identity theft) or how something works (search spiders).

Let's look first at the speech of description.

### ETHICAL CHOICE POINT

#### Informing or Persuading?

You want to raise money for repairs of the local children's community center and plan to give your persuasive speech on this topic. Right now, however, you have to give a speech of description and you wonder if it would be ethical for you to give this speech of description detailing all the problems with the center. You want to be truthful but you also want the audience to conclude that the community center needs money for repairs. You wonder if it would be unethical to deliver a speech of information that is actually persuasive in large part.
➤ *What are your ethical choices in this situation?*

# Speeches of Description

In a speech of description you're concerned with explaining an object, person, event, or process. Here are a few examples.

### Describing an Object or Place

- the structure of DNA
- the parts of a telephone
- the geography of Africa
- the hierarchy of a corporation
- the components of a computer system

### Describing a Person, Real or Generalized

- the power of Nancy Pelosi, Bill Gates, Tiger Woods, or Meg Whitman
- the significance of Benjamin Franklin, Rosa Parks, or Martin Scorsese
- the contributions of a philanthropist
- the vegan and the vegetarian

### Describing an Event or Process

- the attacks of September 11, 2001
- the events leading to war with Iraq
- organizing a bodybuilding contest
- how a book is printed
- purchasing stock online
- how a child acquires language

## Thesis

The thesis of a speech, as explained in Chapter 4, is your single most important concept; it is what you most want your audience to remember. The thesis of a speech of description simply states what you'll describe in your speech. For example:

- The child acquires language in four stages.
- There are three steps to purchasing stock online.
- Four major events led to the war with Iraq.

## Main Points

The main points of your speech are the major subdivisions of the thesis. You derive your main points from the thesis by asking strategic questions. For example:

- What are the four stages in child language acquisition?
- What are the three steps to purchasing stock online?
- What events led to the war with Iraq?

## Support

Obviously you don't want simply to list your main points but to flesh them out—to make them memorable, interesting, and, most of all, clear. You do this by using a variety of materials that amplify and support your main ideas; you include examples, illustrations, testimony, statistics, and the like, as has already been explained. So, for example, in describing the babbling stage of language learning, you might give examples of babbling, the age at which babbling first appears, the period of time that babbling lasts, or the differences between the babbling of girls and boys.

Because this is a speech of description, give extra consideration to the types of description you might use in your supporting materials. Try to describe the object or event with lots of different descriptive categories. With physical categories, for example, ask yourself questions such as these: What color is it? How big is it? What is it shaped like? How much does it weigh? What is its volume? How attractive/unattractive is it? Also consider social, psychological, and economic categories. In describing a person, for example, consider such categories as friendly/unfriendly, warm/cold, rich/poor, aggressive/meek, and pleasant/unpleasant.

Consider how you might use presentation aids. In describing an object or a person, show your listeners a picture; show them the inside of a telephone, pictures of the brain, the skeleton of the body. In describing an event or process, show them a diagram or flowchart to illustrate the stages or steps; for example, the steps involved in buying stock, in publishing a newspaper, in putting a parade together.

## Organization

Consider using a spatial or a topical organization when describing objects and people. Consider using a temporal pattern when describing events and processes. For example, if you were to describe the layout of Philadelphia, you might start from the north and work down to the south (using a spatial pattern). If you were to describe the achievements of Thomas Edison, you might select Edison's three or four major contributions and discuss each of these equally (using a topical pattern).

If you were describing the events leading up to Iraq war, you might use a temporal pattern, starting with

**PUBLIC SPEAKING CHOICE POINT: Describing**
Juliet wants to give a speech describing Second Life, the virtual reality game she has become a passionate fan of. Some members of her audience have a fairly negative view of virtual gaming thinking it is a waste of time or worse, but she knows that others hold positive views. Juliet wants to acknowledge her understanding of these diverse attitudes. What are Juliet's options for introducing this topic? If you were Juliet, what would you say? How can she keep her speech informative, without interjecting her own passions on the subject?

# RESEARCH LINK

### Evaluating Internet Resources

As you research your topic, keep in mind that anyone can "publish" on the Internet, making it essential that you subject everything you find on the Web to critical analysis. An article on the Internet can be written by world-renowned scientists or by elementary school students; by fair and objective reporters or by people who would spin the issues to serve their own political, religious, or social purposes. It's not always easy to tell which is which. Here are five questions—built around the acronym FACQS—to ask concerning the (1) fairness, (2) accuracy, (3) currency, (4) qualifications, and (5) sufficiency of Internet resources (as well as information from print media, from interpersonal interaction, or from film and electronic media).

- **Fairness.** Does the author of the material present the information fairly and objectively, or is there a bias favoring one position? Some websites, although objective on the surface, are actually organs of some political, religious, or social organization; so it's often useful to go to the home page and look for information on the nature of the organization sponsoring the website. Reviewing a range of research in the area will help you see how other experts view the issue. It will also enable you to see if this author's view of the situation takes into consideration all sides of the issue and if these sides are represented fairly.

- **Accuracy.** Is the information presented accurate? Of course, determining accuracy is not easy, but the more you learn about your topic, the more able you'll be to judge the accuracy of information about the topic. Is the information primary or secondary (see the Research Link in Chapter 4, p. 75)? If it's secondary information, you may be able to locate the primary source material (often a hot link in the Internet article or a reference at the end of a printed text). Check to see if the information is consistent with information found in other sources and if the recognized authorities in the field accept this information.

- **Currency.** When was the information published? When were the sources cited in the article written? Generally, the more recent the material, the more useful it will be. With some topics—for example, unemployment statistics, developments in AIDS research, tuition costs, stem cell research, or attitudes toward the war, same-sex marriage, or organized religion—the currency of the information is crucial to its usefulness, simply because these things change so rapidly. Other topics, such as historical or literary subjects, may well rely on information that was written even hundreds of years ago. Even here, however, new information frequently sheds light on events that happened in the far distant past. To ensure currency, check important figures in a recent almanac, in a newspaper, or at a frequently updated Internet source such as Federal Statistics at www.fedstats.gov. At the same time, it's often helpful to simply search for more recent information, updating your facts and figures as necessary.

- **Qualifications.** Does the author have the necessary credentials? For example, does the author have a background in science or medicine to write authoritatively on health issues? Do an Internet search using the biography sites already discussed (see the Research Link in Chapter 6, p. 111), or simply enter the author's name in your favorite search engine and check on the author's expertise.

- **Sufficiency.** Is the information presented sufficient to establish the claim or conclusion? The opinion of one dietitian is insufficient to support the usefulness of a particular diet; statistics on tuition increases at five elite private colleges are insufficient to illustrate national trends in tuition costs. Generally, the broader your conclusion, the greater the information you'll need to meet the requirements for sufficiency. If you want to claim the usefulness of a diet for all people, then you're going to need a great deal of information from different populations—men and women, old and young, healthy and sickly, and so on.

The next Research Link, "Integrating and Citing Research," appears on page 239.

the earliest and working up to the latest. A temporal pattern also would be appropriate for describing how a hurricane develops or how a parade is put together.

Consider the "Who? What? Where? When? and Why?" pattern of organization. These journalistic categories are especially useful when you want to describe an event or a process. For example, if you're going to describe how to purchase a house, you might want to consider the people involved (who?), the steps you have to go through (what?), the places you'll have to go (where?), the time or sequence in which each of the steps have to take place (when?), and the advantages and disadvantages of buying the house (why?).

Here are two examples showing the bare bones of how a descriptive speech might look. In this first example, the speaker describes four suggestions for reducing energy bills. Notice that the speaker derives the main points from asking a question of the thesis.

| | |
|---|---|
| General purpose: | To inform. |
| Specific purpose: | To describe how you can reduce energy bills. |
| Thesis: | Energy bills can be reduced. (How can energy bills be reduced?) |

I. Caulk window and door seams.

II. Apply weather stripping around windows and doors.

III. Insulate walls.

IV. Install storm windows and doors.

In this second example, the speaker describes the way in which fear works in intercultural communication.

| | |
|---|---|
| General purpose: | To inform. |
| Specific purpose: | To describe the way fear works in intercultural communication. |
| Thesis: | Fear influences intercultural communication. (How does fear influence intercultural communication?) |

I. We fear disapproval.

II. We fear embarrassing ourselves.

III. We fear being harmed.

In delivering such a speech a speaker might begin by saying:

Three major fears interfere with intercultural communication. First, we fear disapproval—from members of our own group as well as from members of the other person's group. Second, we fear embarrassing ourselves, even making fools of ourselves, by saying the wrong thing or appearing insensitive. And third, we may fear being harmed—our stereotypes of the other group may lead us to see its members as dangerous or potentially harmful to us.

Let's look at each of these fears in more detail. We'll be able to see clearly how they influence our own intercultural communication behavior. Consider, first, the fear of disapproval.

The speaker would then amplify and support this fear of disapproval, giving examples of disapproval seen in his or her own experience, the testimony of communication theorists on the importance of such fear, research findings on the effects that such fear might have on intercultural communication, and so on.

# Speeches of Definition

What is leadership? What is a born-again Christian? What is the difference between sociology and psychology? What is a cultural anthropologist? What is safe sex? These are all topics for informative speeches of definition.

A definition is a statement of the meaning of a term. In giving a speech of definition (as opposed to using a definition as a form of supporting material, as explained in Chapter 6, pp. 108–110), you may focus on defining a term, defining a system or theory, or pinpointing the similarities and/or differences among terms or systems. A speech of definition may be on a subject new to the audience or may present a familiar topic in a new and different way. Here are a few examples.

### Defining a Term

- What is a smart card?
- What is perjury?
- What is bipolar disorder?
- What is self-esteem?
- What is restless leg syndrome?
- What is political correctness?

### Defining a System or Theory

- What is the classical theory of public speaking?
- What are the parts of a generative grammar?
- Buddhism: its major beliefs
- What is virtual reality?
- What is futurism?
- The "play theory" of mass communication

### Defining Similar and Dissimilar Terms or Systems

- What do Christians and Muslims have in common?
- How do text and online dictionaries differ?
- Football and soccer: What's the difference?
- Oedipus and Electra: How do they differ?
- Heredity and the environment
- Animal and human rights
- Visible and invisible web

## Thesis

The thesis in a speech of definition is a statement identifying the term or system and your intention to define it or to contrast it with other terms; for example, "Christianity and Islam have much in common" or "There are three main differences between print and online dictionaries."

## Main Points

You derive the main points for a speech of definition by asking questions of your thesis; for example, if your thesis is "Christianity and Islam have much in common," then the logical question is, What are they? What do Christianity and Islam have in common? Your answers to this question would then constitute your main points. If your thesis is that text and online dictionaries differ in three major ways, then the logical question is What are the three ways? How do text and online dictionaries differ? Here your main points would be the ways in which these dictionaries differ.

## Support

Once you have each of your main points, support them with examples, testimony, and the like. For example, one of your main points in the Christianity–Islam example may be that both religions believe in the value of good works. You might then quote from the New Testament and from the Quran to illustrate this belief, or you might give examples of noted Christians and Muslims who exemplified this characteristic, or you might cite the testimony of religious leaders who talked about the importance of good works.

Because this is a speech of definition, you'll want to give special attention to all your definitions, as discussed earlier (Chapter 6, pp. 108–110).

## Organization

In addition to the obvious organizational pattern of multiple definitions, consider using a topical order, in which each main idea is treated equally. In either case, however, proceed from the known to the unknown. Start with what your audience knows and work up to what is new or unfamiliar. Let's say you want to explain the concept of phonemics (with which your audience is totally unfamiliar). The specific idea you wish to get across is that each phoneme stands for a unique sound. You might proceed from the known to the unknown and begin your definition with something like this:

> We all know that in the written language each letter of the alphabet stands for a unit of the written language. Each letter is different from every other letter. A *t* is different from a *g* and a *g* is different from a *b* and so on. Each letter is called a "grapheme." In English we know we have 26 such letters.
>
> We can look at the spoken language in much the same way. Each sound is different from every other sound. A *t* sound is different from a *d* and a *d* is different from a *k* and so on. Each individual sound is called a "phoneme."
>
> Now, let me explain in a little more detail what I mean by a "phoneme."

# PUBLIC SPEAKING SAMPLE ASSISTANT

## An Informative Speech

This informative speech was delivered by Steve Zammit of Cornell University. In this speech Zammit informs his listeners about the nature of the electric heart and claims that the electric heart will significantly influence the treatment of heart problems.

---

### THE ELECTRIC HEART
#### Steve Zammit*

On February 21, 2000, David Letterman returned to the Late Show after his quadruple bypass with a list of the "Top 10 Things You Don't Want to Hear When You Wake Up from Surgery." They include: Number 2—"Hello Mr. Letterman... or should I say Miss Letterman?" and Number 1—"We did what we could, Mr. Letterman, but this is Jiffy Lube." But after the gags, Dave brought his doctors on stage and choked up as he thanked them for "saving my life."

One year later, the *New York Times* of February 1, 2001, announced conditional FDA approval for a medical device that will bring similar results to millions of heart patients. But rather than bypass a clogged artery, this revolutionary device bypasses the heart itself, thus fulfilling the life vision of 55-year-old scientist and heart surgeon Dr. David Lederman. Dr. David Lederman is the inventor of the [VA] Electric Heart.

The Electric Heart is a safe, battery-operated, permanent replacement that is directly implanted into the body. The February 12, 2001, *Telegram and Gazette* predicts that within one generation more than 10 million Americans will be living with terminal heart disease. For them, and for the 100,000 transplant candidates who pray for a new heart when only 2,000 are annually available, hope has been fleeting . . . until now.

So to learn why UCLA transplant surgeon Dr. Steven Marelli calls it the "Holy Grail of Heart Surgery," let's first plug into the heart's development and see how it works. Next, we'll flesh out its current status. So that finally we can see how the device's future impact will be heart-stopping.

In early 1982, Washington dentist Barney Clark's heart was stopping—literally. The world watched as Dr. Robert Jarvik implanted Clark with the first ever artificial heart. After 112 days marked by kidney failure, respiratory problems, and severe mental confusion, the heart stopped. It didn't take a rocket scientist to see that, as the *New York*

Did the speaker **gain attention** right at the start? What specifically caught your attention?

How effective was the **introduction**? What purposes did it accomplish? Would you have sought to accomplish any other purpose(s)? If so, what would you have said?

This speech was delivered several years ago; the references cited were current at the time. As you read the speech, consider the changes you would make, for example, in supporting materials or in research, if you were giving the speech today.

Note that the speech transcript shows the points at which **visual aids** [VA] are to be presented.

Does the speaker **stress relevance and usefulness** to maintain your attention? How would you have stressed relevance and usefulness?

What did you think of the way the speaker phrased the **orientation** to the major propositions of the speech? Did the orientation add clarity? Did it add humor?

Notice the **word choices**, for example, plug, flesh, heart-stopping. Were these effective choices?

*"The Electric Heart," by Steve Zammit, Cornell University. Reprinted with permission.

*Times* of May 16, 1988, declared, artificial heart research was medical technology's version of Dracula. Basically, it sucked. Getting Dracula out of his coffin would require a little thinking outside the box. Enter Dr. David Lederman, who, in a happy coincidence, reported *Forbes* of April 17, 2000, is an actual rocket scientist. In fact, Lederman changed his career path in the early 1970s when he heard a lecture by a physicist who insisted artificial hearts would rise or fall based on fluid mechanics.

Lederman's design can be likened to space flight in that the concept is easy, but the tiniest problems can prevent a launch or cause an explosion. *What separates the Electric Heart from Jarvik's earlier model is the development and implementation of space-age technology.* In particular, the *Pittsburgh Post-Gazette* of January 28, 2001, explains that an artificial heart must simultaneously weigh two pounds, be flexible enough to expand and contract, and be tough enough to absorb 40 million beats a year. The solution is a proprietary titanium compound called Angioflex, the first man-made material on earth that fits the mold.

A typical heart pumps blood through constant muscular contractions regulated by the nervous system. [VA] But Lederman's model propels blood using an internal motor regulated by a microprocessor embedded inside the abdomen. A small external belt transmits energy through the skin to a copper coil, allowing the entire system to be continuously stimulated.

When he returned last February, David Letterman was stimulated by a hospital gown–clad Robin Williams, who performed a zany strip tease. . . . I'll spare you the VA. But to see if Dr. Lederman is himself a tease, we must now evaluate his project's current status as well as the obstacles it faces.

The *Houston Chronicle* of January 31, 2001, reveals that FDA approval of the Electric Heart was based on its wild success when implanted in animals. More than 100 cows have been recipients of the heart, and in Dr. Lederman's words, three hours after surgery, "I have seen the animals standing in their stalls munching hay, with their original hearts in a jar nearby." Sometime in early June, surgical teams will swap an Electric Heart for the failing one in five critically ill human patients, for what Dr. Lederman calls "the most public clinical trials in history." For those skeptics who argue it's a little early to break out the bubbly, Dr. Lederman adamantly agrees. He told the February 5, 2001, *Glasgow Herald*, "At first, you had the Wright brothers. Today, you can easily cross the Atlantic. Our heart is the equivalent of making the flight from Boston to New York," but the trip across the Atlantic is only a matter of time.

What functions did the Dracula **example** serve? Do you feel this was too flippant for a speech on such a serious topic? Do you feel it added the right note of levity?

How would you describe the **level of complexity** in this speech?

Although you can't see the **visual aids** the speaker used, you can imagine what they were. If you were listening to this speech, what would you have liked to have seen in these visuals?

Can you identify **transitions** the speaker used to connect the speech parts?

How successfully did the speaker create **involvement**? If the speaker involved you a great deal, what specifically did the speaker say that got you involved? If not so much, what might the speaker have done to make you feel he was talking about you to you?

How effective was this **analogy**? What purposes did this analogy serve?

Despite the optimism, the beat will not go on until Dr. Lederman convincingly addresses two concerns about practicality. As the *British Medical Journal* of March 17, 2001, explains, organ transplant recipients must take expensive, nauseating drugs to prevent clotting and rejection. Fortunately, Angioflex's producer, Abiomed, revealed in a 2000 Securities and Exchange Commission filing that the material is perfectly seamless and can withstand over 20 years of abuse without cracking. No cracks, no place for clots to form. And since the Electric Heart is made of inert materials, UCLA transplant surgeon Dr. Steven Marelli told the February 7, 2001, *University Wire*, the body will not reject it, an observation confirmed by animal trials. Essentially, Electric Heart recipients will come back without expensive drug therapy.

Speaking of comebacks, just as David Letterman's return culminated in an Emmy nomination, Dr. Lederman will soon be picking up some awards of his own, due to the Electric Heart's impact on individuals and society. As transplant pioneer Robert Jarvik once said, "the artificial heart must not only be dependable, but truly forgettable." But during periods of increased energy demand—including making love—Jarvik's model required a user to be tethered to a power unit in the wall. Lederman's model, in the words of the February 2001 *GQ*, is "The Love Machine." As *GQ* observes, the internal battery can allow "unassisted" exercise for 30 minutes—every man's dream. But the *Boston Globe* of February 1, 2001, reveals that advances in battery technology eventually will allow a sleeping user to be charged for a full day—allowing recipients to emulate the Energizer Bunny in more ways than one.

But by normalizing life for individuals, the Electric Heart will be revolutionizing medicine in society. The March 26, 2001, *Los Angeles Times* notes that 400,000 Americans are diagnosed with heart failure each year. Add the

How effectively did the speaker **integrate research** into the speech?

Does the speaker **limit the amount of information** he communicates so that there is significant depth? Would you have done things differently?

Does the speaker successfully **relate new information** to old?

Of all the **research** cited in the speech, which did you think was the most effective? Which was the least effective? Why?

How effective was this injection of **humor**? How effective was the analogy?

Did the speaker **vary the levels of abstraction** effectively, or would you have wished to hear more high-level or more low-level abstractions?

Here are two examples of how you might go about constructing a speech of definition. In this first example the speaker explains the parts of a résumé and follows a spatial order, going from the top to the bottom of the page.

| | |
|---|---|
| General purpose: | To inform. |
| Specific purpose: | To define the essential parts of a résumé. |
| Thesis: | There are four major parts to a résumé. (What are the four major parts of a résumé?) |

I. Identify your career goals.

II. Identify your educational background.

III. Identify your work experience.

IV. Identify your special competencies.

number of other failing internal organs, as well as a glut of aging baby boomers, and we are a generation away from a crisis. To cope, some researchers have famously approached organ shortages by genetically engineering them to grow in a lab, a process that will still take years. But the Electric Heart is both more immediate, and carries none of the ethical entanglements of manipulating the human genome. As Dr. Ed Berger, vice president of Abiomed, explained in an April 2, 2001, telephone interview, Angioflex is so versatile, it could eventually be used to construct artificial kidneys and lungs.

What influence did the research and its integration into the speech have on your image of the speaker's **credibility**?

How effective do you think the **speech title**, "The Electric Heart," was? What other titles might have worked?

Unfortunately, the *American Journal of Medicine* of February 1, 2001, reports that heart disease disproportionately strikes those in lower socioeconomic brackets, a group that often lacks access to advanced technology. But the April 19, 2001, *Boston Herald* predicts the procedure will eventually retail for about $25,000, the same as a traditional heart bypass. Coupled with the cost savings on drug treatment, the procedure should be affordably covered by most insurance companies, including Medicare. So whether rich or poor, young or old, resting or energized, the Electric Heart will be an equal opportunity lifesaver.

What one thing will you **remember most** from this speech? Why will you remember this? That is, what did the speaker say that made this one thing most memorable?

Although you can never mend a broken heart, Dr. Lederman has done the next best thing. By reviewing the Electric Heart's unusual development and current testing, we have seen its future impact on viewers around the world. On the night of his comeback, David Letterman put a human face on heart disease. But for thousands who find themselves in the comedian's shoes, laughter—and everything else—is insufficient medicine. But soon, Dr. David Lederman will reach audiences with a message of hope. For them, the Electric Heart will not just make the Top 10 List. It will be number one.

How effective was the speaker's **conclusion**? What functions did the conclusion serve? What other functions might it have served?

Now that you've finished reading the speech (don't look back), what were the **major propositions** of the speech? What did you learn from this speech?

*Source:* Stephen Zammit, Cornell University. Reprinted with permission.

In this second example the speaker selects three major types of lying for discussion and arranges these in a topical pattern.

General purpose:    To inform.

Specific purpose:    To define lying by explaining the major types of lying.

Thesis:    There are three major kinds of lying. (What are the three major kinds of lying?)

I. Concealment is the process of hiding the truth.

II. Falsification is the process of presenting false information as if it were true.

III. Misdirection is the process of acknowledging a feeling but misidentifying its cause.

In delivering such a speech, a speaker might begin the speech by saying:

A lie is a lie is a lie. True? Well, not exactly. Actually, there are a number of different ways we can lie. We can lie by concealing the truth. We can lie by falsification, by presenting false information as if it were true. And we can lie by misdirection, by acknowledging a feeling but misidentifying its cause.

Let's look at the first type of lie—the lie of concealment. Most lies are lies of concealment. Most of the time when we lie we simply conceal the truth. We don't actually make any false statements. Rather we simply don't reveal the truth. Let me give you some examples I overheard recently.

Public Speaking Exercise 10.1, "Defining Terms," on page 232 provides an experience for practicing using a wide variety of different types of definitions.

# Speeches of Demonstration

Whether in using demonstration within a speech or in giving a speech devoted entirely to demonstration, you show the audience how to do something or how something operates. This speech is sometimes called a speech of process because the emphasis is on showing the audience how to perform some process or how some process works. Here are some examples of topics of speeches of demonstration.

### Demonstrating How to Do Something

- how to give mouth-to-mouth resuscitation
- how to drive defensively
- how to mix colors
- how to ask for a raise
- how to burglarproof your house
- how to use Excel to organize your finances

### Demonstrating How Something Operates

- how the body maintains homeostasis
- how perception works
- how divorce laws work
- how an MRI works
- how e-mail works
- how a hurricane develops
- how emotional contagion works
- how a heart bypass operation is performed

## Thesis

The thesis for a speech of demonstration identifies what you will show the audience how to do, or how something operates. For example:

- E-mail works through a series of electronic connections from one computer to a server to another computer.
- You can burglarproof your house in three different ways.
- Three guidelines will help you get that raise.

## Main Points

You can then derive your main points by asking a simple How or What question of your thesis:

- How do these electronic connections work?
- What are the ways of burglarproofing a house?
- What are the guidelines for asking for a raise?

In the first example, your main points would be the ways in which the electronic connections work. In the second, they would be the ways you can use to burglarproof your home. And, in the third example, your main points would be the guidelines you should follow in asking for a raise.

**PUBLIC SPEAKING CHOICE POINT: Unexpected Happenings**
Harry, a first-year culinary arts student, is the third speaker in a series of five, demonstrating how to prepare stir fried vegetables. Unfortunately, the first speaker, a fourth-year student, presented a really excellent speech on the exact same dish. What are some of Harry's options for dealing with this situation? If you were Harry, what would you say (if anything) in reference to the earlier speaker?

## Support

You then support each of your main ideas with a variety of materials. For example, you might show diagrams of houses that use different burglarproofing methods, demonstrate how various locks work, or show how different security systems work.

Presentation aids are especially helpful in speeches of demonstration. Good examples of visual aids are the signs in restaurants demonstrating the Heimlich maneuver. These signs demonstrate the sequence of steps with pictures as well as words. The combination of verbal and graphic information makes it easy to understand this important process. In a speech on the Heimlich maneuver, however, it might be best to use only the pictures so that the written words would not distract your audience from your oral explanation.

## Organization

In most cases a temporal pattern will work best in speeches of demonstration. Demonstrate each step in the sequence in which it's to be performed. In this way, you'll avoid one of the major difficulties in demonstrating a process—backtracking. Don't skip steps, even if you think they're familiar to the audience. They may not be. Connect each step to the next with appropriate transitions. For example, in explaining the Heimlich maneuver, you might say:

Now that you have your arms around the choking victim's chest, your next step is to ...

Assist your listeners by labeling the steps clearly; for example, "the first step," "the second step," and so on.

**PUBLIC SPEAKING CHOICE POINT: Support**

Rose is planning to give an informative speech on defensive driving and is considering what sorts of support she might use. What types of presentation aids might she use?

It's often helpful when demonstrating to give a broad general picture and then present each step in turn. For example, suppose you were talking about how to prepare a wall for painting. You might begin with a general overview to give your listeners a general idea of the process, saying something like this:

> In preparing the wall for painting, you want to make sure that the wall is smoothly sanded, free of dust, and dry. Sanding a wall isn't like sanding a block of wood. So let's look at the proper way to sand a wall.

Here are two examples of the speech of demonstration. In this first example, the speaker explains the proper way to paint a wall by rag rolling. As you can see, the speaker uses a temporal organizational pattern and covers three stages in the order in which they would be performed.

| | |
|---|---|
| General purpose: | To inform. |
| Specific purpose: | To demonstrate how to rag roll. |
| Thesis: | Rag rolling is performed in three steps. (What are the three steps of rag rolling?) |

I. Apply the base coat of paint.

II. Apply the glaze coat.

III. Roll a rag through the wet glaze.

In the next example, the speaker identifies and demonstrates how to listen actively.

| | |
|---|---|
| General purpose: | To inform. |
| Specific purpose: | To demonstrate three techniques of active listening. |
| Thesis: | We can become active listeners. (How can we become active listeners?) |

I. Paraphrase the speaker's meaning.

II. Express understanding of the speaker's feelings.

III. Ask questions.

In delivering the speech, the speaker might begin by saying:

> Active listening is a special kind of listening. It's listening with total involvement, with a concern for the speaker. It's probably the most important type of listening you can engage in. Active listening consists of three steps: paraphrasing the speaker's meaning, expressing understanding of the speaker's feelings, and asking questions.
>
> Your first step in active listening is to paraphrase the speaker's meaning. What is a paraphrase? A paraphrase is a restatement in your own words of the speaker's meaning. That is, you express in your own words what you think the speaker meant. For example, let's say that the speaker said....

**PUBLIC SPEAKING CHOICE POINT: Informative Strategies**
Rene, a lawyer specializing in the rights of those with disabilities and who is wheelchair bound himself, is planning to give an informative speech on the legal requirements of the American Disabilities Act and is considering the strategies he might use. What options does Rene have for introducing his speech? Should he make reference to his own disability and if so, what might he say? How might he organize his speech? What types of presentation aids might he use?

Public Speaking Exercise 10.2, "A Two-Minute Information Speech," on page 232 offers some suggestions for preparing brief information speeches of description, definition, and demonstration.

# Next Steps

The informative speech, which this current chapter examined, is often a large part of the persuasive speech, which the next chapter discusses.

# Essentials of Informing Your Audience

This chapter considered the informative speech, first surveying some general principles and then examining three main types of informative speaking (speeches of description, definition, and demonstration).

## Principles of Informative Speaking

1. Among the principles of communicating information are:

- Look to your audience.
- Stress the relevance and the usefulness of the information to your audience.
- Limit the amount of information you communicate.
- Adjust the level of complexity.
- Relate new information to old.
- Vary the levels of abstraction.
- Make your speech easy to remember.

### Speeches of Description

**2.** Speeches of description examine a process or procedure, an event, an object, or a person.

### Speeches of Definition

**3.** Speeches of definition define a term, system, or theory, or similarities and/or differences among terms.

### Speeches of Demonstration

**4.** Speeches of demonstration show how to do something or how something operates.

# Essential Terms

informative speaking **(213)**
levels of abstraction **(216)**
definition, speeches of **(217)**

demonstration, speeches of **(217)**

description, speeches of **(217)**

# Public Speaking Exercises

### 10.1 Defining Terms

Select one of the following terms and define it, using at least three of the different types of definition considered in Chapter 6 (etymology, authority, negation, specific examples, or direct symbolism): communication, love, friendship, conflict, leadership, audience. You'll find it helpful to visit a few online dictionaries or thesauruses, for example: www.m-w.com/netdict.htm; http://humanities.uchicago.edu/forms_unrest/ROGET.html.

### 10.2 A Two-Minute Informative Speech

Prepare and deliver a two-minute informative speech in which you do one of the following:

- Explain a card game: Explain the way a card game such as solitaire, poker, gin rummy, bridge, canasta, or pinochle is played.

- Explain a board game: Explain the way a board game such as chess, backgammon, Chinese checkers, Go, Othello, Scrabble, Yahtzee, or Monopoly is played.

- Explain food preparation: Explain how to make a pie, a soup, a western omelet, a pizza, roast beef, a dip, or a casserole (any kind you'd like).

- Explain a sport: Explain the way a sport such as football, baseball, basketball, hockey, soccer, tennis, or golf is played.

# Log*On!* my**speech**lab

### Informing Your Audience

Visit MySpeechLab (www.myspeechlab.com) for further discussions of informative speaking and a variety of speeches and videos illustrating the nature of these types of speeches. This is also a good place to revisit My Outline on MSL; it will help you fine tune the structure and organization of your information speeches. You might find it interesting to take a look at some of the classic and contemporary speeches (over 100 are offered) and watch the video of an informative speech. In connection with this chapter's Research Link, see the additional guides for evaluating source material.

# 11

# Persuading Your Audience

## WHY READ THIS CHAPTER?

**Because it will enable you to influence an audience by helping you to:**

- exert influence fairly and ethically through public speaking
- avoid engaging in fallacious reasoning yourself and recognize it in the speeches of others
- organize and develop speeches on facts, values, and policies that change your listeners' attitudes or move your listeners to action

*Setting goals is the first step in turning the invisible into the visible.*

—ANTHONY ROBBINS

The previous chapter focused on informative speaking; it examined the goals of such speaking, essential principles for communicating information, and the varied types of informative speeches. This chapter looks at persuasive speaking, specifically the goals of persuasive speaking, the three major persuasive proofs, the essential principles of persuasion, and the varied types of persuasive speeches you might give.

# Goals of Persuasive Speaking

Generally, the word **persuasion** refers to the process of influencing another person's attitudes, beliefs, values, and/or behaviors. Briefly, as discussed in Chapter 5, an *attitude* is a tendency to behave in a certain way. For example, if you have a positive attitude toward science fiction, then you're likely to watch science fiction movies or read science fiction books; if you have a negative attitude, you'll be likely to avoid such movies and books. A *belief* is a conviction in the existence or reality of something or in the truth of some assertion. For example, some believe that God exists, that democracy is the best form of government, or that soft drugs lead to hard drugs. A *value* is an indicator of what you feel is good or bad, ethical or unethical, just or unjust. Many people in your audience will positively value "college education" or "free speech" and negatively value "discrimination" or "war." In the context of persuasion, the word *behavior* refers to overt, observable actions such as voting for a particular person, contributing money to the Red Cross, or buying a hybrid automobile.

Your persuasive speeches may focus on your listeners' attitudes, beliefs, values, or behaviors. In your persuasive speeches, you may want to accomplish any one of the following three general goals.

## To Strengthen or Weaken Attitudes, Beliefs, or Values

Persuasion often aims to strengthen audience views. For example, religious sermons usually seek to strengthen the existing beliefs of the audience. Similarly, many public service announcements try to strengthen existing beliefs about, say, recycling, smoking, or safe sex. At times, however, you may want to weaken the existing beliefs of the audience—to suggest that what they currently believe may not be entirely true. For example, you might want to weaken the favorable attitudes people might have toward a particular political party or policy. This type of speech is often used in combination with additional efforts designed to gradually weaken existing beliefs and ultimately to change them.

## To Change Attitudes, Beliefs, or Values

Sometimes you'll want to change your audience's thinking. You might want to change their attitudes about the college's no-smoking rules, to change their beliefs about television's influence on viewer violence, or to change their values about the efficacy of war.

## To Motivate to Action

Ultimately, your goal is to get people to do something—for example, to vote for one person rather than another, to donate money to a fund for the homeless, or to take a course in criminology.

It's useful to think of influence as occurring on a **persuasion continuum** ranging from one extreme to another. Let's say that you want to give a persuasive speech on same-sex marriage. You might visualize your audience as existing on a continuum ranging from strongly in favor to strongly opposed, as shown in Figure 11.1. Your task is to move your audience in the direction of your persuasive purpose. You can center your message on strengthening, weakening, or changing your listeners' attitudes, beliefs, or values about same-sex marriage; or you can center your message on moving the listeners to act—to protest, write letters, or sign a petition.

Strongly in favor of same-sex marriage ____ : ____ : ____ : ____ : ____ : ____ : ____ Strongly opposed to same-sex marriage

**FIGURE 11.1**

**The Persuasion Continuum**

Any movement along the continuum would be considered persuasion.

If your purpose is to persuade the audience to oppose same-sex marriage, then in Figure 11.1 any movement toward the right will be successful persuasion; if your purpose is to persuade listeners to support same-sex marriage, then any movement toward the left will be successful persuasion. Notice, however, that it's quite possible to give a speech in which you hope to move your listeners in one direction but actually to succeed in moving them in the other direction. This "negative persuasion" effect can occur, for example, when the audience perceives the speaker as dishonest or self-promoting.

Now that we've considered the general goals of persuasive speaking, let's turn to some principles that can help you become an effective persuader.

# The Three Persuasive Proofs

As mentioned in the first chapter, classical rhetoric (as well as contemporary research) identifies three kinds of persuasive proofs: logical (or *logos*), emotional (or *pathos*), and credibility (or *ethos*).

## Logical Proof

When a speaker persuades listeners with **logical proof**—arguments focusing on facts and evidence rather than on emotions or credibility claims—the listeners

**PUBLIC SPEAKING CHOICE POINT: Selecting Arguments**

Rose is preparing a persuasive speech on a question of policy, arguing that owners of phone-in psychic services should be prosecuted for fraud. What are some of Rose's options for persuading her audience to accept her thesis?

are more likely to remain persuaded over time and are more likely to resist counterarguments that may come up in the future (Petty & Wegener, 1998). We'll look at the three main categories of logical appeals and then at some fallacies of reasoning.

## Reasoning from Specific Instances and Generalizations

In **reasoning from specific instances** (or examples), you examine several specific instances and then conclude something about the whole. This form of reasoning, known as *induction*, is useful when you want to develop a general principle or conclusion but cannot examine the whole. For example, you sample a few communication courses and conclude something about communication courses in general; you visit several Scandinavian cities and conclude something about the whole of Scandinavia. Critically analyze reasoning from specific instances (your own or those of speakers you're listening to) by asking the following questions.

- **Were enough specific instances examined?** Two general guidelines will help you determine how much is enough. First, the larger the group you wish to cover with your conclusion, the greater the number of specific instances you should examine. If you wish to draw conclusions about members of an entire country or culture, you'll have to examine a considerable number of people before drawing even tentative conclusions. On the other hand, if you're attempting to draw a conclusion about a bushel of 100 apples, sampling a few is probably sufficient. Second, the greater the diversity of items in the class, the more specific instances you will have to examine. Some classes or groups of items are relatively homogeneous, whereas others are more heterogeneous; this will influence how many specific instances constitute a sufficient number. Pieces of spaghetti in boiling water are all about the same; thus, sampling one usually tells you something about all the others. On the other hand, communication courses are probably very different from one another, so valid conclusions about the entire range of communication courses will require a much larger sample.

- **Are there significant exceptions?** When you examine specific instances and attempt to draw a conclusion about the whole, take into consideration the exceptions. Thus, if you examine the GPA of computer science majors and discover that 70 percent have GPAs above 3.5, you may be tempted to draw the conclusion that computer science majors are especially bright. But what about the 30 percent who have lower GPAs? How much lower are these scores? This may be a significant exception that must be taken into account when you draw your conclusion and would require you to qualify your conclusion in significant ways. Exactly what kind of or how many exceptions will constitute "significant exceptions" will depend on the unique situation.

## Reasoning from Causes and Effects

In **reasoning from causes and effects,** you may go in either of two directions. You may reason from cause to effect (from observed cause to unobserved effect) or from effect to cause (from observed effect to unobserved cause). In testing your own reasoning from cause to effect or from effect to cause and in evaluating the causal reasoning of others, ask yourself the following questions.

- **Might other causes be producing the observed effect?** If you observe a particular effect (say, high crime or student apathy), you need to ask if causes other than the one you're postulating might be producing these effects. Thus, you might postulate that poverty leads to high crime, but there might be other factors actually causing the high crime rate. Or poverty might be one cause but not the most important cause. Therefore, explore the possibility of other causes producing the observed effects.

- **Is the causation in the direction postulated?** If two things occur together, it's often difficult to determine which is the cause and which is the effect. For example, a lack of interpersonal intimacy and a lack of self-confidence often occur in the same person. The person who lacks self-confidence seldom has intimate relationships with others. But which is the cause and which is the effect? It might be that the lack of intimacy "causes" low self-confidence; it might also be, however, that low self-confidence "causes" a lack of intimacy. Of course, it might also be that some other previously unexamined cause (a history of negative criticism, for example) might be producing both the lack of intimacy and the low self-confidence.

## Reasoning from Sign

**Reasoning from sign** involves drawing a conclusion on the basis of the presence of clues or symptoms that frequently occur together. Medical diagnosis is a good example of reasoning by sign. The general procedure is simple. If a sign and an object, event, or condition are frequently paired, the presence of the sign is taken as proof of the presence of the object, event, or condition. For example, fatigue, extreme thirst, and overeating serve as signs of hyperthyroidism, because they frequently accompany the condition. In using reasoning from sign and in evaluating the reasoning by sign of others, ask yourself the following questions.

- **Do the signs necessitate the conclusion drawn?** Given extreme thirst, overeating, and the like, how certain may you be of the "hyperthyroid" conclusion? With most medical and legal matters we can never be absolutely certain, but we can be certain beyond a reasonable doubt.

- **Are there other signs that point to the same conclusion?** In the thyroid example, extreme thirst could be brought on by any number of factors. Similarly, the fatigue and the overeating could be attributed to other causes. Yet taken together, the three signs seem to point to only one reasonable diagnosis. Generally, the more signs that point toward the conclusion, the more confidence you can have that it's valid.

■ **Are there contradictory signs?** Are there signs pointing toward contradictory conclusions? For example, if the butler had a motive and a history of violence (signs supporting the conclusion that the butler was the murderer) but also had an alibi (a sign pointing to the conclusion of innocence), then the conclusion of guilt would have to be reconsidered or discarded.

## Listening to Logical Arguments and the Fallacies of Reasoning

When listening to logical or seemingly logical arguments, in addition to asking yourself the questions suggested for the various types of reasoning, also listen for what are called the *fallacies of reasoning*: arguments that appear to address issues but really don't. Here are 10 such fallacies (Lee & Lee, 1972, 1995; Pratkanis & Aronson, 1991; Herrick, 2004). Learn to spot fallacies in the speeches of others, and be sure to avoid them in your own speeches.

■ **Anecdotal evidence.** Often you'll hear people use **anecdotal evidence** to "prove" a point: "Women are like that; I know, because I have three sisters." "That's the way Japanese managers are; I've seen plenty of them." One reason this type of "evidence" is inadequate is that it relies on too few observations; it's usually a clear case of over-generalizing on the basis of too few instances. A second reason anecdotal evidence is inadequate is that one person's observations may be unduly clouded by his or her own attitudes and beliefs; your personal attitudes toward women or Japanese-style management, for example, may influence your perception of their behaviors.

■ **Straw man.** A **straw man** argument (like a man made of straw) is a contention that's easy to knock down. In this fallacy, a speaker creates an easy-to-destroy simplification of an opposing position (that is, a straw man) and then proceeds to smash it. But, of course, if the opposing case were presented fairly and without bias, it wouldn't be so easy to demolish.

■ **Appeal to tradition.** Often used as an argument against change, the **appeal to tradition** claims that some proposed innovation is wrong or should not be adopted because it was never done before. This fallacious argument is used repeatedly by those who don't want change. But, of course, the fact that something has not been done before says nothing about its value or whether or not it should be done now.

■ **Bandwagon.** In the **bandwagon** fallacy, often referred to as an argument *ad populum* (to the people), the speaker tries to persuade the audience to accept or reject an idea or proposal because "everybody's doing it" or because the "right" people are doing it. The speaker urges you to jump on this large and popular bandwagon—or be left out by yourself. This is a popular technique in political elections; campaigns trumpet the results of polls in an effort to get undecided voters to jump on the bandwagon of the leading candidate. After all, you don't want to vote for a loser. When this technique is used ethically—when it's true—it's referred to as social proof (discussed later in this chapter, p. 252).

■ **Testimonial.** The **testimonial** technique involves using the image associated with some person to secure your approval (if you respect the person) or your rejection (if you don't respect the person). This is the technique of

# RESEARCH LINK

### Integrating and Citing Research

Even the best and most extensive research would count for little if you didn't integrate it into your speech. By integrating and acknowledging your sources of information in your speech, you'll give fair credit to those whose ideas and research findings you're using, and you'll lessen the risk that anything you say can be interpreted as plagiarism (see pp. 11–13). At the same time you'll help establish your own reputation as a responsible researcher and thus increase your own credibility. Here are a few suggestions for integrating your research into your speech (additional suggestions are presented in Table 11.1, pp. 240–241):

### Cite the Sources in Your Speech

Cite at least the author; if appropriate, cite the publication and the date. Check out some of the speeches reprinted in this book and on any of the many Internet sites, and note how the speakers have integrated their sources in the speech. In your written preparation outline, give the complete bibliographical reference.

Here is an example of how you might cite your source:

> My discussion of the causes of anorexic nervosa is based on the work of Dr. Peter Rowan of the Priory Hospital in London. In an article titled "Introducing Anorexia Nervosa," which I last accessed on October 5, 2007, Rowan notes that "this is a disorder of many causes that come together." It's these causes that I want to cover in this talk.

Although it's possible to overdo oral source citations—to give more information than listeners really need—there are even greater dangers in leaving out potentially useful source information. Because your speeches in this course are learning experiences, it will be better to err on the side of being more rather than less complete.

### Integrate the Citation Smoothly

Avoid lead-in expressions such as "I have a quote here" or "I want to quote an example." Let the audience know that you're quoting by pausing before the quote, taking a step forward, or—to read an extended quotation—referring to your notes. If you want to state more directly that this is a quotation, you might do it this way:

> Recently, Mary Kay Ash put this in perspective: [pause] "A woman can no more duplicate the male style of leadership than an American businessman can exactly reproduce the Japanese style."

### Include Written Citations in Outline

In addition to the oral citation, you'll most likely want to include a listing of your references in your preparation outline. In citing references, first find out what style manual is used in your class or at your school. Generally, it will be a style manual developed by the American Psychological Association (APA), the Modern Language Association (MLA), or the University of Chicago (*The Chicago Manual of Style*). Different colleges and even different departments within a given school often rely on different formats for citing research, which, quite frankly, makes a tedious process even worse.

Fortunately, a variety of websites provide guides to the information you'll need to cite any reference in your speech and will prove excellent complements to Table 11.1. Good starting points are MySpeechLab (www.myspeechlab.com) and Purdue University (http://owl.english.purdue.edu/handouts/research). Both cover APA and MLA style formats and provide examples for citing books, articles, newspaper articles, websites, e-mail, online postings, electronic databases, and more.

The next Research Link, "Museums," appears on page 289.

advertisers who use actors dressed up to look like doctors or plumbers or chefs to sell their products. Sometimes this technique takes the form of using only vague and general "authorities," as in "experts agree," "scientists say," "good cooks know," or "dentists advise."

■ **Transfer.** In **transfer** the speaker associates her or his idea with something you respect (to gain your approval) or with something you detest (to gain your rejection). For example, a speaker might portray a proposal

## TABLE 11.1 The Oral Citation

Here are a few examples and notes on citing your sources in your speech. The written citations would be included at the end of your speech in a list of references. The American Psychological Association (APA) style is used here.

| SOURCE TO BE CITED AND WRITTEN CITATION | ORAL CITATION | RESEARCH AND PRESENTATION NOTES |
|---|---|---|
| **Book**<br>Knapp, M. (2008). *Lying and deception in human interaction.* Boston, MA: Penguin. | Mark Knapp, an authority on nonverbal communication, and the author of *Lying and Deception in Human Interaction* notes some of the cues to look for when judging lying. | Try to establish the importance of the author to add weight to your argument. |
| **Magazine Article**<br>Dixit, J. (February, 2010). The power of first experiences. *Psychology Today* (February, 2010), 60–69. | A February 2010 article in *Psychology Today* magazine notes, and here I'm quoting the author, Jay Dixit, "your first love may come to define what loves means for you." | If the magazine is well known, as is *Psychology Today,* it's sufficient to name the magazine. If it were less well known, then you might establish its credibility for your listeners by noting, for example, its reputation for fairness, its longevity, its well-known authors. |
| **Newspaper Article**<br>Layton, L. Salmonella prompts food recall. *Washington Post* (March 5, 2010). Retrieved from http://www.washingtonpost .com If a letter to the editor or an editorial, then insert [Letter to the Editor] or [Editorial] after the article title. | An article in the online *Washington Post,* one of the world's great newspapers, dated March 5, 2010 reports that . . . | It sometimes helps to establish the credibility of the newspaper—some are more reputable than others. And always include reference to the date of the article. You should also indicate whether it was a regular news item or a letter to the editor or an editorial. |
| **Encyclopedia**<br>Religion: Year in Review 2009. In Encyclopædia Britannica. Retrieved from http://www .britannica.com | The online version of the Encyclopædia Britannica, accessed March 5, 2010, identifies several important interfaith conflicts in 2009. These include . . . | It isn't necessary to say "http://www .britiannica.com." Your audience will know how to access the encyclopedia—especially if they're in this course. |
| **Research Study**<br>Vishwanath, A. From belief-importance to intention, *Communication Monographs* (June 2009), 177–206. | In the July 2009 issue of *Communication Monographs,* one of the official journals of the National Communication Association, research conducted by . . . | In citing a research study, make it clear that what you're reporting is from the primary source and not a magazine's summary of the research (that is, a secondary source). |
| **Website**<br>Child Support Services. Retrieved from http://www.ny .gov. Include the author's name if one is given. | The official New York State website, which you can access at http://www .ny.gov, contains a wealth of information on child support services. | Like blogs, websites vary in accuracy and credibility. Be sure to establish the credibility of the site. |
| **Blog**<br>Huffington, Arianna (2010, March 5). No SAT Scores. The Huffington Post. Retrieved from http://www.huffingtonpost.com | Just this week, Arianna Huffington, perhaps the most widely read of all bloggers and author—you may have seen her on television; she's a frequent guest—reports on colleges not using SAT scores. . . . | Anyone can maintain a blog. If the blog is used for more than examples or illustrations, you need to establish the authority of the blogger and the currency of the post. |
| **Television Show**<br>National Geographic. (2010, March 7). The Truth about Crop Circles. | National Geographic covered this issue in detail earlier this week. In May of this year, Charlie Rose interviewed Smith on *The Nation* on PBS, and Smith agreed that . . . | It's helpful to name the network as well as the specific show. If the program is an interview, then identify the person being interviewed and perhaps the interviewer. |

**TABLE 11.1    The Oral Citation    (*Continued*)**

| SOURCE TO BE CITED AND WRITTEN CITATION | ORAL CITATION | RESEARCH AND PRESENTATION NOTES |
|---|---|---|
| **Personal Interview** Because this is not retrievable, this is not included in the reference list. | In an e-mail interview I conducted with James Wilder, the sheriff of Forest County, in September of this year, Wilder wrote that . . . | State how the interview was conducted—in person, by telephone, or through e-mail—and establish the currency of the interview. |
| **Classroom Lecture** Windes, R. (2011, October 3). Communication at Queens College. | In a lecture last week in History of American Public Address, Professor Russel Windes noted that . . . | Citations of classroom lectures should include the professor's name, the course, and the approximate time the comment was made. |
| **Statistics** Disability in the United States Center for Disease Control and Prevention. Retrieved from http://www.cdc.gov | The Center for Disease Control and Prevention website, which I read earlier this week—provides sobering statistics on the numbers of people with disabilities. They note . . . | It's important with most statistics to stress the authority of the source that collected the statistics (.gov sites are more reliable than .com sites) and the recency of the statistics. Providing information on when you accessed the website will further help you establish the currency of the statistics. |

for condom distribution in schools as a means for "saving our children from AIDS" (to encourage acceptance) or as a means for "promoting sexual promiscuity" (to encourage disapproval). Sports-car manufacturers try to get you to buy their cars by associating them with high status and sex appeal; promoters of exercise clubs and diet plans attempt to associate them with health, self-confidence, and interpersonal appeal.

- **Plain folks.** Using the **plain folks** device, the speaker identifies himself or herself with the audience. The speaker is good—the "reasoning" goes—because he or she is one of the people, just plain folks like everyone else. Of course, the speaker who presents himself or herself as plain folks often is not. And even if he or she is plain folks, it has nothing to do with the issue under discussion.

- **Card-stacking.** In the pseudo-argument known as **card-stacking,** the speaker selects only evidence and arguments that support his or her case and may even falsify evidence or distort facts to better fit the case. Despite these misrepresentations, the speaker presents the supporting materials as "fair" and "impartial."

- **Thin entering wedge.** In using the **thin entering wedge,** a speaker argues against a proposal or new development on the grounds that it will be a "thin entering wedge" that will open the floodgates to all sorts of catastrophes (Chase, 1956). Though often based on no evidence, this argument has been used throughout history to oppose change. Some examples are "wedge" claims that school integration and interracial marriage will bring the collapse of American education and society, same-sex unions will destroy the family, and banning smoking in all public places will lead to the collapse of the restaurant industry.

- **Agenda-setting.** In **agenda-setting** a speaker contends that XYZ is the issue and that all others are unimportant and insignificant. This kind of fallacious appeal is heard frequently, as in "Balancing the budget is the key to the city's survival" or "There's only one issue confronting elementary education in our largest cities, and that is violence." In almost all situations, however, there are many issues and many sides to each issue. Often the person proclaiming that X is the issue really means, "I'll be able to persuade you if you focus solely on X and ignore the other issues."

## Emotional Proof

**Emotional appeals** (or motivational appeals) are appeals to your listeners' feelings, needs, desires, and wants, and can be powerful means of persuasion (Wood, 2000). Specifically, when you use emotional appeals, you appeal to those forces that energize, move, or motivate people to develop, change, or strengthen their attitudes or ways of behaving. For example, one motive might be the desire for status. This desire might motivate someone to enter a high-status occupation or to dress a certain way.

Developed in the late 1960s, one of the most useful analyses of human motives remains Abraham Maslow's fivefold **hierarchy of needs,** reproduced in Figure 11.2 (Maslow, 1970; Benson & Dundis, 2003). One of the assumptions contained in this theory is that people seek to fulfill the needs at the lowest level first. Only when those needs are satisfied do the needs at the next level

**FIGURE 11.2**
**Maslow's Hierarchy of Needs**
How would you describe the satisfied and unsatisfied needs of members of your public speaking class? Which of these needs would, according to Maslow, be most motivating for your class?

*Source:* Based on Abraham Maslow, *Motivation and Personality.* New York: HarperCollins, 1970.

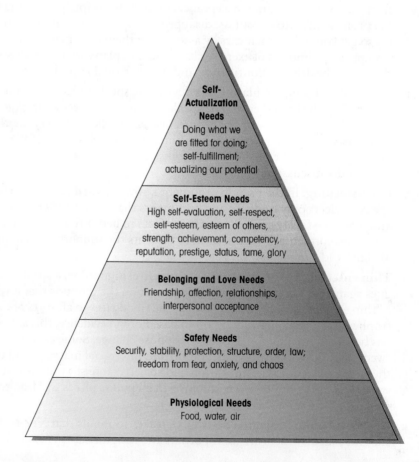

**Self-Actualization Needs**
Doing what we are fitted for doing; self-fulfillment; actualizing our potential

**Self-Esteem Needs**
High self-evaluation, self-respect, self-esteem, esteem of others, strength, achievement, competency, reputation, prestige, status, fame, glory

**Belonging and Love Needs**
Friendship, affection, relationships, interpersonal acceptance

**Safety Needs**
Security, stability, protection, structure, order, law; freedom from fear, anxiety, and chaos

**Physiological Needs**
Food, water, air

begin to influence behavior. For example, people would not concern themselves with the need for security or freedom from fear if they were starving (if their need for food had not been fulfilled). Similarly, they would not be concerned with friendship if their need for protection and security had not been fulfilled. The implication for you as a speaker is that you have to know what needs of your audience are unsatisfied. These are the needs you can appeal to in motivating them.

Here are several useful motivational appeals organized around Maslow's hierarchy. As you review these, try to visualize how you would use each one in your next speech.

## Physiological Needs

In many parts of the world, and even in parts of the United States, the basic physiological needs of people are not fully met. These are powerful motivating forces. In many of the poorest countries of the world, the speaker who promises to meet fundamental physiological needs is the one the people will follow. Most college students in the United States, however, have their physiological needs for food, water, and air well satisfied, so these issues will not prove helpful in motivating and persuading them.

## Safety Needs

Those who do not have their basic safety and freedom-from-fear needs met will be motivated by appeals to security, protection, and freedom from physical harm and from psychological distress. You see appeals to this need in advertisements for burglar protection devices for home and car, in political speeches promising greater police protection on the streets and in schools, and in the speeches of motivational gurus who promise psychological safety and freedom from anxiety. Sometimes the safety motive is seen in individuals' desire for order, structure, and organization—motives clearly appealed to in advertisements for personal data assistants like the cell phones and information management software. Many people fear what is unknown, and order and structure seem to make things predictable and hence safe.

## Belonging and Love Needs

Belonging and love needs are extremely powerful; most people are motivated to love and be loved. If you can teach your audience how to be loved and how to love, your audience will be not only attentive but also grateful. We also want affiliation—friendship and companionship. We want to be a part of a group, despite our equally potent desire for independence and individuality. Notice how advertisements for singles clubs, cruises, and dating services appeal to this need for affiliation. On this basis alone they successfully gain the attention, interest, and participation of thousands.

## Self-Esteem Needs

We have a need for positive **self-esteem:** a favorable self-image, a view of ourselves that casts us in the best possible light. We want to see ourselves as self-confident, worthy, and contributing human beings. Inspirational speeches, speeches of the "you're the greatest" type, never seem to lack receptive and suggestible audiences. People want to achieve in whatever they do. In using the achievement motive, be explicit in stating how your speech, ideas, and recommendations will contribute to the listeners' achievements. At the same time, recognize that different cultures will view achievement very differently. To some, achievement may mean financial success, to others it may mean group popularity, to still others it may mean security. Show your listeners how what you have to say will help them achieve the goals they seek, and you'll likely have an active and receptive audience.

People also want power, control, and influence (1) over themselves—to be in control of their own destiny, to be responsible for their own successes—and (2) over others, that is, to be influential. Because of this you'll motivate your listeners when you make them see that they can increase their power, control, and influence if they learn what you have to say or do as you suggest.

## Self-Actualization Needs

At the top of Maslow's hierarchy is the self-actualization motive. According to Maslow (1970), this motive influences attitudes and behaviors only after all other needs are satisfied. Regardless of how satisfied or unsatisfied your other desires may be, you have a desire to self-actualize—to become what you feel you're fit for. If you see yourself as a poet, you must write poetry. If you see yourself as a teacher, you must teach. Even if you don't pursue these as occupations, you nevertheless have a desire to write poetry or to teach. Appeals to self-actualization needs—to the yearning "to be the best you can be"—encourage listeners to strive for their highest ideals and are often welcomed by the audience.

## Listening to Emotional Appeals

Emotional appeals are all around you, urging you to do all sorts of things—usually to buy a product or to support a position or cause. As you listen to these inevitable appeals, consider the following:

- **Emotional appeals do not constitute proof.** No matter how passionate the speaker's voice or bodily movement, no matter how compelling the language, passion does not prove the case a speaker is presenting.

- **Feelings are not open to public inspection.** You really can't tell with certainty what the speaker is feeling. The speaker may, in fact, be using facial management techniques or clever speechwriters to communicate emotions without actually feeling them.

- **Emotional appeals may be used to divert attention from the lack of real evidence.** If emotional appeals are being used to the exclusion of argument and evidence, or if you suspect that the speaker seeks to arouse your emotions so you forget that there's no evidence, ask yourself why.

- **Emotional appeals may be to high or low motives.** A speaker can arouse feelings of love and peace but also feelings of hatred and war. In asking for charitable donations, an organization may appeal to high motives such as your desire to help those less fortunate than you, or to lower motives such as guilt and fear.

- **Be especially on the lookout for the appeal to pity.** This is what logicians call *argumentum ad misericordiam*, as in "I really tried to do the work, but I've been having terrible depression and find it difficult to concentrate."

Public Speaking Exercise 11.1, "Constructing Motivational Appeals," page 268 provides an opportunity to practice formulating motivational appeals for a variety of different theses.

## Credibility Proof

Your **credibility** is the degree to which your audience regards you as a believable spokesperson. If your listeners see you as competent and knowledgeable, of good character, and charismatic or dynamic, they will find you credible. As a result, you'll be more effective in changing their attitudes or in moving them to do something. Credibility is not something you have or don't have in any objective sense; rather, it's a function of what the audience thinks of you.

What makes a speaker credible will vary from one culture to another. In some cultures people would see competence as the most important factor in, say, their choice of a teacher for their preschool children. In other cultures the most important factor might be the goodness or morality of the teacher or perhaps the reputation of the teacher's family.

At the same time, each culture may define each of the factors in credibility differently. For example, *character* may mean following the rules of a specific religion in some cultures and following the individual conscience in others. To take another example, the Quran, the Torah, and the New Testament will be ascribed very different levels of credibility depending on the religious beliefs of the audience. And this will be true even when all three religious books say essentially the same thing on a given point.

### Competence

Your perceived **competence** is the knowledge and expertise an audience thinks you have. The more knowledge and expertise the audience sees you as having, the more likely the audience will believe you. Similarly, you're likely to believe a teacher or doctor if you think he or she is knowledgeable on the subject at hand. You can demonstrate your competence to your audience in a variety of ways.

- **Tell Listeners of Your Competence.** Let the audience know of any special experience or training that qualifies you to speak on this specific topic. If you're speaking on communal living and you've lived on a commune yourself, then say so in your speech. Tell the audience of your unique personal experiences when these contribute to your

**ETHICAL CHOICE POINT**

**Fear as a Persuasive Strategy?**

You're a student teacher in an elementary school and are required to teach your eighth-grade class the unit on sex education. Your objective, which is mandated by the state syllabus but also is consistent with your own feeling, is to get students to avoid sexual relationships until they are much older. But you know from talking with students that many of them intend to have sexual relationships at the earliest opportunity; in fact, some are currently sexually active. You wonder if it would be ethical to use fear appeals to scare the students about the potential dangers of sex. For example, you could show them photos of people with advanced cases of sexually transmitted diseases, youngsters living in poverty because they now have children to support, and so on. You believe that attitudes and behavior should be motivated by reason and logic and so you wonder if it would be ethical to use such fear appeals. ➤ *Given that you want to be effective but also true to your beliefs, what are some of your ethical choices in this matter?* ➤ *What would you do?*

credibility. This recommendation to tell listeners of your competence generally applies to most audiences you'll encounter in the United States. But in some cultures—notably collectivist cultures such as those of Japan, China, and Korea, for example—to stress your own competence or that of your corporation may be taken as a suggestion that your audience members are inferior or that their corporations are not as good as yours. In other cultures—notably individualist cultures such as those of Scandinavia, the United States, and western Europe, for example—if you don't stress your competence, your listeners may assume it's because you don't have any.

**PUBLIC SPEAKING CHOICE POINT: Establishing Credibility**
Evelyn is planning a speech on baseball. She fears, however, that simply because she's a woman, her audience is not going to perceive her as credible—even though she knows more about baseball than any other person in the room. What options does Evelyn have for making her audience receptive to her speech? How might she introduce her speech?

- **Cite a Variety of Research Sources.** Make it clear to your audience that you've thoroughly researched your topic. Do this by mentioning some of the books you've read, persons you've interviewed, and articles you've consulted. Weave these references throughout your speech. Don't bunch them together at one time.

- **Stress the Competencies of Your Sources.** If your audience isn't aware of them, then emphasize the particular competencies of your sources. In this way it becomes clear to the audience that you've chosen your sources carefully so as to provide the most authoritative sources possible. For example, saying simply, "Senator Cardova thinks . . ." does nothing to establish the senator's credibility. Instead, consider saying something like "Senator Cardova, who headed the finance committee for three years and was formerly a professor of economics at MIT, thinks. . . ."

## Character

An audience will see you as credible if they perceive you as being someone of high moral **character,** someone who is honest, and someone they can trust. When an audience perceives your intentions as good for them (rather than for your own personal gain), they'll think you credible and they'll believe you. You can establish your high moral character in a number of ways.

- **Stress Fairness.** If delivering a persuasive speech, stress that you've examined both sides of the issue (if indeed you have). If you're presenting both sides, then make it clear that your presentation is accurate and fair. Be particularly careful not to omit any argument the audience may already have thought of—this is a sure sign that your presentation isn't fair or balanced. Tell the audience that you would not advocate a position if you did not base it on a fair evaluation of the issues.

■ **Stress Concern for Audience.** Make it clear to the audience that you're interested in their welfare rather than seeking self-gain. If the audience feels that you are "out for yourself," they'll justifiably downgrade your credibility. Make it clear that the audience's interests are foremost in your mind. Tell your audience how the new legislation will reduce *their* taxes, how recycling will improve *their* community, how a knowledge of sexual harassment will make *their* workplace more comfortable and stress free.

■ **Stress Concern for Enduring Values.** We view speakers who are concerned with small and insignificant issues as less credible than speakers who demonstrate a concern for lasting truths and general principles. Thus, make it clear to the audience that your position—your thesis—is related to higher-order values; show them exactly how this is true.

Here, for example, Kofi Annan (2006), in giving his farewell speech as secretary general of the United Nations on September 19, 2006, stressed his concern for enduring values:

> Yes, I remain convinced that the only answer to this divided world must be a truly United Nations. Climate change, HIV/AIDS, fair trade, migration, human rights—all these issues, and many more, bring us back to that point. Addressing each is indispensable for each of us in our village, in our neighborhood, and in our country. Yet each has acquired a global dimension that can only be reached by global action, agreed and coordinated through this most universal of institutions.

## Charisma

**Charisma** is a combination of your personality and dynamism as seen by the audience. An audience will perceive you as credible (and believable) if they like you and if they see you as friendly and pleasant rather than aloof and reserved. Similarly, audiences favor the dynamic speaker over the hesitant, nonassertive speaker. They'll perceive you as less credible if they see you as shy, introverted, and soft-spoken rather than as an extroverted and forceful individual. (Perhaps people feel that a dynamic speaker is open and honest in presenting herself or himself but that a shy, introverted individual may be hiding something.) As a speaker there's much that you can do to increase your charisma and, hence, your perceived credibility.

■ **Demonstrate a Positive Outlook.** Show the audience that you have a positive orientation to the public speaking situation and to the entire speaker–audience encounter. We see positive and forward-looking people as more credible than negative and backward-looking people. Stress your pleasure at addressing the audience. Stress hope rather than despair; stress happiness rather than sadness.

■ **Demonstrate Enthusiasm.** The lethargic speaker, the speaker who somehow plods through the speech, is the very opposite of the charismatic speaker. Try viewing a film of Martin Luther King Jr. or Billy Graham speaking—they're totally absorbed with the speech and with the audience. They're excellent examples of the enthusiasm that makes a charismatic speaker.

- **Be Emphatic.** Use language that is emphatic rather than colorless and indecisive. Use gestures that are clear and decisive rather than random and hesitant. Demonstrate a firm commitment to the position you're advocating; the audience will be much more likely to agree with a speaker who believes firmly in the thesis of the speech.

## Listening to Credibility Appeals and Character Attacks

When you listen to credibility appeals, evaluate them critically. Here are three questions you'll find helpful to ask in assessing credibility appeals:

- **Is the dimension of credibility used relevant to the issue at hand?** For example, are the politician's family members (nice though they may be) relevant to his or her position on gun control or social security or immigration? Is the politician's former military service (or the lack of it) relevant to the issue being discussed?

- **Are credibility appeals being used instead of argument and evidence?** In typical examples of invalid credibility appeals, speakers may emphasize their educational background (to establish "competence"), appear at religious rituals (to establish "moral character"), or endeavor to present themselves as take-charge, alpha-type individuals (to demonstrate "charisma"). When done to divert attention from the issues or to mask the absence of evidence, such appeals are meaningless.

- **Are the credibility appeals true?** The actor who advertises toothpaste dressed as a dentist is still an actor doing a modeling job, not a dentist. Too often people unconsciously attribute credibility to a performance because of a uniform. Even when the endorser is a real dentist, remember that this dentist is getting paid for the endorsement. Although this doesn't necessarily make the endorsement false, it does (or should) make you wonder.

In addition to these general questions, become conscious of fallacious strategies that focus on attacking the person. Be alert for fallacies like the following in the speeches of others, and eliminate them from your own reasoning.

- **Personal interest. Personal interest** attacks may take either of two forms. In one form the speaker disqualifies someone from having a point of view because he or she isn't directly affected by an issue or proposal or doesn't have firsthand knowledge; for example, a speaker might dismiss an argument on abortion merely because the argument was made by a man. In another form the speaker disqualifies someone because he or she will benefit in some way from a proposal. For example, arguing that someone is rich, middle class, or poor and thus will benefit greatly from a proposed tax cut does not mean that the argument for the tax cut is invalid. The legitimacy of an argument can never depend on the gender (or culture) of the individual. Nor can it depend on the gain that a person may derive from the position advocated. The legitimacy of an argument can be judged only on the basis of the evidence and reasoning presented.

- **Character attacks.** Often referred to as *ad hominem* arguments, **character attacks** involve accusing another person (usually an opponent) of some wrongdoing or of some character flaw. The purpose is to discredit the person or to divert attention from the issue under discussion. Arguments

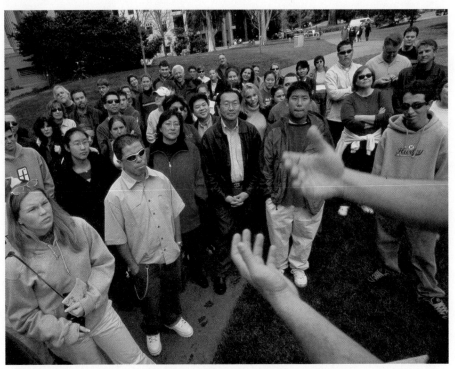

**PUBLIC SPEAKING CHOICE POINT: Negative Audience**
Alan is planning to give a speech in favor of the college's restricting access to certain lifestyle websites. Alan knows that his audience is opposed to his position, so he wonders what types of arguments will work best. What are some of Alan's options? What types of appeals do you think would work best if this speech was given to your class?

such as "How can we support a candidate who has smoked pot [or avoided the military]?" or "Do you want to believe someone who has been unfaithful on more than one occasion?" are often heard in political discussions but probably have little to do with the logic of the argument.

- **Name-calling.** In **name-calling,** often referred to as "poisoning the well," the speaker gives an idea, a group of people, or a political philosophy a bad name ("bigoted," "soft on terrorism,") to try to get listeners to condemn an idea without analyzing the argument and evidence. The opposite of name-calling is the use of "glittering generalities," in which the speaker tries to make you accept some idea by associating it with things you value highly ("democracy," "free speech," "academic freedom"). By using these "virtue words," the speaker tries to get you to ignore the evidence and simply approve of the idea.

# Principles of Persuasive Speaking

You can become more successful in strengthening or changing attitudes or beliefs and in moving your listeners to action by following these guidelines for persuasive speaking.

## Focus on Your Audience

Just as the first principle of informative speaking was to focus on your audience, so it is with persuasion. Begin thinking about your persuasive strategies in terms of the audience's existing beliefs, attitudes, and values. The more you know about your audience, the more you'll be able to address their needs and tailor your persuasive appeals to them specifically. At this point you may want to review the discussion of audience analysis and adaptation presented in Chapter 5, pages 84–104.

## Identify with Your Audience

A closely related principle is that of identification, a process of demonstrating a similarity with your audience. If you can show your audience that you and they share important attitudes, beliefs, and values, you'll clearly advance your persuasive goal. Other similarities are also important. For example, in some cases similarity of cultural, educational, or social background may help you identify yourself with your audience. Be aware, however, that insincere or dishonest identification is likely to backfire and create problems. So avoid even implying similarities between yourself and your audience that don't exist.

As a general rule, never ask the audience to do what you have not done yourself; always demonstrate that you have done what you want the audience to do. If you don't, the audience will rightfully ask, "Why haven't you done it?" In addition, besides doing whatever it may be, show your listeners that you're pleased to have done it. For example, tell them of the satisfaction you derived from donating blood or from reading to blind students.

**PUBLIC SPEAKING CHOICE POINT:** **Stimulating Positive Responses**
Peggy wants to give a persuasive speech arguing that violent computer games should be banned for children under 16 years of age. She knows her audience will be against her so she wonders how she might introduce the topic and get the audience on her side? What are some of Peggy's options for stimulating positive responses in her listeners?

## Secure a Yes Response

Research evidence clearly supports the importance of securing a **yes response** in influencing further compliance (Goldstein, Martin, & Cialdini, 2008). If you can get your listeners to give a yes response to some related issue, they will be more likely to give another yes response (ideally to your thesis). Even if the yes response is to some small request, it will still pave the way to a yes response for a larger request. For example, when homeowners first agreed to install a small "drive safely" sign in their window, they were more likely to agree to a major request (installing a large sign on their perfectly manicured lawns) than were those homeowners who were not asked to install the small sign first.

## Anticipate Selective Exposure

People listen in accordance with the principle of **selective exposure.** This principle or law has two parts: It states that (1) listeners actively seek out information that supports their opinions, beliefs, values, decisions, and behaviors; and (2) listeners actively avoid information that contradicts their existing opinions, beliefs, attitudes, values, decisions, and behaviors.

Of course, if you're very sure that your opinions and attitudes are logical and valid, then you may not bother to seek out supporting information. Similarly, you may not actively avoid contradictory messages. People exercise selective exposure most often when their confidence in their own opinions and beliefs is weak.

If you want to persuade an audience that holds attitudes different from your own, anticipate selective exposure operating and proceed inductively; that is, hold back on your thesis until you've given your evidence and argument. Only then relate this evidence and argument to your initially contrary thesis.

If you were to present them with your thesis first, your listeners might tune you out without giving your position a fair hearing. So become thoroughly familiar with the attitudes of your audience if you want to succeed in making these necessary adjustments and adaptations.

Let's say you're giving a speech on the need to reduce spending on college athletic programs. If your audience were composed of listeners who agreed with you and wanted to cut athletic spending, you might lead with your thesis. Your introduction might go something like this:

> Our college athletic program is absorbing money that we can more profitably use for the library, science labs, and language labs. Let me explain how the money now going to unnecessary athletic programs could be better spent in these other areas.

On the other hand, suppose you were addressing alumni who strongly favored the existing athletic programs. In this case, you might want to lead with your evidence and then state your thesis.

> Our college library, science labs, and computer labs are badly in need of upgrades. Let's see how we can all profit from these upgrades and then we'll consider from where this money might come.

## Use Positive Labeling

People generally act in ways consistent with the way in which they are labeled, especially if the label is a favorable one that reflects positively on the individual. So if you describe your listeners as possessing a particular attitude or trait (and for ethical reasons, you need to truly believe that they actually do possess such attitudes or traits), they'll be more apt to act in accordance with the label (Goldstein, Martin, & Cialdini, 2008). For example, let's say that you want to motivate your audience to denote time to working with students who have learning disabilities. If you describe your audience as caring, compassionate, and helpful, for example, they'll be more apt to think of themselves in that way and be more apt to agree to requests that other caring, compassionate, and helpful people do.

## Ask for Reasonable Amounts of Change

The greater and more important the change you want to encourage in your audience, the more difficult your task will be. Put in terms of the continuum of persuasion introduced earlier, this principle suggests that you'll be more successful if you ask for small movements in the direction of your speech purpose. The reason is simple: As listeners we normally demand a greater number of reasons and a lot more evidence before we make important choices—such as, say, deciding to change careers, move to another state, or invest in stocks.

On the other hand, we may be more easily persuaded (and demand less evidence) on relatively minor issues—whether to take a course in "Small Group Communication" rather than "Persuasion" or to give to the United Heart Fund instead of the American Heart Fund.

Generally, people change gradually, in small degrees over a long period of time. Persuasion, therefore, is most effective when it strives for small changes and works over a period of time. For example, a persuasive speech stands a better chance when it tries to get a drinker to attend just one AA meeting rather than advocating giving up alcohol for life. If you try to convince your audience to change their attitudes radically or to engage in behaviors to which they're initially opposed, your attempts may backfire. In this type of situation, listeners may tune you out, closing their ears to even the best and most logical arguments.

So in your classroom speeches, set reasonable goals for what you want the audience to do. Remember you have only perhaps 10 minutes, and in that time you cannot move the proverbial mountain. Instead, ask for small, easily performed behaviors. Encourage your listeners to visit a particular website (perhaps even one dedicated to beliefs or values that they do not currently share), to vote in the next election, or to buy the new virus protection software.

## Provide Social Proof

You provide **social proof** when you give your listeners examples of other people doing what you want them to do (Surowiecki, 2005; Goldstein, Martin, & Cialdini, 2008). So, for example, let's say you want your listeners to turn off their cell phones during classes. How might you achieve this? Consider these two alternatives:

1. So many people leave on their cell phones which annoy others. This is just an example of gross inconsideration for the rights of others.
2. So many people are turning off their cell phones and acting with consideration for others.

Which strategy is likely to prove more effective? In (1) you offer what is called **negative social proof**—you're showing your listeners that many people do what they should not do. And, they may reason, if everyone is doing it, why shouldn't I? In (2) you offer **positive social proof**—you're showing your listeners that many people do what you want them to also do. And, again, they are more likely to do what others are doing—namely what you want them to do. This "herd instinct" is a powerful impulse.

## Motivate Your Listeners with Limited Choices

If you want to persuade your listeners, you have to motivate them to believe or to act in some way. One way to motivate, as explained in Chapter 7 (pp. 139–144), is to use the motivated sequence—the organizational structure in which you

**TABLE 11.2   The Motivated Sequence as a Persuasive Strategy**

This table summarizes the motivated sequence as used in persuasive speeches.

| STEP AND PURPOSE | AUDIENCE QUESTION SPEAKER SHOULD ANSWER | IDEAL AUDIENCE RESPONSE | CAUTIONS TO OBSERVE |
|---|---|---|---|
| **Attention:** Focus listeners' attention on you and your message. | Why should I listen? Is this worth my time? | ■ This sounds interesting.<br>■ Tell me more. | Make attention relevant to speech topic. |
| **Need:** Demonstrate that there is a problem that affects them. | Why do I need to know or do anything? | ■ Ok, I understand; there's a problem.<br>■ Something needs to be done. | Don't overdramatize the need. |
| **Satisfaction:** Show listeners how they can satisfy the need. | How can I do anything about this? | ■ I can change things.<br>■ I know what I can do.<br>■ I'm empowered. | Answer any objections listeners might have to your plan. |
| **Visualization:** Show listeners what the situation will be like with the need satisfied. | How would anything be different or improved? | ■ *Wow!* Things look a lot better this way.<br>■ That change was really needed. | Be realistic; don't visualize the situation as perfect. |
| **Action:** Urge listeners to act. | What can I do to effect this change? | ■ Let me sign up.<br>■ Here's my contribution.<br>■ I'll participate. | Be specific. Ask for small changes and behaviors. |

gain your listeners' attention, demonstrate that a need exists, demonstrate how that need can be satisfied by their believing or doing what you say, showing them what things will be like if the need is satisfied as you suggested, and urging them to do something to solve the problem.

In using this principle, it is more effective to offer the listeners a limited number of choices in acting as you want them to act. For example, if you want your listeners to participate more in community affairs, be specific and suggest a limited number of ways in which they can participate. If you suggest too many choices, your listeners are more likely to do nothing (Schwartz, 2004; Goldstein, Martin, & Cialdini, 2008).

Table 11.2 summarizes the motivated sequence as a persuasive strategy and will help you develop your speeches whether they deal with questions of fact, value, or policy—the topics to which we turn later in this chapter.

# Culture and Persuasion

Cultural differences are especially important in persuasion; the appeals you'd use to influence one cultural group would not be the same you'd use for a different group. You can appreciate the importance of this by looking at seven dimensions of culture with persuasive strategies in mind (Hall, 1976; Hall & Hall, 1987; Hofstede, Hofstede, & Minkov, 2010; Singh & Pereira, 2005).

## Individualist and Collectivist Cultures

As you will recall from Chapter 3, individualist cultures (such as the United States, Australia, United Kingdom, Netherlands, Canada, New Zealand, Italy, Belgium, Denmark, and Sweden) emphasize the individual, individual success, and individual responsibility. In collectivist cultures (such as Guatemala, Ecuador, Panama, Venezuela, Colombia, Indonesia, Pakistan, China, Costa Rica, and Peru), the group or family or organization is more important than the individual. In appealing to members of individualistic cultures, you'll want to emphasize such themes as independence, nonconformity, and uniqueness. You'll also be well advised to stress your competence; if you don't, your listeners may assume it's because you don't have any. In a speech to members of a collectivist culture, on the other hand, successful appeals will emphasize the importance of family, of loyalty (to brand names or local organizations), and of national identity and pride (Han & Shavitt, 1994; Dillard & Marshall, 2003). In collectivist cultures, to stress your own competence or that of your corporation may prove insulting; it may be taken as a suggestion that your audience members are inferior or that their corporations are not as good as yours.

## High- and Low-Power-Distance Cultures

In high-power-distance cultures (such as Mexico, Brazil, India, and the Philippines), there is a large difference between those who have and those who don't have power. In low-power-distance cultures (such as Denmark, New Zealand, Sweden, and to a lesser extent the United States), there is little difference. When you are addressing members of a high-power-distance culture, references to important and prominent people and to what they believe and advocate will prove effective. In a low-power distance culture, however, these appeals will prove less effective than will, say, references to or testimonials from people much like the people you want to influence.

## High- and Low-Uncertainty-Avoidance Cultures

In some cultures, people do little to avoid uncertainty and have little anxiety about not knowing what will happen next. In some other cultures, however, uncertainty is strongly avoided and there is much anxiety about uncertainty. Members of high-ambiguity-tolerance cultures don't feel threatened by uncertainty; such cultures include, for example, Singapore, Jamaica, Denmark, Sweden, Hong Kong, Ireland, Great Britain, Malaysia, India, Philippines, and the United States. Members of low-ambiguity-tolerance cultures do much to avoid uncertainty and have much anxiety about not knowing what will happen next; these cultures include, for example, Greece, Portugal, Guatemala, Uruguay, Belgium, El Salvador, Japan, Yugoslavia, Peru, France, Chile, Spain, and Costa Rica. Audiences high in uncertainty avoidance want information from experts (or supported by experts)—they want to know very clearly where they can go for information and guidance. These audiences also value tradition, so appeals to the past will prove effective. Audiences low in uncertainty avoidance are more ready to accept the new and the different.

## Masculine and Feminine Cultures

Some cultures emphasize stereotypically masculine values of strength, status, and success; examples include Japan, Austria, Venezuela, Italy, Switzerland, Mexico, Ireland, Jamaica, Great Britain, and Germany. Other cultures emphasize stereotypically feminine values of intimacy, relationships, and fidelity; for example, Sweden, Norway, Netherlands, Denmark, Costa Rica, Yugoslavia, Finland, Chile, Portugal, and Thailand. The message here is clear; audience members with "masculine" cultural beliefs will be motivated by appeals to achievement, adventure, and enjoyment and will welcome the "hard sell." Listeners from cultures high in "femininity" will be motivated by "soft sell" appeals and by appeals to harmony and aesthetic qualities.

It should be mentioned that some may find these terms likely to further stereotyping and offer substitutes such as achievement orientation versus people orientation. But since *masculine* and *feminine* are the terms under which this research is conducted and the terms you'd use in your Internet searches, they are used here with the caveat that they are intended to capture the way lots of people think of these two cultural orientations and not to further stereotyping (Lustig & Koester, 2009).

## High- and Low-Context Cultures

As noted earlier in connection with the discussion of speech organization (Chapter 7, pp. 136–146), in some cultures information is part of the context and does not have to be verbalized explicitly; these high-context cultures are also collectivist, as seen in the Japanese, Arabic, Latin American, Thai, Korean, Apache, and Mexican cultures. In low-context cultures, which are also individualist cultures, information is made explicit and little is taken for granted. Low-context cultures include those of Germany, Sweden, Norway, and the United States. Listeners from high-context cultures will favor appeals that are indirect and implied; listeners from low-context cultures will want detail, directness, and explicitness.

## Short- and Long-Term Oriented Cultures

Some cultures (Puerto Rico, Ghana, Egypt, Trinidad, Nigeria, and Dominican Republic are examples) teach a short-term orientation, an orientation that emphasizes the present with such beliefs as *spend now* and *enjoy yourself now*. Appeals that are addressed to these present and immediate concern—how to enjoy yourself—will likely prove effective here. Other cultures (South Korea, Taiwan, Japan, China, Ukraine, and Germany are examples) teach a long-term orientation, an orientation that promotes the importance of future rewards, and would be especially persuaded by appeals that address these future rewards, for example, the promise of wealth or promotion, the importance of saving, the need for a healthy diet, the importance of insurance.

## Indulgent and Restrained Cultures

Cultures also differ in their emphasis on indulgence (these cultures are also largely short-term oriented) or restraint (these cultures are also largely long-term oriented). Cultures high in indulgence (Venezuela, Mexico, Puerto Rico, El Salvador, Nigeria, and Colombia are examples) are concerned with two main values: (1) the feeling that you may do as you wish, that you aren't obligated to do what others want you to do and (2) having leisure time. Together, these values define happiness—a major concern of cultures high in indulgence. Cultures low in indulgence, or high in restraint (Pakistan, Egypt, Latvia, Ukraine, Albania, and Belarus are examples) foster the curbing of gratification; too much fun is not honorable. Appeals to be thrifty or to save or study for the future, for example, are likely to be well received by cultures high in restraint (they're looking toward the future) and less well received by cultures high in indulgence (they want to enjoy themselves now). Similarly, friendships are more highly valued in indulgent than in restrained cultures and so examples and appeals to the importance of friendship will be received very differently by the different cultures.

# Persuasive Speeches on Questions of Fact

**Questions of fact** concern what is or is not true, what does or does not exist, what did or did not happen. Some questions of fact are easily answered. These include many academic questions you're familiar with: Who was Aristotle? How many people use the Internet to get news? When was the first satellite launched? Questions of fact also include more mundane questions: What's on television? When is the meeting? What's Jenny's e-mail address? You can easily find answers to these questions by looking at some reference book, finding the relevant website, or asking someone who knows the answer.

The questions of fact that we deal with in persuasive speeches are a bit different. Although these questions also have answers, the answers are not that easy to find and in fact may never be found. The questions concern controversial issues for which different people have different answers. Daily newspapers and Internet websites abound in questions of fact. For example, on March 23, 2010, Google News (**www.news.google.com**) contained articles suggesting such questions of fact as: What social security powers were extended in Thailand? What is the quarrel between Google and China? What are the NFL's new playoff overtime rules? What is the carbon tax plan? What led to the fall of ACORN?

## Thesis

For a persuasive speech on a question of fact, you'll formulate a thesis based on a factual statement such as:

- This company has a glass ceiling for women.
- The plaintiff was slandered (or libeled or defamed).
- The death was a case of physician-assisted suicide.
- Gay men and lesbians make competent military personnel.
- Television violence leads to violent behavior in viewers.

If you were preparing a persuasive speech on, say, the first example given above, you might phrase your thesis as "This company discriminates against women." Whether or not the company does discriminate is a question of fact; clearly the company either does or does not discriminate. Whether you can prove it does or it doesn't, however, is another issue.

## Main Points

Once you've formulated your thesis, you can generate your main points by asking the simple question "How do you know this?" or "Why would you believe this is true (factual)?" The answers to one of these questions will enable you to develop your main points. The bare bones of your speech might then look something like this:

| | |
|---|---|
| General purpose: | To persuade. |
| Specific purpose: | To persuade my listeners that this company discriminates against women. |
| Thesis: | This company discriminates against women. [**How can we tell that this company discriminates against women?**] |

I. Women earn less than men.

II. Women are hired less often than men.

III. Women occupy fewer managerial positions than men.

Make sure that you clearly connect your main points to your thesis in your introduction, when introducing each of the points, and again in your summary. Don't allow the audience to forget that when women earn lower salaries than men, it directly supports the thesis that this company discriminates against women.

## Support

Having identified your main points, you will then begin searching for information to support them. Taking the first point, you might develop it something like this:

I. Women earn less than men.

A. Over the past five years, the average salary for editorial assistants was $6,000 less for women than it was for men.

B. Over the past five years, the entry-level salaries for women averaged $4,500 less than the entry-level salaries for men.

C. Over the past five years, the bonuses earned by women were 20 percent below the bonuses earned by men.

The speech in the Public Speaking Sample Assistant (pp. 263–265) focuses entirely on a question of fact; the thesis itself is a question of fact. In other speeches, however, you may want just one of your main points to center on a question of fact. So, for example, let's say you're giving a speech advocating that the military give gay men and lesbians full equality. In this case, one of your points might focus on a question of fact: You might seek to establish that gay men and lesbians make competent military personnel. Once you've established that, you'd then be in a better position to argue for equality in military policy.

In a speech on questions of fact, you'll want to emphasize logical proof. Facts are your best support. The more facts you have, the more persuasive you'll be in dealing with questions of fact. For example, the more evidence you can find that women earn less than men, the more convincing you will be in proving that women do in fact earn less and, ultimately, that women are discriminated against.

Use the most recent materials possible. The more recent your materials, the more relevant they will be to the present time and the more persuasive they're likely to be. Notice, in our example, that if you said that in 1980 women earned on average $13,000 less than men, it would be meaningless in proving that the company discriminates against women *now*.

## Organization

Speeches on questions of fact probably fit most clearly into a topical organizational pattern, in which each reason for your thesis is given approximately equal weight. Notice, for example, that the outline of the speech under "Main Points" (p. 257) uses a topical order: Each of the reasons pointing to discrimination is treated as an equal main point.

# Persuasive Speeches on Questions of Value

**Questions of value** concern what people consider good or bad, moral or immoral, just or unjust. Google News (March 23, 2010), for example, identified such questions of value as these: What is the value of the Health Reform bill? What is the value of a tax on carbon? Should there be a limit on political campaign spending? Are subsidies for Airbus helpful to the economy? Should Kim Kardashian and Reggie Bush end their relationship?

Speeches on questions of value will seek to strengthen audiences' existing attitudes, beliefs, or values. This is true of much religious and political speaking; for example, people who listen to religious speeches usually are already believers, so these speeches strive to strengthen the beliefs and values the people already hold. In a religious setting, the listeners already share the speaker's values and are willing to listen. Speeches that seek to change audience values are much more difficult to construct. Most people resist change. When you try to get people to change their values or beliefs, you're fighting an uphill (though not necessarily impossible) battle.

Be sure that you clearly define the specific value on which you're focusing. For example, let's say that you're developing a speech to persuade high school students to attend college. You want to stress that college is of value, but what type of value do you focus on? The financial value (college graduates earn more money than nongraduates)? The social value (college is a lot of fun and a great place to make friends)? The intellectual value (college will broaden your view of the world and make you a more critical and creative thinker)? Once you clarify the type of value on which you'll focus, you'll find it easier to develop the relevant points. You'll also find it easier to locate appropriate supporting materials.

## Thesis

Theses devoted to questions of value might look something like this:

- The death penalty is unjustifiable.
- Bullfighting is inhumane.
- Discrimination on the basis of affectional orientation is wrong.
- Chemical weapons are immoral.
- Human cloning is morally justified.
- College athletics minimize the importance of academics.

## Main Points

As with speeches on questions of fact, you can generate the main points for a speech on a question of value by asking a strategic question of your thesis, such as "Why is this good?" or "Why is this immoral?" For example, you can take the first thesis given above and ask, "Why is the death penalty unjustifiable?" The answers to this question will give you the speech's main points. The body of your speech might then look something like this:

General purpose:   To persuade.

Specific purpose:   To persuade my listeners that the death penalty is unjustifiable.

Thesis:   The death penalty is unjustifiable. **[Why is the death penalty unjustifiable?]**

I. The criminal justice system can make mistakes.

II. The death penalty constitutes cruel and unusual punishment.

III. No one has the moral right to take another's life.

## Support

To support your main points, search for relevant evidence. For example, to show that mistakes have been made in capital punishment cases, you might itemize three or four high-profile cases in which people were put to death and later, through DNA, found to have been innocent.

At times, and with certain topics, it may be useful to identify the standards you would use to judge something moral or justified or fair or good. For example, in the "bullfighting is inhumane" speech, you might devote your first main point to defining when an action can be considered inhumane. In this case, the body of your speech might look like this:

I. An inhumane act has two qualities.

  A. It is cruel and painful.

  B. It serves no human necessity.

II. Bullfighting is inhumane.

  A. It is cruel and painful.

  B. It serves no necessary function.

Notice that in the example of capital punishment, the speaker aims to strengthen or change the listeners' beliefs about the death penalty. The speaker is not asking the audience to do anything about capital punishment, but merely to believe that it's not justified. However, you might also use a question of value as a first step toward persuading your audience to take some action. For example, once you got your listeners to see the death penalty as unjustified, you might then ask them to take certain actions—perhaps in your next speech—to support an anti–death penalty politician, to vote for or against a particular proposition, or to join an organization fighting against the death penalty.

## Organization

Like speeches on questions of fact, speeches on questions of value often lend themselves to topical organization. For example, the speech on capital punishment cited earlier uses a topical order. But even within this topical order there is another level of organization, an organization that begins with those items on which there is the least disagreement or opposition and moves on to the items on which your listeners are likely to see things very differently. It's likely that even listeners in favor of the death penalty would agree that mistakes can be made; and such listeners probably would be willing to accept evidence that mistakes have in fact been made—especially if you cite reliable statistical evidence and expert testimony. By starting with this issue, you secure initial agreement and can use that as a basis for approaching areas where you and the audience are more likely to disagree.

## Persuasive Speeches on Questions of Policy

When you move beyond a focus on value to urging your audience to do something about an issue, you're then into a question of policy. For example, in a speech designed to convince your listeners that bullfighting is inhumane, you'd be focusing on a question of value. If you were to urge that bullfighting should therefore be declared illegal, you'd be urging the adoption of a particular policy.

Items on Google News (March 23, 2010) that suggested questions of policy included these: What should be the policy of the United States and Mexico to combat drugs? Should advertisers rehire Tiger Woods? What should Google do in China? How can the popular drain from manufacturing areas be reversed? What should be our policy concerning the taxing of carbon?

**Questions of policy** concern what should be done, what procedures should be adopted, what laws should be changed; in short, what policy should be followed. In some speeches you may want to defend or promote a specific policy; in others you may wish to argue that a current policy should be discontinued. Table 11.3 summarizes and compares questions of fact, value, and policy.

## Thesis

Persuasive speeches frequently revolve around questions of policy and may use theses such as the following:

**TABLE 11.3    Questions of Fact, Value, and Policy**

This table summarizes the three types of persuasive speeches in terms of their purposes, examples of the types of questions such speeches deal with, and the questions the audience is likely to ask and that you will likely want to have answers for somewhere in your speech.

| QUESTION PURPOSES | EXAMPLES | QUESTIONS AUDIENCE MAY WANT ANSWERED |
|---|---|---|
| **Questions of Fact** To persuade listeners that something is true or false | ■ Higgins is guilty (not guilty). ■ What he did was criminal (legal). ■ The stock market will go much higher (much lower). | ■ Is this the most likely interpretation of the issue? ■ Are other, more likely, explanations possible? ■ How do we know that this is true or that this is false? |
| **Questions of Value** To persuade listeners in the value of something, that something is good, moral, or just | ■ Higgins deserves the chair (to go free). ■ Universal health care is essential (not essential). | ■ Why is this good or just or the right thing to do? Are there alternatives that would be more just or fairer? ■ The war is just (unjust) |
| **Questions of Policy** To persuade listeners that this is the policy to adopt or not adopt | ■ The verdict must be guilty (not guilty). ■ Plan B needs to be enacted (discarded). ■ The war needs to be continued (discontinued). | ■ Might there be better courses of action to follow? ■ Are there downsides to this course of action? |

■ Hate speech should be banned on college campuses.

■ Our community should adopt a zero tolerance policy for guns in schools.

■ Abortion should be available on demand.

■ Music CDs should be rated for violence and profanity.

■ Medical marijuana should be legalized.

■ Smoking in cars should be banned.

As you can tell from these examples, questions of policy almost invariably involve questions of values. For example, the argument that hate speech should be banned at colleges is based on the value judgment that hate speech is wrong. To argue for a zero tolerance policy on guns in schools implies that you think it's wrong for students or faculty to carry guns to school.

## Main Points

You can develop your speech on a question of policy by asking a strategic question of your thesis. With policy issues, the question will be "Why should this policy be adopted?" or "Why should this policy be discontinued?" or "Why is this policy better than what we now have?" Taking our first example, we might ask, "Why should hate speech be banned on campus?" From the answers to this question, you would develop your main points, which might look something like this:

I.  Hate speech encourages violence against women and minorities.

II. Hate speech denigrates women and minorities.

III. Hate speech teaches hate instead of tolerance.

## Support

You would then support each main point with a variety of supporting materials that would convince your audience that hate speech should be banned from college campuses. For example, you might cite the websites put up by certain groups that advocate violence against women and minority members, or quote from the lyrics of performers who came to campus. Or you might cite examples of actual violence that had been accompanied by hate speech or hate literature.

In some speeches on questions of policy, you might simply want your listeners to agree that the policy you're advocating is a good idea. In other cases you might want them to do something about the policy—to vote for a particular candidate, to take vitamin C, to diet, to write to their elected officials, to participate in a walkathon, to wear an AIDS awareness ribbon, and so on.

## Organization

Speeches on questions of policy may be organized in a variety of ways. For example, if the existing policy is doing harm, consider using a cause-to-effect pattern. If your policy is designed to solve a problem, consider the problem-solution pattern. For example, in a speech advocating zero tolerance for guns in school, the problem–solution pattern would seem appropriate; your speech would be divided into two basic parts:

I.  Guns are destroying our high schools. **[problem]**

II. We must adopt a zero tolerance policy. **[solution]**

Questions of policy are often well suited to organization with the motivated sequence. Here is an example how a talk about hate speech might employ the motivated sequence.

### Attention

I.  Here are just a few of the examples of hate speech I collected right here on campus. [Show slides 1–7]

### Need

II. Hate speech creates all sorts of problems.

A. Hate speech encourages violence.

B. Hate speech denigrates women and minorities.

C. Hate speech teaches intolerance.

### Satisfaction

III. If we're to build an effective learning environment, hate speech must go.

# PUBLIC SPEAKING SAMPLE ASSISTANT

## A Persuasive Speech

Here is an excellent persuasive speech. "The Home of the Slaves," given by Jayme Meyer of the University of Texas at Austin at the American Forensic Association's National Individual Events tournament in 2004. The speech is used here with the permission of Jayme Meyer.

### THE HOME OF THE SLAVES
#### Jayme Meyer*

History books tell us that slavery ended after the Civil War. Try telling that to Andrea. At the age of 4, she was sold by her mother and enslaved for 12 years. Locked in a basement with 16 other children, the *New York Times Magazine* of January 25, 2004, explains, Andrea was raped almost every night while her owner got rich. Tragically, Andrea and her companions were not victims of an inadequate Third World government, but, according to the September 2003 *National Geographic,* they are among the almost 150,000 slaves currently held here in the United States.

Unlike the slaves of our early history, these slaves are lured to America with false promises of a better life through well-paying jobs or marriage. But as the *Boston Globe* of April 17, 2003, elaborates, once they arrive, these immigrants are forced to work in "brothels, sweatshops, fields, or private homes." And the terror doesn't stop there. The *San Antonio Express News* of April 3, 2003, reveals that slavery is now the third-largest source of money for organized crime, generating $19 billion annually, money that is often used for other criminal activity, including drug trafficking and arms smuggling, producing more crime for all of us to deal with here at home.

So in order to break this cycle of slavery, we must first, explore the extent of slavery in the United States; next, understand why this problem keeps us in chains; and finally, implement some solutions to what John Miller of the U.S. State Department calls in the *Washington Post* of January 1, 2004, "the emerging human rights issue of the 21st century."

The 13th Amendment was supposed to end slavery in December 1865, but even today slaves are forced into the U.S. and slavery fosters additional crime. Kristiina Kangaspunta of the United Nations tells the Associated Press of May 13, 2003, that the United States is now one of the top three human trafficking destinations in the world, with most slaves originating from Thailand, Russia, or the Ukraine. The January 25, 2004, *New York Times Magazine* explains that traffickers promise slaves

This is a particularly dramatic story designed **to gain attention** and **to suggest the topic** of the speech. Did it gain your attention? If not, what else might the speaker have done?

Is 150,000 people a lot? How might the speaker have dramatized this number and made its **significance** more apparent to an audience of college students?

This elaboration continues to dramatize the situation of modern slavery and presents it as a problem for the listeners. Was the speaker successful in **convincing** you that this is a problem for society and for you? If not, what else might the speaker have done to convince you that this problem really affected you personally?

Here the speaker provides an excellent **orientation** to the speech and identifies the three major sections of the speech: (1) the present state of slavery in the United States, (2) the reasons this is a problem, and (3) ways of solving the problem.

The **organizational pattern** is also identified; the first two sections present the problem and the third presents the solution. In what other ways could this speech have been organized?

Here the speaker begins to explain the current state of slavery and makes us see it as a horrendous crime.

The speaker continues to introduce current material (note that the speech was delivered in 2004) from reliable sources and

*"The Home of the Slaves" by Jayme Meyer of the University of Texas at Austin, given at the American Forensic Association's National Individual Events tournament in 2004. The speech is used here with the permission of Jayme Meyer.

better lives in the U.S. as waiters, actors, models or nannies. But after tricking them into paying their own way into Mexico, the traffickers smuggle them across the border and force them into a nightmare world of brutality. According to the U.S. Department of State's *Trafficking in Persons Report* of June 11, 2003, slaves are exposed to appalling working conditions, sexually transmitted diseases from rape and forced prostitution, poor nutrition, and even torture. For instance, four girls between the ages of 14 and 17 were recently discovered working in an underground brothel in Plainfield, New Jersey. The same *New York Times Magazine* described the conditions when the police found them: the emaciated girls slept on rotting mattresses, used a doorless, filthy bathroom, and were surrounded by morning-after pills and abortion-inducing medications.

Although we may not personally be enslaved, all of us are affected by America's slave trade. According to the summer/fall 2003 *Brown Journal of World Affairs*, the profits made from slavery are often invested in the mainstream economy, giving criminal networks more power because of their immense wealth. And the more they make, the more we're affected. As M2 Presswire of October 14, 2003, explains, crime syndicates use the billions of dollars generated by slavery to fund other criminal activities, including drug trafficking, arms smuggling, and money laundering. While 150,000 slaves suffer the immediate evils of slavery, all of us are endangered by its long-term implications.

We pride ourselves on our freedoms, but 150,000 people within our borders are denied theirs because of slavery's lucrative nature and ineffective legislation. The *Agence France Presse* of August 1, 2003, reports the results of an International Labour Organization study: modern-day slavery is "more lucrative . . . than drug trafficking." As the aforementioned *Trafficking in Persons Report* reveals, slave owners make up to thousands of dollars for each child laborer and tens of thousands for each brothel worker. And, as a February 24, 2004, article on the Florida State University Web page notes, "unlike drugs, humans can be recycled . . . so it's a better investment for the traffickers." And according to the *National Geographic* of September 2003, countless people take advantage of its lucrative nature: Juan, Ramiro, and Jose Ramos forced men and women from Mexico to pick fruit in Florida. Sardar and Nadira Gasanov made women from Uzbekistan work in strip clubs in West Texas. Louisa Satia and Kevin Nanji tricked a 14-year-old girl from Cameroon into working as their private servant in Maryland after raping her and imprisoning her in their house—and the list goes on.

And unfortunately, current laws are simply not strong enough. The Trafficking Victims Protection Act of 2000 has done a good job of protecting some victims, giving former slaves temporary U.S. visas and offering protection from their traffickers. But helping victims

makes us feel he is **well prepared and knowledgeable,** which adds to his **credibility.**

The speaker makes a great effort to make the topic of these enslaved individuals **significant for a group of listeners** who are probably quite comfortable and secure. Did the speaker succeed in making you feel that this problem affects you? If not, what else might the speaker have done?

Here the speaker moves from general statements about slavery to a specific case of four girls. Moving from the **abstract to the specific** is a useful technique for making your listeners understand and feel the problem.

The speaker cleverly **answers the potential audience question** ("Why should this concern me?") by relating the problem to one that creates additional crime from which we all suffer. Was the speaker successful in getting you to feel that this is important to you? How much do you care about these other problems—drug trafficking, arms smuggling, and money laundering? If you don't care very much, what might the speaker have done to make you care?

What has the speaker done throughout this speech to **identify with the audience**? What else might the speaker have done?

Would selective exposure play a role in this speech? If so, what could the speaker do to **anticipate selective exposure?**

What kinds of **logical appeals** does the speaker use in this speech? How effective are they?

Again, the speaker cleverly weaves in **specific examples** along with the generalizations and gives the problem a human face.

What types of **emotional appeals** can you find throughout this speech? How effective are they? How might they have been made even more effective?

Can you find any examples of the **principles of persuasion** discussed in this chapter, for example, identification or social proof?

after they are discovered doesn't get to the root of the problem; getting traffickers off the streets would. The *San Antonio Express News* of April 3, 2003, states that while $60 million per year is spent on the cause, only 75 traffickers were actually prosecuted in 2000, simply not enough for the problem that Assistant Secretary of State Richard Armitage tells the *Weekly Standard* of October 6, 2003, will "outstrip the illicit trade in guns and narcotics within a decade."

We thought we abolished slavery in 1865, but the fight obviously is not over. Action from the UN and the United States government, as well as our own attention, can help protect those who have lost all freedom. The United Nations needs to follow through with its international database of human trafficking. As a UN press release of May 16, 2003, states, the database, now consisting of about 3,000 cases, tracks the "countries of origin, transit and destination of trafficked persons." This database needs to be continuously updated in order to give governments accurate information to prosecute those who traffic human beings. The U.S. government needs to work in conjunction with the UN to help populate the database, and then must utilize the information once it is available. This database will help us find a way to stop the flow of slaves into the United States, allowing us to get to the root of the problem.

Once this information is acquired, United States lawmakers must also take swift action. The Trafficking Victims Protection Act of 2000 was definitely a good first step. However, it needs to refocus its funding on the prosecution of traffickers. To reach this goal, more money obviously needs to be spent. According to Mohamed Matted, codirector of the Protection Project at Johns Hopkins University, in his testimony to the House Committee on International Relations on June 24, 2003, this can be done by confiscating traffickers' assets. This money could be used to fund prosecution of other traffickers as well as provide restitution for the victims.

Finally, you and I easily can play our part in abolishing slavery by going to the American Anti-Slavery Group's website at iAbolish.com. Next time you are online, become an e-abolitionist by signing antislavery petitions and joining the site's Freedom Action Network. The Network will send you weekly e-mail newsletters to keep you informed and to alert you to antislavery events in your area. We have condemned past slavery and those who allowed it to persist. But now it's our turn to stand up for what we know is right and help abolish the slavery that plagues our time.

Even though Andrea has been free for about five years, so are those who tortured her for 12. Fearing retribution, she's in constant hiding, dealing with the daily trauma from her years of forced servitude. But after understanding the extent of modern-day slavery and discussing how it came about, we can implement solutions to help people like Andrea see for themselves that we do live in the land of the free, not the home of the slave.

---

This first sentence is an interesting but subtle **transition** between the problem, already discussed, and the solution, which is about to be discussed. Would you have preferred a more obvious and direct transition?

Does the speaker convince you that the United Nations can help in combating this problem? If so, what specifically did the speaker say that convinced you? If not, what would have convinced you? What kinds of **evidence** would you want the speaker to produce?

The **second part of the solution** concerns lawmakers. Does the speaker make an effective case for the role that laws and lawmakers must play in human trafficking?

What types of **credibility appeals** can you identify throughout this speech? Would you have used credibility appeals differently? What would you have said?

The third part of the solution is to act on a personal level, specifically to participate in a particular Internet group devoted to the speech's ultimate aim—the elimination of human slavery. Here the speaker seeks to **motivate you to action**. Is this something you might do after reading this speech? If not, what might the speaker have said to move you to action?

Is the speaker asking for **reasonable amounts** of **change**? If not, what correction would you suggest?

Here the speaker **returns to the introduction**, and you know that he is nearing the end of his speech.

The speaker here **summarizes** the main points that were introduced in the introduction and developed throughout the speech.

Now that you've read the entire speech, what **title** would you use if it had been prepared for presentation in your public speaking class?

**Visualization**

IV. Banning hate speech will help us build an environment conducive to learning.

   A. Students will not fear violence.

   B. Women and minorities will not feel as if they are second-class citizens.

   C. Tolerance can replace intolerance.

**Action**

V. Sign my petition urging the administration to take action, to ban hate speech.

If you're persuading your listeners that one policy will be more effective than another (say, that a new policy will be better than the present policy), then a comparison-and-contrast organization might work best. Here you might divide each of your main points into two parts—the present policy and the proposed plan—so as to effectively compare and contrast them on each issue. For example, the body of a speech urging a new health care plan might look something like this:

I. The plans are different in their coverage for psychiatric problems.

   A. The present plan offers nothing for such problems.

   B. The proposed plan treats psychiatric problems with the same coverage as physical problems.

II. The plans differ in their deductibles.

   A. The present plan has a $2,000 deductible.

   B. The proposed plan has a $500 deductible.

III. The plans differ in the hospitalization allowances.

   A. In the present plan two days are allowed for childbirth; in the proposed plan four days are allowed.

   B. In the present plan all patients are assigned to large wards; in the proposed plan all patients are assigned to semiprivate rooms.

Public Speaking Exercise 11.2, "Questions of Fact, Value, and Policy," on page 268 invites you to try your hand at identifying contemporary issues in terms of their being questions of fact, value, or policy.

## Next Steps

Informative and persuasive speeches are the main types of speeches and all others are variations of these basic types. Nevertheless, it's useful to examine these special occasion speeches as a group, as Special Occasion Speeches, the topic of the next chapter.

# Essentials of Persuading Your Audience

In this chapter we looked at the persuasive speech: its goals, the principles of persuasion, and the three main types of persuasive speeches.

## The Goals of Persuasive Speaking

1. Persuasive speaking has three general goals:
   - To strengthen or weaken attitudes, beliefs, or values
   - To change attitudes, beliefs, or values
   - To motivate to action

## The Three Persuasive Proofs

2. The three persuasive proofs are:
   - Logical proof, the evidence and arguments
   - Emotional proof, the motivational appeals
   - Ethical proof or credibility appeals

## Principles of Persuasive Speaking

3. Among the important principles for persuasive speaking are:
   - Focus on your audience.
   - Identify with your audience.
   - Secure a yes response.
   - Anticipate selective exposure.
   - Use positive labeling.
   - Ask for reasonable amounts of change.
   - Provide social proof.
   - Motivate your listeners.

## Culture and Persuasion

4. Among the important cultural differences that impact on persuasive are:
   - Individualism and collectivism
   - High and low power distance
   - High and low uncertainty avoidance
   - Masculine and feminine
   - High and low context
   - Long- and short-term orientation
   - Indulgence and restraint

## Persuasive Speeches on Questions of Fact

5. Persuasive speeches on **questions of fact** focus on what is or is not true. In a speech on a question of fact:
   - Emphasize logical proof.
   - Use the most recent materials possible.
   - Use highly competent sources.
   - Clearly connect your main points to your thesis.

## Persuasive Speeches on Questions of Value

6. Speeches on **questions of value** focus on issues of good and bad, justice or injustice. In designing speeches to strengthen or change attitudes, beliefs, or values:
   - Define clearly the specific value on which you're focusing.
   - Begin with shared assumptions and beliefs, then progress gradually to areas of disagreement.
   - Use sources that the audience values highly.

## Persuasive Speeches on Questions of Policy

7. Speeches on **questions of policy** focus on what should or should not be done, what procedures should or should not be adopted. In designing speeches to move listeners to action:
   - Prove that the policy is needed.
   - Emphasize that the policy you're supporting is practical and reasonable.
   - Show your listeners how the policy will benefit them directly.
   - When asking for action, ask for small, easily performed, and very specific behaviors.
   - Use an organizational pattern that best fits your topic.

# Essential Terms

agenda-setting **(241)**
anecdotal evidence **(238)**
appeal to tradition **(238)**
bandwagon **(238)**
card-stacking **(241)**
character **(246)**

character attacks **(248)**
charisma **(247)**
competence **(245)**
credibility **(245)**
emotional appeals **(242)**
hierarchy of needs **(242)**

logical proof **(235)**
name-calling **(249)**
negative social proof **(252)**
personal interest **(248)**
persuasion **(234)**
plain folks **(241)**

positive social proof **(252)**
questions of fact **(256)**
questions of policy **(260)**
questions of value **(258)**
reasoning from causes and
　effects **(237)**

reasoning from sign **(237)**
reasoning from specific
　instances **(236)**
selective exposure **(251)**
social proof **(252)**
straw man **(238)**

testimonial **(238)**
thin entering wedge **(241)**
transfer **(239)**
yes response **(250)**

# Public Speaking Exercises

## 11.1 Constructing Motivational Appeals

Here are five theses you might use or hear in a persuasive speech. Select one of these and develop two or three motivational appeals that you might use in a speech to members of this class.

> Universal health care is a human right.
>
> Same-sex marriage should be legalized in all 50 states.
>
> Capital punishment should be declared illegal.
>
> Smoking should be banned throughout the entire college (buildings and grounds).
>
> Tenure for college teachers should be abolished.

## 11.2 Questions of Fact, Value, and Policy

Understanding how purposes and theses can be identified from a wide variety of questions of fact, value, and policy will help you construct more effective speeches. To develop this understanding, select a newspaper (Sunday's edition will work best), a weekly newsmagazine, or an Internet news site and identify the questions of fact, value, and policy covered in this one issue (as was done in this chapter). From these, select one question of fact, value, or policy and develop a general purpose, a specific purpose, a thesis that would be appropriate for a speech in this class, and two or three main ideas that you might want to develop based on this thesis.

# Log*On!* my**speech**lab PEARSON

## Persuading Your Audience

Visit MySpeechLab (www.myspeechlab.com) for additional insights into the nature of persuasion and into the strategies of persuasive speaking. You'll also find texts and videos of a variety of types of persuasive speeches. You may also want to revisit the Outlining Wizard for help with organizing your persuasive speeches and watch some of the excellent persuasive speeches. Take the self-test on the ethics of persuasion; it will raise some interesting questions. In connection with this chapter's Research Link guidelines for citing sources are provided for both MLA (Modern Language Association) and APA (American Psychological Association) formats.

# 12

# Speaking on Special Occasions

## WHY READ THIS CHAPTER?

**Because it will enable you to develop additional types of public speeches by helping you to:**

- prepare and present a variety of special occasion speeches, including speeches designed to secure good-will, to praise another person, to present or accept an award, or to honor or celebrate some occasion

- present a group's thinking in a variety of public speaking formats

- apply special occasion insights and guidelines to all kinds of speeches

*Life affords no higher pleasure than that of surmounting difficulties, passing from one step of success to another, forming new wishes and seeing them gratified.*

—SAMUEL JOHNSON

In addition to the many varieties of informative and persuasive speeches, there are several types of speeches usually called "special occasion speeches," with which you'll want to achieve some familiarity. In this chapter we'll consider speeches to introduce someone, to present or accept an award, to secure goodwill or apologize, to dedicate something, to congratulate a graduating class (the commencement speech), to eulogize someone, to bid farewell, or to toast. We'll also look at some of the ways in which you might present the thinking of a group to an audience after the group has brainstormed or problem-solved. We'll conclude the chapter with a look at the role of culture in the special occasion speech.

# The Speech of Introduction

In Chapter 3 (see Public Speaking Sample Assistant on pp. 60–61) we examined the speech designed to introduce you or another person to an audience. The aim of that speech is to help listeners learn something about you or another person. The **speech of introduction** considered here is a bit different and is usually designed to introduce a speaker or a topic that a series of speakers will address. For example, before a speaker addresses an audience, another speaker often sets the stage by introducing both the speaker and the topic. At conventions, where a series of speakers address an audience, a speech of introduction might introduce the general topic on which the speakers will focus and perhaps provide connecting links among the several presentations.

In a speech of introduction, your main purpose is to gain the attention and arouse the interest of the audience. Your speech should pave the way for favorable and attentive listening. The speech of introduction is basically informative and follows the general patterns already discussed for an informative speech. The main difference is that instead of discussing a topic's issues, you discuss who the speaker is and what the speaker will talk about. In your speeches of introduction, follow these general principles:

- **Establish the significance of the speech.** Focus the audience's attention and interest on the main speaker and on the importance of what the speaker will say.

- **Establish relevant connections among the speaker, the topic, and the audience.** Answer your listeners' inevitable question: Why should we listen to this speaker on this topic?

- **Stress the speaker's credibility.** For example, tell the audience what has earned this speaker the right to speak on this topic to this audience (see Chapter 11).

- **Speak in a style and manner that is consistent with the main speech.** Introduce the speaker with the same degree of formality that will prevail during the actual speech. Otherwise, the speaker will have to counteract an inappropriate atmosphere created by the speech of introduction.

- **Be brief (relative to the length of the main speech).** If the main speech is to be brief—say, 10 to 20 minutes—your introduction should be no longer than 1 or 2 minutes. If, on the other hand, the main speech is to be an hour long, then your introduction might last 5 to 10 minutes or even longer.

■ **Don't cover the substance of the topic the speaker will discuss.** Also remember that clever stories, jokes, startling statistics, or historical analogies, which are often effective in speeches of introduction, will prove a liability if the main speaker intended to use this same material.

■ **Don't oversell the speaker or topic.** Present the speaker in a positive light, but don't create an image that the speaker will find impossible to live up to.

# The Speech of Presentation or Acceptance

We'll consider speeches of presentation and speeches of acceptance together, both because they're frequently paired and because the same general principles govern both types of speeches. In a **presentation speech** you seek to (1) place an award or honor in some kind of context and (2) give the award an extra air of dignity or status. A speech of presentation may focus on rewarding a colleague for an important accomplishment (being named Teacher of the Year) or on recognizing a particularly impressive performance (winning an Academy Award). It may honor an employee's service to a company or a student's outstanding grades or athletic abilities.

The **acceptance speech** is the other side of this honoring ceremony. Here the recipient accepts the award and attempts to place the award in some kind of context. At times the presentation and the acceptance speeches are rather informal and amount to a simple "You really deserve this" and an equally simple "Thank you." At other times—for example, in the presentation and acceptance of a Nobel Prize—the speeches are formal and are prepared in great detail and with great care. Such speeches are frequently reprinted in newspapers throughout the world. Somewhere between these two extremes lie average speeches of presentation and acceptance.

In your speeches of presentation, follow these two principles:

■ **State the reason for the presentation.** Make clear why this particular award is being given to this particular person.

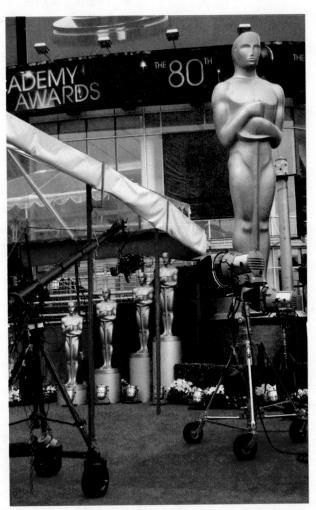

**PUBLIC SPEAKING CHOICE POINT: Presenting an Award**
You have been asked to present the Academy Award for best supporting actor (select your own favorite). The speech is to last no longer than one minute (approximately 150 words). What are your options? What would you say to improve upon the actual speeches given at these award shows?

- **State the importance of the award.** The audience (as well as the group authorizing or sponsoring the award) will no doubt want to hear something about this. You might point out the importance of the award by referring to the previous recipients (assuming they're well known to the audience), emphasizing the status of the award (assuming that it's a prestigious award), or describing the award's influence on previous recipients.

In preparing and presenting your speech of acceptance, follow these three principles:

- **Thank the people responsible for giving you the award.** Thank the academy members, the board of directors, the student body, your teammates, etc.
- **Acknowledge those who helped you achieve the award.** Be specific without being overly detailed.
- **Put the award into personal perspective.** For example, you might tell the audience what the award means to you right now and perhaps what it will mean to you in the future.

Here is an exceptionally moving and provocative acceptance speech that clearly illustrates how closely tied together the speaker, the audience, and the occasion are. This is the acceptance speech by actor Elizabeth Taylor on receiving the Jean Hersholt Humanitarian Award, given for her work on behalf of people with AIDS. The speech was transcribed from television.

---

## Speech of Acceptance

### Elizabeth Taylor*

I have been on this stage many times as a presenter. I have sat in the audience as a loser. And I've had the thrill and the honor of standing here as a winner. But, I never, ever thought I would come out here to receive this award.

It is the highest possible accolade I could receive from my peers. And for doing something I just have to do, that my passion must do.

I am filled with pride and humility. I accept this award in honor of all the men, women, and children with AIDS who are waging incredibly valiant battles for their lives—those to whom I have given my commitment, the real heroes of the pandemic of AIDS.

I am so proud of the work that people in Hollywood have done to help so many others, like dearest, gentle Audrey. And while she is, I know, in heaven, forever guarding her beloved children, I will remain here as rowdy an activist as I have to be and, God willing, for as long as I have to be. [Applause]

Tonight I am asking for your help. I call upon you to draw from the depths of your being, to prove that we are a human race, to prove that our love outweighs our need to hate, that our compassion is more compelling than our need to blame, that our sensitivity to those in need is stronger than our greed, that our ability to reason overcomes our fear, and that at the end of each of our lives we can look back and be proud that we have treated others with the kindness, dignity, and respect that every human being deserves.

Thank you and God bless.

*Reprinted by permission.

# The Speech to Secure Goodwill

The **goodwill speech** is part information and part persuasion. On the surface, the speech informs the audience about a product, company, profession, institution, or person. Beneath this surface, however, lies a more persuasive purpose: to heighten the image of a person, product, or company—to create a more positive attitude toward this person or thing. Many speeches of goodwill have a further persuasive purpose: to get the audience ultimately to change their behavior toward the person, product, or company.

A special type of goodwill speech is the speech of self-justification, in which the speaker seeks to justify his or her actions to the audience. Political figures do this frequently. Richard Nixon's "Checkers Speech," his Cambodia-bombing speeches, and, of course, his Watergate speeches are clear examples of speeches of self-justification. Edward Kennedy's Chappaquiddick speech, in which he attempted to justify what happened when Mary Jo Kopechne drowned, is another example. In securing goodwill, whether for another person or for yourself, consider the following suggestions:

- **Demonstrate the contributions that deserve goodwill.** Show how the audience may benefit from this company, product, or person. Or at least— in the speech of self-justification—show that the listeners have not been hurt; or, if they have been hurt, that the injury was unintentional.

- **Stress uniqueness.** In a world dominated by competition, the speech to secure goodwill must stress the uniqueness of the specific company, person, profession, situation, and so on. Distinguish your subject clearly from all others; otherwise, any goodwill you secure will be spread over the entire field.

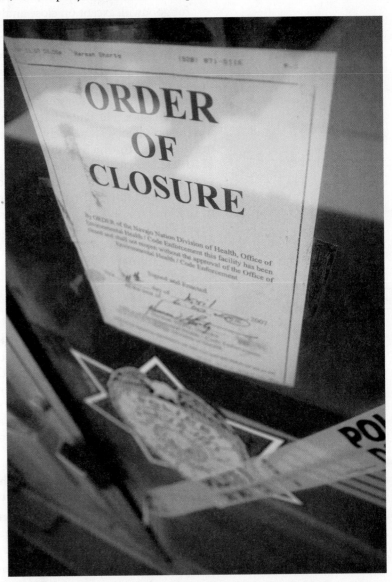

**PUBLIC SPEAKING CHOICE POINT: Securing Goodwill**

Jimmy has been asked by his catering firm—which was cited by the Board of Health for several health violations a year ago—to present to the local Board of Education the firm's case for the catering contract for the entire elementary school district. The board members agree to hear Jimmy but are generally reluctant to hire his firm because of its history of unsafe practices. What are some of the things Jimmy could say to secure goodwill (and another chance)?

- **Establish credibility.** Speeches to secure goodwill must also establish credibility, thereby securing goodwill for the individual or commodity. To do so, concentrate on those dimensions of credibility discussed in Chapter 11. Demonstrate that the person is competent, of good intention, and of high moral character.

- **Don't be obvious.** The effective goodwill speech looks, on the surface, very much like an objective informative speech. It will not appear to ask for goodwill, except on close analysis.

Another type of goodwill speech is the speech of **apology,** a speech in which the speaker apologizes for some transgression and tries to restore his or her credibility. A particularly dramatic example of this type of speech, given by President William Jefferson Clinton, is presented here. The speech was given to the nation on August 17, 1998, after Clinton testified to a grand jury about a variety of issues. The issue that the nation and the media focused on, however, was the president's affair with a White House intern, Monica Lewinsky, including the extent to which he misled the country and the question of whether he obstructed justice. This speech was almost universally criticized for not expressing enough of an apology, for not asking for forgiveness, and for attacking the opposition rather than taking responsibility. The speech is presented in the Public Speaking Sample Assistant below. (If you wish to learn more about this speech and some of the critical reactions to it, visit *The American Communication Journal* online at **www.uark.edu/~aca** and go to Volume Two, Issue Two [February, 1999].)

## The Speech of Dedication

The **dedication speech** is designed to give some specific meaning to, say, a new research lab, a store opening, or the start of the building of a bridge. This speech is usually given at a rather formal occasion. You'll need to do some research on exactly what it is that is being dedicated. For example, if it's a bridge, then you'll want to learn something about why the bridge was built, when it was constructed, and who designed it. In preparing a dedication speech, consider the following suggestions:

- **State the reason you're giving the dedication.** For example, you might identify the connection you have to the project.

- **Explain exactly what is being dedicated.** If it's the opening of the bridge linking Roosevelt Island to Manhattan say so early in your dedication.

- **Note who is responsible for the project.** Tell the audience, for example, who designed the bridge, who constructed it, and who paid for it.

- **Explain why this project is significant.** What advantages will it create? For example, you might describe the relevance the bridge has to your audience; that is, what changes will occur as a result of this bridge and how the bridge will benefit your listeners.

On page 276 is a particularly effective speech of dedication, presented by Archbishop Desmond Tutu at the Dedication of the Freedom Center on June 10, 2004, at the World Financial Center, New York City.

## PUBLIC SPEAKING SAMPLE ASSISTANT

### Speech to Secure Goodwill (Apology)

#### *President William Jefferson Clinton*

Good evening. This afternoon in this room, from this chair, I testified before the Office of Independent Counsel and a grand jury. I answered their questions truthfully, including questions about my private life, questions no American citizen would ever want to answer.

Still I must take complete responsibility for all my actions, both public and private. And that is why I am speaking to you tonight.

As you know, in a deposition in January, I was asked questions about my relationship with Monica Lewinsky. While my answers were legally accurate, I did not volunteer information. Indeed I did have a relationship with Miss Lewinsky that was not appropriate. In fact, it was wrong.

It constituted a critical lapse in judgment and a personal failure on my part for which I am solely and completely responsible.

But I told the grand jury today, and I say to you now, that at no time did I ask anyone to lie, to hide or destroy evidence, or to take any other unlawful action.

I know that my public comments and my silence about this matter gave a false impression. I misled people. Including even my wife. I deeply regret that.

I can only tell you I was motivated by many factors. First, by a desire to protect myself from the embarrassment of my own conduct. I was also very concerned about protecting my family. The fact that these questions were being asked in a politically inspired lawsuit which has since been dismissed was a consideration too.

In addition, I had real and serious concerns about an independent counsel investigation that began with private business dealings 20 years ago—dealings, I might add, about which an independent federal agency found no evidence of any wrongdoing by me or my wife over two years ago.

The independent counsel investigation moved on to my staff and friends. Then into my private life. And now the investigation itself is under investigation. This has gone on too long, cost too much, and hurt too many innocent people.

Now this matter is between me, the two people I love most—my wife and our daughter—and our God. I must put it right. And I am prepared to do whatever it takes to do so.

Nothing is more important to me personally, but it is private. And I intend to reclaim my family life for my family. It's nobody's business but ours. Even presidents have private lives. It is time to stop the pursuit of personal destruction and the prying into private lives and get on with our national life.

Our country has been distracted by this matter for too long, and I take my responsibility for my part in all of this. That is all I can do. Now it is time, in fact it is past time, to move on. We have important work to do, real opportunities to seize, real problems to solve, real security matters to face.

And so tonight I ask you to turn away from the spectacle of the past seven months, to repair the fabric of our national discourse and to return our attention to all the challenges and all the promise of the next American century.

Thank you for watching and good night.

## The Commencement Speech

The **commencement speech** recognizes and celebrates the end of some training period, such as the listeners' school or college years. The commencement speech is designed to congratulate and inspire the recent graduates and is often intended to mark the transition from school to the next stage in life. Usually the person asked to give a commencement speech is a well-known personality. The speakers at college graduations—depending on the prestige of the institution—are often important men and women in the world: presidents, senators, religious leaders, Nobel Prize winners, famous scientists, and people of similar accomplishment. Or a commencement speech may be given by a student who has achieved some exceptional goal; for example, the student

# PUBLIC SPEAKING SAMPLE ASSISTANT

## Speech of Dedication

### *Archbishop Desmond Tutu\**

Good afternoon. I am a pastor. They have said I should be brief. Have you ever met a brief pastor?

Governor Pataki, Mayor Bloomberg, distinguished ladies and gentlemen:

The world still shudders with horror when it looks back on what happened here on September the eleventh and still feels a deep sympathy for those who were injured here and those who died here as well as for their loved ones.

The Freedom Center will symbolize the indomitable spirit of the people of this land, the indomitable spirit of people of other lands, of the people of this city who may have been down, but most certainly not out. It will be a testimony to their resilience as they rise like the proverbial phoenix from the ashes. There is a renewed resolve to make the world safer for freedom and to eradicate those conditions that can make people so desperate that they are driven to commit dastardly acts of desperation. What Martin Luther King, Jr., said about injustice applies to poverty; and abject poverty anywhere poses a threat to affluence everywhere.

It is apt, so apt, so fitting that this designation of the Freedom Center should occur in the week when we commemorate D-Day—when the Allies launched the drive that ultimately defeated Adolf Hitler and the awfulness that was Nazism. We showed then attributes that we have sometimes forgotten. But it is when we are united as the free world was united then, that we can and will—as happened then—we can and will defeat the enemies of freedom, of goodness, of justice, of compassion, of caring. We realized then, and we need to realize now, that we are bound together by a common humanity, by a common vulnerability, bound together by our common passion for freedom that we can't go it alone, that we are bound up in the bundle of life. We used to say to our white compatriots in South Africa: "you will never be free until we blacks are free, for freedom is indivisible."

As we stand here, looking to the future of the Freedom Center, we feel how the record of the glorious quest for freedom of the Pilgrim fathers and mothers; of those who were escaping persecution and destitution in Europe; the quest of freedom of such as a Nelson Mandela, of an Aung San Suu Kyi, of a Mahatma Gandhi, of a Martin Luther King, Jr., and many, many others of this and other lands—let us all dedicate ourselves, inspired by the splendid examples that have gone before, dedicate ourselves anew to a common commitment to strive for freedom for all. For we can ultimately be free only together. We can be human only together. We can be prosperous only together. We can be safe and secure only together.

Thank you.

with the highest grade point average or the recipient of a prestigious award. In giving a commencement speech, consider the following:

- **Organize the speech in a temporal pattern.** Beginning with the past, commenting on the present, and projecting into the future is one easy to develop and follow pattern.

- **Do your research.** Learn about the school, the student body, the goals and ambitions of the graduates, and integrate these into your speech.

- **Be brief.** Recognize that your audience has other things on their minds—the graduation party, for example—and may become restless if your speech is too long.

- **Congratulate the graduates.** But also congratulate the parents, friends, and instructors who also contributed to this day.

- **Motivate the graduates.** Offer the graduates some kind of motivational message, some guidance, some suggestions for taking their education and using it in their lives.
- **Offer your own good wishes to the graduates.**

# The Speech of Inspiration

A great many special occasion speeches aim to inspire the audience, as you've seen in the speeches already covered. Some speeches, however, are designed primarily to inspire; raising the spirits of an audience is their primary objective. Many religious speeches are of this type. Similarly, speeches that corporate leaders give to stockholders when introducing a new product or a new CEO, for example, would be designed to inspire investors. A commanding officer might give a speech of inspiration to the troops before going into battle. And, of course, there are the speeches of professional motivational speakers who seek to arouse the audience to feel better about themselves by organizing their lives, taking chances, giving up drugs, or doing any of a variety of things.

Before reading some suggestions for preparing and presenting an **inspirational speech,** consider the speech by Nikki Giovanni in the accompanying Public Speaking Sample Assistant box on page 278. This is a particularly impressive inspirational speech given by Virginia Tech faculty member and poet Giovanni after 32 students and faculty were killed at the college on April 16, 2007.

- **Demonstrate your oneness with the audience.** Try to show in some way that you and your listeners have significant similarities. Notice in this accompanying speech the repeated use of "we": It makes listeners feel connected to the speaker.

- **Demonstrate your own intense involvement.** Display to the audience the kind of intensity you want them to show. You cannot make others feel emotions if you don't feel them yourself.

- **Stress emotional appeals.** Inspiring an audience has to do more with emotions than with logic. Use appeals that are consistent with the nature of the event. In Nikki Giovanni's speech you see appeals to pity, loyalty to friends and institution, and empathy for others.

- **Stress the positive.** Especially, end your speech on a positive note. Inspirational speeches are always positive. Note the positiveness in Giovanni's speech: "We will prevail. We will prevail. We will prevail."

## ETHICAL CHOICE POINT

### Telling the Truth

You'll be delivering the commencement speech to a graduating class at the high school you attended. In all honesty, you thought the education you received was especially poor; the teachers were unconcerned, the science and computer labs were 30 years old, and all the money went to athletic programs. You want to criticize the poor educational training the high school provided and urge students to approach college with a new perspective. At the same time, you want to appeal to a wider audience—the school board, the community at large, the city government—and get them to provide the school with better facilities and additional staff. Given that a commencement speech is usually a positive, congratulatory exercise, you wonder if you should present this somewhat negative picture. ▶*What are your ethical choices for being honest and yet being consistent with the nature of the situation?*

# PUBLIC SPEAKING SAMPLE ASSISTANT

## Speech of Inspiration

### *Professor Nikki Giovanni\**

We are Virginia Tech.

We are sad today, and we will be sad for quite a while. We are not moving on, we are embracing our mourning.

We are Virginia Tech.

We are strong enough to stand tall tearlessly, we are brave enough to bend to cry, and we are sad enough to know that we must laugh again.

We are Virginia Tech.

We do not understand this tragedy. We know we did nothing to deserve it, but neither does a child in Africa dying of AIDS, neither do the invisible children walking the night away to avoid being captured by the rogue army, neither does the baby elephant watching his community being devastated for ivory, neither does the Mexican child looking for fresh water, neither does the Appalachian infant killed in the middle of the night in his crib in the home his father built with his own hands being run over by a boulder because the land was destabilized. No one deserves a tragedy.

We are Virginia Tech.

The Hokie Nation embraces our own and reaches out with open heart and hands to those who offer their hearts and minds. We are strong, and brave, and innocent, and unafraid. We are better than we think and not quite what we want to be. We are alive to the imaginations and the possibilities. We will continue to invent the future through our blood and tears and through all our sadness.

We are the Hokies.

We will prevail.

We will prevail.

We will prevail.

We are Virginia Tech.

# The Eulogy

The **eulogy** is a speech of tribute in which you seek to praise someone who has died. In the eulogy you attempt to put the person's life and contributions in perspective and show them in a positive light. This type of speech is often given at a funeral or at the anniversary of the person's birth or death. This is not the time for a balanced appraisal of the individual's life. Rather, it's a time for praise. In developing the eulogy, consider the following:

- **Relate the person to the audience.** Stress the connection between the life you're celebrating to yourself, to those in the audience, and, if appropriate, to the larger audience—for example, the scientific community, the world of book lovers, or those who have devoted their lives to peace.

- **Be specific.** Show that you really knew the person or know a great deal about the person. The best way to do that is to give specific examples from the person's life. Then combine the specifics with the more general so that the audience can see these specifics as being a part of some larger whole—for example, after you mention the several books that an author wrote, frame the author's contribution in a more general way within the mystery genre or contemporary poetry genre.

- **Portray a deserving person.** Make the audience see that this person is deserving of the praise you are bestowing on him or her by explaining

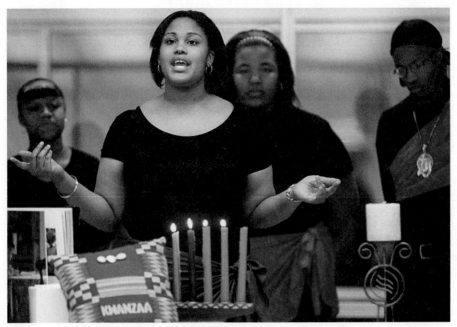

**PUBLIC SPEAKING CHOICE POINT: A Speech of Inspiration**
Tonya wants to give a speech of inspiration to her class on the topic of Kwanzaa. What are some of Tonya's options for sharing the inspirational aspects of this holiday? What are some ways she might introduce the topic to gain attention and then conclude effectively?

what this person accomplished and how this person influenced—for example—the world of patient care, the design of safer cars, and so on.

- **Show the audience what they can learn from this individual.**

An especially moving eulogy appears in the accompanying Public Speaking Sample Assistant box on page 280. The eulogy (abridged here) was written and presented by Tiffany Grosso at the funeral mass of her best friend, Audra, at St. Ann's Church, Yonkers, New York, on January 30, 2010. A complete text of this eulogy is available at **www.myspeechlab.com.**

# The Farewell Speech

In the **farewell speech** you say goodbye to an organization or to colleagues and signal that you're moving on. In this speech you'll want to express your positive feelings to those you're leaving. Generally, the farewell speech is given after you've achieved some level of distinction within a company or other group or organization that you're now leaving. In developing a farewell speech, consider the following:

- **Thank those who contributed.** Give thanks and credit to those who made life interesting, helped you in your position, taught you essential principles, and so on.
- **Note your achievements modestly.** Put them in a positive light, but do it gently and with modesty.

# PUBLIC SPEAKING SAMPLE ASSISTANT

## Eulogy

### Tiffany Grosso

Audra was powerful even though she'd probably tell you different. She would say that she was this meek, shy little girl but I beg to differ. I first met Aud at the age of 9 and she punched me in the stomach on the softball field of PS 32 because she thought I messed with her big sister Andrea. Oh, she was determined alright, determined to seek the truth in life. Long ago, Audra chose to take the challenge of looking at herself in order to grow. She allowed all of us to witness this side of her through her most recent journey with cancer as she sought to make sense of the senseless. Seeking the lesson in it all. The lesson she would later teach.

Teacher. From as young as I can remember Audra wanted to be a teacher, she just knew she was one and she took that vocation very seriously. As you know Audra was a reading teacher and we can all remember just how sad she was when she had to retire due to the cancer. It was extremely difficult for her and she even questioned being forgotten. Storybooks. Novels. Menus. Ads. Billboards. Emails. Facebook. Bills. Newspapers. etc. . . . How can we not be grateful to that one person who opened up a world of wonder! How can we not acknowledge that person who taught us how to READ? Every letter, word, phrase, sentence, paragraph, chapter coming together, imparting knowledge and enjoyment is a medal pinned on the chest of that caring teacher that taught us how to read. A gift for our lifetime! FORGET? NEVER!

Audra's biological children. James, Adam and Olivia. The loss of James was almost too much to bear for Audra and Tom. But Audra fought to go on and have the children she so dearly wanted. They are the epitome of the word miracle, Adam and Olivia. The joy, light and love they brought to her is indescribable. If we ever question Audra's closeness to us we need to look no further than the twins. Audra is in their eyes, their hearts, their souls and of course their silly little personalities. I know she is with James now and will be forever watching over Addie and Livie loving them the way only a mother could.

Tom, Audra's husband you were Audra's soul mate—she loves you well beyond this lifetime! Please know you have succeeded in giving her the love, happiness and security she had always craved. You were a safe haven of love with whom she could be whoever she wanted. You kept her laughing until the very last day. She cherished you most.

Mrs. Tufo, Alicia and Andrea. Audra's mom and sisters. The ties that bind the four of you could never be broken. The love you have for one another is unique and unmatched. No words could describe the love and gratitude she felt for you all.

Audra's friends. Aud loved each and every one of you for the unique gifts that made you special. Please know who you are and what you meant to each other.

As for me, Aud and I saw life through a similar lens and this connected us profoundly at a very young age. She was a gift to me. "Old soul mates" we called one another and no words can express how precious her friendship is to me and always will be. I will miss her the rest of my life.

Everything we do has a ripple effect. Most of the time we do not get to see firsthand just what it is we are affecting. Through Audra's journey though it was obvious that she was affecting us all on some level with her story. Rippling out her words, wisdom, grace and yes fight! Let us choose to remember Audra for the beautiful woman that she was—a woman who loved, fought, mothered and taught. Let us remember her story and allow it to be the first pebble cast in our lives to ripple far beyond touching every shore in a positive way. For if we do this our dear Audra will NEVER be forgotten.

Audra's last lesson:

**"But my hope today is that as you go about your day you stop and feel blessed to be doing WHATEVER it is you are doing BECAUSE YOU CAN."**

- **Express your enjoyment of the experience.** This is a time for positive reflection, not for critical evaluation, so put aside the negative memories, at least for this speech.

- **State your reasons for leaving.** This isn't always appropriate, but when it is do tell your listeners your reason for leaving and your plans for the future.

- **Express good wishes to those who remain.**
- **Offer some words of wisdom.** Tell the audience what you learned and what you now want to pass on to those remaining.

Here is an example of a farewell speech, delivered by Cal Ripken Jr. on his retirement from baseball (**www.americanrhetoric.com/speeches/calripkenjr.htm**).

---

## Farewell Speech

### Cal Ripken Jr.*

As a kid, I had this dream.

And I had the parents that helped me shape that dream.

Then, I became part of an organization, the Baltimore Orioles—the Baltimore Orioles, to help me grow that dream. Imagine playing for my hometown team for my whole career.

And I have a wife and children to help me share and save the fruits of that dream.

And I've had teammates who filled my career with unbelievable moments.

And you fans, who have loved the game, and have shared your love with me.

Tonight, we close a chapter of this dream—my playing career.

But I have other dreams.

You know, I might have some white hair on top of this head—well, maybe on the sides of this head. But I'm really not that old.

My dreams for the future include pursuing my passion for baseball. Hopefully, I will be able to share what I have learned. And, I would be happy if that sharing would lead to something as simple as a smile on the face of others.

One question I've been repeatedly asked these past few weeks is, "How do I want to be remembered?" My answer has been simple: to be remembered at all is pretty special.

I might also add that if, if I am remembered, I hope it's because, by living my dream, I was able to make a difference.

Thank you.

*Reprinted with permission from the Ripkin Baseball Group, www.RipkinBaseball.com.

---

# The Toast

The **toast** is a brief speech designed to celebrate a person or an occasion. You might, for example, toast the next CEO of your company, a friend who just got admitted to a prestigious graduate program, or a colleague on the occasion of a promotion. Often toasts are given at weddings or at the start of a new venture. The toast is designed to say hello or good luck in a relatively formal sense. In developing your toast consider the following:

- **Be brief.** Realize that people want to get on with the festivities and don't want to listen to an overly long speech.
- **Focus attention on the other person(s).** Often speakers get so involved that they begin to focus on themselves instead of the person being toasted.

- **Avoid inside jokes.** Inside jokes that only you and the person you're toasting understand are out of place and will likely distance you from the audience. Remember that the toast is not only for the benefit of the person you're toasting but for the audience as well.

- **End your speech clearly.** When you raise your glass in the toast—an almost obligatory part of toasting—make the audience realize that they should drink and that your speech is at an end.

# Presenting the Group's Thinking

A great deal of your social and professional life will revolve around your participation in groups—groups for developing ideas, increasing self-awareness, learning, and solving problems. At times the thinking of the small group needs to be presented to a larger audience; for example, when a small group of workers investigate a new wage and benefits proposal and then report back to the entire union membership, or when representatives of university academic departments report their proposals to the administration or to the entire university. As a backdrop for this discussion take a look at "A Primer of Small Group Communication" (pp. 286–288). If you'd like more information on small group communication, two complete chapters—"Small Group Communication" and "Members and Leaders"—are available at MySpeechLab (**www.myspeechlab.com**).

Let's begin by looking at some general guidelines for presenting groups' ideas to wider audiences; then we'll examine some more specific suggestions for various group formats.

## General Speaking Guidelines

If a group develops a solution to a problem, it will generally seek some way to put this solution into operation. Often it's necessary to convince others that the solution is workable and cost effective. Try these suggestions:

- **Present the solution in a non-threatening manner.** New solutions often frighten people. For example, if your solution might lead people to feel insecure about their jobs, then alleviate these worries before you try to explain the solution in any detail. As a general rule it's best to proceed slowly, especially if you anticipate objections or hostility from your listeners.

- **Present new solutions tentatively.** In the excitement of inspiration, you may not have thought through all of the practical implications of your proposed solution. If you present your ideas tentatively and they're shown to be impractical or unworkable, you will be less hurt psychologically and—most important—more willing to present new solutions again.

- **Try to link changes to known problems in the organization.** For example, if you're going to ask employees to complete extensive surveys, then show them how this extra work will correct a long-standing problem and benefit them and the organization.

- **Say why you think the solution will work.** Give the advantages of your plan over the existing situation and explain why you think your solution should be implemented. The patterns for organizing a public speech (see Chapter 7) will help you make an effective presentation.

- **State the negatives.** There usually are some negatives with most ideas and it may be necessary to identify these. And, of course, explain why you think the positives outweigh any potential drawbacks.

- **Relate your solution to the members' needs and interests.** Show how your solution is directly related to the needs and interests of those whom the solution will affect. Show others how your solution will benefit them.

## Speaking in the Panel Group

In a **panel** the group members are cast in the role of "experts" and participate informally and without any set pattern of who speaks when. The procedure is similar to that of any small group interaction, except that the panel is discussing the issue before an audience; the audience is present but does not participate in the actual discussion. Normally a moderator guides the discussion.

A variation is the two-panel format, with an expert panel and a lay panel. The expert panel consists of the members who participated in the group and who ideally are more knowledgeable than the lay panel members. The topic is then discussed as the lay and the expert panel members interact. This is the format followed by many talk shows, such as those featuring Jerry Springer and Oprah Winfrey. On these shows the moderator is the host (Springer, Winfrey). The "expert panel" is the group of guests (the dysfunctional family, the gossip columnists, the political activists). And the lay panel consists of the members of the studio audience who ask questions or offer comments.

Here are a few suggestions for making the panel format more effective:

- As moderator, always treat panel members and their questions with respect. You'll notice this on the popular talk shows: No matter how stupid the question may be, the moderator treats it as serious, though often restructuring it just a bit so that it makes more sense. Treat questions objectively; don't try to bias either a question or its answer through your verbal or nonverbal responses.

- As a panel member, speak in short turns. The group's interaction should resemble a conversation rather than individual public speeches. Resist the temptation to tell long stories or go into too much detail.

- Try to spread the conversation around the group. Generally, try to give each member the same opportunity to speak.

## Speaking in the Symposium and Team Presentations

In a **symposium** each member delivers a prepared presentation, a public speech. All speeches are addressed to different aspects of a single topic. The symposium leader introduces the speakers, provides transitions from one speaker to another, and may provide periodic summaries.

In a **team presentation**, a format popular in business settings, two or three members of a group will report the group's findings to a larger group. In some situations team presentations may amount to "position papers" and may include both majority and minority reports, as at the Supreme Court. Or if, say, a group considered a range of new scheduling systems, members of a team might each present one of the proposed systems and the advantages and disadvantages of each.

Here are a few suggestions for making symposia and team presentations more effective:

- Coordinate your presentations very carefully. Team presentations and symposia are extremely difficult to synchronize. Make sure that everyone knows exactly what he or she is responsible for. Make sure there's no (or very little) overlap among the presentations.

- Much as you would rehearse a public speech, try to rehearse these presentations and their coordination. This is rarely possible to do in actual practice, but it is very helpful to "rehearse" mentally or imaginatively, going through the proceedings in your mind in advance.

- Adhere carefully to time limits. If you speak for more time than allotted, that time will be deducted from the minutes available to a later speaker. As you can appreciate, violating time limits will severely damage the entire group's presentation.

- Provide clear transitions between the presentations. Internal summaries work especially well as connectives between one speech and the next: "Now that Judy has explained the general proposal, Peter and Margarita will explain some of the advantages and disadvantages of the proposal. First, we'll hear from Peter with the advantages and then from Margarita with the disadvantages."

A variation of the symposium is the **symposium–forum,** which consists of a symposium (with prepared speeches, as just explained) and a **forum,** with questions from the audience and responses by the speakers. The leader introduces the speakers and moderates the question-and-answer session. The suggestions for making these presentations more effective are essentially the same as for the panel and the symposium.

## Oral and Written Reports

In many cases, the small group leader will make a presentation of the group's findings, recommendations, or decisions to some larger group— for example, to the class as a whole, the entire student body, the board of directors, the union membership, or the heads of departments.

Depending on the specific situation, these reports may be similar to speeches of information or speeches

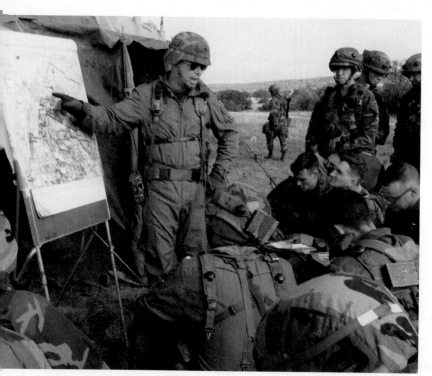

**PUBLIC SPEAKING CHOICE POINT: Presenting the Group's Thinking**
Jack needs to present the group's decisions on airlifting supplies to those who will actually deliver the supplies. What are some options Jack has for presenting these decisions? What public speaking guidelines should Jack be especially careful to follow?

of persuasion. For example, if you are the group leader, your task may be simply to inform the wider group of the findings or recommendations of your committee—the proposed ways to increase morale, the new pension scheme, the new developments in competing organizations. In other cases your report will be largely persuasive; for example, you may need to convince the larger group to provide increased funding so that your group's recommendations can be implemented.

In some situations, both a brief oral report and a more extensive written report are required. A good example is the press conference. At a press conference you deliver an oral report to members of the press, who also receive a written report. The press will then question you for further details. In some cases you may want to use a computer-assisted presentation and prepare handouts of your slides, your speaker's notes, or selected slides with space for your listeners to write notes (see Chapter 6). Here are a few suggestions for more effective oral and written reports.

- Write the written report as you would a term paper, and from that develop a summary of the report in the form of a public speech, following the 10 steps explained in Chapter 2 and elaborated throughout this text.

- Don't read the written report. Even though the oral and the written report may cover essentially the same content, they're totally different in development and presentation. The written report is meant to be read; the oral report is meant to be listened to.

- In some instances it's helpful to distribute the written report and to use your oral presentation to highlight the most essential aspects of the report. Listeners may then refer to the report as you speak—a situation not recommended for most public speeches.

- In some instances you might distribute the written report only after you have completed your oral report. Generally, however, people don't like this procedure; they prefer the option of thumbing through the report as they listen or reserving reading until after they've heard the oral report.

Now that you've finished the first part of your public speaking training, there is still much to learn. Take a look at the inside back cover for some suggestions for continuing your study of public speaking.

# The Special Occasion Speech in Cultural Perspective

Like all forms of communication, the special occasion speech must be developed with a clear understanding of the influence of culture. For example, the discussion of the speech of introduction suggested that you not oversell the speaker; excessive exaggeration is generally evaluated negatively in much of the United States. On the other hand, exaggerated praise often is expected in some Latin cultures.

Similarly, the discussion of the speech of goodwill suggested that you present yourself as being worthy of the goodwill rather than as a supplicant begging for it. In some cultures, however, this attitude might be seen as arrogant and

# A Primer of Small Group Communication

Understanding the nature and functions of small groups and learning to use these groups effectively and efficiently will help you throughout your social and professional career.

## What Is a Small Group?

A group is (1) a collection of individuals who (2) are connected to one another by some common purpose, (3) are interdependent, (4) have some degree of organization among them, and (5) see themselves as a group.

## Types of Small Groups

**Idea-generation groups** are small groups that exist solely to generate ideas and often follow a formula called brainstorming. Brainstorming is a technique for bombarding a problem and generating as many ideas as possible. This technique involves two stages. The first is the brainstorming period proper; the second is the evaluation period. Brainstorming follows four general rules. (1) Don't Criticize. (2) Strive for Quantity. (3) Combine and Extend Ideas. (4) Develop the Wildest Ideas Possible.

**Personal growth groups,** sometimes referred to as support groups, aim to help members cope with particular difficulties—such as drug addiction, not being assertive enough, having an alcoholic parent, being an ex-convict, or having a hyperactive child or a promiscuous spouse. Other groups are more clearly therapeutic and are designed to change significant aspects of an individual's personality or behavior. Still other groups are devoted to making healthy individuals function even more effectively. Three well-known types of personal growth groups: the encounter group, the assertiveness training group, and the consciousness-raising group.

- **Encounter groups,** also known as "sensitivity groups" or "T [Training]-groups," for example, constitute a form of psychotherapy; these groups try to facilitate members' personal growth and foster their ability to deal effectively with other people.

- **Assertiveness training groups** aim to increase the willingness of its members to stand up for their rights and to act more assertively in a wide variety of situations.

- **Consciousness-raising groups** aim to help people cope with the problems society confronts them with. The members of a consciousness-raising group all have one characteristic in common (for example, they may all be women, unwed mothers, gay fathers, or recently unemployed executives). It's this commonality that leads the members to join together and help one another.

**Information sharing groups** enable members to acquire new information or skills through a sharing of knowledge. In most information-sharing groups, all members have something to teach and something to learn. In some, however, the interaction takes place because some members have information and some don't.

- In **educational** or **learning groups,** the members pool their knowledge to the benefit of all, as in the popular law and medical student learning groups.

- A different type of learning group is the **focus group,** a small group assembled for a kind of in-depth interview. The aim here is to discover what people think about an issue or product; for example, what do young executives earning more than $100,000 think about buying a foreign luxury car?

**Problem-solving groups** are those in which individuals meet to solve a problem or to reach a decision. They are traditionally described as taking place in a series of steps:

- **Define and Analyze the Problem.** Define the problem as an open-ended question ("How can we improve the company website?") rather than as a statement ("The company website needs to be improved") or a yes/no question ("Does the website need improvement?"). The open-ended question allows greater freedom of exploration.

- **Establish Criteria for Evaluating Solutions.** Before any solutions are proposed, you need to decide how to evaluate them. At this stage you identify the standards or criteria that you'll use in evaluating solutions or in selecting one solution over another.

- **Identify Possible Solutions.** At this stage identify as many solutions as possible. Focus on quantity rather than quality.

- **Evaluate Solutions.** After all the solutions have been proposed, you go back and evaluate each according to the criteria you have established. For example, to what extent does incorporating reviews of area restaurants meet the evaluation criteria? Will it increase the budget? Each potential solution should be matched against the criteria.

- **Select the Best Solution(s).** At this stage the best solution or solutions are selected and put into operation. For instance, in the company website example, if "reviews of area restaurants" and "listings of new positions" best met the evaluation criteria, the group might then incorporate these two new items in the redesign of the website.

- **Test Selected Solution(s).** After solutions are put into operation, test their effectiveness. The group might, for example, poll employees about the website changes, examine the number of hits, or analyze the advertising revenue. If the solutions you have adopted prove ineffective, you will need to go back to one of the previous stages and repeat part of the process.

## Decision-Making Methods

Groups may use different decision-making methods in deciding, for example, which criteria to use or which solutions to accept. Generally, groups use one of three methods: decision by authority, majority rule, or consensus.

- **Decision by Authority.** In decision by authority, members voice their feelings and opinions, but the leader, boss, or CEO makes the final decision.

- **Decision by Majority Rule.** With this method the group members agree to abide by the majority decision and may vote on various issues as the group works toward solving its problem.

- **Decision by Consensus.** In some situations *consensus* means unanimous agreement; for example, a criminal jury must reach a unanimous decision to convict or acquit a defendant. In most business groups, however, consensus means that members agree that they can live with the solution; they agree that they can do

whatever the solution requires (Kelly, 1994). Consensus is especially important when the group wants each member to be satisfied with and committed to the decision and the decision-making process as a whole.

## Member Roles

Group member roles fall into three general classes—group task roles, group building and maintenance roles, and individual roles:

- **Group task roles** are those that help the group focus more specifically on achieving its goals. In serving any of these roles, you act not as an isolated individual but rather as a part of the larger whole. The needs and goals of the group dictate the task roles you serve. As an effective group member you would serve several of these functions, for example: contributor of new ideas, information seeker of facts and opinions, elaborator, coordinator, critic, recorder, and energizer.

- **Group building and maintenance roles** are those that focus not only on the task to be performed but also on interpersonal relationships among members, for example, encourage other members, offer compromises, and set standards.

- **Individual roles** are counterproductive; they hinder the group's productivity and member satisfaction, largely because they focus on serving individual rather than group needs, for example, being aggressive or disagreeable, seeking recognition for oneself, jokes, dominates, or pleads for special interests.

## Member Participation

- **Be Group or Team Oriented.** Pool your talents, knowledge, and insights so as to arrive at a better solution than any one person could have developed.

- **Center Conflict on Issues.** Avoid personal attacks.

- **Be Critically Open-Minded.** Advance any solutions or conclusions tentatively rather than with certainty. Be willing to alter your suggestions and revise them in light of the discussion.

- **Ensure Understanding.** Make sure that your ideas are understood by all participants.

## Groupthink

Groupthink is a way of thinking that people use when agreement among members has become excessively important. Groupthink is most likely to occur when there is high stress, when like-minded individuals are isolated from others, and when there is an especially strong and opinionated leader. Overemphasis on agreement among members tends to shut out realistic and logical analysis of a problem or of possible alternatives. Watch for such signs as these: the illusion of invulnerability, the assumption of morality, intolerance of differences of opinion, self-censorship, the assumption of unanimity, and gatekeeping (preventing contrary evidence from being discussed).

## Leaders in Small Group Communication

Leadership is defined in two very different ways in research and theory: (1) Leadership is the process of influencing the thoughts, feelings, and behaviors of group members and establishing the direction that others follow; leadership and influence are parts of the same skill. (2) Leadership is the process of empowering others; the leader is the person who helps others to maximize their potential and to take control of their lives.

## Functions of Leadership

It often falls to the leader to provide members with necessary materials prior to the meeting.

### Before-Discussion Functions

These may include, for example, arranging a convenient meeting time and place; informing members of the purposes and goals of the meeting; providing them with materials they should read or view; and recommending that they come to the meeting with, for example, general ideas or specific proposals.

### During-Discussion Functions

The leader has much to do here:

- **Activate the Group Agenda.** Most groups have an agenda (a list of tasks the group wishes to complete).
- **Promote Effective Group Interaction.** One of the leader's functions is to stimulate the members to interact effectively. A leader also serves this function when members act as individuals rather than as a group. In this instance the leader needs to focus the members on their *group* task.
- **Empower Group Members**. An important function in at least some leadership styles (though not limited to leadership) is to empower others—to help other group members (but also your relational partner, co-workers, employees, other students, or siblings) to gain increased power over themselves and their environment. Some ways to empower others include the following: (1) Raise the person's self-esteem. Compliment, reinforce. Resist faultfinding. (2) Share skills as well as decision-making power and authority. (3) Be constructively critical. (4) Encourage growth in all forms: academic, relational, and professional, among others.
- **Keep Members on Track.** Don't allow the discussion to go off on tangents or take unnecessary detours.
- **Ensure Member Satisfaction.** If a group is to be effective, the leader must help the group serve not only the surface purposes of, say, solving the problem, but also the underlying or interpersonal purposes that motivated many of the members to come together in the first place.
- **Manage Conflict.** When there is conflict—whether openly expressed or hidden in subtle nonverbal cues—the leader needs to address it.

### After-Discussion Functions

Such functions might include summarizing the group's discussion, organizing future meetings, or presenting the group's decisions to some other group.

## RESEARCH LINK

### Museum Collections and Exhibits

Not too long ago, museums weren't even included in research discussions; good museums were so far away from most people that the possibility of visiting any given museum was remote. Now, however, you have the world of museums literally at your fingertips. Every museum collects all sorts of information pertaining to its major focus; for example, to natural history, science, or art. Visiting a few museum websites is well worth your while. A few exceptionally good sites are those of the Franklin Institute Science Museum at http://sln.fi.edu/, London's Museum of Natural

History at www.nhm.ac.uk, the Metropolitan Museum of Art, at www.metmuseum.org/home.asp), and the Smithsonian Institution at www.si.edu/. An especially good site if you don't know what museum you'd like to visit is www.comlab.ox.ac.uk/archive/other/museums/usa.html, where you will find links to museums, archives, and galleries throughout the United States.

So take a break and visit the Smithsonian or any of the numerous art, science, or history museums online. Have fun.

disrespectful to the audience. In some Asian cultures, for example, pleading for goodwill would be seen as suitably modest and respectful of the audience.

In introducing or in paying tribute to someone, consider the extent to which you wish to focus on the person's contribution to the group or to individual achievement. An audience with a predominantly collectivist orientation (see Chapter 3) will expect to hear group-centered achievements, whereas an audience of predominantly individualist orientation will expect to hear more individually focused achievements.

Culture also will influence the way in which an acceptance speech should be framed. Not surprisingly, collectivist cultures would suggest that you give a lot of credit to the group, whereas individualist cultures would suggest that taking self-credit is appropriate when it's due. Thus, if you were accepting an award for a performance in a movie, an extreme collectivist orientation would lead you to give great praise to others and to claim that without others you never could have accomplished what you did. An extreme individualist orientation would lead you to accept the award and the praise for yourself; after all, you did it! In the media business, as you see from the numerous televised award shows, everyone gives thanks to almost everyone connected with the project. That's the custom; the collectivist form of expression has become the norm, at least in the context of show business.

## Next Steps

Now that you've completed what might be called your formal training in public speaking, there is still a great deal to learn so consider continuing your study of public speaking. A few suggestions are offered on the inside back cover.

# Essentials of Speaking on Special Occasions

This chapter discussed special occasion speeches, highlighting a variety of specific types, and placed special occasion speeches in a cultural context.

## The Speech of Introduction

1. The **speech of introduction** introduces another speaker or series of speakers. In this speech: Establish a connection among speaker, topic, and audience; establish the speaker's credibility; be consistent in style and manner with the major speech; be brief; avoid covering what the speaker intends to discuss; and avoid overselling the speaker.

## The Speech of Presentation

2. The **speech of presentation** explains why the presentation is being made, and the speech of acceptance expresses thanks for the award. In the speech of presentation, state the reason for the presentation and state the importance of the award. In the **speech of acceptance**, thank those who gave the award, thank those who helped, and state the meaning of the award to you.

## The Speech to Secure Goodwill

3. The **speech to secure goodwill** attempts to secure or, more often, to regain the speaker's place in the listeners' good graces. In this speech: Stress benefits the audience may derive; stress uniqueness; establish your credibility and the credibility of the subject; avoid being obvious in securing goodwill; and avoid pleading for goodwill.

## The Speech of Dedication

4. The **speech of dedication** gives specific meaning to some event or object. In this speech: Explain why you're giving the speech; explain what is being dedicated; state who is responsible for the event or object; and say why this is significant, especially to your specific listeners.

## The Commencement Speech

5. The **commencement speech** celebrates the end of some training period. In this speech: Consider the values of a temporal organizational pattern; learn something about the training organization and demonstrate this knowledge in your speech; be brief; congratulate the larger audience, not only those who went through the training; offer some motivational message; and offer your own good wishes.

## The Inspirational Speech

6. The **inspirational speech** aims to inspire the audience, to lead listeners to think in a positive direction. In this speech you demonstrate your connection with the audience and your intense involvement using emotional appeals and stressing the positive.

## The Eulogy

7. The **eulogy** seeks to praise someone who has died. In this speech: Show the connection between yourself and the person you're eulogizing; be specific; combine specifics with the general; stress that the person is deserving of your praise; and show your listeners what they can learn from this person.

## The Farewell Speech

8. The **farewell speech** signals a transition between what was and what will be. In this speech: Thank those who helped you; portray the positives of the past; explain your reasons for making the transition; and offer some words of wisdom, some motivational message.

## The Toast

9. The **toast** celebrates a person or an occasion. In the toast: Be brief; focus attention on the person or event you're toasting; avoid references that listeners may not understand; and make it clear that this is the end of your speech when you raise your glass.

## Presenting the Group's Thinking

10. Among the formats that typically involve **public presentations of group conclusions** are the panel, the symposium (or symposium-forum) and team presentations, and oral and written reports

## The Special Occasion Speech in Cultural Perspective

11. The special occasion speech needs to be developed with an awareness of the **cultural norms and rules** specific to the occasion and to the audience members. Especially relevant here is the distinction between individualist and collectivist cultures.

# Essential Terms

acceptance speech **(271)**      goodwill speech **(273)**       symposium **(283)**
apology **(274)**                inspirational speech **(277)**  symposium–forum **(284)**
commencement speech **(275)**    forum **(284)**                 team presentation **(283)**
dedication speech **(274)**      panel **(283)**                 toast **(281)**
eulogy **(278)**                 presentation speech **(271)**
farewell speech **(279)**        speech of introduction **(270)**

# Public Speaking Exercises

### 12.1 Developing the Speech of Introduction

Prepare a speech of introduction approximately two minutes in length. For this experience you may assume that the speaker you introduce will speak on any topic you wish. Do, however, assume a topic appropriate to the speaker and to your audience—your class. You may wish to select your introduction from one of the following suggestions:

1. Introduce a historical figure to the class.

2. Introduce a contemporary religious, political, or social leader.

3. Prepare a speech of introduction that someone might give to introduce you to your class.

4. Introduce a famous media (film, television, radio, recording, writing) personality—alive or dead.

5. Introduce a series of speeches debating the pros and cons of a cultural emphasis in college courses.

### 12.2 Developing the Special Occasion Speech

Select one of the special occasion speeches discussed in this chapter and create a scenario in which such a speech might be given—for example, you're presenting an award to the Teacher of the Year or you're giving a eulogy at a funeral or you're toasting the union of two people, or you're trying to secure the goodwill of high school seniors to your college. Prepare the speech, approximately 3 minutes in length should do it, and present it.

# LogOn! myspeechlab

Visit MySpeechLab (www.myspeechlab.com) for a variety of useful resources on the special occasion speech. For those who wish more information on small group communication to complement the discussion of "Presenting the Group's Thinking" in this chapter, two complete chapters from my *Essentials of Human Communication*, 7th edition (2011) are available on MSL: "Small Group Communication" and "Members and Leaders in Small Group Communication." You may also find it interesting to read the full eulogy of the one presented in the chapter in abbreviated form and another eulogy given by a professor of speech. A variety of additional special occasion speeches are also provided.

# Glossary

**abstraction** A general concept derived from a class of objects; a partial representation of some whole; the quality of abstractness, or non-concreteness.

**abstraction process** The process by which a general concept is derived from specifics; the process by which some (never all) characteristics of an object, person, or event are perceived by the senses or included in some term, phrase, or sentence.

**accent** The stress or emphasis placed on a syllable when it is pronounced.

**acceptance speech** A speech in which the speaker accepts an award or honor of some kind and attempts to place the award in some kind of context.

**active listening** A process of putting together into some meaningful whole the listener's understanding of the speaker's total message—the verbal and the nonverbal, the content and the feelings.

**ageist language** Language that insults people because of their age, usually directed against older people.

**agenda-setting** A fallacy or pseudo-argument in which a speaker contends that only certain issues are important and others are not—in an attempt, for example, to focus attention on the strong points of a plan and divert attention from the weak points.

**alliteration** A figure of speech in which the initial sound in two or more words is repeated.

**allness** The assumption that all can be known or is known about a given person, issue, object, or event.

**analogy** Comparison of two things; analogies may be literal (in which items from the same class are compared) or figurative (in which items from different classes are compared).

**anecdotal evidence** A fallacious persuasive tactic in which the speaker offers specific examples or illustrations as "proof."

**antithesis** A figure of speech in which contrary ideas are presented in parallel form, as in Charles Dickens's opening lines in *A Tale of Two Cities*: "It was the best of times, it was the worst of times."

**antithetical sentences** A type of sentence patterning in which contrasting ideas are placed together in parallel style

**apology** A type of excuse in which you acknowledge responsibility for the behavior, generally ask forgiveness, and claim that the behavior will not happen again.

**appeal to tradition** A fallacy often used as an argument against change, as when a speaker claims that a proposed plan should not be adopted because it was never done before.

**articulation** The movements of the speech organs as they modify and interrupt the air stream from the lungs, forming sounds.

**assimilation** A process of message distortion in which messages are reworked to conform to our own attitudes, prejudices, needs, and values.

**attention** The process of responding to a stimulus or stimuli; usually some consciousness of responding is implied.

**attitude** A predisposition to respond for or against an object, person, or position.

**audience analysis** The process of discovering useful information about the listeners so that a speech may be better tailored to this specific group of people.

**audience** A group of people listening to the same message or speech.

**bandwagon** A persuasive technique in which the speaker tries to gain compliance by saying that "everyone is doing it" and urges you to jump on the bandwagon.

**belief** Confidence in the existence or truth of something; conviction.

**bias** Preconceived ideas that predispose you to interpret meaning on the basis of these ideas rather than on the basis of the evidence and argument.

**brainstorming** A technique for generating ideas either alone or, more usually, in a small group.

**card-stacking** A fallacy in reasoning in which the speaker selects only the evidence and arguments that support the case, and may even falsify evidence and distort the facts to better fit the case; despite these misrepresentations, the speaker presents the supporting materials as "fair" and "impartial."

**cause-effect pattern** An organizational pattern in which the speech is divided into two parts: causes and effects. It is especially useful when you wish to demonstrate causal connection between two events or elements.

**causes and effects, reasoning from** A form of reasoning in which you reason that certain effects are due to specific causes or that specific causes produce certain effects.

**channel** The vehicle or medium through which signals are sent.

**character attacks** A fallacy—often referred to as *ad hominem*—in which a speaker accuses another person (usually an opponent) of some serious wrongdoing or of some serious character flaw that has nothing to do with the issues under discussion in an attempt to discredit the person or to divert attention from the issues.

**character** One of the qualities of **credibility;** an individual's honesty and basic nature; moral qualities.

**charisma** One of the qualities of **credibility;** an individual's dynamism or forcefulness

**clarity** A quality of speaking style which makes a message easily intelligible

**cliché** An overused expression that has lost its novelty and part of its meaning and that calls attention to itself because of its overuse; "tall, dark, and handsome" as a description of a man is a cliché.

**cognitive restructuring** A technique involving a change in thinking to reduce stress and anxiety.

**collectivist culture** A culture in which the group's goals rather than the individual's are given primary importance and where, for example, benevolence, tradition, and conformity are given special emphasis. Opposed to **individualistic culture.**

**commencement speech** A speech given to celebrate the end of some training period, often at school graduation ceremonies.

**communication apprehension** Fear or anxiety over communicating; may be trait apprehension (a fear of communication generally, regardless of the specific situation) or state apprehension (a fear that is specific to a given communication situation).

**competence** One of the qualities that undergird personal **credibility;** encompasses a person's ability and knowledge.

**conclusion** The final part of a public speech which usually contains a summary of the main points and a wrap up

**connotation** The feeling or emotional aspect of meaning, generally viewed as consisting of the evaluative (for example, good/bad), potency (strong/weak), and activity (fast/slow) dimensions; the associations of a term. See also **denotation.**

**context** The physical, psychological, social, and temporal environment in which communication takes place.

**credibility** The degree to which a receiver perceives the speaker to be believable; **competence**, **character**, and **charisma** (dynamism) are credibility's major dimensions.

**criticism** The reasoned judgment of some work; although often equated with faultfinding, criticism can involve both positive and negative evaluations

**cultural identifiers** Terms or phrases used to refer to cultural qualities such as race or age.

**cultural sensitivity** An awareness of the rules for communicating in varied cultural settings.

**culture** The relatively specialized lifestyle of a group of people—consisting of their values, beliefs, artifacts, ways of behaving, and ways of communicating—that is passed on from one generation to the next.

**database** An organized collection of information.

**dedication speech** A special occasion speech in which you commemorate the opening or start of a project.

**definition** A statement explaining the meaning of a term, phrase, or concept.

**definition, speech of** An informative speech devoted to explaining the meaning of a concept.

**delivery outline** A brief outline of a speech that the speaker uses during the actual speech presentation.

**demonstration, speech of** A speech in which the speaker shows the audience how to do something or how something operates.

**denotation** Referential meaning; the objective or descriptive meaning of a word. See also **connotation.**

**description, speech of** A speech in which you explain an object, person, event, or process.

**descriptive categories** Ways in which a speaker might describe an object or person, for example, physical categories of height or weight or psychological categories of happy or compulsive

**directness** A quality of speech in which the speaker's intentions are stated clearly and directly.

**display rules** Cultural norms for what is and what is not appropriate to display in public.

**door-in-the-face technique** A persuasive strategy in which the speaker first makes a large request that will be refused and then follows with the intended and much smaller request.

**emotional appeals** Persuasive strategies designed to influence the emotions of the audience.

**empathy** The feeling of another person's feeling; feeling or perceiving something as another person does.

**ethics** The branch of philosophy that deals with the rightness or wrongness of actions; the study of moral values.

**ethnic expressions** Words and phrases that are associated with specific ethnic groups.

**ethnocentrism** The tendency to see others and their behaviors through our own cultural filters, often as distortions of our own behaviors; the tendency to evaluate the values and beliefs of our own culture more positively than those of another culture.

**eulogy** A speech of tribute in which the speaker praises someone who died.

**euphemism** A polite word or phrase used to substitute for some taboo or otherwise offensive term; often used as a persuasive strategy to make the negative appear positive.

**example** A form of supporting material in which a specific instance is used to illustrate a concept.

**extemporaneous speech** A speech that is thoroughly prepared and organized in detail and in which certain aspects of style are predetermined.

**fact, questions of** Questions that concern what is or is not true, what does or does not exist, what did or did not happen; questions that, potentially at least, have answers.

**fact–inference confusion** A misevaluation in which a person makes an inference, regards it as a fact, and acts upon it as if it were a fact.

**fallacies of language** Ways of using language that may appear logical on the surface but in fact have no logical foundation and are often (though not always) used to persuade (for example, weasel words, euphemisms, and jargon).

**farewell speech** A speech designed to say goodbye to a position or to colleagues and to signal that you're moving on.

**figures of speech** Stylistic devices and ways of expressing ideas that are used to achieve special effects.

**flexibility** The ability to adjust communication strategies on the basis of the unique situation.

**flip chart** A presentation aid consisting of sheets of paper for writing key terms or numbers while presenting a speech.

**foot-in-the-door technique** A persuasive strategy in which the speaker first asks for something small (to get a foot in the door) and then, once a pattern of agreement has been achieved, follows with the real and larger request.

**forum** A question-and-answer period that often follows a public speech or small group presentation.

**gender** The psychological sex role of an individual.

**general purpose** The overall aim of your speech, for example, to inform or to persuade

**goodwill speech** A special occasion speech in which the speaker seeks to make the image of a person, product, or company more positive.

**heterosexist language** Language that assumes all people are heterosexual and thereby denigrates lesbians and gay men.

**hierarchy of needs** A view of human needs that argues that certain basic needs (e.g., for food and shelter) have to be satisfied before higher-order needs (e.g., for self-esteem or love) can be effective in motivating listeners.

**high-context culture** A culture in which much of the information in communication is in the context or in the person rather than explicitly coded in the verbal messages. **Collectivist cultures** are generally high-context. Opposed to **individualist low-context culture.**

**hyperbole** A figure of speech in which something is exaggerated for effect but is not intended to be taken literally.

**idioms** Expressions that are unique to a specific language and whose meaning cannot be deduced simply from an analysis of the individual words.

**illustration** A specific instance drawn in greater detail than a brief example.

**imagery** A quality of language that appeals to the senses.

**I-messages** A type of message in which the speaker takes responsibility for the message.

**immediacy** A quality of interpersonal effectiveness; a sense of contact and togetherness; a feeling of interest in and liking for the other person.

**impromptu speech** A speech given without any explicit prior preparation.

**indiscrimination** A misevaluation that results when someone categorizes people, events, or objects into a particular class and responds to them only as members of the class; a person's failure to recognize that each individual is unique.

**individualist culture** A culture in which the individual's rather than the group's goals and preferences are given primary importance. Opposed to **collectivist culture.**

**informative speech** A speech designed to communicate information to an audience rather than to persuade.

**inspirational speech** A special occasion speech designed to raise the spirits of the audience, to inspire them

**introduction** The first part of the speech which generally seeks to gain attention and orient the audience.

**introduction, speech of** A speech designed to introduce the speaker himself or herself to an audience or a speech designed to introduce another speaker or group of speakers.

**irony** A figure of speech employed for special emphasis, in which a speaker uses words whose literal meaning is the opposite of the speaker's actual message or intent.

**jargon** The technical language of any specialized group, often a professional class, which is unintelligible to individuals not belonging to the group; "shop talk."

**levels of abstraction** The different levels of specificity ranging from the highly abstract to the very specific.

**listening** An active process of receiving messages sent orally; this process consists of five stages: receiving, understanding, remembering, evaluating, and responding.

**logical appeals** Persuasive appeals that focus on facts and evidence rather than on emotions or credibility.

**low-context culture** A culture in which most of the information in communication is explicitly stated in the verbal messages. **Individualist cultures** are usually low-context cultures. Opposed to **high-context culture.**

**main points** The major concepts or arguments of your speech.

**manuscript speech** A speech designed to be read verbatim from a script.

**mean** The arithmetic average.

**median** The middle score in an array of scores.

**memorized speech** A method of oral presentation in which the entire speech is committed to memory and then recited.

**message** Any signal or combination of signals that serves as a **stimulus** for a receiver.

**metaphor** A figure of speech in which there is an implied comparison between two unlike things; for example, "That CEO is a jackal."

**metonymy** A figure of speech in which some particular thing is referred to by something with which it is closely associated, for example, *Rome* for the *Catholic Church* or the *White House* for the United States Government.

**models** Replicas of actual objects.

**motivated sequence** An organizational pattern for arranging the information in a discourse to motivate an audience to respond positively to the speaker's purpose.

**name-calling** An often-used fallacy in which the speaker gives an idea a derogatory name to try to get you to condemn the idea without analyzing the argument and evidence.

**narrative** An illustration told in story form.

**negative social proof** Examples of other people doing what you don't want the audience to do.

**noise** Anything that interferes with a person's receiving a message as the source intended the message to be received. Noise is present in a communication system to the extent that the message received is not the message sent.

**nonverbal communication** Messages without words; communication by means of space, gestures, facial expressions, touching, vocal variation, and silence, for example.

**objectivity** A quality of language which is largely denotative.

**oral style** The style of spoken discourse that, when compared with written style, consists of shorter, simpler, and more familiar words; more qualification, self-reference terms, allness terms, verbs and adverbs; and more concrete terms and terms indicative of consciousness of projection—for example, "as I see it."

**organization** The pattern of a speech.

**orientation** In public speaking, a preview of what is to follow in the speech.

**outline** A blueprint or pattern for a speech.

**oxymoron** A figure of speech in which two opposite qualities are combined as in *bittersweet.*

**panel** A small group presentation format in which participants speak informally and without any set pattern.

**parallel sentence** A type of sentence patterning in which all sentences in a series follow the same grammatical structure.

**pauses** Silent periods in the normally fluent stream of speech. Pauses are of two major types: filled pauses (interruptions in speech that are filled with such vocalizations as "er" or "um") and unfilled pauses (silences of unusually long duration).

**performance visualization** A technique designed specifically to reduce the outward signs of apprehension and also to reduce the negative thinking that often creates anxiety.

**periodic sentence** A type of sentence in which the key word is placed at the end of the sentence

**personal interest** A persuasive fallacy that attempts to divert attention from the issues and arguments in one of two ways: (1) The speaker argues that the opponent should be disqualified because he or she isn't directly affected by the proposal or doesn't have firsthand knowledge, or (2) the speaker tries to disqualify someone because he or she will benefit in some way from the proposal.

**personal style** A quality of style in which speech resembles conversation.

**personification** A figure of speech in which human characteristics are attributed to inanimate objects for special effect; for example, "After the painting, the room looked cheerful and energetic."

**persuasion** The process of influencing attitudes and behavior.

**persuasive speech** A speech designed to strengthen or change the attitudes or beliefs of the audience or to move them to take some kind of action.

**pie chart** A type of presentation aid which divides a whole into pieces and represents these as pieces of a pie.

**pitch** The highness or lowness of the vocal tone.

**plagiarism** The act or process of passing off the work (ideas, words, illustrations) of others as your own.

**plain folks** An often-used fallacy in which the speaker presents himself or herself as one of the people, just "plain folks" like everyone else, even when that image is false or is not relevant to the issue at hand.

**polarization** A form of fallacious reasoning in which only two extremes are considered; also referred to as "black-or-white" or "either/or" thinking or a two-valued orientation.

**policy, questions of** Questions that focus on what should be done (the policy that should be adopted).

**positive labeling** A persuasive technique in which the audience is labeled in ways that are consistent with the way you want them to act.

**positive social proof** Examples of people who do as you wish your listeners do.

**preparation outline** A thorough outline (or blueprint) of the speech.

**presentation** The actual delivery of a speech.

**presentation aid** A visual or auditory form of supporting material.

**presentation software** Computer software for preparing materials for a public speech.

**presentation speech** A special occasion speech in which a speaker presents an award or some sign of recognition.

**problem solution pattern** An organizational system often useful in persuasive speeches in which the speaker presents the problem and then the solution.

**pronunciation** The production of syllables or words according to some accepted standard; as presented, for example, in a dictionary.

**proxemics** The study of the communicative function of space; the study of how people unconsciously structure their space—the distance between people in their interactions, the organization of space in homes and offices, and even the design of cities.

**public speaking** Communication in which the source is one person and the receiver is an audience of many persons.

**questions of fact** Issues revolving around potentially answerable questions.

**questions of policy** Issues focused on what should or should not be done, what is and what is not a valuable policy.

**questions of value** Issues focused on what is good or bad, just or unjust.

**racist language** Language that denigrates or is derogatory toward members of a particular race.

**rate** The speed at which you speak, generally measured in words per minute.

**reliability** A quality of research or support that can be counted on as accurate and trustworthy.

**repetition** Repeating something in exactly the same words.

**research** A systematic search for information; an investigation of the relevant information on a topic; an inquiry into what is known or thought about a subject.

**restatement** Repeating an idea in different words.

**rhetoric** The study of the means of persuasion.

**rhetorical question** A figure of speech in which a question is asked to make a statement rather than to secure an answer.

**selective exposure, principle of** A principle of persuasion that argues that listeners actively seek out information that supports their opinions, beliefs, and values while actively avoiding information that would contradict these opinions, beliefs, and values.

**self-affirmation** A positive statement about oneself.

**self-esteem** The value you place on yourself; your self-evaluation; usually refers to the positive value a person places on himself or herself.

**sexist language** Language derogatory to one gender, usually women.

**sign, reasoning from** A form of reasoning in which the presence of certain signs (clues) are interpreted as leading to a particular conclusion.

**signpost phrases** Phrases that signal where you are in a speech.

**simile** A figure of speech in which a speaker compares two unlike things using the words *like* or *as*.

**slang** Language used by special groups that is not considered proper by the general society; language made up of the argot, cant, and jargon of various groups and known by the general public.

**social proof** Examples of other people who do or don't do as you want the audience to do.

**spatial pattern** An organizational scheme in which the main topics of a speech are arranged in spatial terms, for example, high to low or East to West.

**specific instances, reasoning from** A form of reasoning in which several specific instances are examined and then a conclusion about the whole is formed.

**specific purpose** The aim of your speech put in concrete, specific terms.

**state apprehension** A fear that is specific to a given communication situation.

**static evaluation** An orientation that fails to recognize that the world is characterized by constant change; an attitude that sees people and events as fixed rather than as constantly changing.

**statistics** Summary numbers such as the mean (or average) or the median (or most common score).

**straw man** An argument (like a person made of straw) that is set up only to be knocked down. In this fallacy a speaker creates a "straw man"—an easy-to-destroy simplification of the opposing position—and then proceeds to demolish it.

**supporting materials** Those examples, statistics, testimony and the like that amplify or give evidence in support of a main idea.

**symposium** A small group presentation format in which each member of the group delivers a relatively prepared talk on some aspect of the topic. Often combined with a **forum.**

**symposium–forum** A moderated group presentation with prepared speeches on various aspects of a topic, followed by a question-and-answer session with the audience.

**synecdoche** A figure of speech in which a part of an object is used to stand for the entire object as in *green thumb* for gardener.

**systematic desensitization** A theory and technique for dealing with a variety of fears (such as communication apprehension) in which you gradually desensitize yourself to behaviors you wish to eliminate.

**taboo topics** Subjects that are best avoided because they violate a culture's principles of appropriateness.

**team presentation** A public presentation shared by several members of a team.

**template outline** An outline in which the essential parts of the speech are identified with spaces for these essential parts to be filled in; a learning device for developing speeches.

**temporal pattern** An organizational scheme in which the main points of a speech are arranged chronologically, for example, from past to present.

**testimonial** A persuasive and often fallacious technique in which the speaker uses the authority or image of some positively evaluated person to gain your approval or of some negatively evaluated person to gain your rejection.

**testimony** A form of supporting material consisting of the opinions or eyewitness report of another person.

**thesis** The main assertion of a message—for example, the theme of a public speech.

**thin entering wedge** A persuasive fallacy in which a speaker argues against a position on the grounds that it is a thin entering wedge that will open the floodgates to all sorts of catastrophes, though there is no evidence to support such results.

**toast** A brief speech designed to celebrate a person or an occasion.

**topic generators** Computer programs that generate a variety of subject matter topics, often useful for speeches and compositions.

**topical pattern** An organizational pattern in which a topic is divided into its component parts.

**topoi** A system for analyzing a topic according to a pre-established set of categories.

**trait apprehension** A general fear of communication, regardless of the specific situation.

**transfer** A persuasive technique in which a speaker associates an idea with something you respect to gain your approval or with something you dislike to gain your rejection.

**transitions** Words, phrases, or sentences that connect the parts of a speech and that serve as guides to help listeners follow the speaker's train of thought.

**tree diagram** A method for narrowing a topic in which each topic is branched off into subtopics and each of these subtopics is branched off into additional subtopics.

**value** Relative worth of an object; a quality that makes something desirable or undesirable; ideals or customs about which we have emotional responses, whether positive or negative.

**value, questions of** Questions that focus on the goodness or badness, the morality or immorality of an act.

**volume** The relative loudness of the voice.

**weasel words** Words whose meanings are difficult (slippery like a weasel) to pin down to specifics.

**you-messages** A type of message in which the speaker avoids personal responsibility for the message and blames the other person.

# References

Alessandra, T. (1986). How to listen effectively. *Speaking of success* [videotape series]. San Diego, CA: Levitz Sommer Productions.

Allan, K., & Burridge, K. (2007). *Forbidden words: Taboo and the censoring of language.* Cambridge, UK: Cambridge University Press.

Allen, R. L. (1997, October 6). People—the single point of difference—listening to them. *Nation's Restaurant News, 31,* 130.

Annan, K. (2007) *General Assembly Sixty-first Session 10th plenary meeting.* Retrieved from http://unbisnet.un.org

Arliss, L. P. (1991). *Gender communication.* Englewood Cliffs, NJ: Prentice-Hall.

Axtell, R. E. (1990). *Do's and taboos of hosting international visitors.* New York, NY: Wiley.

Axtell, R. E. (1993). *Do's and taboos around the world* (3rd ed.). New York, NY: Wiley.

Axtell, R. E. (2007). *Essential do's and taboos. The complete guide to international business and leisure travel.* Hoboken, NJ: Wiley.

Ayres, J. (1986). Perceptions of speaking ability: An explanation for stage fright. *Communication Education, 35,* 275–287.

Ayres, J. (2005, April). Performance visualization and behavioral disruption: A clarification. *Communication Reports, 18,* 55–63.

Ayres, J., & Hopf, T. S. (1992). Visualization: Reducing speech anxiety and enhancing performance. *Communication Reports, 5,* 1–10.

Ayres, J., & Hopf, T. S. (1993). *Coping with speech anxiety.* Norwood, NJ: Ablex.

Ayres, J., Hopf, T., & Ayres, D. M. (1994, July). An examination of whether imaging ability enhances the effectiveness of an intervention designed to reduce speech anxiety. *Communication Education, 43,* 252–258.

Barker, L. L. (1990). *Communication* (5th ed.). Englewood Cliffs, NJ: Prentice-Hall.

Barker, L. L., Edwards, R., Gaines, C., Gladney, K., & Holley, F. (1980). An investigation of proportional time spent in various communication activities by college students. *Journal of Applied Communication Research, 8,* 101–109.

Bates, D. G., & Fratkin, E. M. (1999). *Cultural anthropology* (2nd ed.). Boston, MA: Allyn & Bacon.

Beatty, M. J. (1988). Situational and predispositional correlates of public speaking anxiety. *Communication Education, 37,* 28–39.

Beck, A. T. (1988). *Love is never enough.* New York, NY: Harper & Row.

Bellafiore, D. (2005). *Interpersonal conflict and effective communication.* Retrieved from http://www.drbalternatives.com/articles/cc2.html

Benson, S. G., & Dundis, S. P. (2003, September). Understanding and motivating health care employees: Integrating Maslow's hierarchy of needs, training and technology. *Journal of Nursing Management, 11,* 315–320.

Bodie, G. D. (2010). A racing heart, rattling knees, and ruminative thoughts: Defining, explaining, and treating public speaking anxiety. *Communication Education 59,* 70–105.

Bok, S. (1978). *Lying: Moral choice in public and private life.* New York, NY: Pantheon.

Borchardt, J. K. (2006, November). Harness the power of metaphors. *Writer, 119,* 28–30.

Brownback, S. (1998, May 15). Free speech: Lyrics, liberty and license. *Vital Speeches of the Day, 64,* 454–456.

Brownell, J. (2010). *Listening: Attitudes, principles, and skills* (4th ed.). Boston, MA: Allyn & Bacon.

Burgoon, J. K., & Bacue, A. E. (2003). Nonverbal communication skills. In J. O. Greene & B. R. Burleson (Eds.), *Handbook of communication and social interaction skills* (pp. 179–220). Mahwah, NJ: Erlbaum.

Burke, K. (1950). *A rhetoric of motives.* New York, NY: Prentice-Hall.

Butler, M. M. (2005). Communication apprehension and its impact on individuals in the work place. Howard University. *Dissertation Abstracts International: A. The Humanities and Social Sciences, 65* (9-A), 3215.

Capra, F. (Producer & Director), & Goodrich, F. (Writer), & Hackett, A. (Writer). (1946). *It's a Wonderful Life.* United States: RKO Studio. Retrieved from http://www.americanrhetoric.com/MovieSpeeches

Chang, H. C., & Holt, G. R. (1996, Winter). The changing Chinese interpersonal world: Popular themes in interpersonal communication books in modern Taiwan. *Communication Quarterly, 44,* 85–106.

Chase, S. (1956). *Guides to straight thinking, with 13 common fallacies.* New York, NY: HarperCollins.

Cialdini, R. T. (1984). *Influence: How and why people agree to things*. New York, NY: Morrow.

Cialdini, R. T., & Ascani, K. (1976). Test of a concession procedure for inducing verbal, behavioral, and further compliance with a request to give blood. *Journal of Applied Psychology, 61*, 295–300.

Coates, J., & Cameron, D. (1989). *Women, men, and language: Studies in language and linguistics*. London, UK: Longman.

Crawford, L. (2005). *Speech before World Pharma IT Congress*. Retrieved from http://www.fda.gov

Dalton, J. (1994, March 1). The character of readiness. *Vital Speeches of the Day, 60*, 296–299.

deBono, E. (1967). *Lateral thinking*. New York, NY: Harper Paperbacks.

deBono, E. (1976). *Teaching thinking*. New York, NY: Penguin.

Dejong, W. (1979). An examination of self perception mediation of the foot in the door effect. *Journal of Personality and Social Psychology, 37*, 2221–2239.

DeVito, J. A. (1974). *General semantics: Guide and workbook* (Rev. ed.). DeLand, FL: Everett/Edwards.

DeVito, J. A. (1996). *Brainstorms: How to think more creatively about communication (or about anything else)*. Boston, MA: Allyn & Bacon.

Dillard, J. P., & Marshall, L. J. (2003). Persuasion as a social skill. In J. O. Greene & B. R. Burleson (Eds.), *Handbook of communication and social interaction skills* (pp. 479–514). Mahwah, NJ: Erlbaum.

Dodd, C. (2007). *Senator Dodd speaks at Rev. Jesse Jackson's Wall Street Summit. Chris Dodd United States Senator for Connecticut*. Retrieved from http://dodd.senate.gov

Dwyer, K. K. (2005). *Conquer your speech anxiety* (2nd ed.). Belmont, CA: Wadsworth.

Eisenberg, N., & Strayer, J. (1987). *Empathy and its development*. New York, NY: Cambridge University Press.

Ekman, P., Friesen, W. V., & Ellsworth, P. (1972). *Emotion in the human face: Guidelines for research and an integration of findings*. New York, NY: Pergamon Press.

Ellis, A. (1988). *How to stubbornly refuse to make yourself miserable about anything, yes anything*. Secaucus, NJ: Lyle Stuart.

Emmert, P. (1994). A definition of listening. *Listening Post, 51*, 6.

Erber, R., & Erber, M. W. (2011). *Intimate relationships: Issues, theories, and research* (2nd ed.). Boston, MA: Allyn & Bacon.

Feinstein, D. (2006, October 23). *Gang violence: An environment of fear*. Speech delivered at the Gang Summit hosted by the U.S. Department of Justice. Retrieved from http://feinstein.seate.gov/public

Fensholt, M. (2003, June). There's nothing wrong with taking written notes to the podium. *Presentations, 17*, 66.

Floyd, J. J. (1985). *Listening: A practical approach*. Boston, MA: Allyn & Bacon.

Fraser, B. (1990, April). Perspectives on politeness. *Journal of Pragmatics, 14*, 219–236.

Freedman, J., & Fraser, S. (1966). Compliance without pressure: The foot-in-the-door technique. *Journal of Personality and Social Psychology, 4*, 195–202.

Frey, K. J., & Eagly, A. H. (1993, July). Vividness can undermine the persuasiveness of messages. *Journal of Personality and Social Psychology, 65*, 32–44.

Gamble, T. K., & Gamble, M. W. (2003). *The gender communication connection*. Boston, MA: Houghton Mifflin.

Gates, B. (2004) *Bill Gates—United Nations Media Leaders Summit on HIV/AIDS*. Retrieved from http://www.gatesfoundation.org/speeches-commentary/Pages/bill-gates-un-media-summit-hiv.aspx

Glucksberg, S., & Danks, J. H. (1975). *Experimental psycholinguistics: An introduction*. Hillsdale, NJ: Erlbaum.

Goldstein, N. J., Martin, S. J., & Cialdini, R. B. (2008). *Yes! 50 scientifically proven ways to be persuasive*. New York, NY: Free Press.

Goshgarian, G. (2010). *Exploring language*, (12th ed.). New York, NY: Longman.

Gudykunst, W. B., & Kim, Y. Y. (Eds.). (1992). *Readings on communication with strangers: An approach to intercultural communication*. New York, NY: McGraw-Hill.

Gudykunst, W., & Nishida, T. (1984). Individual and cultural influence on uncertainty reduction. *Communication Monographs, 51*, 23–36.

Gudykunst, W., Yang, S., & Nishida, T. (1985). A cross-cultural test of uncertainty reduction theory: Comparisons of acquaintance, friend, and dating relationships in Japan, Korea, and the United States. *Human Communication Research, 11*, 407–454.

Hall, E. T. (1976). *Beyond culture*. Garden City, NY: Doubleday.

Hall, E. T., & Hall, M. R. (1987). *Hidden differences: Doing business with the Japanese*. New York, NY: Doubleday.

Hall, J. A. (2006). Women's and men's nonverbal communication: Similarities, differences, stereotypes and origins. In V. Manusov & M. L. Patterson (Eds.), *The Sage handbook of nonverbal communication* (pp. 201–218). Thousand Oaks, CA: Sage.

Hammond, R. A., & Axelrod, R. (2006, December). The evolution of ethnocentrism. *Journal of Conflict Resolution, 50*, 926–936.

Han, S. P., & Shavitt, S. (1994). Persuasion and culture: Advertising appeals in individualistic and collectivist societies. *Journal of Experimental Social Psychology, 30*, 326–350.

Hanley, S. J., & Abell, S. C. (2002, Fall). Maslow and relatedness: Creating an interpersonal model of self-actualization. *Journal of Humanistic Psychology, 42*, 37–56.

Harris, M., & Johnson, O. (2000). *Cultural anthropology* (5th ed.). Boston, MA: Allyn & Bacon.

Hayakawa, S. I., & Hayakawa, A. R. (1990). *Language in thought and action* (5th ed.). New York, NY: Harcourt Brace Jovanovich.

Hecht, M. L., Collier, M. J., & Ribeau, S. (1993). *African American communication: Ethnic identity and cultural interpretation*. Thousand Oaks, CA: Sage.

Hendry, J. (1995). *Wrapping culture: Politeness, presentation, and power in Japan and other societies*. New York, NY: Oxford University Press.

Hensley, C. W. (1994, March 1). Divorce—the sensible approach. *Vital Speeches of the Day, 60*, 317–319.

Henslin, J. M. (2000). *Essentials of sociology: A down-to-earth approach* (3rd ed.). Boston, MA: Allyn & Bacon.

Herrick, J. A. (2004). *Argumentation: Understanding and shaping arguments*. State College, PA: Strata Publishing.

Hesketh, B., & Neal, A. (2006). Using 'war stories' to train for adaptive performance: Is it better to learn from error or success? *Applied Psychology: An International Review, 55*, 282–302.

Higgins, J. M. (1994). *101 creative problem solving techniques*. New York, NY: New Management Publishing.

Himle, J. A., Abelson, J. L., & Haghightgou, H. (1999, August). Effect of alcohol on social phobic anxiety. *American Journal of Psychiatry, 156*, 1237–1243.

Hofstede, G., Hofstede, G., & Minkov, M. (2010). *Cultures and organizations: Software of the mind* (3rd ed.). New York, NY: McGraw-Hill.

Holmes, J. (1995). *Women, men and politeness*. New York, NY: Longman.

Howard, Ronald. (Director), & Goldsman, A. (Writer) & Nasar, S. (Writer). (2001).

Jaffe, C. (2007). *Public speaking: Concepts and skills for a diverse society* (5th ed.). Belmont, CA: Wadsworth.

Jaksa, J. A., & Pritchard, M. S. (1994). *Communication ethics: Methods of analysis* (2nd ed.). Belmont, CA: Wadsworth.

James, D. L. (1995). *The executive guide to Asia–Pacific communications*. New York, NY: Kodansha International.

Jandt, F. E. (2000). *Intercultural communication* (3rd ed.). Thousand Oaks, CA: Sage.

Joel, B. (1993). *Commencement Address Billy Joel*. Retrieved from http://www.berklee.edu/commencement/past/bjoel.html

Johannesen, R. L. (1996). *Ethics in human communication* (5th ed.). Prospect Heights, IL: Waveland Press.

Johnson, K. G. (Ed.). (1991). *Thinking creatically: Thinking creatively, thinking critically*. Concord, CA: International Society for General Semantics.

Kiel, J. M. (1999, September). Reshaping Maslow's hierarchy of needs to reflect today's educational and managerial philosophies. *Journal of Instructional Psychology, 26*, 167–168.

Korzybski, A. (1933). *Science and sanity: An introduction to non-Aristotelian systems and General Semantics*. Concord, CA: International Society for General Semantics.

Kramarae, C. (1981). *Women and men speaking*. Rowley, MA: Newbury House.

Lee, A. M., & Lee, E. B. (1972). *The fine art of propaganda*. San Francisco, CA: International Society for General Semantics.

Kucinich, D. J. (2007, January 8). *Rep. Dennis Kucinich: Out of Iraq and Back to the American City*. Retrieved from http://www.politicalaffairs.net/article/articleview/4666/

Lee, A. M., & Lee, E. B. (1995, Spring). The iconography of propaganda analysis. *ETC.: A Review of General Semantics, 52*, 13–17.

Lustig, M. W., & Koester, J. (2006). *Intercultural competence: Interpersonal communication across cultures* (5th ed.). New York, NY: Allyn & Bacon.

Mackay, H. B. (1991, August 15). How to get a job. *Vital Speeches of the Day, 57*, 656–659.

Maggio, R. (1997). *Talking about people: A guide to fair and accurate language*. Phoenix, AZ: Oryx Press.

*Many Americans uneasy with mix of religion and politics*. (2006, August 24). *The Pew Research Center for the People & the Press*. Retrieved from http://people-press.org/reports/pdf/287.pdf

Marien, M. (1992, March 15). Education and learning in the 21st century. *Vital Speeches of the Day, 58*, 340–344.

Martin, M. M., & Rubin, R. B. (1994, Winter). Development of a communication flexibility measure. *The Southern Communication Journal, 59*, 171–178.

Martin, M. M., & Rubin, R. B. (1995). A new measure of cognitive flexibility. *Psychological Reports, 76*, 623–626.

Maslow, A. (1970). *Motivation and personality*. New York, NY: HarperCollins.

Matsumoto, D. (2006). Culture and nonverbal communication. In V. Manusov & M. L. Patterson (Eds.), *The Sage handbook of nonverbal communication* (pp. 219–235). Thousand Oaks, CA: Sage.

Maxwell, J. (1987, September 1). Economic forecasting. *Vital Speeches of the Day, 53*, 685–686.

McCroskey, J. C. (2001). *An introduction to rhetorical communication* (8th ed.). Boston, MA: Allyn & Bacon.

McKerrow, R. E., Gronbeck, B. E., Ehninger, D., & Monroe, A. H. (2000). *Principles and types of speech communication* (14th ed.). Boston, MA: Allyn & Bacon.

Meade, C. H. (2000). The misunderstood vividness effect: Roles in which vividness can enhance persuasion. University of Georgia. *Dissertation Abstracts International: B. The Physical Sciences and Engineering, 61* (January), 3323.

Midooka, K. (1990, October). Characteristics of Japanese style communication. *Media, Culture and Society, 12*, 477–489.

Mora, A. (2006). *Acceptance Speech by Alberto Mora*. Retrieved from http://www.jfklibrary.org/Education+and+Public+Programs/Profile+in+Courage+Award/Award+Recipients/Alberto+Mora/Acceptance+Speech+by+Alberto+Mora.htm

Nelson, A. (1986, June 1). The sanctuary movement. *Vital Speeches of the Day, 52*, 482–485.

Neuliep, J. W., Chaudoir, M., & McCroskey, J. C. (2001). A cross-cultural comparison of ethnocentrism among Japanese and United States college students. *Communication Research Reports, 18*, 137–146.

Nordahl, H. M., & Wells, A. (2007). *Changing beliefs in cognitive therapy*. New York, NY: Wiley.

Osborn, A. (1957). *Applied imagination* (Rev. ed.). New York, NY: Scribner's.

Obama, B. (2006) *Dr. Martin Luther King Memorial Dedication Speech*. Retrieved from http://obama.senate.gov

Obama, B. (2006). *World Aids Day Speech*. Retrieved January 14, 2007, from http://obama.senate.gov

Pearson, J. C., West, R., & Turner, L. H. (1995). *Gender and communication* (3rd ed.). Dubuque, IA: William C. Brown.

Pei, M. (1956). *Language for everybody*. New York, NY: Pocket Books.

Perkins, D. F., & Fogarty, K. (2006). Active listening: A communication tool. Retrieved from http://edis.ifas.ufl.edu

Peterson, H. (Ed.). (1965). *A treasury of the world's great speeches*. New York, NY: Simon & Schuster.

Petty, R. E., & Wegener, D. T. (1998). Attitude change: Multiple roles for persuasion variables. In D. T. Gilbert, S.

T. Fiske, & G. Lindzey (Eds.), *The handbook of social psychology* (4th ed., Vol. 1, pp. 323–390). New York, NY: McGraw-Hill.

Pratkanis, A., & Aronson, E. (1991). *Age of propaganda: The everyday use and abuse of persuasion*. New York, NY: W. H. Freeman.

Rankin, P. (1929). Listening ability. *Proceedings of the Ohio State Educational Conference's Ninth Annual Session*.

Reynolds, C. L., & Schnoor, L. G. (Eds.). (1991). *1989 championship debates and speeches*. Normal, IL: American Forensic Association.

Richardson, M. M. (1995, January 15). Taxation with representation. *Vital Speeches of the Day, 61,* 201–203.

Richmond, V. P., & McCroskey, J. C. (1998). *Communication: Apprehension, avoidance, and effectiveness* (5th ed.). Boston, MA: Allyn & Bacon.

Riggio, R. E. (1987). *The charisma quotient*. New York, NY: Dodd, Mead.

Rodman, G. (2001). *Making sense of media: An introduction to mass communication*. Boston, MA: Allyn & Bacon.

Rogers, C. (1970). *Carl Rogers on encounter groups*. New York, NY: Harrow Books.

Rogers, L. (2001). *Sexing the brain*. New York, NY: Columbia University Press.

Salopek, J. (1999, September). Is anyone listening? *Training and Development, 53,* 58.

Schnoor, L. G. (Ed.). (1994). *1991 and 1992 championship debates and speeches*. River Falls, WI: American Forensic Association.

Schnoor, L. G. (Ed.). (2000). *Winning orations of the Interstate Oratorical Association*. Mankato, MN: Interstate Oratorical Association.

Schnoor, L. G. (Ed.). (2006). *Winning orations of the Interstate Oratorical Association*. Mankato, MN: Interstate Oratorical Association.

Schwartz, M., and the Task Force on Bias-Free Language of the Association of American University Presses. (1995). *Guidelines for bias-free writing*. Bloomington, IN: Indiana University Press.

Singh, N., & Pereira, A. (2005). *The culturally customized web site*. Oxford, UK: Elsevier Butterworth-Heinemann.

Smith, T. E., & Frymier, A. B. (2006, February). Get 'real': Does practicing speeches before an audience improve performance? *Communication Quarterly, 54,* 111–125.

Sojourner, R. J., & Wogalter, M. S. (1998). The influence of pictorials on the comprehension and recall of pharmaceutical safety and warning information. *International Journal of Cognitive Ergonomics, 2,* 93–106.

Sprague, J., & Stuart, D. (2008). *The speaker's handbook* (8th ed.). Belmont, CA: Wadsworth.

Steil, L. K., Barker, L. L., & Watson, K. W. (1983). *Effective listening: Key to your success*. Reading, MA: Addison-Wesley.

Stephan, W. G., & Stephan, C. W. (1992). *Improving intergroup relations*. Thousand Oaks, CA: Sage.

Schwarzenegger, A. (2007). *Prepared Text of Gov. Schwarzenegger's Remarks to Tackle California's Broken Health Care System*. Retrieved from http://gov.ca.gov/index.php?/print-version/speech/5066/

Tannen, D. (1990). *You just don't understand: Women and men in conversation*. New York, NY: Morrow.

von Oech, R. (1990). *A whack on the side of the head: How you can be more creative* (Rev. ed.). New York, NY: Warner.

Watts, R. J. (2004). *Politeness*. Cambridge, UK: Cambridge University Press.

Watzlawick, P. (1978). *The language of change: Elements of therapeutic communication*. New York, NY: Basic Books.

Watzlawick, P., Beavin, J., & Jackson, D. D. (1967). *Pragmatics of human communication: A study of interactional patterns, pathologies, and paradoxes*. New York, NY: Norton.

Werner, E. K. (1975). *A study of communication time*. Master's thesis, University of Maryland, College Park. Cited in A. Wolvin & C. Coakley. (1988). *Listening* (3rd ed.). Dubuque, IA: William C. Brown.

Westbrook, D., Kennerley, H., & Kirk, J. (2007). *An introduction to cognitive behavior therapy: Skills and applications*. Thousand Oaks, CA: Sage.

Withers, L. A., & Vernon, L. L. (2006, January). To err is human: Embarrassment, attachment, and communication apprehension. *Personality and Individual Differences 40,* 99–110.

Wolpe, J. (1957). *Psychotherapy by reciprocal inhibition*. Stanford, CA: Stanford University Press.

Wolvin, A. D., & Coakley, C. G. (1996). *Listening*. Dubuque, IA: William C. Brown.

Wood, W. (2000). Attitude change: Persuasion and social influence. *Annual Review of Psychology, 51,* 539–570.

Wright, W. (1999). *Born that way: Genes–behavior–personality*. New York, NY: Knopf.

Young-Hong, Z. (2004, May). A study of group counseling for dispelling communication apprehension of undergraduates. *Chinese Journal of Clinical Psychology, 12,* 156–157.

# Index

Page numbers followed by t or f indicate tables and figures, respectively.

Abstraction, 169, 292
  levels of, 216, 294
Abstraction process, 292
Accent, 204, 292
  listening and, 40–41
Acceptance speech, 271–272, 292
Accuracy, 171–175, 220
Acknowledging differences, 99
Action
  asking for, 143–144
  bodily, 204–209
  persuasive speech and, 234, 253t
Active listening, 26–27, 292
Active sentences, 188
Active verbs, 178
Adaptation during speech, 100–102
Additions in articulation, 203
Advantages-disadvantages pattern of
  organization, 136t
Affectional orientation
  audience analysis and, 91
  wording of speech and, 181–182, 185
Affiliations, audience, 94
Age of audience, 89–90
Ageist language, 181–182, 185, 292
Agenda-setting fallacy, 241–242, 292
Alcohol, apprehension and, 16
Alliteration, 178, 292
Allness, 173, 292
Almanacs, 111
Amount of information in speech, 215
Analogies, 108, 292
Analysis. See Audience analysis
Anecdotal evidence, 238, 292
Annotated preparation outline, 157–161
Antithesis, 179, 292
Antithetical sentences, 188, 292
Apologies, 154, 274, 275, 292
Appeals to tradition, 238, 292
Appearance, 205
Apprehension, 13–18, 293
  alcohol and, 16
  breathing and, 16
  chemicals and, 16
  cognitive restructuring and, 16–17
  conspicuousness and, 15
  culture and, 15–16
  drug use and, 16
  enlarged conversation and, 15
  experience and, 15
  physical activity and, 16
  positive thinking and, 16–17

practice and, 16
preparation and, 16
presentation aids and, 115
self-affirmations and, 17
similarity and, 15–16
state, 14, 296
systematic desensitization and, 17–18
trait, 13–14, 296
visualization and, 15, 17
Appropriateness, 65–66, 180–185
Arguments, sidestepping opposing, 170
Articulation of speech, 202–203, 292
Assertiveness training groups, 286
Assimilation, 29, 292
Attack
  character, 248–249, 292–293
  criticism as, 34t
  personal, 248–249
Attention, 57, 81–82, 96–97, 217, 292
  gaining, 140–141, 145–147
  persuasive speech and, 253t
Attitudes, 292
  of audience, 88, 97
  persuasive speech and, 234
Audience, 85–102, 87f, 292. See also
    Audience analysis
  appropriate topics and, 66
  attention of, 81–82, 96–97, 217
  attitudes of, 88, 97
  beliefs of, 88, 97–98
  collecting data on, 86–88, 87f
  complimenting, 147–148
  concern for, 247
  culture and, 101
  defined, 5
  diversity of, 85–86
  empathy and, 88
  ethics and, 85, 107
  favorability of, 97–99
  as focus of speech, 73–74, 81–82, 213,
    250
  identifying with, 250
  immediate, 4f, 5
  inference and, 88
  interviewing, 88
  knowledge of, 99–100
  misleading statements and, 107
  motivating, 150–151, 252–253, 253t
  observation and, 86
  organization and, 132–133
  orienting, 57–58, 149
  persuasive speech and, 250–256

relating to, 97
remote, 4f, 5
responses from, 101–102
rewarding, 96–97
similarities with, 148
size of, 94
speaker-audience-topic relationship,
    147–148
uniqueness of, 85
values of, 88, 98
willingness of, 96–97
yes response from, 250
Audience analysis, 47f, 52, 89–102, 292.
    See also Audience
  acknowledging differences and, 99
  affectional orientation and, 91
  affiliations and, 94
  age and, 89–90
  attitudes and, 97
  beliefs and, 94, 97–98
  context characteristics and, 94–96
  credibility of speaker and, 100
  culture and, 93, 101
  educational level and, 91–92
  favorability of audience and, 97–99
  gender and, 90–91
  income and, 93
  intellectual level and, 91–92
  knowledge of audience and, 99–100
  location of speech and, 94–95
  occupation and, 93
  organization of speech and, 98–99
  physical environment and, 94–95
  political beliefs and, 94
  psychology and, 96–100
  purpose of speech and, 96
  relational status and, 93–94
  religion/religiousness and, 92
  size of audience and, 94
  sociology and, 89–96
  special interests and, 94
  during speech, 100–102
  time of day and, 96
  values and, 98
  "what if" questions and, 101
  willingness of audience and, 96–97
Audiotapes, 118t
Auditory imagery, 179–180
Authority, definition by, 109

Backchannel cues, 24, 26
Bandwagon fallacy, 238, 292

Bar graph, 116f
Behavior, 34–35, 34t
Beliefs, 292
    about public speaking, 47–48
    of audience, 88, 94, 97–98
    persuasive speech and, 234
Belonging needs, 242f, 243
Bias, 29, 292
Biographical material, 111
Blogs, oral citation of, 240t
Bodily action, 204–209
Books, oral citation of, 240t
Brainstorming, 67, 292
Breathing, apprehension and, 16
Broadcast news, oral citation of, 240t

Card-stacking fallacy, 241, 292
Cause-effect pattern, 139, 262, 292
Causes and effects, reasoning from, 237, 292
CDs, 118t
Central idea. See Thesis
Changes
    in behavior, persuasive speech and, 251–252
    to speech, 193
Channel, 10, 292
Character, 246–247, 293
Character attacks, 248–249, 292–293
Charisma, 247–248, 293
Chartboards, 118t
Chemicals, apprehension and, 16
Choice, persuasive speech and, 252–253, 253t
Citing sources of research, 239, 240–241t, 246
Claim and proof pattern of organization, 136t
Clarity, 175–178, 293
Classroom
    listening in, 30, 31t
    oral citation of lectures, 241t
    public speaking, 49–50
Clichés, 176, 293
Closure, 151–152
Cognitive restructuring, 16–17, 293
Collectivist culture, 42–43, 254, 289, 293
Commencement speech, 275–277, 293
Communication, nonverbal, 41, 294
Communication apprehension, 13–18, 293
    alcohol and, 16
    breathing and, 16
    chemicals and, 16
    cognitive restructuring and, 16–17
    conspicuousness and, 15
    culture and, 15–16
    drug use and, 16
    enlarged conversation and, 15
    experience and, 15
    physical activity and, 16
    positive thinking and, 16–17
    practice and, 16
    preparation and, 16
    presentation aids and, 115
    self-affirmations and, 17
    similarity and, 15–16
    state, 14
    systematic desensitization and, 17–18

    trait, 13–14
    visualization and, 15, 17
Compare and contrast pattern of organization, 136t
Competence, 245–246, 293
Complexity of speech, 215
Compliments, 147–148
Computer-assisted presentations, 115, 119–125, 123f, 124f
Conclusion of speech, 47f, 58, 293
    common faults of, 154–155
    introducing new material in, 154
    organization of, 150–152
Connectives, 153
Connotation, 169–170, 293
Consciousness-raising groups, 286
Conspicuousness, apprehension and, 15
Constructive criticism, 34
Context, 8–10, 293, 294
    characteristics of, 94–96
    culture and, 9–10, 144–145, 255, 294
    physical, 8
    sociopsychological, 8
    temporal, 9
Conversation, public speaking as, 15
Correcting errors in speech, 208
Credibility, 100, 147, 293
    presentation aids and, 115
Credibility appeals, 245–249
Criticism, 30–43, 293
    as attack, 34t
    behavior and, 34–35, 34t
    constructive, 34
    culture and, 42–43
    ethics and, 35
    evaluating, 37
    listening to, 36–37
    objectivity and, 33–34
    owning, 35
    positive reinforcement and, 33
    specificity and, 33
    as support, 34t
Cues
    backchannel, 24, 26
    listening, 50
Cultural context, 9–10, 144–145, 255, 294
Cultural identifiers, 293
Cultural sensitivity, 293
Culture, 293
    accent and, 40–41
    apologies and, 154
    apprehension and, 15–16
    audience analysis and, 93, 101
    audience attention and, 82
    collectivist, 42–43, 254, 289, 293
    context and, 9–10, 144–145, 255, 294
    credibility appeals and, 245
    criticism and, 42–43
    direct language and, 168
    display rules and, 101
    ethnocentrism and, 41, 293
    eye contact and, 41
    feminine, 255
    gender and, 42, 255
    high-context, 144–145, 255, 294
    high-power-distance, 254
    high-uncertainty-avoidance, 254
    identifiers of, 183–185

    individualist, 42–43, 254, 289, 293, 294
    indulgent, 255–256
    language and, 37, 40–41
    listening and, 37, 40–42
    long-term oriented, 254
    low-context, 144–145, 255, 294
    low-power-distance, 254
    low-uncertainty-avoidance, 254
    masculine, 255
    nonverbal communication and, 41
    objectivity and, 170
    organization of speech and, 144–145
    persuasive speech and, 253–256
    power-distance, 254
    proxemics and, 207
    restrained, 255–256
    sensitivity to, 253–256
    short-term oriented, 254
    special occasion speech and, 285, 289
    taboos and, 66
    topic selection and, 51, 66
    uncertainty-avoidance, 254
    wording of speech and, 183–185
Currentness of research, 220

Data
    audience, 86–88, 87f
    organization of, 155
Databases, 174, 293
Decision-making groups, 287
Declarative statements, 77, 159
Dedication speech, 274, 276, 293
Definition, speech of, 222–223, 226–228, 293
    defined, 217
    main points of, 223
    organization of, 223, 226–228
    support of, 223
    thesis of, 222–223
Definitions, 293
    categories of, 222
    as supporting materials, 108–110
Delivery of speech. See Presentation
Delivery outline, 161–163, 293
Demonstration, speech of, 228–231, 293
    defined, 217
    main points of, 229
    organization of, 229–231
    support of, 229
    thesis of, 228–229
Demonstration categories, 228
Denotation, 169–170, 293
Description, speech of, 218–221, 293
    defined, 217
    main points of, 218
    organization of, 219, 221
    support of, 219
    thesis of, 218
Descriptive categories, 218, 293
Desensitization, systematic, 17–18, 296
Designing slides, 120–125
Development of main points, 47f, 55–56, 131–133
Diction, 194
Diluting one's position, 154
Direct language, 168
Direct sentences, 187–188
Directness, 208, 293

Directories, 199–200
Disabilities, wording of speech and, 182–183
Display rules, 101, 293
Disqualifiers, 187
Diversity of audience, 85–86
Door-in-the-face technique, 293
Dress, 205
Drug use, apprehension and, 16
DVDs, 118t

Economy of wording, 175
Educational groups, 286
Educational level of audience, 91–92
Effective presentation, 194–195
Emotional appeals, 242–245, 242f, 293
Empathy, 293
    audience and, 88
    listening and, 28–29
Emphasis, 248
Encounter groups, 286
Encyclopedias, 111
    oral citation of, 240t
Enlarged conversation, apprehension and, 15
Enthusiasm, 247
Errors in speech, correcting, 208
Establishing needs, 141
Ethics, 10–13, 293
    audience and, 85, 107
    correcting errors and, 208
    criticism and, 35
    defined, 10
    fair use and, 11
    of fear appeals, 245
    of getting help from others, 161
    informing vs. persuading, 217
    listening and, 29–30
    of lying, 277
    objective view of, 10
    plagiarism and, 10–13
    research use and, 57
    sidestepping opposing arguments and, 170
    subjective view of, 10
    supporting materials and, 107
    of telling the truth, 277
    thesis and, 80
Ethnic expressions, 183, 293
Ethnocentrism, 41, 293. See also Culture
Ethos, 235
Etymology, definition by, 109
Eulogies, 278–279, 280, 293
Euphemisms, 170, 293
Evaluation, 22f, 24, 37
Evidence, anecdotal, 238, 292
Examples, 106–108, 293
    gaining attention through, 146
    specific, definition by, 109
Experience, apprehension and, 15
Expert testimony, 110–112
Exposure, selective, 251, 295
Expression
    ethnic, 183
    facial, 206
Extemporaneous speech, 197–198, 293
Eye contact, 205–206, 208
    culture and, 41

Facial expression, 206
Fact
    gaining attention through, 146
    questions of, 256–258, 261t, 293, 295
Fact-fiction pattern of organization, 137t
Fact-inference confusion, 172–173, 293
Fair use, 11
Fairness
    persuasive speech and, 247
    of research, 220
Fallacies of language, 238–242, 248–249, 293
    agenda-setting, 241–242, 292
    appeal to tradition, 238, 292
    anecdotal evidence, 238, 292
    bandwagon, 238, 292
    card-stacking, 241, 292
    straw man, 238, 296
    testimonial, 238–239, 296
    thin entering wedge, 241, 296
    transfer, 239, 241, 296
Farewell speech, 279–281, 293
Favorability of audience, 97–99
Fear appeals, 245
Feedback
    listening and, 30
    on presentation, 193
Feeling empathy, 29
Feminine culture, 255
Figurative analogies, 108, 292
Figures of speech, 178–179, 294
Filtering, listening and, 28, 29
Flexibility, 294
Flip charts, 117, 118t, 294
Focus groups, 286
Focus of speech, 73–74, 81–82, 213, 250
Foot-in-the-door technique, 294
Formality, 180
Forum presentations, 284, 294, 296
Friend-or-foe factor, listening and, 28

Gaining attention, 140–141, 145–147
Gallup Poll website, 86
Gender, 9, 294
    audience analysis and, 90–91
    culture and, 42, 255
    listening and, 42
    wording of speech and, 181–182, 185
General appearance, 205
General purpose of speech, 51, 294
Gesture, 206–207
Gimmicks, 154
Goodwill speech, 273–274, 275, 294
Government publications, 134
Graphs as presentation aids, 115, 116f
Groups. See Small groups
Groupthink, 288

Handouts, 118t
Hesitations, 187
Heterosexist language, 181–182, 185, 294
Hierarchy of needs, 242–245, 242f, 294
High-context culture, 144–145, 255, 294
High-power-distance culture, 254
High-uncertainty-avoidance culture, 254
Humor, 147
Hyperbole, 178, 294
Hypothetical examples, 107

I-messages, 35, 294
Idea generation, 68–69, 69f, 70t, 286. See also Main points
Identifiers, cultural, 183–185, 293
Identifying with the audience, 250
Idiolect, 37
Idioms, 177–178, 294
Illustration, 106–108, 117, 294
    gaining attention through, 146
Imagery, 179–180, 294
Immediacy, 186, 294
Immediate audience, 4f, 5
Impromptu speech, 195–196, 294
Income of audience, 93
Indexes, newspaper, 174
Indiscrimination, 173–175, 294
Individualist culture, 42–43, 254, 289, 293, 294
Indulgent culture, 255–256
Inexperience, 15
Inference, 88
Infinitive phrase, 73
Information sharing groups, 286
Informative speech, 51, 72, 73, 212–231, 294
    abstraction in, 216, 292
    amount of information in, 215
    audience as focus of, 213
    audience attention and, 81
    complexity of, 215
    of definition, 222–223, 226–228, 293
    of demonstration, 228–231, 293
    of description, 218–221, 293
    main points of, 56, 218, 223, 229
    memorability of, 217
    organization of, 219, 221, 223, 226–228, 229–231
    persuasive speech vs., 217
    poorly constructed, sample of, 38–40
    principles of, 213–217
    relating types of information in, 216
    relevance of, 213–215
    sample of, 38–40, 224–227
    support of, 219, 223, 229
    thesis of, 218, 222–223, 228–229
    usefulness of, 213–215
Inspirational speech, 277, 278
Integration of research, 239
Intellectual level of audience, 91–92
Intensifiers, 187
Intercultural openness, 144–145. See also Culture
Internal summary transitions, 217
Internet, 199–200. See also Websites
    databases, 174, 293
    directories, 199–200
    museum sites, 289
    oral citations and, 240–241t
    search engines, 199–200
Interviews
    of audience, 88
    personal, oral citation of, 241t
    as research, 25
Introduction, speech of, 60–61, 270–271, 294
Introduction of speech, 47f, 57–58, 294
    common faults of, 154
    organization of, 145–149
Irony, 178, 294

Jargon, 170, 294
Journals, 94–95

Knowledge of audience, 99–100

Labeling, positive, 295
Language. *See also* Wording of speech
  abstraction and, 169, 292
  accuracy of, 171–175
  ageist, 181–182, 185, 292
  allness in, 173, 292
  culture and, 37, 40–41, 168
  directness of, 168
  disabilities and, 182–183
  fact-inference confusion in, 172–173, 293
  fallacies of, 238–242, 248–249, 293
  figures of speech and, 178–179, 294
  heterosexist, 181–182, 185, 294
  idiolect and, 37
  idioms, 177–178, 294
  indiscrimination in, 173–175, 294
  informative (*See* Informative speech)
  listening and, 37, 40–42
  nationality and, 183–184
  objectivity of, 169–170
  orality of, 171, 294–295
  persuasive (*See* Persuasive speech)
  phrasing sentences and, 186–189
  polarization in, 171–172, 295
  power and, 186–187
  racist, 181–184, 295
  religion and, 184–185
  sexist, 181–182, 185, 295
  static evaluation in, 173, 296
  vulgar, 187
Leadership in small groups, 288
Learning groups, 286
Lectures, oral citation of, 241t
Levels of abstraction, 216, 294
Libraries, 55
Limiting length of examples, 107
Limiting purpose of speech, 74
Limiting scope of speech, 51
Limiting topic of speech, 69–72, 70t, 71f
Line graph, 116f
Listening, 22–30, 22f, 294
  accent and, 40–41
  active, 26–27, 292
  assimilation and, 29, 292
  attention and, 57
  backchannel cues and, 24, 26
  bias and, 29, 292
  in the classroom, 30, 31t
  to credibility appeals, 248–249
  to criticism, 36–37
  cues for, 50
  culture and, 37, 40–42
  defined, 22
  to emotional appeals, 244–245
  empathy and, 28–29
  ethics and, 29–30
  ethnocentrism and, 41
  evaluating and, 22f, 24
  feedback and, 30
  filtering and, 28, 29
  friend-or-foe factor and, 28
  gender and, 42
  language and, 37, 40–42

to logical arguments, 238–242
  message senders and, 101
  nonverbal communication and, 28, 41
  offensive, 28
  open-mindedness and, 29, 35, 36
  prejudging and, 29
  receiving and, 22–23, 22f
  remembering and, 22f, 23–24
  responding and, 22f, 24, 26
  speech and, 37, 40–42
  total meaning, 27–28
  understanding and, 22f, 23
  verbal messages and, 28
Literal analogies, 108, 292
Location of speech, 94–95
Logical appeals, 235–242, 294
Logos, 235
Long-term delivery improvement program, 193–194
Long-term oriented culture, 254
Love needs, 242f, 243
Low-context culture, 144–145, 255, 294
Low-power-distance culture, 254
Low-uncertainty-avoidance culture, 254
Lying, 107, 277

Magazines, oral citation of, 240t
Main points, 294. *See also* Idea generation
  of speech of definition, 223
  of speech of demonstration, 229
  of speech of description, 218
  development of, 47f, 55–56, 131–133
  generating, 77, 80–81
  limiting number of, 132
  organization of, 135–145
  of persuasive speech, 257, 259, 261–262
  proof of, 55
  support of, 47f, 55
Manuscript speech, 196–197, 294
Maps, 116–117
Masculine culture, 255
Maslow, Abraham, 242–245, 242f
Maslow's hierarchy of needs, 242–245, 242f, 294
Materials. *See* Supporting materials
Mean, 112, 294
Median, 294
Member participation, 287–288
Member roles, 287
Memorability of speech, 217
Memorized speech, 195, 294
  drawbacks of, 48
Message, 4f, 5–6, 294
Message patterns, 217
Message senders, 101
Metaphor, 179, 294
Metonymy, 179, 294
Mindfulness, 49
Misleading statements, 107
Mode, statistical, 112
Models, 115, 294
Motivated sequence pattern of organization, 139–145, 160–161, 253t, 294
Motivating the audience, 150–151, 234, 252–253, 253t
Movement, 207
Multiple definition pattern of organization, 136t

Museum research, 289
MySearchLab, 8f, 86
MySpeechFeed, 214f
MySpeechLab, 69f

Name-calling, 249, 294
Narrative, 106–108, 146, 294
Nationality, wording of speech and, 183–184
Needs
  establishing, 141
  hierarchy of, 242–245, 242f, 294
  persuasive speech and, 253t
  satisfying, 141–143
Negation, definition by, 109
Negative social proof, 252, 294
News items
  broadcast, oral citation of, 240t
  gaining attention through, 146
  oral citation of, 240t
  sources of, 174
  topic selection and, 68
Noise, 4f, 6, 8, 294
Nonverbal communication, 28, 41, 294
Notes
  taking, 27
  use of during speech, 208
Numerical data, 111, 112–114
  gaining attention through, 146

Objective view of ethics, 10
Objectivity, 294
  criticism and, 33–34
  of language, 169–170
Observation of audience, 86
Occupation of audience, 93
Offensive listening, 28
Omissions in articulation, 203
Open-mindedness, 29, 35, 36
Open subtlety, 208
Oral citation, 240–241t
Oral reports, 284–285
Oral style, 171, 294–295
Orality of language, 171
Organization, 130–164, 295
  advantages-disadvantages pattern of, 136t
  audience and, 98–99, 132–133
  cause-effect pattern of, 139, 262
  claim and proof pattern of, 136t
  compare and contrast pattern of, 136t
  of conclusions, 150–152
  culture and, 144–145
  of data, 155
  of speech of definition, 223, 226–228
  delivery outline for, 293
  of speech of demonstration, 229–231
  of speech of description, 219, 221
  developing main points and, 131–133
  fact-fiction pattern of, 137t
  flexibility and, 294
  of introduction, 145–149
  of main points, 132, 135–145
  motivated sequence pattern of, 139–145, 253t, 294
  multiple definition pattern of, 136t
  of outline, 130f, 155–164
  of persuasive speech, 258, 260, 262, 266

pro and con pattern of, 136t
problem-solution pattern of, 138–139, 262, 266
of references, 156, 158
spatial pattern of, 137–138
structure-function pattern of, 136t
of supporting materials, 47f, 56
temporal pattern of, 135, 137, 296
thesis and, 81
topical pattern of, 135, 258, 260, 296
of transitions, 153–154, 156
Who? What? Why? Where? When? pattern of, 137t, 221
wording of speech and, 133
Orientation, 57–58, 149, 295
Outline of speech, 130f, 155–164, 295
annotated preparation, 157–161
data in, 155
declarative statements in, 159
delivery, 161–163, 293
motivated sequence organization, 160–161
preface to, 155
preparation, 155, 157–161, 160, 295
references in, 156, 158
samples of, 157–164
symbols in, 156, 159
template, 160–161, 296
topical organization, 157–159, 162–163
transitions in, 156
written citations in, 239
Owning criticism, 35
Oxymoron, 179, 295

Panel groups, 283, 295
Parallel sentences, 188, 295
Pathos, 235
Pattern of messages, 217
Pauses in speech, 202, 295
People as presentation aids, 117
Percentages, statistical, 112–113
Performance visualization, 17, 295
apprehension and, 15, 17
persuasive speech and, 253t
of satisfied needs, 142–143
Periodic sentences, 188, 295
Personal attacks, 248–249
Personal growth groups, 286
Personal interest attacks, 248, 295
Personal interests, 67
Personal style, 185–186, 295
Personification, 179, 295
Persuasion, 295
continuum of, 235, 235f
Persuasive speech, 51, 72, 73, 234–266, 235f, 242f, 253t, 295
audience and, 82, 250–256
change and, 251–252
choice and, 252–253, 253t
credibility appeals and, 245–249
culture and, 253–256
door-in-the-face technique and, 293
emotional appeals and, 242–245, 242f, 293
foot-in-the-door technique and, 294
goals of, 234–235, 235f
informative speech vs., 217
listening to, 238–242, 244–245

logical appeals and, 235–242, 294
main points of, 56, 257, 259, 261–262
motivated sequence pattern of organization and, 253t
motivating listeners and, 252–253, 253t
organization of, 258, 260, 262, 266
poorly constructed, sample of, 78–79
positive labeling and, 251
principles of, 249–253
on questions of fact, 256–258, 261t, 293
on questions of policy, 260–262, 261t, 266, 295
on questions of value, 258–260, 261t, 296
reasoning and, 236–238
sample of, 263–265
selective exposure and, 251, 295
social proof and, 252
support of, 257–258, 259–260, 262
thesis of, 256–257, 259, 260–261
Photographs, 117
Phrase/key-word organization of outline, sample of, 164
Phrasing sentences, 186–189
Physical activity, apprehension and, 16
Physical context, 8
Physical environment, 94–95
Physical noise, 6
Physiological needs, 242f, 243
Physiological noise, 6
Pie graph, 115, 116f, 295
Pitch of speech, 201–202, 295
Plagiarism, 10–13, 295
fair use and, 11
Plain folks fallacy, 241, 295
Polarization, 171–172, 295
Policy, questions of, 260–262, 261t, 266, 295
Political beliefs, 94
Polling sites, 86
Popular journals, 94–95
Positive labeling, 251, 295
Positive reinforcement, 33
Positive sentences, 188
Positive social proof, 252, 295
Positive thinking, 247
apprehension and, 16–17
Posture, 206
Power, wording of speech and, 186–187
Power-distance culture, 254
Practice
apprehension and, 16
effective, 48
Preface to outline, 155
Prejudging, listening and, 29
Preparation, apprehension and, 16
Preparation outline, 155, 157–161, 160, 295
Presentation, 47f, 59, 62, 194–209, 295
articulation and, 202–203, 292
bodily action during, 204–209
context of, 8–10
effectiveness and, 194–195
extemporaneous, 197–198, 293
feedback on, 193
impromptu, 195–196, 294
long-term delivery improvement program and, 193–194
from manuscript, 196–197, 294
from memory, 195

methods of, 195–198
pauses in, 202, 295
pitch of, 201–202, 295
pronunciation and, 202–204, 295
questions during, 208–209
rehearsal of, 192–194
speech rate of, 200–201, 295
team, 296
vocal delivery of, 198, 200–204
volume of, 198, 200, 296
Presentation aids, 114–126, 295
audiotapes as, 118t
CDs as, 118t
chartboards as, 118t
computers as, 119–125, 123f, 124f
DVDs as, 118t
flip charts as, 117, 118t
graphs as, 115, 116f
handouts as, 118t
illustrations as, 117
maps as, 116–117
media of, 118t, 123f, 124f
models as, 115
people as, 117
photographs as, 117
purpose of, 114–115
rehearsal with, 125–126
slides as, 118t, 120–125, 123f, 124f
transparencies as, 118t
types of, 115–117, 116f
use of, 117–125
videotapes as, 118t
whiteboards as, 117, 118t
word charts as, 115–116
Presentation software, 119–125, 123f, 124f, 295
Presentation speech, 271–272, 295
Previews, 153
Primary sources, 75
Pro and con pattern of organization, 136t
Problem-solution pattern of organization, 138–139, 262, 266, 295
Problem-solving groups, 286–287
Pronouns, 185
Pronunciation of speech, 202–204, 295
Proof of main points, 55
Proxemics, 207, 295
Psychological noise, 6
Psychology, 96–100
Public speaking defined, 295
Purpose of speech, 51, 72–74
audience analysis and, 96
audience as focus of, 73–74
infinitive phrase and, 73
limiting, 74
specific terms and, 74
thesis versus, 76–77

Questionnaires, 86–88, 87f
Questions
of fact, 256–258, 261t, 293, 295
gaining attention through, 146
of policy, 260–262, 261t, 266, 295
rhetorical, 179, 295
during speech, 208–209
tag, 187
of value, 258–260, 261t, 295, 296
wording of speech and, 186

Quotations, gaining attention through, 146

Racist language, 181–184, 295
Rate of speech, 200–201, 295
Raw numbers, 112
Reasoning, 236–238, 292, 296
Receiving, 22–23, 22f
References, 156, 158
Rehearsal of speech, 47f, 59, 192–194
   with presentation aids, 125–126
Relating to audience, 97
Relating types of information, 216
Relational status of audience, 93–94
Relevance of examples, 107
Relevance of speech, 213–215
Reliability, 220, 295
Religion
   of audience, 92
   wording of speech and, 184–185
Remembering, 22f, 23–24
Remote audience, 4f, 5
Repetition, 176, 217, 295
Research, 295
   accuracy of, 220
   almanacs and, 111
   biographical material and, 111
   citing sources of, 239, 240–241t, 246
   currentness of, 220
   encyclopedias and, 111
   ethics of using, 57
   expert testimony and, 110–112
   fairness of, 220
   government publications and, 134
   indexes and, 174
   integration of into speech, 239
   Internet (*See* Internet)
   interviewing for information and, 25
   journals and, 94–95
   libraries and, 55
   museums and, 289
   MySearchLab and, 8f, 86
   MySpeechFeed and, 214f
   MySpeechLab and, 69f
   news sources and, 174
   notetaking and, 27
   numerical data and, 111
   oral citation of, 240–241t
   principles of, 53
   sources of, 75
   statistics and, 111
   studies, oral citation of, 240t
   sufficiency of, 220
   time management and, 7
   topic and, 47f, 53
   website (*See* Websites)
Response
   from audience, 101–102
   listening and, 22f, 24, 26
Restatement, 176, 295
Restrained culture, 255–256
Restructuring, cognitive, 16–17, 293
Reviews, 153–154
Rewarding audience, 96–97
Rhetoric, 295
Rhetorical questions, 179, 295
Rules, display, 101, 293

Safety needs, 242f, 243
Satisfaction, persuasive speech and, 253t
Satisfying needs, 141–143
Scholarly journals, 94–95
Scope of speech, 51
Search directories, 72
Search engines, 199–200
Secondary sources, 75
Selective exposure, 251, 295
Self-actualization needs, 242f, 244
Self-affirmation, 17, 295
Self-critical statements, 187
Self-defeating thinking, 16–17
Self-esteem, 295
Self-esteem needs, 242f, 243–244
Self-justification, 273
Semantic noise, 6
Sensitivity, cultural, 293
Sentence phrasing, 186–189
Sexist language, 181–182, 185, 295
Sexual orientation
   audience analysis and, 91
   wording of speech and, 181–182, 185
Short sentences, 187
Short-term oriented culture, 254
Sidestepping opposing arguments, 170
Sign reasoning, 237–238, 296
Signal *vs.* noise, 6
Signpost phrases, 154, 175–176, 217, 296
Silent sounds in articulation, 204
Similarity
   apprehension and, 15–16
   with audience, 148
Simile, 179, 296
Size of audience, 94
Slang, 180–181, 187, 296
Slides, 118t, 123f, 124f
   designing, 120–125
   speech with, sample of, 120–121
Small groups, 286–288
   forum presentations, 284, 294
   groupthink in, 288
   members of, 287–288
   oral reports and, 284–285
   panel, 283, 295
   presenting conclusions of, 282–285
   symposium presentations, 283–284, 296
   team presentations, 283–284
   written reports and, 284–285
Social proof, 252, 294, 295, 296
Sociology, 89–96
Sociopsychological context, 8
Software, presentation, 115, 119–125, 123f, 124f, 295
Sources, citing, 240–241t, 246
Spatial pattern of organization, 137–138, 296
Speaker, 4f, 5
Speaker-audience-topic relationship, 147–148
Special interests of audience, 94
Special occasion speech, 51, 72, 270–289
   of acceptance, 271–272, 292
   of commencement, 275–277, 293
   culture and, 285, 289
   of dedication, 274, 276, 293
   eulogies as, 278–279, 280, 293
   of farewell, 279–281, 293

of goodwill, 273–274, 275, 294
of inspiration, 277, 278
of introduction, 270–271, 294
oral reports and, 284–285
panel groups and, 283
of presentation, 271–272
presenting conclusions of small groups and, 282–285
sample of, 275, 276, 278, 280, 281
small group communication and, 286–288
symposium presentations and, 283–284
team presentations and, 283–284
toasts as, 281–282, 296
written reports and, 284–285
Specific examples, definition by, 109
Specific instances, reasoning from, 236–237, 296
Specific purpose, 296
Specific terms, purpose of speech and, 74
Specificity
   criticism and, 33
   wording of speech and, 175
Speech. *See* Language; Wording of speech; *specific type of speech, e.g.* Informative speech
Speech rate, 200–201, 295
Spelling, 176–177
State apprehension, 14, 296
Static evaluation, 173, 296
Statistics, 111, 112–114, 296
   gaining attention through, 146
   oral citation of, 241t
Straw man, 238, 296
Strong verbs, 178
Structure-function pattern of organization, 136t
Subjective view of ethics, 10
Substantive topics, 65
Substitutions in articulation, 203
Subtlety, open, 208
Sufficiency of research, 220
Summarizing speech, 150
Supporting materials, 55, 106–114, 296
   analogies as, 108
   biographical, 111
   criticism and, 34t
   of speech of definition, 223
   definitions as, 108–110
   of speech of demonstration, 229
   of speech of description, 219
   ethics and, 107
   examples as, 106–108, 109
   hypothetical examples as, 107
   illustrations as, 106–108
   narratives as, 106–108
   numerical data as, 111, 112–114
   organization of, 47f, 56
   of persuasive speech, 257–258, 259–260, 262
   plagiarism and, 10–13
   research of, 111
   statistics as, 111, 112–114
   testimony as, 110–112
Surveys, 67–68
Symbols, 156, 159
Symposium-forum presentations, 296
Symposium presentations, 283–284, 296

Synecdoche, 179, 296
Systematic desensitization, 17–18, 296

Taboo topics, 66, 296
Tactile imagery, 180
Tag questions, 187
Team presentations, 283–284, 296
Television shows, oral citation of, 240t
Template outline, 160-161, 296
Temporal context, 9
Temporal pattern of organization, 135, 137, 296
Terms, specific, purpose of speech and, 74
Tertiary sources, 75
Testimonial, 296
Testimonial technique, 238–239
Testimony, 110–112, 296
Thesis, 52, 74–82, 296
    central idea of speech and, 52, 77
    of speech of definition, 222–223
    of speech of demonstration, 228–229
    of speech of description, 218
    development of, 47f, 55–56
    ethics and, 80
    focusing audience attention through, 81–82
    generating main ideas and, 77, 80–81
    organization and, 81
    of persuasive speech, 256–257, 259, 260–261
    purpose of speech *versus*, 76–77
Thin entering wedge fallacy, 241, 296
Thinking empathy, 29
Time constraints, 48
Time management, 7, 192
Time of day, 96
Title of speech, 59
Toasts, 281–282, 296
Topic generators, 68–69, 69f, 70t, 296
Topic of speech
    appropriate, 65–66
    brainstorming and, 67, 292
    central idea and, 52
    culture and, 51, 66
    idea generator system and, 68–69, 69f, 70t, 296
    limiting, 69–72, 70t, 71f
    news items and, 68
    orienting the audience and, 57–58
    personal interests and, 67
    research and, 47f, 53
    search directories and, 72
    selection of, 47f, 50–52, 65–72, 68–69, 69f, 70t, 71f

speaker-audience-topic relationship, 147–148
    substantive, 65
    surveys and, 67–68
    taboo, 66, 296
    thesis and, 52
    *Topoi* and, 70–71, 70t, 296
    tree diagrams and, 71–72, 71f, 296
Topical pattern of organization, 135, 157–159, 162–163, 258, 260, 296
*Topoi* system of topics, 70–71, 70t, 296
Total meaning listening, 27–28
Tradition, appeals to, 238, 292
Trait apprehension, 13–14, 296
Transfer fallacy, 239, 241, 296
Transitions in speech, 47f, 58, 296
    internal summary, 217
    organization of, 153–154
    outline of, 156
Transparencies, 118t
Tree diagrams, 71–72, 71f, 296
Truth-telling, 277

Uncertainty-avoidance culture, 254
Understanding, 22f, 23
Unfamiliar terms, 180
Uniqueness of audience, 85
United States Government publications, 134
Usefulness of speech, 213–215

Values
    of audience, 88, 98, 296
    persuasive speech and, 234, 247
    questions of, 258–260, 261t, 295, 296
Verbal messages, listening and, 28
Verbs, 178
Videotapes, 118t
Visual imagery, 179
Visualization, 17, 295
    apprehension and, 15, 17
    persuasive speech and, 253t
    of satisfied needs, 142–143
Vividness, 178–180
Vocal delivery, 198, 200–204
Voice, 194
Volume of speech, 198, 200, 296
Vulgar language, 187

Weasel words, 170, 296
Websites, 174. *See also* Internet
    database, 174, 293
    directory, 199–200
    Gallup Poll, 86
    museum, 289
    MySearchLab, 8f, 86

MySpeechFeed, 214f
MySpeechLab, 69f
    oral citation of, 240t
    outlining, 130f
    polling site, 86
    research and, 199–200
    search engine, 199–200
    topic generator, 69f
"What if" questions, 101
Whiteboards, 117, 118t
Who? What? Why? Where? When? pattern of organization, 137t, 221
Willingness of audience, 96–97
Wire services, 174
Word charts, 115–116
Wording of speech, 47f, 59, 77, 80–81, 133, 175–186. *See also* Language
    affectional orientation and, 181–182, 185
    ageism and, 181–182, 185
    appropriateness of, 180–185
    central idea and, 77
    clarity and, 175–178
    clichés and, 176, 292
    commonly confused words and, 176–177
    culture and, 183–185
    declarative sentences and, 77
    disabilities and, 182–183
    economy of, 175
    ethnic expressions and, 183
    figures of speech and, 178–179, 294
    formality and, 180
    gender and, 181–182, 185
    heterosexism and, 181–182, 185, 294
    idioms and, 177–178
    imagery and, 179–180
    immediacy and, 186, 294
    nationality and, 183–184
    personal style and, 185–186
    phrasing sentences and, 186–189
    power and, 186–187
    racism and, 181–184, 295
    religion and, 184–185
    repetition and, 176
    restatement and, 176
    sexism and, 181–182, 185, 295
    signpost phrases and, 154, 175–176, 217, 296
    slang and, 180–181, 296
    specificity and, 175
    unfamiliar terms and, 180
    vividness and, 178–180
Written reports, 284–285

Yes response, 250
You-messages, 35, 296

# Credits

## Text Credits

**Page 57:** speech by Elizabeth Hobbs, also published in WINNING ORATIONS, 2006 Edition.
**Page 58:** speech by Sarah Collins, also published in WINNING ORATIONS, 2006 Edition.
**Page 58:** speech by Kristen K. Gunderson, also published in WINNING ORATIONS, 2006 Edition.
**Page 113:** speech by Meaghan Hagensick, also published in WINNING ORATIONS, 2008 Edition.
**Page 148:** reprinted with permission from Eastman & Eastman, on behalf of the author.
**Page 150:** speech by Linse Christensen, also published in WINNING ORATIONS, 2006 Edition.
**Page 151:** speech by Sarah Hoppes, also published in WINNING ORATIONS, 2008 Edition.
**Page 216:** speech by Betsy Heffernan, also published in WINNING ORATIONS, 1991 Edition.
**Page 263:** "The Home of the Slaves" by Jayme Meyer of the University of Texas at Austin, given at the American Forensic Association's National Individual Events tournament in 2004. The speech is used here with the permission of Jayme Meyer.

## Photo Credits

**Pages i** (bottom row, right), **iii, 1, 18:** pr2is, Shutterstock; **Pages, i** (bottom row, left), **46,** and **62:** © Keith Hunter/CORBIS All Rights Reserved; **Pages i** (middle row, right), **64,** and **82:** George Clerk, iStockphoto; **Pages i** (bottom row, center), **167,** and **189:** Derek Abbott, iStockphoto; **Pages i** (middle row, left), **233** and **266** A.G.E. FotoStock/© Images of Birmingham/AGE Fotostock; **Pages i** (top), **269, 289:** John Lund/Sam Diephuisc/Jupiter Images; **Page 3:** Comstock Images/Getty Images; **Pages 7, 25, 55, 75, 94, 111, 134, 174, 199, 220, 239,** and **289:** Martin Plsek/Shutterstock; **Page 9:** Kevin Galvin, AGE Fotostock America, Inc.; **Page 12:** Richard Cummins, Lonely Planet Images/Photo 20–20; **Page 13:** Carlos Moura/Shutterstock; **Pages 13, 35, 57, 80, 85, 107, 161, 170, 208:** Carlos Moura/Shutterstock; **Pages 14, 32, 172:** Getty Images Inc. RF; **Page 16:** Photodisc/Getty Images; **Pages 21** and **43:** Ikon Images/Andy Baker, Getty Images, Inc.; **Page 23:** Karin Hildebrand Lau, Shutterstock; **Page 27:** © moodboard/Alamy Images Royalty Free; **Page 30:** Alamy Images; **Page 36:** © Alamy Images; **Page 51:** © Artiga Photo/Corbis; **Page 52:** TebNad, Shutterstock; **Page 59:** Chris O'Meara, AP Wide World Photos; **Page 66:** PhotoEdit Inc.; **Page 81:** iStockphoto; **Pages 84** and **102:** Robert Cocquyt, iStockphoto; **Page 88:** © Gary Conner/PhotoEdit; **Page 97:** © Syracuse Newspapers/David Lassman/The Image Works; **Page 99:** © 2002, Ira Wyman/PictureDesk International, Newscom; **Pages 105,** and **126:** MaleWitch, iStockphoto International/Royalty Free. Courtesy of www.istockphoto.com; **Page 113:** AFP/Getty Images; **Page 117:** David J. Sams; **Page 126:** © Andres, iStockphoto; **Pages 129** and **164:** Nicholas Roemmelt, iStockphoto; **Page 143:** Jon Feingersh, Getty Images/Iconica; **Page 148:** Barry Rosenthal, Getty Images, Inc./Taxi; **Page 149:** Jaimie Duplass, Shutterstock; **Page 152:** Robert Mecea, Getty Images, Inc./Liaison; **Page 180:** Photolibrary, Photolibrary.com; **Page 182:** © Bill Aron/PhotoEdit; **Page 186:** Paul Barton; **Pages 191** and **210:** Andrey Plis, iStockphoto; **Page 201:** © David Young-Wolff/PhotoEdit; **Page 204:** Getty Images, Inc./Riser; **Page 205:** Getty Images, Inc./Reportage; **Pages 212** and **231:** Shutterstock; **Page 219:** Newscom; **Page 229:** Jeff Greenberg, Alamy Images; **Page 230:** Don Mason, Getty Images, Inc./Blend Images; **Page 231:** Bob Daemmrich, The Image Works; **Page 236:** NovaStock, Superstock Royalty Free; **Page 246:** Israel Pabon, Shutterstock; **Page 249:** © Ed Kashi/CORBIS; **Page 250:** © Moviestore Collection Ltd./Alamy Images; **Page 271:** egd/Shutterstock; **Page 273:** Donovan Quintero, AP Wide World Photos; **Page 279:** © Syracuse Newspapers/Suzanne Dunn/The Image Works; **Page 284:** © Bob Mahoney/The Image Works.